URAL-ALTAISCHE BIBLIOTHEK
FORTSETZUNG DER »UNGARISCHEN BIBLIOTHEK«

Herausgegeben von
OMELJAN PRITSAK und WOLFGANG SCHLACHTER

XIV

INTRODUCTION TO ALTAIC LINGUISTICS

BY

NICHOLAS POPPE

1965

Otto Harrassowitz · Wiesbaden

INTRODUCTION TO ALTAIC LINGUISTICS

BY

NICHOLAS POPPE

1965

OTTO HARRASSOWITZ · WIESBADEN

This text was developed pursuant to a contract between the United States Office of Education and the American Council of Learned Societies and is published with the permission of the United States Office of Education
April 1963

Alle Rechte vorbehalten
© Otto Harrassowitz, Wiesbaden 1965
Otto Harrassowitz GmbH & Co. KG, Kreuzberger Ring 7c-d, D-65205 Wiesbaden,
produktsicherheit.verlag@harrassowitz.de
Photographische und photomechanische Wiedergaben nur mit ausdrücklicher Genehmigung des Verlages

TABLE OF CONTENTS

PREFACE IX

ABBREVIATIONS X

0. INTRODUCTORY 1

1. THE ALTAIC LANGUAGES 7
    1.1. The Mongolian Languages 7
        1.11. Santa 9
        1.12. Monguor 9
        1.13. Dagur 9
        1.14. Mogol 10
        1.15. Oirat 10
        1.16. Buriat 12
        1.17. Mongol 13
        1.171. Khalkha 13
        1.172. Dariganga 14
        1.173. Chakhar 14
        1.174. Urat 14
        1.175. Kharchin-Tumut 14
        1.176. Khorchin 14
        1.177. Ujumchin 15
        1.178. Ordos 15
        1.18. Mongolian script 15
        1.181. The Oirat script 18
        1.19. Periodization of Mongolian language history 18
        1.191. Ancient Mongolian 21
        1.192. Middle Mongolian 21

    1.2. The Manchu-Tungus Languages 24
        1.21. Languages of the Manchu group 27
        1.211. Juchen 27
        1.212. Manchu 28
        1.213. Goldi 30
        1.214. Ulcha 30
        1.215. Orochi 30
        1.216. Oroki 30
        1.217. Udehe 31
        1.22. Languages of the Tungus group 31
        1.221. Negidal 31
        1.222. Evenki 31
        1.223. Lamut 32
        1.224. Solon 32

    1.3. The Chuvash-Turkic Languages 33
        1.31. Chuvash 36

Table of Contents

    1.32. The Turkic languages 38
        1.321. Yakut 38
        1.322. The Tuva-Khakas group 39
        1.323. The Kypchak group 41
        1.324. The Chaghatai group 47
        1.325. The Turkmen group 49
    1.33. The Cyrillic alphabets of Chuvash and the Turkic peoples . . 53
    1.34. Historical periodization of the Turkic languages 57
        1.341. The language of the Huns 57
        1.342. Volga and Danube Bulgarian 58
        1.343. Ancient Turkic 59
        1.344. Middle Turkic 67
        1.345. New Turkic 73

1.4. Korean 75

2. HISTORY OF INVESTIGATION OF THE ALTAIC LANGUAGES . . 79

  2.1. History of Mongolian Linguistics 79
    2.11. Beginnings 79
    2.12. Schmidt 80
    2.13. Kowalewski 80
    2.14. Golstunskiĭ 81
    2.15. Pozdneyev 81
    2.16. Castrén 82
    2.17. Ramstedt 83
    2.18. Kotwicz 85
    2.19. Rudnev 86
    2.110. Žamtsarano 87
    2.111. Vladimirtsov 87
    2.112. Haenisch 89
    2.113. Pelliot 89
    2.114. Mostaert 90
    2.115. Poppe 91
    2.116. Lewicki 91
    2.117. Ligeti and his pupils 92
    2.118. Cleaves 92
    2.119. Mongolian linguistics in Japan 93
    2.120. Summary 94

  2.2. History of Manchu-Tungus Linguistics 95
    2.21. Beginnings 95
    2.22. Zakharov 95
    2.23. Grube 96
    2.24. Hauer 96
    2.25. Sinor 97
    2.26. Tsintsius 97
    2.27. Vasilevich 98
    2.28. Petrova 99
    2.29. The pupils of Tsintsius 99
    2.230. Manchu-Tungus linguistics in Japan 100

  2.3. History of Chuvash and Turkic Linguistics 100
    2.31. The beginnings 100
    2.32. Böhtlingk 101

2.33.	Radloff	102
2.34.	Ilminskiĭ	103
2.35.	Katanov	104
2.36.	Piekarski	105
2.37.	Ashmarin	105
2.38.	Melioranskiĭ	106
2.39.	Malov	106
2.310.	Samoilovich	107
2.311.	Dmitriev	108
2.312.	Dyrenkova	109
2.313.	Borovkov	109
2.314.	Kononov	110
2.315.	Baskakov	110
2.316.	Thomsen	111
2.317.	Grønbech	112
2.318.	F. W. K. Müller	113
2.319.	Von Le Coq	114
2.320.	Bang-Kaup	114
2.321.	Brockelmann	115
2.322.	Von Gabain	116
2.323.	Menges	117
2.324.	Pritsak	119
2.325.	Räsänen	120
2.326.	Jarring	120
2.327.	Deny and French turcology	121
2.328.	Kowalski	122
2.329.	Zajączkowski	123
2.330.	Németh and Hungarian turcology	123

3. THE ALTAIC THEORY 125

4. MUTUAL INFLUENCES WITHIN THE ALTAIC GROUP 157

    4.1. Altaic Borrowings in Mongolian 158
        4.11. Turkic loan-words in Mongolian 158
        4.12. Manchu-Tungus loan-words in Mongolian 160

    4.2. Altaic Borrowings in Manchu-Tungus 160
        4.21. Turkic loan-words in Manchu-Tungus 160
        4.22. Mongolian loan-words in Manchu-Tungus 161

    4.3. Altaic Borrowings in Chuvash-Turkic Languages 161
        4.31. Mongolian borrowings in Turkic 161
        4.32. Turkic borrowings in Chuvash 162
        4.33. Mutual borrowings in Turkic 162

    4.4. Altaic Borrowings in Korean 163

5. CONTACTS OF ALTAIC LANGUAGES WITH OTHER LANGUAGES 165

    5.1. Chinese Elements in Altaic Languages 165
        5.11. Chinese elements in Turkic 165
        5.12. Chinese elements in Mongolian 166
        5.13. Chinese elements in Manchu-Tungus 166
        5.14. Chinese elements in Korean 166

    5.2. Tibetan Elements in Altaic Languages 167

Table of Contents

    5.3. Ancient Indo-European Elements in Altaic Languages. . 167
        5.31. Sanskrit, Tokharian, and Sogdian elements in Turkic 167
        5.32. Iranian elements in Modern Turkic languages 168
        5.33. Iranian elements in Chuvash 169
        5.34. Ancient Indo-European loan-words in Mongolian 169
    5.4. Semitic Influences upon Altaic 170
    5.5. Modern European Influences upon Altaic 171

6. ALTAIC INFLUENCES UPON OTHER LANGUAGES 173
    6.1. Altaic Elements in Indo-European Languages 173
    6.2. Altaic Elements in Georgian 175
    6.3. Altaic Elements in Uralic 175
        6.31. Altaic elements in Samoyed 175
        6.32. Altaic elements in Hungarian 176
        6.33. Chuvash elements in Finno-Ugric 176
        6.34. Turkic elements in Finno-Ugric 176

7. CHARACTERISTIC STRUCTURAL FEATURES OF THE ALTAIC
   LANGUAGES 177
    7.1. Long Vowels 177
        7.11. Long vowels in Turkic 177
        7.12. Long vowels in Chuvash 178
        7.13. Long vowels in Mongolian 178
        7.14. Long vowels in Manchu-Tungus 179
        7.15. Long vowels in Korean 180
    7.2. Stress and Pitch 180
    7.3. Vowel Harmony 181
        7.31. Vowel harmony in Turkic 181
        7.32. Vowel harmony in Chuvash. 183
        7.33. Vowel harmony in Mongolian 184
        7.34. Vowel harmony in Manchu-Tungus 184
        7.35. Vowel harmony in Korean 185
        7.36. Consonant harmony 185
        7.37. Summary 186
    7.4. Internal Sandhi 186
    7.5. Word Structure 189
        7.51. Agglutination. 189
        7.52. The stem 190
        7.53. The suffixes 191
        7.531. The possessive suffixes 191
    7.6. The Parts of speech. 192
        7.61. Nouns and verbs 192
        7.62. The pronouns. 193
        7.63. Substantive and adjective 195
        7.64. Verbal forms 195

8. BRIEF COMPARATIVE SURVEY OF ALTAIC LANGUAGES 197
    8.1. Sound Correspondences 197
        8.11. Consonants 197
        8.12. Vowels 202

9. INDICES 204

PREFACE

This manual for university students represents, in concise form, the contents of the author's lectures on Altaic linguistics, held at various times at the University of Washington and the Columbia University, New York. In the process of writing this book, the author was helped by his friend, Professor Omelian Pritsak, Harvard University, who made many useful suggestions and supplied some bibliographic data. Likewise, the undersigned owes some information about the history of the Korean language to Professor Ki-Moon Lee, University of Seoul. Some bibliographic data on Korean linguistics were obtained from Professor Johannes Rahder, Yale University. The undersigned takes pleasure in expressing his heartfelt thanks to the colleagues mentioned. It goes without saying that the author alone is responsible for all the shortcomings found in this book.

The undersigned wishes also to mention that the drawings on pp. 8, 27, and 35 were made by Mr. Osman Nedim Tuna, University of Washington.

In conclusion, it should be said that the present book was written under a contract of the Department of Health, Education, and Welfare of the United States of America.

April 22. 1965   Nicholas Poppe
                                                     University of Washington

I. ABBREVIATIONS

A. Books and journals

ABAW	=	Abhandlungen der Berliner Akademie der Wissenschaften (Berlin)
ADAW	=	Abhandlungen der Deutschen Akademie der Wissenschaften zu Berlin (Berlin)
AGSKl.	=	Abhandlungen der Geistes- und Sozialwissenschaftlichen Klasse der Akademie der Wissenschaften und der Literatur (Mainz)
ALH	=	Acta Linguistica Academiae Scientiarum Hungaricae (Budapest)
AM	=	Asia Major (Leipzig)
AM – Neue Folge	=	Asia Major – Neue Folge (Leipzig)
AM New Ser.	=	Asia Major – New Series (London)
AmJSL	=	American Journal of Semitic Languages
AO	=	Archiv Orientální (Praha)
AOH	=	Acta Orientalia Academiae Scientiarum Hungaricae (Budapest)
APAW	=	Abhandlungen der Preussischen Akademie der Wissenschaften (Berlin)
ASAL	=	American Studies in Altaic Linguistics, Vol 13 of the Uralic and Altaic Series (Bloomington, Indiana)
BOH	=	Bibliotheca Orientalis Hungarica (Budapest – Leipzig)
BSOAS	=	Bulletin of the School of Oriental and African Studies (London)
CAJ	=	Central Asiatic Journal (The Hague – Wiesbaden)
CO	=	Collectanea Orientalia (Wilna)
DRAN	=	Dokladï Rossiïskoï Akademii Nauk, Seriya B (Leningrad)
DWAW	=	Denkschriften der Wiener Akademie der Wissenschaften (Wien)
FUF	=	Finnisch-Ugrische Forschungen (Helsinki)
HJAS	=	Harvard Journal of Asiatic Studies (Cambridge, Mass.)
HO	=	Handbuch der Orientalistik (Leiden – Köln)
IAN	=	Izvestiya Akademii Nauk (St. Petersburg, Petrograd, Leningrad)
IAN – OLYa	=	Izvestiya Akademii Nauk SSSR, Otdelenie Literaturï i Yazïka (Moskva – Leningrad)
IAN – OON	=	Izvestiya Akademii Nauk SSSR, Otdelenie Obščestvennïx Nauk (Leningrad, Moscow)
IORYaS	=	Izvěstiya Otděleniya Russkago Yazïka i Slovesnosti (St. Petersburg)
IRGO	=	Izvěstiya Russkago Geografičeskago Obščestva (St. Petersburg)
JA	=	Journal Asiatique (Paris)
JAOS	=	Journal of the American Oriental Society (Baltimore)
JLSJ	=	Journal of the Linguistic Society of Japan (Tokyo)

Abbreviations

JRAS	= Journal of the Royal Asiatic Society
JSFOu	= Journal de la Société Finno-Ougrienne (Helsinki)
KCsA	= Kőrösi Csoma Archivum (Budapest)
Kl. f. Spr., Lit. u. Kunst	= Klasse für Sprachen, Literatur und Kunst
KSz	= Keleti Szemle (Budapest)
L	= Language, Journal of the Linguistic Society of America (Washington D. C.)
LUÅ – NF	= Lunds Universitets Årsskrift, N. F. (Lund)
Mél. As.	= Mélanges Asiatiques (St. Pétersbourg)
MIO	= Mitteilungen des Instituts für Orientforschung (Berlin)
MSFOu	= Mémoires de la Société Finno-Ougrienne (Helsinki)
MS	= Monumenta Serica (Peking)
MSOS	= Mitteilungen des Seminars der Orientalischen Sprachen, Abt. II, West-Asiatische Studien
O	= Oriens (Leiden)
OZ	= Ostasiatische Zeitschrift
PhTF	= Philologiae Turcicae Fundamenta (Aquis Mattiacis 1959)
RO	= Rocznik Orientalistyczny (Kraków)
SA	= Studia Altaica (Wiesbaden 1957)
SBAW	= Sitzungsberichte der Berliner Akademie der Wissenschaften, Philologisch-historische Klasse (Berlin)
SBFAW	= Sitzungsberichte der Finnischen Akademie der Wissenschaften (Helsinki)
SM	= Studia Mongolica (Ulanbator)
Sov. Étn.	= Sovetskaya Etnografiya (Leningrad, Moskva)
StOF	= Studia Orientalia edidit Societas Orientalis Fennica (Helsinki)
SV	= Sovetskoe Vostokovedenie (Leningrad – Moskva)
SWAW	= Sitzungsberichte der Wiener Akademie der Wissenschaften (Wien)
TIYa	= Trudï Instituta Yazïkoznaniya (Moskva)
TP	= T'oung Pao (Leiden)
UAB	= Ural-Altaische Bibliothek (Wiesbaden)
UAJ	= Ural-Altaische Jahrbücher (Wiesbaden)
UAS	= Uralic and Altaic Series (Bloomington, Indiana)
Uč. Zap. Kaz. Un-ta	= Učeniya Zapiski Imperatorskago Kazanskago Universiteta (Kazań)
Uč. Zap. LGU	= Učenïe Zapiski Leningradskogo Gosudarstvennogo Universiteta, Seriya filologičeskix nauk (Leningrad)
UJ	= Ungarische Jahrbücher (Berlin)
UZIV	= Učenïe Zapiski Instituta Vostokovedeniya (Moskva)
Vo. Ya.	= Voprosï Yazïkoznaniya (Moskva)
Word	= Word, Journal of the Linguistic Circle of New York (New York)
WZKM	= Wiener Zeitschrift für die Kunde des Morgenlandes (Wien)
YaS	= Yafetičeskiï Sbornik (Leningrad)
ZDMG	= Zeitschrift der Deutschen Morgenländischen Gesellschaft (Wiesbaden)
ZE	= Zeitschrift für Ethnologie
ZIRGO	= Zapiski Imperatorskago Geografičeskago Obščestva (St. Petersburg)
ZKV	= Zapiski Kollegii Vostokovedov (Leningrad)
ZSPh	= Zeitschrift für Slavische Philologie

Abbreviations

ZVO = Zapiski Vostočnago Otděleniya Imperatorskago Russkago Arxeologičeskago Obščestva (St. Petersburg)

ŽMNP = Žurnal Ministerstva Narodnago Prosvěščeniya (St. Petersburg)

B. Languages

Alt.	= Altai Turkic		Mo.	= Written Mongolian
AMo	= Ancient Mongolian		Mog.	= Mogol
AT	= Ancient Turkic		MT	= Middle Turkic
Az.	= Azerbaijan		Oir.	= Oirat
Bash.	= Bashkir		Ord.	= Ordos, cf. Urdus
Bur.	= Buriat		Oroch.	= Orochi
Chuv.	= Chuvash		Orok.	= Oroki
Kum.	= Kuman		Sol.	= Solon
Dag.	= Dagur		Soy.	= Soyot
Ev.	= Evenki (Tungus)		Tat.	= Tatar
Go.	= Goldi (Nanai)		Tel.	= Teleut
Karak.	= Karakalpak		Trkm.	= Turkmenian
Kaz.	= Kazakh		Turk.	= Turkish (which is spoken in Turkey)
Kh.	= Khalkha			
Kha.	= Khakas		Tuv.	= Tuvinian
Kirg.	= Kirghiz		Ud.	= Udehe
Koib.	= Koibal		Uig.	= Uighur, Uighuric
Lam.	= Lamut (Even)		Urd.	= Urdus, cf. Ordos
Ma.	= Manchu		Yak.	= Yakut
MMo	= Middle Mongolian		Yen.	= Yenisei inscriptions
Mng.	= Monguor			

0. INTRODUCTORY

0.1. The present *Introduction to Altaic Linguistics* is designed as a manual for university students. It is by no means a learned work presenting new material or new ideas to scholars who themselves are altaicists, although it might be of some use to a scholar, let us say, in the Turkic field who wishes to learn something about Mongolian in general or a particular Mongolian (or Tungus, etc.) language. And *vice versa*, a scholar in the Mongolian (or Tungus or Korean) field might need information on one of the Turkic languages. A general linguist, too, might find some portions of this book useful to him, e.g., as far as bibliography or geographical distribution of some languages is concerned. However, it was neither scholars in the Altaic fields nor general linguists who were being thought of when this book was being written but students and, in particular, students at American universities. This statement needs explanation. Whereas at some European universities chairs of some Altaic languages, such as Turkic and Mongolian, have existed for a considerable length of time, Altaic studies started at American universities only recently. Chairs of Turcology or Mongolian studies are very old in some countries, e.g., in the USSR and former Russia. In the United States, however, there were no chairs of Turcology although Turkish (Osman Turkish or Turkish as spoken in Turkey) was being taught. But Turkish and Turkic are not the same. Teaching Turkish (including literature) is comparable to teaching German (language and literature) which is not identical with the activities of a chair of Germanic languages (which covers all or most of Western Germanic and Nordic languages and Gothic). Therefore, the situation is different in the United States from that in some European countries. Whereas a professor of Turkic linguistics in the USSR, Germany, Finland, Poland, and Hungary might give his students a general picture of what Turkic studies are and what languages they cover, and might even say something about Mongolian or Manchu-Tungus, a student of Turkish in America would not be given detailed information about other Turkic languages. Of course, the situation has improved in the recent years but another obstacle still remains, and this leads us to problems revolving around libraries and books. Altaic studies being a relatively new field in the United States, most of our libraries lack literature, not to mention the fact that literature on Altaic languages is greatly scattered. Whereas some important old books, as for instance Böhtlingk's, Radloff's, or Kowalewski's works are available in some libraries, still articles have been appearing in numerous periodicals which are not found in any library. But even if they were found, it would be too burdensome for a student to look for a large number of articles. Microfilms and other reproductions would not solve the problem because only a small fraction of Altaistic literature is in English. The English-speaking nations are not the cradle of Altaic studies and did not display any interest in these studies in the past. Therefore, the main bulk of literature is in Russian, French, and German. But how many students, including both the freshmen and graduate students, possess a fair reading knowledge of these three languages?

These considerations, the author believes, justify the publication of an introduction which might give the student general information of this type, which might not be the ideal type, but at least gives the student information difficult to obtain under the prevailing conditions in which our students do their work. Thus, it is the student whose interests were taken into consideration when this book was being written.

0.2. A few words should be said about the arrangement of the present book. The first part gives a survey of the Altaic languages, i.e., Mongolian, Manchu-Tungus, Chuvash-Turkic, and Korean. The languages are discussed by the families: Mongolian, Manchu-Tungus, etc. It gives a classification of the Altaic languages and classifications of languages within each family. The reader will notice that what other scholars call Turkic is called here "Chuvash-Turkic", only the *toquz* (nine) and *qïš* (winter) languages being regarded as Turkic as opposed to Chuvash which is a *tăxxăr* (nine) and *xĕl* (winter) language. The geographical distribution of the languages and information on the script concerned is given. The reader will also find a short bibliography appended to the discussion of each language. It should be stressed that bibliographic data are necessarily very brief. In cases in which this is possible, only a few book titles are given. This is the case of Buriat, Tatar, Bashkir, etc. Speaking of Tatar, the author wishes to remark that he gives among the few titles that of his *Tatar Manual* which contains a bibliography of the most important works. Written in English, it will spare the student the effort of looking for information in numerous publications in Russian and Tatar, and he will be much better off if he takes the *Tatar Manual*, reads it and notes the bibliography given in it.

In cases in which there are works giving most of the information, and completely reliable, only their titles, with a few other additional titles, are given. A well-informed reader might still ask why this or that work believed by him to be worthwhile mentioning has been omitted. This may have happened for one of two reasons. Either the work has not been mentioned because there is another one which, in the opinion of the author, is more suitable for a student or non-specialist in that particular field, and which is mentioned in the bibliography given in one of the books recommended; or the title has not been given because the author of these lines does not regard that book as reliable, no matter what the opinion of others is.

The second part of the book presents a brief outline of history of study. History of a science is inevitably connected with names of scholars. It is a list of names and achievements. Therefore, this part contains a number of very short biographical data and bibliographies. Of course, there were more scholars in the past than those whose biographies are given. Thus, the Russian mongolists Orlov (author of a Buriat grammar), Podgorbunskii (author of a Buriat dictionary), Cheremisov (author of another Buriat dictionary), the Russian turcologist K. K. Yudakhin (author of excellent Kirghiz and Uzbek dictionaries), Nikiforov (author of some important works on Yakut), etc. have not been mentioned for the same reason why in a brief outline of history of literature some names are omitted. One should again be reminded of the fact that this is a book for students for whom it would be impossible to know all the names and biographies. The aim of this book is to give students basic facts. It needs no explanation why every altaicist should know who Böhtlingk, Castrén, Radloff or F.W.K. Müller was and why, on the other hand, one will not be handicapped in his study if he does not know who Orlov was.

Among names not mentioned there are very famous ones, e.g., Klaproth, Salemann, Otto Donner, etc., but Salemann was primarily a scholar in the Iranian field, and Donner in the Indo-European and Finno-Ugric fields, not having done anything of primary importance to Altaic studies. As for Klaproth, it is true that he was a great scholar but his works are hopelessly obsolete. The author of these lines would be the first to demand that the biography of Klaproth and many other biographies be included in a *History of Altaic Studies*. Unfortunately, this cannot be done in a manual for students whose primary task is to acquire knowledge of what concerns their work.

The third part of this book gives a brief history of the Altaic theory or, as some scholars prefer to call it, hypothesis. It begins with a survey of hypotheses created in the XVIII century with regard to the mutual relations of various languages, including those which are not now considered as Altaic, and brings the reader to the Ural-Altaic hypothesis as established in the middle of the XIX century. After that comes the Altaic theory (or hypothesis, if the reader prefers this term) as it appears in G. J. Ramstedt's works and the writings of his followers. There are two schools of thought at the present time. Some scholars believe to have proved that the similarities in the Altaic languages are a result of genetic affinity. Other scholars doubt it and, not denying the existence of these similarities, prefer to explain them as old and new borrowings, and speak of the Altaic languages as of a group of genetically unrelated but structurally very similar languages which have borrowed many elements of grammar and vocabulary from each other. Facing these two diametrically opposite theories (justice would demand that both of them be called hypotheses if one of them is), the author had a hard time to remain impartial. Sharing the view that the Altaic languages have more in common than mere borrowings, the author could not help corroborating this view and, on the other hand, pointing out the weakness of the theory of borrowings. The situation being as it is, the author has attempted to present both contrasting theories, making the greatest efforts to avoid polemics which would be utterly out of place in a manual. As long as there are two or more contrasting views, all of them should be given, remembering the old saying *audiatur et altera pars*, especially in cases like this in which both sides include scholars who in their respective fields are commonly recognized authorities. Further investigation will show which of the two schools of thought is closer to the truth.

The subsequent portions of the book deal with problems of mutual influences of the Altaic languages (e.g., Turkic influence on Mongolian), Altaic influences in non-Altaic languages (e.g., Turkic influence on Sayan-Samoyed, or Mari which is a Finno-Ugric language), non-Altaic influences in Altaic languages (e.g., Sogdian elements in Turkic), and structural features common to all Altaic languages.

0.3. Consequently, this book is neither a descriptive nor comparative nor historical grammar of any Altaic language. Brief outlines of grammars of Altaic languages should be looked for elsewhere. Readers interested in general information about phonology, grammar, or features characteristic from the point of view of comparative linguistics, should consult other works, e.g., *Philologiae Turcicae Fundamenta* or *Handbuch der Orientalistik* in cases involving Turkic languages, or the second of the works mentioned, in cases involving Mongolian or Manchu-Tungus languages. The articles contained in these generally important reference works are not equal in value, and some of them are even poor. The better ones are mentioned in bibliographies given in this book.

However, this book is not a bibliography either and should not be regarded even as a substitute for a bibliography. The number of authors and works given here amounts only to a fraction of the existing literature. It should be emphasized that the author did not even set as his task to compile a bibliography of Altaic linguistics or only part of it, such as a bibliography of Mongolian or Turkic languages, etc., or even bibliographies of a few individual languages. There are special bibliographies, e.g., R. Loewenthal's, bibliographies given in the *Fundamenta* or *Handbuch* mentioned above, but none of them is really complete, because no bibliography can ever be complete, new works constantly being published. And least of all can this book be regarded as a bibliography.

Speaking of bibliographies, it should be remarked that some of them (although none of them may be regarded as complete for reasons mentioned above) are reliable, the bibliographic data contained being accurate. Such are the bibliographies appended to the following works:

Baskakov, N. A., *Tyurkskie yazïki*, Moskva 1960.

Bibliografiya Tuvinskoĭ Avtonomnoĭ Oblasti, Moskva 1959, pp. 116–118.

Bibliografičeskiĭ ukazatel literaturï po yazïkoznaniyu, izdannoĭ v SSSR s 1918 po 1957 god, Vïp. 1, Knigi i sborniki na russkom yazïke, izdannïe v SSSR 1918–1955, Moskva 1958.

Bibliografičeskiĭ ukazatel po kazaxskomu yazïkoznaniyu, Alma-Ata 1956.

Cincius, Prof. V. I., *Sravnitelnaya fonetika tunguso-mańčžurskix yazïkov*, Leningrad 1949, pp. 337–339.

Gabain, A. von, *Alttürkische Grammatik*, Mit Bibliographie, Lesestücken und Wörterverzeichnis, auch Neutürkisch, Leipzig 1950, pp. 224–246.

Loewenthal, R., *The Turkic Languages and Literatures of Central Asia*, A Bibliography, 'S-Gravenhage 1957. (Contains some errors).

Matrosova, N. A., *Bibliografiya literaturï, izdannoĭ v Buryat-Mongolskoĭ ASSR v 1948 g.*, Ulan-Udė 1950.

Philologiae Turcicae Fundamenta, Tomus Primus, Aquis Mattiacis 1959.

Sunik, O. P., *Glagol v tunguso-mańčžurskix yazïkax*, Moskva-Leningrad 1962, pp. 354–358.

Tyulyaeva, V. P., *Mongolskaya Narodnaya Respublika*, Bibliografiya knižnoĭ i žurnalnoĭ literaturï na russkom yazïke 1935–1950 gg., Moskva 1953.

Yakovleva, E. N., *Bibliografiya Mongolskoĭ Narodnoĭ Respubliki* (sistematičeskiĭ ukazatel knig i žurnalnïx stateĭ na russkom yazïke), Moskva 1935.

Bibliographies of works on individual Altaic languages are appended to most grammars of languages concerned. The reader will find bibliographical information in each section dealing with a particular language.

In conclusion, mention should be made of the book *Einführung in das Studium der altaischen Philologie und Turkologie*, Wiesbaden 1953 by J. Benzing.

This book having been severely criticized in several reviews (especially by H.W. Duda in *WZKM* 52: 3–4 (1955), pp. 326–345), the author of these lines cannot recommend it to readers, particularly in view of the fact that, besides other errors, its bibliographical data are in many cases incorrect and misleading. An introduction to the study of the Turkic languages by N. A. Baskakov, *Vvedenie v izučenie tyurkskix yazïkov*, Moskva 1962 contains numerous bibliographical notes.

An equally good bibliography of and, to a certain extent, introduction to Altaic studies (linguistics, history, and anthropology) is Denis Sinor's *Introduction à l'étude de l'Eurasie Centrale* (Wiesbaden 1963). It contains rather complete bibliographies of works in the fields of languages and history of the peoples of Central Asia and vast regions of Eastern Europe. Although the title of the book suggests that this is an introduction to the study of languages and history of *all* peoples inhabiting Central Eurasia, including the Iranians, Slavs, etc., it actually deals with Ural-Altaic studies. It omits the non-Altaic and non-Uralic peoples and languages and discusses only literature dealing with Altaic and Finno-Ugric matters, although Central Eurasia counts among its inhabitants also Iranian peoples and even Arabs who live in the Russian Turkestan. Anyway, Sinor's book is very useful and can be recommended most emphatically.

1. THE ALTAIC LANGUAGES

1.0. Altaic languages are Mongolian, Manchu-Tungus, and the Chuvash-Turkic languages. Since recent times, Korean, too, is counted, by some scholars, among the Altaic languages.

1.1. The Mongolian languages.

The Mongolian languages are spread over a large area, in Outer and Inner Mongolia, in some parts of Manchuria, in Eastern Siberia, in the Chinese provinces of Kansu, Sinkiang, and Chinghai, in the lower course of the Volga River (in the European part of the USSR), and in some areas in Afghanistan.

In spite of the vastness of the territory covered, there are only about three million speakers of Mongolian.

The Mongolian group comprises seven languages. The following features are the basis for classification:
1. the developments of the initial *p ($>f, x$, Zero);
2. the developments of *$\bar{a}$ ($> \bar{a}, \bar{o}$) following a syllable containing o;
3. the developments of *$a\gamma u$ ($a\underset{\cdot}{u}/o\underset{\cdot}{u}, \bar{u}$);
4. the preservation or disappearance of the final n in nouns;
5. the preservation of the final r and g or their disappearance. This can be illustrated by the following table:

No.	Features						
1.	f-group		x-group	Zero-group			
2.	*$\bar{a} > \bar{o}$			*$\bar{a} > \bar{a}$		*$\bar{a} > \bar{o}$	
3.	$\bar{u}$		$a\underset{\cdot}{u}$		$\bar{u}$		
4.	-*$n > \emptyset$			-n preserved			-*$n > \emptyset$
5.	-*$r > \emptyset$		final r preserved				
	I	II	III	IV	V	VI	VII

The Roman numerals in the horizontal column of the table refer to the languages:

        I. Santa   V. Oirat
       II. Monguor   VI. Buriat
      III. Dagur   VII. Mongol
      IV. Mogol

The same can be represented as a system of concentric circles: (See page 8).

Examples illustrating the correspondences:

1. Santa *funie* "mist", Monguor *funi* "smoke", Dagur *xoni* id., Oirat (Kalmuck) *uńār* "mist", Buriat *unin* "smoke", *uńār* "mist", Khalkha *uńār* "mist".

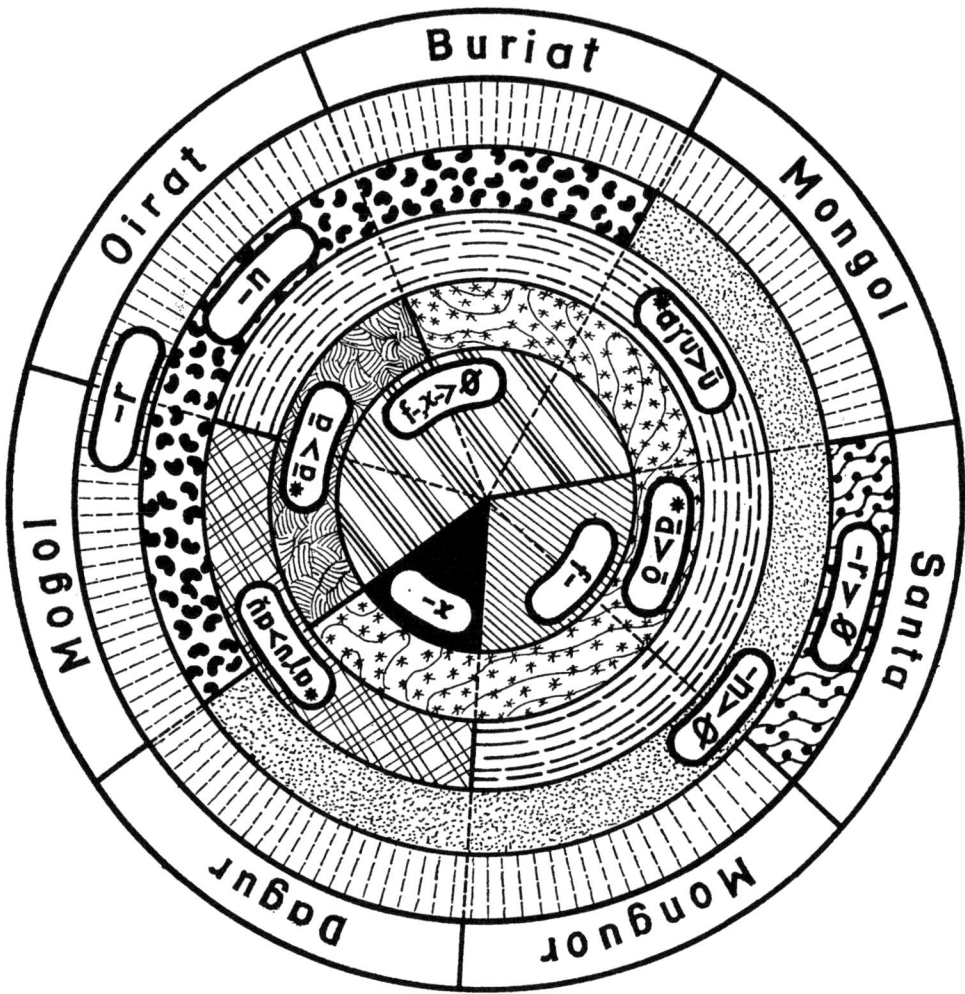

2. S *dolon* "seven", M *dolōn* id., D *dolōn* id., O *dolān* id., B *dolōn* id., Kh. *dolōn* id.

3. S *ula* "mountain", M *ula* id., D *aṵla* id., Mogol *oṵla* id., O *ūl* id., Kh. *ūl* id.

4. S, M *mori* "horse", D *mor̆/mori* id., Mog. *morin* id., O *mörṇ* id., B *morin* id., Kh. *mor̆* id.

5. S *gaja* "earth, ground, soil", M *gajiär* id., D *gajir* id., Mog. *γajar* id., O *gazṛ* id., B *gazar* id., Kh. *gazar* id.

Bibliography:

Poppe, N., *Introduction to Mongolian Comparative Studies*, Helsinki 1955, pp. 14–24.

— *Vergleichende Grammatik der altaischen Sprachen*, Teil 1, Vergleichende Lautlehre, Wiesbaden 1960, pp. 1–3.

1.11. Santa.

Santa is spoken in the Chinese province of Kansu, to be exact, east of the city of Kaoho (former Hochou). It is spoken by about 150,000 people. Some authors call this language the Tunghsian language, i. e., "the language of the Eastern Village" which is not, however, quite correct.

Bibliography:

Mostaert, A., C.I.C.M., "The Mongols of Kansu and their Language," *Bulletin of the Catholic University of Peking*, 8 (1931), pp. 75–89.
Todaeva, B. X., *Mongolskie yazïki i dialektï Kitaya*, Moskva 1960, pp. 88–107.
— *Dunsyanskiĭ yazïk*, Moskva 1961.

1.12. Monguor.

Monguor *moŋguor* is spoken in parts of the provinces Kansu and Chinghai in China. The number of speakers amounts to about 60,000. The inhabitants of the Linhsia district of Kansu, numbering approximately 8,000 people, speak a special dialect of Monguor.

Bibliography:

Róna-Tas, A., "Remarks on the Phonology of the Monguor Language," *AOH* 10: 3 (1960), pp. 263–267.
de Smedt, A., C.I.C.M., et Mostaert, A., C.I.C.M., "Le dialecte monguor parlé par les Mongols du Kansu occidental, Ière partie, Phonétique," *Anthropos* 24–25, correct. 26, p. 253.
— *Le dialecte Monguor parlé par les Mongols du Kansu occidental, IIe partie, Grammaire*, Peking 1945.
— *Le dialecte Monguor parlé par les Mongols du Kansu occidental, IIIe partie, Dictionnaire monguor-français*, Pei-ping 1933.
Schröder, Dominik, *Aus der Volksdichtung der Monguor I. Teil, Das weisse Glücksschaf (Mythen, Märchen, Lieder)*, Wiesbaden 1959.
Todaeva, B. X., *Baoańskiĭ yazïk*, Moskva 1964. (Description of the Linhsia dialect).

1.13. Dagur.

Dagur *dagūr* is spoken by about 25,000 people in North-Western Manchuria, to be exact, in the vicinity of the city of Hailar and in the valley of the river Nonni, mainly in the vicinity of the city of Tsitsikar. Dagur comprises three dialects, namely the Hailar dialect, Butkha, and the Tsitsikar dialect.

Bibliography:

Martin, S. E., *Dagur Mongolian Grammar, Texts, and Lexicon, Based on the Speech of Peter Onon*, UAS 4, 1961.
Poppe, N. N., *Dagurskoe narečie*, Leningrad 1930.
— "Über die Sprache der Daguren," *AM* 10 (1934), pp. 1–32, 183–220.

1.14. Mogol.

Mogol *moɣul* is spoken in Afghanistan, mainly in the provinces of Herāt and Maimana, and in the Baghlān region of the Badakhshān province. The number of speakers is not even approximately known.

Bibliography:

Iwamura, Sh. and Schurmann, H. F., "Notes on Mongolian Groups in Afghanistan," *Silver Jubilee Volume of the Zinbun-Kagaku-Kenkyusyo, Kyoto University*, Kyoto 1954, pp. 480–517.

Iwamura, Sh., with the collaboration of Natsuki Osada and the late Tadashi Yamasaki, *The Zirni Manuscript, A Persian-Mongolian Dictionary and Grammar*, with "Preliminary Remarks on the Zirni Manuscript" by Nicholas Poppe, Kyoto University 1961.

Ligeti, L., "La lexique moghol de R. Leech," *AOH* 4: 1–3 (1954), pp. 119–158.

— "O mongolskix i tyurkskix yazïkax i dialektax Afganistana," *ibid.*, pp. 93–117.

— "Les voyelles longues en moghol," *AOH* 17 (1964), pp. 1–48.

Pritsak, O., "Das Mogholische," *HO* 5: 2 (1964), pp. 159–184.

1.15. Oirat.

Oirat *öröd* to which Kalmuck also belongs is spread over a vast territory. Oirat dialects are spoken in the north-western part of the Mongolian People's Republic (Outer Mongolia), in Zoongaria, in Alashan, in the province of Chinghai, and in the lower course of the Volga River (in the USSR) where the Autonomous Kalmuck Republic is located.

The Oirat dialects spoken in the Mongolian People's Republic are Dörböt *dörwöd*, Bayit *bayid*, Torgut *torɣūd*, Zakhachin *zaxčin*, Mingat *miŋgad*, and Dambi-Ölöt *dämb-ölöd*.

Dörböt is spoken in the Ubsa-Nur aimak (i.e., province) by approximately 25,000 people. In the same province Bayit is spread (approximately 16,000 speakers). Zakhachin (10,000 speakers) and Dambi-Ölöt (5,000 speakers) are spread in the Kobdo aimak. Torgut is spoken hardly by more than 5,000 people in the aimaks Kobdo and Bayan-Ölgei. Mingat is also spoken in the Kobdo aimak, the number of speakers not exceeding 2,000 people.

Consequently, the total number of Oirats in the Mongolian People's Republic amounts to approximately 63,000.

Torgut is also spoken in the Bayangol autonomous district and in the Khubuksar autonomous county of the Sinkiang-Uighur autonomous region, in China. Bayit is the language of one part of the population of the Bayangol district. Ölöt is spoken in the Tarbagatai district of the same region. The total number of speakers of Oirat dialects in Sinkiang amounts to 60,000.

Besides, various Oirat groups live in Alashan and in the province of Chinghai. No details with regard to the Sinkiang, Alashan, and Chinghai Oirats are available.

The largest group of Oirats are the Kalmucks. The latter are descendants of those Oirats who left Zoongaria in the first half of the XVII century and came to the banks of the Volga River in its lower course. They call themselves *xalmg*, hence Kalmucks. They inhabit the Kalmuck Autonomous Socialist Soviet Republic, USSR. The number of speakers amounts there to about 100,000. Kalmuck comprises the dialects Torgut, Dörböt, and Buzawa *buzāw*. A small group of Moslem Kalmucks, the so-called Sart-Kalmucks (approximately 3,000 people) live in the Karakol district of the Kirghiz SSR. The Kalmucks living in the Kalmuck Republic are Buddhists.

Consequently, the total number of Oirat speakers in Mongolia, China, and the USSR probably amounts to 300,000.

The Oirats use the Oirat alphabet which was created by Zaya Pandita, a learned monk, on the basis of the Mongolian alphabet, in 1648. The written language is Written Oirat, based on Colloquial Mongolian of the XVII century.

The Oirat alphabet is given in 1.181.

In spite of the fact that the Oirat alphabet is more precise than the old Mongolian alphabet, it was constantly losing ground to the latter. However, it was still used by the Oirats in Outer Mongolia until 1944 when it was replaced by the new Mongolian alphabet based on the Cyrillic alphabet. It is still being used by the Oirats in Sinkiang, Alashan, and Chinghai. It was also used by the Kalmucks until the Russian revolution of 1917. Soon after the revolution, it was replaced by an alphabet based on the Cyrillic alphabet. In 1931, the latter was replaced by a romanized alphabet but in 1937 it was again replaced by the Cyrillic script.

The letters of the alphabet in use at the present time are given in the table *infra*.

THE KALMUCK ALPHABET

Phonemic transcription is given in / /; *italics* transliterate signs used only in Russian loan words; alternative variants are given in ( ).

А а	/a/	Ә ә (Ä ä)/ää/		Б б	/b/	В в	/v/	Г г	/g/
һ	/γ/	Д д	/d/	Е е	/e, ye/	Ё ё	*yo*	Ж ж	*ž*
Җ җ (дж)	/ǰ/	З з	/z/	И и	/i/	Й й	/y/	К к	/k/
Л л	/l/	М м	/m/	Н н	/n/	ң (нъ)	/ŋ/	О о	/o/
Ө ө	/ö/	П п	/p/	Р р	/r/	С с	/s/	Т т	/t/
У у	/u/	Ү ү	/ü/	Ф ф	*f*	Х х	/x/	Ц ц	/c/
Ч ч	/č/	Ш ш	/š/	Щ щ	*šč*	ъ	'	ы	*i*
ь	'	Э э	/e/	Ю ю	*yu*	Я я	*ya*		

Bibliography:

Kara, G., "Notes sur les dialectes oïrat de la Mongolie Occidentale," *AOH* 8: 2 (1959), pp. 111–168.

Kotwicz, Wl., *Opït grammatiki kalmïckogo razgovornogo yazïka*, Izd. II, Rževnice u Pragi 1929. (The most complete and best of all grammars of Kalmuck.)

Ramstedt, G. J., *Kalmückisches Wörterbuch*, Helsinki 1935. (Contains also a concise grammar.)
— *Kalmückische Sprachproben, Erster Teil, Kalmückische Märchen*, MSFOu 27: 1–2 (1909–1919).
Street, J. C., "Kalmyk Shwa," *American Studies in Altaic Linguistics*, UAS 13 (1962), pp. 263–291.
Todaeva, B. X., "Materïalï po fol̇kloru sinczyanskix mongolov," *Tyurko-mongol̇skoe yazïkoznanie i folkloristika*, Moskva 1960, pp. 228–264.
Vladimircov, B. Ya., *Obrazcï mongol̇skoĭ narodnoĭ slovesnosti (S–Z. Mongoliya)*, Leningrad 1926.

1.16. Buriat.

Buriat *buŕād* is the northernmost Mongolian language. It is spread mainly in the Buriat Autonomous Socialist Soviet Republic, East Siberia. Various groups of Buriats live also in the Irkutsk and Chita regions (in East Siberia) and in the area called Barga in Manchuria. Some Buriats live also in the Mongolian People's Republic. Buriat is spoken by approximately 300,000 people. The main dialects are Khori, Barguzin, Ekhirit-Bulgat, Alar, Tunka, Nižneudinsk, Tsongol, Sartul, and Bargu-Buriat. Of these, Tsongol and Sartul are transitional dialects, forming a bridge between Buriat and Khalkha. Bargu-Buriat is spoken in the Barga region mentioned above.

The Buriats used until 1931 the Mongolian alphabet and Written Mongolian as their literary language. In 1931, a romanized alphabet was introduced which in 1938 was replaced by the present alphabet based on Cyrillic. The literary language is based on the Khori dialect.

THE BURIAT ALPHABET

Phonemic transcription is given in / /; *italics* transliterate signs used only in Russian loan-words.

А а	/a/	Б б	/b/	В в	*v*	Г г	/g/	Д д	/d/	Е е	/ye/
Ё ё	/yo/	Ж ж	/ž/	З з	/z/	И и	/i/	Й й	/y/	К к	*k*
Л л	/l/	М м	/m/	Н н	/n/	О о	/o/	Ө ө	/öö/	П п	/p/
Р р	/r/	С с	/s/	Т т	/t/	У у	/u/	Ү ү	/ü/	Ф ф	/f/
Х х	/x/	Һ һ	/h/	Ц ц	*c*	Ч ч	*č*	Ш ш	/š/	Щ щ	*šč*
ъ	'	ы	/ii/	ь	'	Э э	/e/	Ю ю	/yu, yü/	Я я	/ya/

Bibliography:

Bosson, J. E., *Buriat Reader*, supervised and edited by Nicholas Poppe, UAS 8 (1963).
Čeremisov, K. M., *Buryat-mongol̇sko-russkiĭ slovaŕ*, Moskva 1951.
Cïdendambaeva, B., *Russko-buryat-mongol̇skiĭ slovaŕ*, pod redakcieĭ –, Moskva 1954.
Poppe, N., *Buriat Grammar*, UAS 2 (1960).

1.17. Mongol.

Mongol *moŋgol*, or Mongolian in the narrower sense, is the largest language among its immediate relatives. It comprises a number of dialects spoken in the Mongolian People's Republic and Inner Mongolia, including parts of Manchuria. The total number of speakers amounts to about 2,200,000, including about 650,000 in Outer Mongolia and 1,465,000 in Inner Mongolia.

1.171. Khalkha.

Khalkha *xalx* is the most important dialect of Mongolian. It is spoken by almost 650,000 people, i.e., 75% of the total population of the Mongolian People's Republic. Being the official language of the only independent Mongolian nation, it serves also as the basis of the literary language which uses Cyrillic script.

Khalkha comprises a number of subdialects. The subdialects spoken in the eastern and southern parts of the Mongolian People's Republic display some features common to Mongolian dialects spoken in parts of Inner Mongolia.

THE CYRILLIC ALPHABET IN USE IN THE MONGOLIAN PEOPLE'S REPUBLIC

Phonemic transcription is in / /; *italics* transliterate signs used in loan-words.

А а	/a/	Б б	/b/	В в	/b/	Г г	/g/	Д д	/d/	Е е	/yö/
Ё ё	/yo/	Ж ж	/ǰ/	З з	/ʒ/	И и	/i/	Й й	/y/	К к	*k*
Л л	/l/	М м	/m/	Н н	/n/	О о	/o/	Ө ө	/ö/	П п	/p/
Р р	/r/	С с	/s/	Т т	/t/	У у	/u/	Ү ү	/ü/	Ф ф	*f*
Х х	/x/	Ц ц	/c/	Ч ч	/č/	Ш ш	/š/	Щ щ	*šč*	ъ	'
ы	/ii/	ь	/ĭ/	Э э	/e/	Ю ю	/yu, yü/	Я я	/ya/		

Bibliography:

Bosson, J. E., *Modern Mongolian*, UAS 38 (1964).
Bese, L., "Remarks on a Western Khalkha Dialect," *AOH* 13: 3 (1961), pp. 279–294.
Luvsandėndėva, A., *Mongolsko-russkiĭ slovaŕ*, pod obščeĭ redakcieĭ –, Moskva 1957.
Poppe, N., *Khalkha-Mongolische Grammatik*, Mit Bibliographie, Sprachproben und Glossar, Wiesbaden 1951.
— *Mongolische Volksdichtung, Sprüche, Lieder, Märchen und Heldensagen, Khalkha-mongolische Texte mit Übersetzung und Anmerkungen*, Wiesbaden 1955.
Street, J. C., *Khalkha Structure*, UAS 24 (1963).
Troxel, D. A., *Mongolian Vocabulary (Modern Khalkha Language), Mongolian-English, English-Mongolian*, Department of the Army, TM 30–537, Washington 1953.

1.172. Dariganga.

Dariganga *dariganga* is spoken in the southern part of the Mongolian People's Republic. The number of speakers in all seven *sumuns* (counties) amounts to 16,000.

Bibliography:

Róna-Tas, A., "A Study of the Dariganga Phonology," *AOH* 10: 1 (1960), pp. 1–29.
— "Dariganga Folklore Texts," *ibid.* 10: 2 (1960), pp. 171–183.
— "Dariganga Vocabulary," *ibid.* 13: 1–2 (1961), pp. 147–174.

1.173. Chakhar.

Chakhar *čaxar* is spoken in the aimak (district, province) Chakhar, Inner Mongolia. The exact number of speakers is unknown but it certainly amounts to several hundred thousand.

Bibliography:

Hattori, Sh., "Phonemic Structure of Mongol (Chakhar Dialect)," *JLSJ* 19–20 (1951), pp. 68–102.
Jagchid, S. and Dien, A. E., *Spoken Chahar Mongolian*, Inter-University Program for Chinese Language Studies. (Place and date of publication are not indicated).

1.174. Urat.

Urat *urad* is spoken in the Ulān Tsab aimak in Inner Mongolia. It is very close to Chakhar and Khalkha. This dialect has not been studied. The number of speakers is unknown.

1.175. Kharchin-Tumut.

Kharchin *xarčin* and Tumut *tümd* are names of two large tribes. Their dialect, Kharchin-Tumut, is spoken mainly in the Jou Uda aimak, Inner Mongolia, and in the adjacent areas.

The Kharchin-Tumut are a numerous group, at least 300,000 people.

Bibliography:

Nomura, M., "On Short Vowels in the Wang-fu Dialect of the Kharachin Right Banner, Inner Mongolia, "*Annual Report of the Institute of Ethnology* 3 (1940–41).
— "Remarks on the Diphthong [wa] in the Kharachin Dialect of the Mongol Language," *JLSJ* 16 (1950), pp. 126–142.
— "Supplementary Notes and Additions to Remarks on the Diphthong [wa] in the Kharachin Dialect," *ibid.* 17–18, pp. 149–155.
— "On some Phonological Developments in the Kharachin Dialect," *SA*, Wiesbaden 1957, pp. 132–136.

1.176. Khorchin.

Khorchin *xoršin* is spoken in the Jerim aimak, Inner Mongolia. The exact number of speakers is unknown but this dialect is said to be one of the most widely spoken.

Bibliography:

Bosson, J. and Unensečen, B., "Some Notes on the Dialect of the Khorchin Mongols," *UAS* 13 (1962), pp. 23–44.

1.177. Ujumchin.

Ujumchin *üjümüčin* is spoken mainly in the Shilingol aimak in Inner Mongolia and by emigrants from that area in the adjacent parts of the Mongolian People's Republic.

Bibliography:

Kara, G., "Sur le dialecte *üjümüčin*," *AOH* 14: 2 (1962), pp. 145–172.
— "Un glossaire *üjümüčin*", *AOH* 16: 1 (1963), pp. 1–43.

1.178. Ordos.

Ordos *urdus* is spoken in the Yeke Ju *yeke ǰū* aimak, in the former Ordos region which is located in the bend of the Yellow River. It is one of the best-investigated dialects in Inner Mongolia.

Bibliography:

Mostaert, A., C.I.C.M., "Le dialecte des mongols Urdus (Sud)," *Anthropos* 21–22 (1926–27), corr. 25, p. 725.
— *Textes oraux ordos*, Peip'ing 1937 (contains also a concise grammar).
— *Folklore ordos (Traduction des Textes oraux ordos)*, Peip'ing 1947.
— *Dictionnaire ordos* I–III, Peking 1941–44.

1.18. Mongolian script.

The Mongolian script is still used by all Mongols speaking Mongolian in the narrower sense (*vide* 1.17) and was until recently used also by the Buriats. In 1944, a new script based on the Cyrillic alphabet was introduced in the Mongolian People's Republic. The Buriats abandoned the old script in 1931. However, there are still numerous people in Outer Mongolia and among the Buriats who use the old script for their private purposes. It is still the only script known to almost 1.5 million Mongols in Inner Mongolia.

The date of introduction of the Mongolian script is unknown. The first document written in Mongolian script dates approximately from 1225. It is an inscription on a stele erected in honor of Chingis Khan's nephew, Yesunke, who excelled everyone at a contest in archery which took place soon after Chingis Khan's return from his campaign in Turkestan. The orthography and the grammatical forms of words in that inscription are consistent and betray a rather long usage, and therefore, it is improbable that the inscription in question represents the first attempt at writing. It is to be assumed that the Mongols had known how to write for a considerable time before, and it will not be wrong to assume that writing became known to the Mongols some time in the XII century.

The Mongolian alphabet had been borrowed from the Uighurs, a civilized Turkic people (*vide* 1.3434). The Uighurs had borrowed it from the Sogdians who were an Iranian people. The Sogdian alphabet is, in its turn, of Aramaic origin, i.e., one of the northern Semitic alphabets.

As for the language used by the Mongols for written communication, it was Written Mongolian which is basically still the same in Inner Mongolia and in all countries where Written Mongolian is used side by side with the new official alphabets.

The Mongolian script is vertical and consists of 21 basic letters. Two main periods can be established in the history of the Mongolian script. The first period lasted until the XVII century. During the first period, expecially in the XIII–XIV centuries, the letters still had the shape of the Uighur letters almost without any changes. Later on, the shape of the letters slightly changed, and some additional letters were introduced in order to render foreign sounds, mainly Tibetan and Sanskrit.

The second period began in the XVII century when an extensive Buddhist literature was created which consisted entirely of translations chiefly from Tibetan. Numerous Buddhist works were published xylographically. In these printed books, the letters changed their shapes and acquired their present forms. During this period, the written language also changed. Obsolete and unintelligible ancient words, especially old borrowings from Uighur, were replaced by new words and expressions. An extensive Buddhist terminology was

Table of Mongolian Letters of the Pre-classical Period

Initial	Medial	Final	Transcription	Initial	Medial	Final	Transcription
			a				s
			e				š
			i				t d
			o u				l
			ö ü				m
			n				č ǰ
			ng				ǰ y
							k g
			q				
			γ ġ				r
			b				v

1.1. The Mongolian Languages

Number	Transcription	Characters		
		Initial	Medial	Final
1	a	ᠠ	ᠠ	ᠠ ᠠ
2	e	ᠡ	ᠡ	ᠡ ᠡ
3	i	ᠢ	ᠢ	ᠢ
4	o u	ᠣ	ᠣ	ᠣ
5	ö ü	ᠥ	ᠥ ᠥ	ᠥ
6	n	ᠨ	ᠨ ᠨ	ᠨ
7	ng		ᠩ	ᠩ
8	q	ᠬ	ᠬ	ᠬ
9	γ	ᠭ	ᠭ ᠭ	ᠭ ᠭ
10	b	ᠪ	ᠪ	ᠪ
11	p	ᠫ	ᠫ	
12	s	ᠰ	ᠰ	ᠰ ᠰ
13	š	ᠱ	ᠱ	ᠱ
14	t d	ᠲ	ᠳ ᠳ	ᠳ
15	l	ᠯ	ᠯ	ᠯ
16	m	ᠮ	ᠮ	ᠮ
17	č	ᠴ	ᠴ	
18	ǰ	ᠵ	ᠵ	
19	y	ᠶ	ᠶ	ᠶ
20	k g	ᠭ	ᠭ	ᠭ
21	k	ᠺ	ᠺ	
22	r	ᠷ	ᠷ	ᠷ
23	v	ᠸ	ᠸ	
24	h	ᠾ	ᠾ	

created. Ancient and rare grammatical forms were replaced by newer forms. The spelling was also modernized. The language of the xylographic publications of the XVII–XVIII centuries is called Classical Mongolian. The modern Written Mongolian language is its direct continuation and differs from the former mainly in vocabulary.

The letters of the Mongolian alphabet are shown in two tables. The first table (p. 16) gives the alphabet of the pre-classical period (mainly the XIII and XIV centuries). The second table (p. 17) gives the letters in their modern shapes as they appear in books printed in modern printing shops.

Bibliography:

Grønbech, K., and Krueger, J. R., *An Introduction to Classical (Literary) Mongolian*, Wiesbaden 1955.
Haltod, M., Hangin, J. G., Kassatkin, S., and Lessing, F. D., *Mongolian-English Dictionary*, Berkeley and Los Angeles 1960.
Poppe, N., *Grammar of Written Mongolian*, Wiesbaden 1954.

1.181. The Oirat script.

The Mongolian script, particularly the Written Mongolian language, were unintelligible to the Oirats. When Buddhist missionaries started their activities among the Oirats in the XVII century, it was found that Mongolian Buddhist writings could not be understood by the Oirats. Therefore, a special Oirat script and a new literary language had to be introduced. This task was solved by the learned monk Zaya Pandita, a Mongol by birth. He reformed the Mongolian script and compiled in 1648 a new Oirat alphabet based on the old Mongolian alphabet. The basis of the written language was Colloquial Mongolian of the XVII century.

It is to be noted that this reform was first carried out among the Volga Oirats, i.e., Kalmucks, who had come to the banks of the Volga in the first half of that century.

The Oirat script and literature in the Oirat language reached their acme in the first half of the XVIII century which was followed by a rapid decline. Writing became less and less literate and many Oirats in northwestern Mongolia passed to the Mongolian script and Written Mongolian.

The Oirats in the Mongolian People's Republic use the Cyrillic alphabet given in 1.171, and the Kalmucks use the Cyrillic alphabet given in 1.15. The Oirat script is, however, still in use in Alashan and in Sinkiang.

The Oirat alphabet is given on pp. 19–20.

Bibliography:

Popov, A., *Grammatika kalmĭckago yazika*, Kazań 1851. (Grammar of Written Kalmuck, i.e., Oirat.)
Pozdněev, A., *Kalmĭcko-russkiĭ slovaŕ*, S. Peterburg 1911.
— *Kalmĭckaya xrestomatiya dlya čteniya v starših klassax kalmĭckix narodnix škol*, II izdanie, S. Peterburg 1907.
Zwick, H. A., *Handwörterbuch der westmongolischen Sprache*, Donaueschingen 1853.

1.19. Periodization of Mongolian language history.

Three main periods have been established in the history of the Mongolian languages: the ancient period, the middle period, and the modern period.

Number	Separately	Initially	Medially	Finally	Transcription
1.	᠊ ᠊	᠊	᠊	᠊ ᠊	a
2.	᠊	᠊	᠊	᠊	e
3.	᠊	᠊	᠊	᠊	i
4.	᠊	᠊	᠊	᠊	o
5.	᠊	᠊	᠊	᠊	u
6.	᠊	᠊	᠊	᠊	ö
7.	᠊	᠊	᠊	᠊	ü
8.		᠊	᠊	᠊	n
9.		᠊	᠊		x
10.		᠊	᠊		γ
11.		᠊	᠊	᠊	b
12.		᠊	᠊		p
13.		᠊	᠊	᠊	s
14.		᠊	᠊	᠊	š

Number	Initially	Medially	Finally	Transcription
15.	ᠣ	ᠣ		t
16.	ᠠ	ᠠ	ᠠ	d
17.	ᠯ	ᠯ	ᠯ	l
18.	ᠮ	ᠮ	ᠮ	m
19.	ᠴ	ᠴ		c
20.	ᠽ	ᠽ		z
21.	ᠶ	ᠶ		y
22.	ᠺ	ᠺ ᠺ к.	ᠺ	k
23.	ᠭ	ᠭ		g
24.	ᠷ	ᠷ	ᠷ	r
25.	ᠸ	ᠸ		v
26.			ᠩ	ŋ

1.191. Ancient Mongolian.

Ancient Mongolian was probably spoken until the XII century. Written Mongolian was based on Ancient Mongolian, cf., Mo. *sayā-* "to milk", AMo. **sagā-* id. > Solon *sagā-* id.; Mo. *oyūr* "mortar", AMo. **ogūr* > Sol. *oyor* id.; Mo. *imayān* "goat", AMo. **imagān* id. > Sol. *imayān* id.

It is to be assumed that Ancient Mongolian had at least two dialects. One of the dialects still preserved the initial $f < *p$ which is still found in some positions in Monguor and Santa. In the other dialect $*p > f$ had already developed into h. Written Mongolian was based on the latter dialect because it has not preserved $*p$ or $*f$ and left the initial $*h$ unmarked.

There is no material directly referring to Ancient Mongolian, but there is material enabling the linguist to draw some conclusions indirectly. These materials consist of ancient borrowings in the Tungus languages, such as Evenki and Solon, and borrowings in Turkic languages, e.g., Kazakh which preserves such forms as *köbögön* "children" < AMo. **köbegǖn*, Mo. *köbegün* "son, boy".

1.192. Middle Mongolian.

Middle Mongolian was spoken from the XII to the XV (or XVI) century. The main feature of Middle Mongolian was the preservation of $f < *p$- in one or some dialects, and the preservation of $h < *p$- in the other dialects.

Middle Mongolian comprised at least three dialects. They can be called conventionally Southern Middle Mongolian, Eastern Middle Mongolian, and Western Middle Mongolian.

Southern Middle Mongolian was the source of present Monguor, Santa, and Dagur. Eastern Middle Mongolian was the ancestor of Buriat and Mongol (i.e., Mongolian in the narrower sense). Western Middle Mongolian was the ancestor of Mogol and Oirat.

There is no material on Southern Middle Mongolian. Eastern Middle Mongolian is well represented by the language of the texts in the so-called ḥPʻags-pa script, the language of the *Secret History of the Mongols*, and various Sino-Mongolian glossaries of the XIV century.

The ḥPʻags-pa script was introduced by the order of Emperor Khubilai in 1269. His idea was to give the peoples of his vast Sino-Mongolian Empire a unified script. It was his personal lama, on whom he had bestowed the title of ḥPʻags-pa ("Honorable"), and who compiled the new alphabet based on Tibetan. The only documents written in this script and in Middle Mongolian are several inscriptions on steles, a number of the so-called *pʻai-tzu*, i.e., credentials of official messengers, and a few fragments of the well-known didactic work by Sakya Pandita, the uncle of ḥPʻags-pa Lama, *Subhaṣitaratnanidhi*. The ḥPʻags-pa script disappeared from usage after the fall of the Yüan dynasty (1368).

A by far more important document of Eastern Middle Mongolian is the *Secret History*, a legendary history of the ancestors of Chingis Khan and a vivid description of some events which took place during his lifetime. This work may have been written in 1240, although some scholars accept a later date as the more probable.

The *Secret History* had been originally written in Written Mongolian and with the letters of the Mongolian script. The original manuscript has not been preserved but numerous excerpts from this work are present in the text of the later historical work, *Altan Tobči* "The Golden Button". The Mongolian text of the original work was transcribed during the Ming time (i.e., the time of the dynasty which succeeded the Mongolian Yüan dynasty in China), in the XIV century, with Chinese characters, and an interlineal Chinese translation was added. This text is of great value because it is the largest continuous narrative text of that time.

Another important source for the study of Eastern Middle Mongolian is the Sino-Mongolian glossaries of the Ming time, such as *Hua-I i-yü* (1389) which contains also Mongolian texts in Chinese transcription.

Western Middle Mongolian can be studied on the basis of numerous Arabic-Mongolian and Persian-Mongolian glossaries compiled by Moslem scholars in

The ḥP'ags-pa Script
Consonants

	p		$č^c$
	b		$ǰ$
	v		$š$
	m		$ž$
	t		y
	t^c		k
	d		k^c
	n		g
	r		q
	l		$γ$
	c^c		$η$
	j		h
	s		$\cdot$
	z		y
	$č$		$\underset{\smile}{u}$

Vowels

൩	–	a
ㅈ ㅈ	∧ ∧	o
ড	ও	u
⊏	⊏	e
ㄲ ㄲ	ㄱ ㄱ	ė
൝ ൝	ㅈ ㅈ	ö
ඕ	ඕ	ü
ට	ට	i

the XIII and XIV centuries. The Mongolian words are transcribed with the letters of the Arabic alphabet. The largest and the most important of the Moslem sources is the Arabic-Persian-Chaghatai (Turkic)-Mongolian dictionary compiled on the basis of the Arabic-Persian dictionary of al-Zamakhšarī.

There are also some minor Armenian-Mongolian and Georgian-Mongolian glossaries, and numerous Mongolian words are found in various historical works by Moslem authors and in reports on travel by European travelers such as Plano Carpini, Rubruk, and Marco Polo.

Bibliography:

A. Secret History

Doerfer, G., "Beiträge zur Syntax der Sprache der *Geheimen Geschichte der Mongolen*," *CAJ* 1: 4 (1955), pp. 219–267.

Haenisch, E., "Grammatische Besonderheiten in der Sprache des Manghol un Niuca Tobca'an," *StOF* 14: 3, pp. 1–26.

— *Manghol un Niuca Tobca'an (Yüan-ch'ao pi-shi), die Geheime Geschichte der Mongolen*, Aus der chinesischen Transkription im mongolischen Wortlaut wiederhergestellt, Leipzig 1937.

— *Die Geheime Geschichte der Mongolen*, Aus einer mongolischen Niederschrift des Jahres 1240 von der Insel Kode'e im Keluren-Fluss, Erstmalig übersetzt, Leipzig 1948.
— *Wörterbuch zu Manghol un Niuca Tobca'an (Yüan-ch'ao pi-shi), Geheime Geschichte der Mongolen*, Leipzig 1939.
Hung, W., "The Transmission of the Book Known as *The Secret History of the Mongols*," *HJAS* 14: 3–4, pp. 433–492.
Pelliot, P., *Histoire Secrète des Mongols*, Paris 1949.
Poppe, N., "Die Sprache der mongolischen Quadratschrift und das Yüan-ch'ao pi-shi," *AM-Neue Folge* 1: 1 (1944), pp. 97–115.
Street, J. Ch., *The Language of the Secret History of the Mongols*, New Haven 1957.

B. Sino-Mongolian glossaries and texts

Haenisch, E., *Sino-mongolische Dokumente vom Ende des 14. Jahrhunderts* ADAW, Kl. f. Spr., Lit. u. Kunst, 1950, 4, Berlin 1952.
— *Sino-mongolische Glossare I, Das Hua-I ih-yü*, ibid., 1956, 5, Berlin 1957.
Lewicki, M., *La langue mongole des transcriptions chinoises du XIVe siècle, Le Houa-yi yi-yu de 1389*, Wrocław 1949.
— *La langue mongole des transcriptions chinoises du XIVe siècle II, Vocabulaire-Index*, Wrocław 1959.

C. ḫP'ags-pa script

Haenisch, E., *Steuergerechtsame der chinesischen Klöster unter der Mongolenherrschaft, Eine kulturgeschichtliche Untersuchung mit Beigabe dreier noch unveröffentlichter Phagspa-Inschriften*, Berichte über die Verhandlungen der Sächsischen Akademie der Wissenschaften zu Leipzig, Philologisch-historische Klasse 92 (1940), pp. 1–74.
Ligeti, L., "Le Po kia sing en écriture 'Phags-pa," *AOH* 6: 1–3 (1956), pp. 1–52.
— "Trois notes sur l'écriture 'Phags-pa," ibid., 13: 1–2 (1961), pp. 201–237.
Poppe, N., *The Mongolian Monuments in ḫP'ags-pa Script*, Second Edition translated and edited by John R. Krueger, Wiesbaden 1957.

D. Principal Moslem sources on Western Middle Mongolian

Ligeti, L., "Un vocabulaire mongol d'Istanbul," *AOH* 14: 1 (1962), pp. 3–99.
Poppe, N., "Das mongolische Sprachmaterial einer Leidener Handschrift," *Bulletin de l'Académie des Sciences de l'USSR*, 1927, pp. 1009–1040, 1251–1274; ibid., 1928, pp. 55–80.
— *Mongolskii slovar' Mukaddimat al-Adab* 1–3, Moskva-Leningrad 1938–39.
— "Zur mittelmongolischen Kasuslehre, eine syntaktische Untersuchung," *ZDMG* 103: 1 (1953), pp. 92–125.

1.2. The Manchu-Tungus languages.

The Manchu-Tungus languages comprise two sub-groups:
1. the southern or Manchu group;
2. the northern or Tungus group.

1.2. The Manchu-Tungus Languages

No	FEATURES									
	Disappearance of -g-/-γ-						Preservation of -g-/-γ-			
1.	f-		p-			x-		h-		$\emptyset$
2.										
3.	Preservation of final i					Disappearance of -i				-i preserved
4.	-Vn	-V̄		-V	-V̄		-Vn		-V̄	
5.	-xa	-lta	-lasa	-laha		-kta	-la	-lda/-lla	-lra	-lla
	I	II	III	IV	V	VI	VII	VIII	IX	X

A basis for the classification of the Manchu-Tungus languages is provided by phonologic and morphologic developments.

The following classification is based on the characteristic features listed below:

1. Preservation of g/γ in intervocalic position and its disappearance (Tungus group *versus* the Manchu group).
2. Development of initial $*p$ ($> p, f, x, h$, Zero).
3. Preservation of the final vowel i and its disappearance.
4. Occurrence of the final Vn (vowel plus n) *versus* $\tilde{V}$ (naso-oral vowel).
5. Developments of -$*lasa$.

See table on p. 25.

The Roman numbers in the table refer to the following languages:

      I Manchu
     II Goldi (Nanai)
   III Ulcha
    IV Oroki
     V Udehe (Ude)
    VI Orochi
   VII Negidal
 VIII Evenki (Tungus proper)
    IX Lamut (Even)
     X Solon

The same can be represented as a system of concentric circles (See page 27).

Examples illustrating the correspondences:

1. Manchu *tuveri* < *tüeri* "winter," Juchen *tu'e'erin* (*t'uh-'óh-lin*), Goldi *tuę*, Ulcha *tùę*, Orochi and Udehe *tuę*, Oroki *tuvę*, Negidal *tuɣʷeni*, Evenki and Lamut *tuɣęni*, Solon *tugù* id.
2. Manchu *faxun* "liver," Goldi, Ulcha *pa*, Oroki *paka*, Orochi *xaki*, Udehe *x'ai*, Negidal *xaxin*, Evenki *hākin*, Lamut *hākan*, Solon *āxī* id.
3. Manchu *jili* "the roots of the antlers," Goldi *jeli* "head," Ulcha *dili* id., Oroki *ďili*, Orochi *dili*, Udehe *dili*, Negidal *del*, Evenki *dil*, Lamut *dęl*, Solon *dili/dil* id.
4. Manchu *nadan* "seven," Goldi, Ulcha, Orochi *nadã*, Oroki and Udehe *nada*, Negidal, Evenki, Lamut *nadan*, Solon *nadã* id.
5. Suff. -*lasa*: Goldi, Ulcha -*lta*, Oroki -*lasa/-lta*, Orochi -*kta*, Udehe -*laha*, Negidal -*la*, Evenki -*lda* (-*lᵈra*, -*lra*, -*lla*), Lamut -*lra* (-*lᵈra*, -*lda*, -*lla*), Solon -*lla*.

Bibliography:

Benzing, J., *Die tungusischen Sprachen*, Wiesbaden 1956.
Cincius, V. I., *Sravnitelnaya fonetika tunguso-mańčžurskix yazïkov*, Leningrad 1949, pp. 7–35.
Novikova, K. A., *Proekt edinoĭ fonetičeskoĭ transkripcii dlya tunguso-mańčžurskix yazïkov*, Moskva-Leningrad 1961 (contains also bibliography).

1.2. The Manchu-Tungus Languages

Sunik, O., *Glagol v tunguso-mańčžurskix yazïkax*, Moskva-Leningrad 1962, pp. 11–24.

Vasilevič, G. M., "K voprosu o klassifikacii tunguso-mańčžurskix yazïkov", *VoYa* 1960, 2, p. 43–49.

1.21. Languages of the Manchu Group.

To this group the following languages belong: 1. Juchen; 2. Manchu; 3. Goldi; 4. Ulcha; 5. Oroki; 6. Udehe; 7. Orochi.

1.211. Juchen.

Juchen or Jurchen *jürjin* is an extinct language which was still spoken in Manchuria at the time of the rise of the Mongols in history and still existed in the Ming period of Chinese history (1368–1644). The most important document available is the Juchen section (compiled in the XVI century) of the polyglot collection known as the *Hua-i i-yü*. The Juchen section contains texts (documents) in the Juchen script and in Chinese transcription.

There are also inscriptions carved on steles namely one of 1413 and another one of 1433. The Juchen characters in the inscriptions are different from the Chinese characters. Juchen is close to Manchu and can be regarded as Old-Manchu or a dialect of that language of which Old-Manchu was another dialect.

Bibliography:

Grube, W., *Die Sprache und Schrift der Jučen*, Leipzig 1896.
Ligeti, L., "Note préliminaire sur le déchiffrement des "petits caractères" joutchen," *AOH* 3: 2 (1953), pp. 211–228.
— "Les inscriptions djurchen de Tyr. La formule *oṃ maṇi padme hūṃ*," *ibid.*, 12: 1–3 (1961), pp. 5–26.

1.212. Manchu.

Manchu is the literary language of those Manchu who conquered China and established there the Ch'ing dynasty (1644–1911). It was also their colloquial language. At the present time there are few speakers left, although Manchu is still read and written by the few Manchus, Solons, and Dagurs.

Manchu played an important rôle as the official language in China during the Ch'ing period. The literature in Manchu is rather large but consists mostly of translations from Chinese.

The first attempts at writing were made by the Manchus in 1599. They used at that time the Mongolian script. In 1632 the latter was reformed and additional letters were introduced. The Manchu alphabet is shown in the table (p. 29).

Bibliography:

Austin, W. M., "The Phonemics and Morphophonemics of Manchu," *UAS* 13 (1962), pp. 15–22.
Doerfer, Dr. G., *Der Numerus im Mandschu*, Abh. d. Geistes und Sozialwiss. Kl. d. Ak. d. Wiss. u. d. Lit., Jhg. 1962, 4, Wiesbaden 1963.
Haenisch, E., *Mandschu-Grammatik*, Mit Lesestücken und 23 Texttafeln, Leipzig 1961.
Hauer, E., *Handwörterbuch der Mandschu-Sprache*, Wiesbaden 1952–55.
Ligeti, L., "À propos de l'écriture mandchoue," *AOH* 2 (1952), pp. 235–301.
— "Les anciens éléments mongols dans le mandchou," *ibid.*, 10: 3 (1960), pp. 231–248.
Möllendorff, P. G. von, *A Manchu Grammar with Analyzed Texts*, Shanghai 1892.
Peeters, H., "Manjurische Grammatik," *Monumenta Serica* 5 (1940), pp. 349–418.
Rudnev, A., "Novïya dannïya po živoĭ mandžurskoĭ rěči i šamanstvu," *Zapiski Vostočnago Otděleniya Imperatorskago Russkago Arxeologičeskago Obščestva* 21 (1912), pp. 047–082.

1.2. The Manchu-Tungus Languages

Transcription	Initially	Medially	Finally
a			
e			
i			
o			
u			
û			
n			
q k			
ɣ g			
χ x			
b			
p			
s			
š			
t			
d			
l			
m			
č			
ǰ			
y			
r			
f			
v			

Sinor, D., "Introduction aux études mandjoues," *TP* 42: 1–2 (1953), pp. 70–100.
— "Le verbe mandjou," *Bulletin de la Société Linguistique de Paris* 45 (1949), pp. 146–156.

1.213. Goldi.

Goldi or Nanai *nanai*, as they call themselves, are a small people of 7000 in the lower course of the Amur river.

They did not have a script prior to 1931. Since 1937 the Russian (Cyrillic) alphabet without any additional signs is used.

Bibliography:

Avrorin, A. A., *Grammatika nanaĭskogo yazïka*, I–II, Moskva-Leningrad 1959–1961 (contains a bibliography).
Grube, W., "Goldisch-deutsches Wörterverzeichnis," appended to: L. Schrenck, *Reisen und Forschungen im Amur-Lande* 3, St. Petersburg 1900.
Petrova, T. I., *Kratkiĭ nanaĭsko-russkiĭ slovaŕ*, Leningrad 1935.
— *Nanaĭsko-russkiĭ slovaŕ*, Leningrad 1960.
Poniatowski, S., "Materials to the Vocabulary of the Amur-Golds," *Bibliotheca Universitatis Poloniae* 1923 (quoted from Avrorin's bibliography).

1.214. Ulcha.

Ulcha is spoken by hardly more than 1500 people in an area located downstream of that of the Goldi. Some scholars regard it as an independent language but, according to others, it is a dialect of Nanai. At any rate, it does not possess classificatory features distinguishing it from Goldi.

Bibliography:

Petrova, T. I., *Uĺčskiĭ dialekt nanaĭskogo yazïka*, Leningrad 1936.
Schmidt, P., "The language of the Oltchas," *Acta Universitatis Latviensis* 8 (1923), pp. 229–288.

1.215. Orochi.

Orochi is spoken in the Amur region on the sea-shore. The number of speakers amounts to a few hundred.

Bibliography:

Cincius, V. I., "Očerk morfologii oročskogo yazïka," *Uč. Zap. LGU* 98: 1, Seriya vostokovedčeskix nauk (1949).
Schmidt, P., "The Language of the Oroches," *Acta Universitatis Latviensis* 17 (1928).

1.216. Oroki.

Oroki is spoken by a few hundred people on the island of Sakhalin. It is little explored.

Bibliography:

Ikegami, J., "The Verb Inflection of Orok," *Kokugo Kenkyu* (Inquiries into the Japanese Language) 9 (1959), pp. 34–73.

— "The Substantive Inflection of Orok," *JLSJ* 30 (1956), pp. 77–96.

— "Orok Texts," *Memoirs of the Research Department of the Toyo Bunko* (The Oriental Library) 17 (1958), pp. 85–95.

1.217. Udehe.

Udehe or Ude is spoken by a small group hardly exceeding 1000 speakers along some tributaries of the Amur and Ussuri.

Bibliography:

Šneĭder, E. R., *Kratkiĭ udėĭsko-russkiĭ slovaŕ, S priloženiem grammatičeskogo očerka*, Leningrad 1936.

1.22. Languages of the Tungus Group.

To this group the following languages belong: Negidal, Evenki (or Tungus proper), Lamut, and Solon.

1.221. Negidal.

Negidal *ęlkęmbęy* is spoken by less than 800 people in the basin of the Amgun river.

Bibliography:

Mĭlnikova, K. M. i Cincius, V. I., "Materialĭ dlya issledovaniya negidaĺskogo yazĭka," *Tungusskiĭ Sbornik* I, Leningrad 1931.

Schmidt, P., "The Language of the Negidal," *Acta Universitatis Latviensis* 5, 1922.

1.222. Evenki.

Evenki *ęvęnki* is spoken in various regions of Eastern Siberia, mostly in the northern parts of it, roughly between the Yenisei river and the Okhotsk Sea and between the 50° and 85° of northern latitude. The total number of speakers approximately amounts to 40,000. Evenki is divided in three groups of dialects, the northern, southern, and eastern. Evenki received its script in 1930. First it was based on the Latin alphabet, but since 1938 the Cyrillic alphabet has been used.

THE EVENKI ALPHABET

The phonemic transcription is in / /; *italics* transliterate letters used in Russian words.

А а	/a/	Б б	/b/	В в	/v/	Г г	/g/	Д д	/d, ǰ/	Е е	/e, ye/
Ё ё	/yo/	Ж ж	*ž*	З з	*z*	И и	/i/	Й й	/y/	К к	/k/
Л л	/l/	М м	/m/	Н н	/n/	нг	/ŋ/	О о	/o/	П п	/p/
Р р	/r/	С с	/s/	Т т	/t/	У у	/u/	Ф ф	*f*	Х х	/h/
Ц ц	*c*	Ч ч	/č/	Ш ш	/š/	Щ щ	*šč*	ъ	–	Ы ы	/i/ï/
ь	–	Э э	/ę/	Ю ю	/yu/	Я я	/ya/				

Bibliography:

Konstantinova, O. A., *Ėvenkiĭskiĭ yazïk, Fonetika, Morfologiya*, Moskva-Leningrad 1964. (Grammar, preface containing bibliographical data).
Konstantinova, O. A. i Lebedeva, E. P., *Ėvenkiĭskiĭ yazïk*, Učebnoe posobie dlya pedagogičeskix učilišč, Moskva-Leningrad 1953.
Sunik, O. P., *Glagol v tunguso-mańčžurskix yazïkax*, Moskva-Leningrad 1962 (contains a bibliography).
Vasilevič, G. M., *Očerk grammatiki ėvenkiĭskogo (tungusskogo) yazïka*, Leningrad 1940.
— *Očerki dialektov ėvenkiĭskogo (tungusskogo) yazïka*, Leningrad 1948.
— *Ėvenkiĭsko-russkiĭ slovaŕ*, Moskva 1958 (contains a concise grammar).
— i Aĺkor, Ya. P., *Sbornik materialov po ėvenkiĭskomu (tungusskomu) folkloru*, Leningrad 1936.

1.223. Lamut.

Lamut *ęvęn* is spoken by 9000 people in various parts of the Magadan and Khabarovsk regions (kraĭ) in Kamchatka, and in the Autonomous Yakut Soviet Republic. The Lamut call themselves /ęvęn/. The name Lamut has originated from Evenki *lamudi* "maritime" because many groups of the Lamut live near the sea.

There are three groups of Lamut dialects: the eastern, western, and central.

The Lamut did not have any kind of writing prior to 1931. The present Cyrillic alphabet was introduced in 1937.

THE LAMUT ALPHABET

А а	/a/	Б б	/b/	В в	/v/	Г г	/g/	Д д	/d/	Е е	/e, ye/
Ё ё	/o, yo/	Ж ж	/ž/	З з	/z/	И и	/i/	Й й	/y/	К к	/k/
Л л	/l/	М м	/m/	Н н	/n/	О о	/o/	П п	/p/	Р р	/r/
С с	/s/	Т т	/t/	У у	/u/	Ф ф	/f/	Х х	/h/	Ц ц	/c/
Ч ч	/č/	Ш ш	/š/	Щ щ	/šč/	ъ	—	ь	/'/	Э э	/e/
Ю ю	/yu/	Я я	/ya/	ы	/ï/						

Bibliography:

Bogoraz, V. G., "Materialï po lamutskomu yazïku," *Tungusskiĭ Sbornik* I, Leningrad 1931.
Cincius, V. I., *Očerk grammatiki ėvenskogo (lamutskogo) yazïka*, Leningrad 1947.
— i Rišes, L. D., *Russko-ėvenskiĭ slovaŕ s priloženiem grammatičeskogo očerka*, Leningrad 1952.
Levin, V. I., *Kratkiĭ ėvensko-russkiĭ slovaŕ s priloženiem grammatičeskogo očerka*, Leningrad 1936.
Novikova, K. A., *Očerki dialektov ėvenskogo yazïka*, Moskva-Leningrad 1960 (contains a bibliography).

1.224. Solon.

Solon is spoken by a few thousand people in north-western Manchuria, in the cities of Tsitsikar, Hailar, Butkha, Mergen, and Aigun, and in the northern parts of Manchuria along the Russian frontier. The Solons do not have a system of writing of their own. Those who can write and read use Manchu.

Bibliography:

Poppe, N. N., *Materiali po solonskomu yaziku*, Leningrad 1931.

1.3. The Chuvash-Turkic languages.

The Chuvash-Turkic languages are usually called Turkic but the latter term is inaccurate if applied to Chuvash and Turkic, i.e., Turkish (Osman, Anatolian), Azerbaijan Turkic, Turkmenian, Uzbek, Kazakh, etc., because the Turkic languages, including both those enumerated here and those not mentioned, are descendants of Common Turkic, a z- and š- language (*toquz* "nine", *qïš* "winter"), whereas Chuvash is the descendant of a r- and l- language (*tăxăr* "nine", *xĕl* "winter") which was close to Common Turkic (otherwise called Proto-Turkic) but not identical with the latter. The ancestor of Chuvash and Common Turkic constituted a unity which preceded in time the appearance of Common Turkic. This unity can be called Pre-Turkic. The relationship of Chuvash and the Turkic languages can be represented schematically as follows:

Pre-Turkic					
Proto-Chuvash	Proto-Turkic				
Chuvash	Presently existing Turkic languages				
	I	II	III	IV	V

As for the Roman numbers, they denote the five groups of Turkic languages which will be discussed *infra* (p. 34).

The Chuvash-Turkic languages cover a large territory. Chuvash is spoken in the Volga region, in the USSR. The Turkic languages are spoken in Turkey, in Transcaucasia, in many parts of Daghestan and in the Northern Caucasus, in the Volga region, in Russian Central Asia, in Chinese Turkestan, in Northern Iran, in Afghanistan, in the mountain regions of the Altai and Sayan, and in the northern part of East Siberia.

The Turkic languages are numerous and their speakers amount to no less than 50 million.

There are several classifications of the Chuvash-Turkic (or as most turcologists call them, Turkic) languages but none of them can be regarded as fully satisfactory even as far as they concern only the Turkic (the z- and š-) languages, leaving Chuvash aside. Their main defect lies in the fact that their authors wanted them to be applicable to both the presently spoken Turkic languages and those spoken in ancient times. A classification can, however, be either a synchronous or a diachronous one, but it cannot be both at the same time. It is obvious that a classification of presently spoken languages cannot include languages of the past.

The classification of the Turkic languages is usually based on the following features:

1. the developments of $*d > t, d, z, y$;
2. the developments of the syllables $*a\gamma > a\gamma, a\underline{u}, u(\bar{u}), ia$; $*\ddot{i}\gamma > \ddot{i}\gamma, iq, \ddot{i}$;
3. the preservation or the loss of $*\gamma$ following a consonant, e.g., $*l\gamma > l$.

Some other features may be added to those enumerated.

The most widely accepted classification of the Chuvash-Turkic languages is that by Samoilovich who regards Chuvash as just one of the Turkic languages and divides the whole group into six subgroups:

1	tăxxăr 'nine'	toquz / doquz 'nine'				
2	ura 'foot'	adaq 'foot'	ayaq 'foot'			
3	bol- / pol- (pul-) 'to be'					ol- 'to be'
4	tăv-/tu 'mountain'	taγ 'mountain'	tau 'mountain'	taγ / daγ 'mountain'		
5	*ïγ > ă	ïγ	*ïγ > ï	*ïγ > ïq	*ïγ > ï	
6	yulnă 'remained'	qalγan 'remained'				qalan 'remained'
	I r-group	II d-group	III tau-group	IV taγlïq-group	V taγlï-group	VI ol-group

This classification is, however, obsolete. Not to mention the fact that Chuvash should not be classified without any reservations as a Turkic language, some Turkic languages do not quite fit into this scheme. Samoilovich's classification could also be simplified because the features n°3 (i.e., the preservation or loss of b- in bol-/ol- "to be") and n°6 (i.e., the development *lγ > l) are only additional features, the languages in question being distinguished by a number of other characteristic features. However, Yakut should be included as a special group, because it does not quite fit into Samoilovich's second group. Therefore, Ramstedt's classification is to be preferred, although it needs corrections.

Ramstedt classifies the *toquz*-group (i.e., that group which in this book is called Turkic) into the foolowing five subgroups:

1. Yakut.
2. Northern group: Tuva, Karagas, Abakan dialects, Baraba, Altai, Teleut.
3. Western group: Kirghiz, Kazakh, Nogai, Karai, Kuman, Tatar, Bashkir, Kumyk, Karachai-Balkar.
4. Eastern group: East Turki (Modern Uighur), Uzbek.
5. Southern group: Turkmenian, Anatolian (i.e., Turkish spoken in Turkey, sometimes called also Osmanli or Osman-Turkish), and Azerbaijan Turkic.

On the basis of Samoilovich's and Ramstedt's classifications the following amended classification of the Turkic languages (i.e., z- and š- languages, Chuvash excluded) may be given:

The Turkic languages				
atax	adaq/azaq	ayaq "foot"		
tïa	taγ	tau/tu	taγ/daγ "mountain"	
ï	ïγ	ï	ïq	ï
I	II	III	IV	V
Yakut	Tuva-Khakas	Kypchak	Chaghatai	Turkmen

The Roman numbers denote groups named here after individual languages, each representative of the group concerned.

The same can be represented as a system of concentric circles:

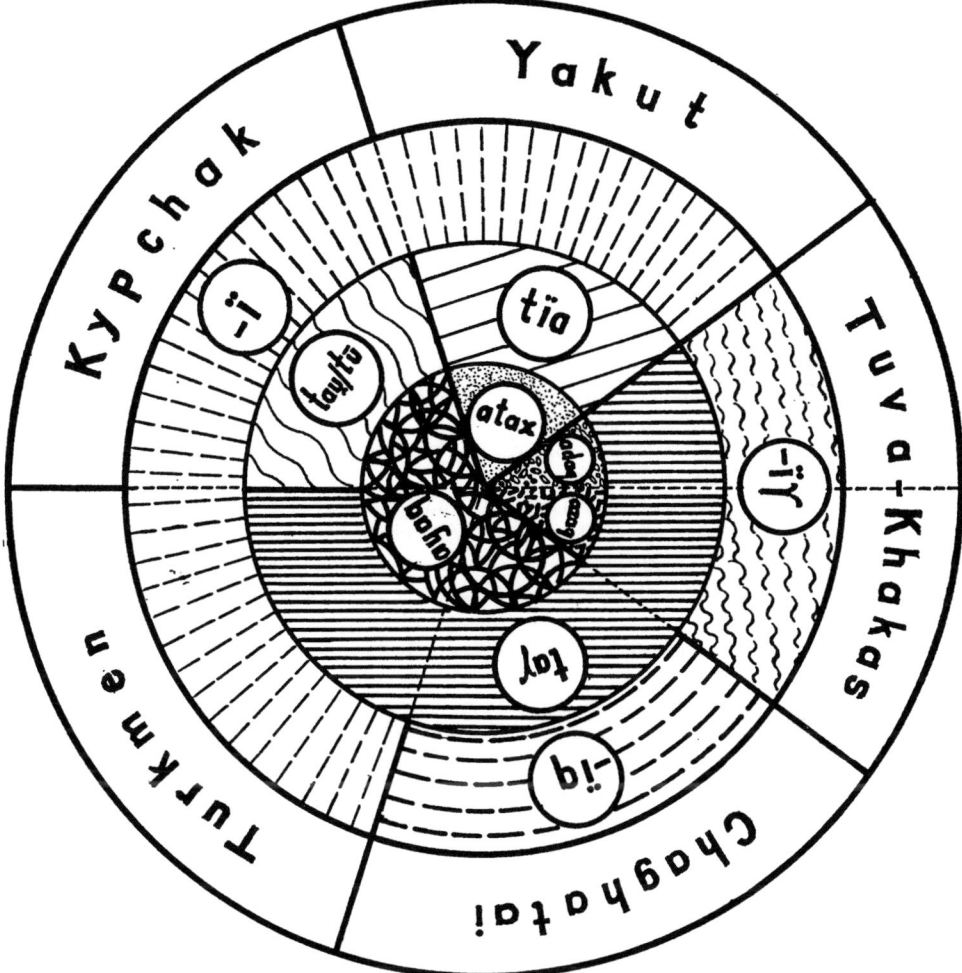

Each of the five groups, with the exception of Yakut, can be divided into still smaller subgroups. The most diversified group is Kypchak which, according to suggestions made by Prof. O. Pritsak, can be divided into the following four subgroups:

1. Karai, Karachai-Balkar, and Kumyk which have $*a\gamma > a\underset{\sim}{u}$ and lack the features characteristic of the other three subgroups;
2. Tatar and Bashkir which also have $*a\gamma > a\underset{\sim}{u}$ but also $*o > u$, $*ö > ü$, $*u > \theta$, $*ü > ö$, $*i > \vartheta$, and $*e > i$, lacking the features characteristic of the remaining subgroups 3 and 4;

3. Nogai, Kazakh, Karakalpak which have *č > š, *š > s, and the consonant *n at the onset of suffixes appearing as n/d/t, depending on the stem-final phoneme;
4. Kirghiz and Altai which have secondary long vowels, labial attraction, and the consonant m at the onset of the suffix -ma- of the negative verb-stem being replaced by p/b, depending on the stem-final phoneme.

Continuing subdivision into still smaller units, one finally arrives at individual languages. Thus Bashkir shares many features with Tatar but has *č > s, *s- > h (*-s- and *-s > ϑ), *z > ð, labial harmony, and other features alien to Tatar.

Bibliography:

Baskakov, N. A., "K voprosu o klassifikacii tyurkskix yazïkov", *IAN-OLYa* 11: 2 (1952).
— "Klassifikaciya tyurkskix yazïkov v svyazi s istoričeskoĭ periodizacieĭ ix razvitiya i formirovaniya", *TIYa* 1 (1952).
— *Tyurkskie yazïki*, Moskva 1960, pp. 91–103.
Benzing, J. and Menges, K. H., *Philologiae Turcicae Fundamenta*, Tomus primus, Aquis Mattiacis 1959, pp. 1–10.
Jyrkänkallio, P., "Übersicht über die türkischen Völker unserer Zeit", *StOF* 14: 10 (1950), pp. 1–31, with 2 maps.
— "A Survey of Present-Day Turkic Peoples, Second Edition translated from the German and revised" by John R. Krueger, *Central Asian Collectanea* 7 (Washington D.C. 1961).
Räsänen, M., *Zur Lautgeschichte der türkischen Sprachen*, StOF 15 (1949), pp. 26–31.
Samoĭlovič, A. N., *Nekotorïe dopolneniya k klassifikacii tureckix yazïkov*, Petrograd 1922.
Wurm, St., *Turkic Peoples of the USSR*, Their Languages and the Development of Soviet Linguistic Policy, London 1954.

1.31. Chuvash

The only surviving *r*-language (*tăxxăr* "nine" versus Turkic *toquz*) is Chuvash which is spoken by almost 1.5 million people in the Chuvash Autonomous Socialist Soviet Republic in the USSR, to be exact, in the middle course of the Volga River. It comprises two main dialects, namely Anatri, i.e., the Lower dialect (spoken downstream), and Viryal, i.e., the Upper dialect (spoken upstream).

Chuvash is the descendant of one of the dialects of the ancient Volga Bulgar which was spoken in the Bulgar kingdom on the banks of the Volga and Kama, existing from the VII century AD to the XIV century. Numerous Bulgarian words were taken by the ancient Hungarians from some dialect close to Volga Bulgar at the time when the Hungarians still lived in the area north of the Caucasus, mainly in the present Kuban region, whence they migrated to present Hungary in the IX century AD.

Another kingdom in that period was the Khazar kingdom. It was situated in the lower courses of the Volga and Don rivers and existed in the VII–X centuries AD. Whether the Khazars spoke a dialect or language closely related to Bulgar, i.e., an *r*-language or dialect, cannot be said for sure because of lack of material unequivocally proving that Khazar was an *r*-language.

There is no doubt that Chuvash is very closely related to Bulgar, because both are *r*- (and *l*-) languages:

Ch. *šĕr*	"one hundred"	= Bulg. *ǰür*	id.	= Turk. *yüz*	id.
Ch. *xĕr*	"daughter"	= Bulg. *hïr*	id.	= Turk. *qïz*	id.
Ch. *pillĕkĕmĕš*	"the fifth"	= Bulg. *biyälim*	id.	= Turk. *bešinč*	id.
Ch. *šul*	"year"	= Bulg. *ǰāl*	id.	= Turk. *yaš*	"age"

The material available on Bulgar is not abundant. It is confined to a few inscriptions in Arabic script on tombstones dating from the XIII-XIV centuries.

The Volga Bulgars used the Arabic script but the Chuvash themselves either lost or never had it and did not know any script at the time when the first Russian missionaries came to them. The first attempts at writing with Russian letters were made in 1730. The present alphabet, based on the Russian alphabet, was introduced after the revolution, having replaced the phonemic alphabet, also based on Russian, which had been introduced in 1871 by Yakovlev. The present Chuvash alphabet is given in the general table of alphabets (*vide* 1.33).

Bibliography:

A. Chuvash

Andreev, N. A., Egorov, V. G., Pavlov, I. P., *Materialï po grammatike sovremennogo čuvašskogo yazïka* I, Čeboksarï 1957.

Ašmarin, N. I., *Materialï dlya isslĕdovaniya čuvašskago yazïka* I–II, Kazań 1898 (the most complete grammar of Chuvash, although obsolete in method).

— *Opït izslĕdovaniya čuvašskago sintaksisa*, č. I, Kazań 1903; č. II, Simbirsk 1923.

— *Thesaurus linguae tchuvaschorum*, I–XVII, Kazań-Čeboksarï 1928–1950 (the most complete dictionary of Chuvash).

Čuvašsko-russkiĭ slovaŕ, Pod redakcieĭ člena-korrespondenta Akademii Pedagogičeskix Nauk M. Ya. Sirotkina, Moskva 1961 (contains a concise grammar).

Egorov, V. G., *Bibliografičeskiĭ ukazateĺ literaturï po čuvašskomu yazïku*, Čeboksarï 1931 (bibliography).

Gorskiĭ, S. P., *Očerki po istorii čuvašskogo literaturnogo yazïka*, Čeboksarï 1959.

Krueger, J. R., *Chuvash Manual, Introduction, Grammar, Reader, and Vocabulary*, UAS 7 (1962).

Krueger, J. R., "Morphophonemic Change in Chuvash Verb", American Studies in Altaic Linguistics, *UAS* 13 (1962), pp. 129–140.

Paasonen, H., *Csuvás szójegyzek*, Budapest 1908 (Chuvash-Hungarian-German dictionary).

Pritsak, O., "Tschuwaschische Pluralsuffixe", *SA* (Wiesbaden 1957), pp. 137–155.

— "Die Herkunft des tschuwaschischen Futurums", *WZKM* 56 (1960), pp. 141–153.

Ramstedt, G. J., "Zur Frage nach der Stellung des Tschuwassischen", *JSFOu* 38: 1 (1922), pp. 1–34.

Russko-čuvasskiĭ slovaŕ, Pod redakcieĭ N. K. Dmitrieva, Moskva 1951 (contains a concise grammar).

B. Bulgar

Baskakov, N. A., *Tyurkskie yazïki*, Moskva 1960, pp. 106–112.

Gombocz, Z., *Die bulgarisch-türkischen Lehnwörter in der ungarischen Sprache*, MSFOu 30 (1912).

Pritsak, O., "Die sogenannte Bulgarische Fürstenliste und die Sprache der Protobulgaren", *UAJ* 26: 1–2 (1954), pp. 61–77.

— *Die bulgarische Fürstenliste und die Sprache der Protobulgaren*, Wiesbaden 1955.

— "Bolgaro-Tschuwaschica", *UAJ* 21 (1959), pp. 274–314.

— "Kultur und Sprache der Hunnen", *Čyževskyj-Festschrift*, herausgegeben von M. Vasmer und D. Gerhard, Berlin 1954, pp. 238–249.

Yusupov, T. B., *Vvedenie v bulgaro-tatarskuyu èpigrafiku*, Moskva-Leningrad 1960.

1.32. The Turkic languages.

The Turkic languages are z- and š- languages, in which z and š correspond to Chuvash r and l respectively. They are descendants of Common Turkic (otherwise called Proto-Turkic). The Turkic languages are spoken in Turkey (both in the European part and in Asia Minor), in the Volga region, in the Caucasus, in Turkestan, in parts of Afghanistan, in Northern Iran, in many parts of Western and Eastern Siberia, and in the Western regions of the Mongolian People's Republic.

They are classified in five groups.

1.321. Yakut.

Yakut is the northernmost Turkic language and is spoken in the Yakut Autonomous Socialist Soviet Republic, in the northern part of East Siberia. The Yakuts call themselves Sakha *saxa*. The name Yakut was given to them by the Tungus who called them *yękē*. The Yakuts number approximately 240,000.

The Yakut language differs considerably from all the other Turkic languages both phonemically and morphologically, as well as with regard to the vocabulary which is less than 50 percent of Turkic origin.

The Yakuts had not had a script prior to the arrival of the first Russian missionaries. The first attempts at writing with the help of the Russian alphabet were made in the XIX century. A romanized alphabet based on the international phonetic transcription was compiled in 1922 by S. A. Novgorodov, a native Yakut trained linguistically at the University of Petrograd in Russia. In 1939 the present alphabet based on Cyrillic was introduced.

The Yakut alphabet is given in the general table of alphabets (1.33).

Bibliography:

Böhtlingk, O., *Über die Sprache der Yakuten* I–II, St. Petersburg 1848–51.

Kałużyński, S., *Mongolische Elemente in der jakutischen Sprache*, Warszawa 1961.

Krueger, J. R., *Yakut Manual*, UAS 25 (1963).
Pekarskiĭ, Ė. K., *Slovaŕ yakutskogo yazïka* I–III, St. Peterburg-Leningrad 1907–1930. (New edition: 1958–1959).
Poppe, N., "Das Yakutische", *PhTF*, pp. 671–84.
Ubryatova, E. I., *Očerk istorii izučeniya yakutskogo yazïka*, Yakutsk 1945 (complete bibliography).
— *Issledovaniya po sintaksisu yakutskogo yazïka*, Moskva-Leningrad 1950.
Xaritonov, L. N., *Sovremennïĭ yakutskiĭ yazïk*, Yakutsk 1947.
— *Tipï glagoĺnoĭ osnovï v yakutskom yazïke*, Moskva-Leningrad 1954.
— *Formï glagoĺnogo vida v yakutskom yazïke*, Moskva-Leningrad 1960.
Yastremskiĭ, S. V., *Grammatika yakutskogo yazïka*, Irkutsk 1900; II edition: Moskva 1938 (obsolete).

1.322. The Tuva-Khakas group.

The Tuva-Khakas group is divided into three subgroups: 1. *adaq*-subgroup; 2. *azaq*-subgroup; 3. *ayaq*-subgroup.

One of the characteristic features of the *adaq*-subgroup is the preservation of ancient *d* as such: *adaq* 'foot'. In the other two subgroups the same word is *azaq* and *ayaq* respectively.

1.3221. The *adaq*-languages are Tuvinian and Karagas.

1.32211. Tuvinian.

Tuvinian (Tuva, Soyot, or Uriankhai) spoken by 100,000 people in the Autonomous Tuva Region, in Eastern Siberia (prior to 1944 a semi-independent people's republic, a satellite of the USSR since 1921), is an *adaq*-language.

The Tuvinians did not have a script of their own prior to 1930 and used the Written Mongolian language. A romanized alphabet was introduced in 1931 which was replaced by the Cyrillic alphabet in 1941.

The Tuvinian alphabet is given in the general table of alphabets (1.33).

Bibliography:

Isxakov, F. G., *Tuvinskiĭ yazïk*, Očerk po fonetike, Moskva-Leningrad 1957.
— i Paĺmbax, A. A., *Grammatika tuvinskogo yazïka*, Moskva 1961.
Katanov, N. F., *Opït izslĕdovaniya uryanxaĭskago yazïka*, Kazań 1903.
Menges, K. H., "Das Sojonische und Karagassische", *PhTF*, pp. 640–670.
Tuvinsko-russkiĭ slovaŕ, pod redakcieĭ A. A. Paĺmbaxa, Moskva 1955 (contains a concise grammar).

1.32212. Karagas.

Karagas (Tofa), closely related to Tuvinian, is spoken by 500–600 people in a locality of the Krasnoyarsk province (kraĭ). They are believed to be descendants of Samoyeds who adopted a Turkic language.

The Karagas have no script of their own and can read and write only Russian.

Bibliography:

Castrén, M. A., *Versuch einer koibalischen und karagassischen Sprachlehre*, St. Petersburg 1857.

Menges, K. H., "Das Sojonische und Karagassische", *PhTF*, pp. 640–670.
Radloff, W., *Proben der Volksliteratur der türkischen Stämme* IX, St. Petersburg 1907.
— *Obrazcï narodnoĭ literaturï tyurkskix plĕmen* II, St. Petersburg 1868.

1.3222. The *azaq*-dialects.

1.32221. Abakan dialects.

The *azaq*-dialects (*azaq* "foot") are spoken by various small groups of Turks inhabiting the Abakan area in Eastern Siberia.

The number of speakers totals 57,000. The tribes in question did not have a script prior to 1924. The presently used alphabet was introduced in 1939. The dialects in question were united under one literary language based on two larger dialects, namely Sagai (and the almost identical Beltir) and Kacha. This unified language received the name Khakas after a tribe mentioned in ancient Chinese annals. The name Khakas is, however, a false reading of the name of the Kirghiz (*qïryïz*), distorted in rendition with Chinese characters. The latter have nothing in common with the speakers of the Sagai, Kacha, and other dialects in that area.

Bibliography:

Baskakov, N. A. i Inkiževkova-Grekul, A. I., *Xakassko-russkiĭ slovaŕ*, Moskva 1953 (contains a concise grammar).
Dïrenkova, N. P., *Grammatika xakasskogo yazïka*, Abakan 1948.
Pritsak, O., "Das Abakan- und Čulymtürkische und das Schorische", *PhTF*, pp. 598–629.

1.32222. Yellow Uighur.

The Yellow Uighurs *sarï uyγur* are a small group living in the Chinese province of Kansu. Their language belongs to the *azaq*-group, cf. *azaq* "foot". The total number of speakers is not known. The Yellow Uighurs do not have a script of their own. Some Yellow Uighurs speak a particular Mongolian dialect.

Bibliography:

Kotwicz, Wł., "La langue mongole parlée par les ouïgours jaunes près de Kan-tcheou", *RO* 16 (1953), pp. 435–465.
Malov, S. E., *Yazïk želtïx uĭgurov*, Alma-Ata 1957.
Mannerheim, C.G.E., "A Visit to the Sarö and Shera Yögurs", *JSFOu* 27: 2, pp. 1–72.

1.3223. The *ayaq*-dialects.

The Tuva-Khakas group includes also some *ayaq*-dialects or languages (*ayaq* "foot"). These represent a link between this group and the Kypchak group. They include the languages Shor, Chulym, Tuba, Kumanda, Chalkan, and Lebed.

1.32231. Shor.

Shor *šor* is spoken by 15,000 people in the northern part of the Altai range and in the Kuznetsk Alataw mountain range, in the river basins of Kondoma, Mrass, and Toḿ.

The Shor, in older Russian literature also called *černevïe tatarï* (i.e., "The Black Forest Tatars") or *Kuznetsk Tatars*, do not have a script of their own and use either the Khakas script or write in Russian. Prior to 1944, however, they had their own script based on Cyrillic.

Bibliography:

Dïrenkova, N. P., *Šorskiĭ fol̀klor*, Moskva-Leningrad 1940.
— *Grammatika šorskogo yazïka*, Moskva-Leningrad 1941.
Pritsak, O., "Das Abakan- und Čulymtürkische und das Schorische", *PhTF*, pp. 630–640.

1.32232. Chulym.

Chulym *čulïm* is the collective name of the dialects Ketsik, Küärik *küärik*, and Chulym proper which are spoken in the basin of the Chulym river, a tributary of the Ob. Some tribes speaking these dialects may be turkicized Ostiaks (i.e., Ugrians) or Kets (i.e., a Palaeoasiatic tribe). Exact numbers of speakers are not known. Chulym has no script. Its speakers use the Russian literary language.

Bibliography:

Baskakov, N. A., *Tyurkskie yazïki*, Moskva 1960, pp. 206–207.
Dul̀zon, A. P., "Čulïmskie tatarï i ix yazïk", *Učenïe Zapiski Tomskogo gosudarstvennogo pedagogičeskogo instituta* 9 (1952) (contains also a bibliography).
Pritsak, O., "Das Abakan- und Čulymtürkische und das Schorische", *PhTF*, pp. 622–630.

1.32233. Tuba and related dialects.

The dialects Tuba (of the so-called Black Forest Tatars), Kumanda, Chalkan, and Lebed are spoken in the northern parts of the Autonomous Altai Mountain Region (Gorno-Altaĭskaya Avtonomnaya Oblast) and are officially counted among the dialects of the Altai language which belongs to the Kypchak group, although they do not belong to the Altai language.

The total number of speakers of these dialects amounts to 16,000.

The dialects in question do not have a script of their own but are served by the literary Altai language (vide 1.32310).

Bibliography:

Baskakov, N. A., *op cit.*, pp. 212–218.
— *Altaĭskiĭ yazïk*, Moskva 1958, pp. 109 ff.
Pritsak, O., "Das Altaitürkische", *PhTF*, pp. 568–598.

1.323. The Kypchak group.

The Kypchak *qïpčaq* group is called so after the Kypchaks or Kumans, a nomad people who were frequently engaged in wars against the Kievan Russian state in the XI–XIII centuries. The Russians called the Kumans Polovtsi.

The Kypchak group comprises the following languages: Karai, Kumyk, Karachai-Balkar, Crimean Tatar, Volga Tatar, Bashkir, Nogai, Kazakh, Kirghiz, Altai (Oirot), and, of course, Kuman which is no longer spoken and was a Middle Turkic language. This is one of the largest groups of Turkic languages presently spoken by more than ten million people.

The languages belonging to the Kypchak group are characterized by the following features: *ayaq* "foot", *taṷ* (*tō*, *tū*) "mountain", the syllable **ïγ* has resulted in *ï*. Some languages are *yoq*-languages, others are *ǰoq*-languages (*yoq*/*ǰoq* "not"), etc.

1.3231. Karai.

Karai or Karaim (Hebrew plural of Karai) who call themselves *qaray* are a small Turkic people professing the Jewish faith. They live in Lithuania (in the cities of Troki and Poniewież), in the Ukraine (near Luck and Halicz), and in the Crimea (near Evpatoria). The total number of speakers amounts to 6,000 people.

The Karai use in their religious books the Hebrew alphabet. Since the beginning of the XX century, the Latin (Polish) and the Cyrillic alphabets are used in secular literature.

The Karai (Hebrew) alphabet

Letters	Names	Transcription and explanation
א	āleph	"Mater lectionis" for *a/ä, o/ö, i/i, ü*
ב	beth	*b*, sometimes *w*
ג	gimel	*g, η* (*η* is also rendered by *nun* and *gimel*)
ד	dāleth	*d*
ה	he	*g* in loan-words
ו	wāw	*v*
ז	zayin	*z*
ח	heth	*x*
ט	ṭeth	*t*
י	yodh	*i/i, y*; palatalization mark of front (especially rounded) vowels and palatal consonants
כ, ך	kaph	*k*
ל	lāmedh	*l*
מ, ם	mēm	*m*
נ, ן	nun	*n*
ס	sāmekh	*s*
ע	'ayin	"Mater lectionis" for *u*
פ, ף	pē	*p*
צ, ץ	ṣādhe	*č* (Halicz *c*)
ק	ḳoph	*q*
ר	resh	*r*
ש	shin	*š*
ת	tāw	*th* in loan-words

Where two letters are given for a single phoneme, the second one is used in final position.

Bibliography:

Foy, K., "Karaimisch-türkische Sprachproben aus Halič in Galizien", *MSOS* 1 (1898), Westasiatische Studien, pp. 172–184.

Kowalski, T., "Język karaimski", Myśl Karaimska I (Wilna 1926).

— Karaimische Texte im Dialekt von Troki, Kraków 1929 (includes a complete bibliography).

Mardkowicz, A., *Karai sez bitigi*, Luck 1935 (a Karai-Polish-German dictionary).

Musaev, K. M. *Grammatika karaimskogo jazïka, Fonetika i morfologiya*, Moskva 1964 (With an introduction containing bibliography).

Pritsak, O., "Das Karaimische", *PhTF*, pp. 318–340.

Zajączkowski, A., *Krótki wykład gramatyki języka zachodnio-karaimskiego*, Luck 1931.

— *Sufiksy imienne i czasownikowe w języku zachodnio-karaimskim*, Kraków 1932.

1.3232. Kumyk.

Kumyk *qumïq* is spoken in Daghestan (Caucasus) by 135,000 people. It has three dialects (Khaidak, Buinak, and Khasaw-Yurt).

The Kumyks used, until 1930, the Arabic script which was superceded by a romanized alphabet. Since 1939 the Cyrillic alphabet has been used. The present Kumyk alphabet is given in the general table (1.33).

Bibliography:

Bammatova, Z. Z., *Russko-kumïkskiĭ slovaŕ*, pod redakcieĭ –, Moskva 1960.

Dmitriev, N. K., *Grammatika kumïkskogo yazïka*, Moskva-Leningrad 1940.

— "Materialï po istorii kumïkskogo yazïka", *Yazïki Severnogo Kavkaza i Dagestana*, t. II, Moskva-Leningrad 1949.

1.3233. Karachai-Balkar.

Karachai *qaračay* and Balkar *balqar/malqar* are two dialects of one language. Karachai is spoken by 70,000 people in the Karachai-Circassian Autonomous region in the Northern Caucasus. Balkar is spoken by 40,000 people in the Autonomous Kabardian-Balkar region in the Northern Caucasus.

Although Karachai and Balkar are two dialects of one language, their alphabets based on Cyrillic are not quite identical.

Bibliography:

Akbaev, I., *Russko-Karačaevskiĭ slovaŕ*, Batalpašinsk 1926.

Aliev, U., *Karačaevo-balkarskaya grammatika* (gorsko-tyurkskiĭ yazïk), Kislovodsk 1930.

Baĭramkulov, U., *Grammatika karačaevskogo yazïka*, Kislovodsk 1930.

Borovkov, A. K., "Karačaevo-balkarskiĭ yazïk", *YaS* 7 (1931).

— "Očerki karačaevo-balkarskoĭ grammatiki", *Yazïki Severnogo Kavkaza i Dagestana* I (1935).

Filonenko, V. I., *Grammatika balkarskogo yazïka*, Naĺčik 1940.

Hebert, R. J., "Karachai Phonology", *UAS* 13 (1962), pp. 97–114.

Pritsak, O., "Das Karatschaische und Balkarische", *PhTF*, pp. 340–368.

Pritsak, O., „Die ursprünglichen türkischen Vokallängen im Balkarischen", *Jean Deny Armağanı*, Ankara 1958, pp. 203–207.
Pröhle, W., "Balkarische Studien", *KSz* 15 (1914–15), 16 (1915–1916).
— "Karatschaisches Wörterverzeichnis", *KSz* 10 (1909).

1.3234. Crimean Tatar.

Crimean Tatar was spoken, prior to World War II, by several hundred thousand people in Crimea. After the reoccupation of Crimea by the Soviets during World War II, the entire population of Crimea was moved to Russian Central Asia on the ground that it had collaborated with the Germans.

Crimean Tatar is now "the language of a small ethnic group living mainly in the Uzbek Republic" (verbatim quotation from N. A. Baskakov, *Tyurkskie yazïki*, Moskva 1960, p. 154). No details with regard to the exact whereabouts or numbers of the Crimean Tatars are available.

Prior to their deportation, the Crimean Tatars were classified in two groups: the South-shore Tatars and the Northern or Steppe Tatars. The South-shore Tatars spoke a dialekt of the Turkish language (Anatolian) spoken in Turkey. They were the descendants of those Turks who moved into the Crimea at the time when the latter was part of the Turkish Empire. The Crimean peninsula was conquered by the Russians at the end of the XVIII century. The Russian conquest and oppression of the Turks by the Russians caused 200,000 Turks to emigrate back to Turkey. Only a few of them remained in the Crimea until the end. They spoke a dialect very little differing from standard Turkish. The speakers of this dialect numbered (1940) hardly more than 50,000.

The Steppe Tatars or the Nogai spoke a language typical of the Kypchak group. Before World War II, their number exceeded 200,000.

Besides, in the Crimea there lived the so-called Krymchaks or the Crimean Jews. They numbered about 5,000. None of the latter survived World War II because all of them were exterminated by the Germans "for being of Jewish origin". They spoke a special dialect of Steppe Tatar.

Prior to the revolution of 1917 in Russia, the Crimean Tatars used the Arabic alphabet. Their literary language was the descendant of the literary language of the Golden Horde (1.3443).

In 1929 a romanized alphabet was introduced which, shortly before World War II, was replaced by a Cyrillic alphabet.

The Crimean Tatar language can be regarded as practically extinct.

Bibliography:

Čoban-Zadė, B., *Naučnaya grammatika krïmsko-tatarskogo yazïka*, Simferopol' 1925.
Doerfer, G., "Das Krimtatarische", *PhTF*, pp. 369–390.
Odabaš, A. i Kaya, I. S., *Rukovodstvo dlya obučeniya krïmsko-tatarskomu yazïku*, Simferopol', izd. III, 1928.
Samoĭlovič, A. N., *Opït kratkoĭ krïmsko-tatarskoĭ grammatiki*, Petrograd 1916.
Zaatov, O., *Polnïĭ russko-tatarskiĭ slovaŕ*, Simferopol' 1906.

1.3235. Tatar.

Tatar *tatar* is spoken by almost five million people mainly in the Autonomous Tatar Republic and in the adjacent parts of the Volga region, and in various places in Western Siberia.

Their language comprises seven dialects. The central dialect is spoken by more than 1.5 million people in the republic. This dialect is also called Kazan Tatar (after the name of the capital) or Kazan Turkic. The Western or Mishar *mišär* dialect is spoken in the Goŕkiĭ, Tambov, Voronež, Ryazań, Penza, Simbirsk, Samara, Saratov and Orenburg regions, in the Autonomous Mordvan Republic, and in the Bashkir Republic. The eastern dialect or the dialect of the Siberian Tatars (in Baraba, Tomsk, Tyumeń, Ishim, Yalutorovsk, Toboĺsk, etc.) is spoken by about 100,000 people.

The other dialects are those of Astrakhan, Kasimov, Teptyar, and Ural Tatars.

Prior to the Soviet regime, the Tatars used the Arabic alphabet. Their literary language was that of the Golden Horde (1.3443).

The present literary language is based on the Central dialect. In 1938 a Cyrillic alphabet was introduced which is shown in the general table of alphabets (1.33).

Bibliography:

Baĭčura, U. S., *Zvukovoĭ sostav tatarskogo yazïka*, Kazań, I 1959; II 1960.

Gazizov, R. S., *Sopostaviteĺnaya grammatika tatarskogo i russkogo yazïkov*, Kazań 1959.

Kurbangaliev, M., Gazizov, R., Kuleev, I., *Tatarsko-russkiĭ slovaŕ*, Izd. II, Kazań 1931.

Poppe, N., *Tatar Manual*, UAS 20 (1963) (grammar, texts, glossary, and bibliography).

Tatarsko-russkiĭ slovaŕ, Kazań 1950.

Thomsen, K., "Das Kasantatarische und die westsibirischen Dialekte", *PhTF* pp. 407–421.

Weil, G., *Tatarische Texte*, Berlin 1930.

1.3236. Bashkir.

Bashkir *bašqort* is spoken by 900,000 people in the Autonomous Bashkir Soviet Republic in the Volga region. It is phonemically quite different from Tatar which is closest to it: *č > s, *s- > h, *-s- and *-s > ϑ (= Engl. *th* in *thin*), *z > ð (= Engl. *th* in *the*), etc.

Formerly, the Bashkir did not have a literary language of their own but used the same literary language and script as the Tatars. The present Cyrillic alphabet was introduced in 1940. The basis of the literary language is the hill dialect which is spoken in the hilly parts of the north-eastern and south-eastern regions of the republic.

The Bashkir alphabet is given in the general table.

Bibliography:

Baškirsko-russkiĭ slovaŕ, Moskva 1958 (Contains a concise grammar by K. Z. Axmerov.)

Dmitriev, N. K., *Grammatika baškirskogo yazïka*, Moskva-Leningrad 1948.
Poppe, N., *Bashkir Manual*, UAS 21 (1963) (grammar, texts, glossary, and bibliography.)
Yuldašev, A. A., *Sistema slovoobrazovaniya i spryaženiya glagola v baškirskom yazïke*, Moskva 1958.

1.3237. Nogai.

Nogai is spoken by 40,000 people in the Stavropol̂ region and in the Autonomous Circassian region in the Northern Caucasus. It has three dialects.

Prior to the revolution in Russia, the Nogai did not have a literary language of their own. Some of them knew the Arabic script. In 1938 the present Cyrillic alphabet and a literary language based on spoken Nogai was introduced.

Bibliography:

Baskakov, N. A., *Nogaĭskiĭ yazïk i ego dialektï*, Moskva-Leningrad 1956.
— *Russko-nogaĭskiĭ slovaŕ*, pod redakcieĭ –, Moskva 1956.
— *Nogaĭsko-russkiĭ slovaŕ*, pod redakcieĭ — (Contains a concise grammar).
Menges, K., "Die aralo-kaspische Gruppe", *PhTF*, pp. 434–488.

1.3238. Kazakh and Karakalpak.

Kazakh *qazaq* is spoken by 3.5 million people in the Kazakh Union Republic. A dialect of this language is Karakalpak *qaraqalpaq* spoken in the Autonomous Karakalpak Republic which is part of the Uzbek Union Republic. The number of speakers of Karakalpak amounts to almost 175,000. Although Karakalpak has been declared by the Soviet authorities an independent language, it is only a dialect of Kazakh. The other dialects of Kazakh are the North-Western, Southern and Western. The literary Kazakh language is based on the North-Western dialect. The Karakalpak have their own literary language. The Cyrillic alphabets of both groups, which were introduced in 1938, slightly differ from each other.

Prior to the revolution in Russia, the Kazakh and Karakalpak used the Arabic script.

Bibliography:

Balakaev, M. B., *Sovremennïĭ kazaxskiĭ yazïk*, Sintaksis, Alma-Ata 1959.
— *Osnovnïe tipï slovosočetaniĭ v kazaxskom yazïke*, Alma-Ata 1957.
Baskakov, N. A., *Karakalpakskiĭ yazïk* I–II, Moskva 1951–52.
— *Karakalpaksko-russkiĭ slovaŕ*, pod redakcieĭ –, Moskva 1958.
Isengalieva, V. A., *Služebnïe imena i poslelogi v kazaxskom yazïke*, Alma-Ata 1957.
— *Russkie predlogi i ix ėkvivalentï v kazaxskom yazïke*, Alma-Ata 1960.
Maxmudov, S., Musabaev, G., *Kazaxsko-russkiĭ slovaŕ*, Alma-Ata 1954.
Menges, K. H., "Die aralo-kaspische Gruppe", *PhTF*, pp. 434–488.
— *Qaraqalpaq Grammar* I: Phonology, New York 1947.
Musabaev, G. G., *Sovremennïĭ kazaxskiĭ yazïk* I: Leksika, Alma-Ata 1959.
Sarïbaev, S. S., *Bibliografičeskiĭ ukazateĺ po kazaxskomu yazïkoznaniyu*, Alma-Ata 1956 (bibliography).

Voprosi istorii i dialektologii kazaxskogo yazïka I, Alma-Ata 1958.
Wurm, S., "The Karakalpak Language", *Anthropos* 46 (1951), pp. 487–610.

1.3239. Kirghiz.

Kirghiz *qïrγïz* (or Kara-Kirghiz as it is called sometimes) is spoken by almost one million people in the Kirghiz Union Republic. Kirghiz has two main dialects, and these are the northern and the southern dialect. The former has been influenced by Kazakh, the latter betrays Uzbek influence.

Formerly the Arabic alphabet was used. The present alphabet given in the general table was introduced in 1940.

Bibliography:

Batmanov, I. A., *Grammatika kirgizskogo yazïka* I–III, Frunze 1939–1940.
— *Kratkoe vvedenie v izučenie kirgizskogo yazïka*, Frunze 1947.
— *Sovremennïĭ kirgizskiĭ yazïk*, č. I, Frunze 1953.
Hebert, R. J. *Kirghiz Manual*, UAS 33 (Rather poor. By some error, the author of these lines is listed as Hebert's coauthor).
Menges, K., "Die aralo-kaspische Gruppe", *PhTF*, pp. 434–488.
Yudaxin, K. K., *Kirgizsko-russkiĭ slovaŕ*, Moskva 1940 (available also in Turkish translation: Prof. K. K. Yudahin, *Kırgız sözlüğü* I–II, Ankara 1945–1948).

1.32310. Altai.

Altai, which until 1947 was called Oirot, is a group of dialects spoken in the Autonomous Altai region. The total number of speakers is 45,000. The dialects in question are grouped in southern and northern. The southern dialects are: 1. Altai, spoken in the valleys of the rivers Katun, Sema, Pesčanaya, Čariš, Ursul, and Maĭma; 2. Telengit, spoken along the rivers Čulišman and Baškauz, on the southern bank of the Teletsk lake, and along the river Čuĭ; 3. Teleut, spoken in the districts Shebalinsk, Maĭma, and in adjacent areas.

The Altai dialect is the basis of the literary language. Prior to the arrival of Russian missionaries in the XIX century, the Altai Turks did not have a system of writing. Their present alphabet was introduced in 1937.

The literary Altai language serves also the speakers of the Tuba dialect mentioned in 1.32233.

Bibliography:

Baskakov, N. A., *Altaĭskiĭ yazïk*, Moskva 1958.
— i Toščakova, T. M., *Oĭrotsko-russkiĭ slovaŕ*, Moskva 1947 (contains a concise grammar and bibliography).
Dïrenkova, N. P., *Grammatika oĭrotskogo yazïka*, Moskva-Leningrad 1940.
Pritsak, O., "Das Altaitürkische", *PhTF*, pp. 568–598.
Rachmatullin, G. R., *Die Hilfsverben und Verbaladverbien im Altaischen*, Berlin 1928.

1.324. The Chaghatai group.

The Chaghatai group called so after one of the literary Middle Turkic languages includes Uzbek, East Turki and Salar.

1.3241. Uzbek.

Uzbek *özbäk* is the language of six million people inhabiting the Uzbek Union Republic in the USSR, to which an unspecified number of speakers in Afghanistan is to be added. Uzbek comprises a large number of dialects and subdialects which can be roughly classified in two groups: 1. The Iranized dialects which have only six vowel phonemes and no vowel harmony, and 2. those which have from eight to ten vowel phonemes and vowel harmony.

The present literary language is based on the Iranized dialects. Prior to the revolution in Russia, Chaghatai mixed with local Uzbek elements served as the literary language. The use of the Arabic alphabet was discontinued in 1927 and a romanized alphabet was introduced. In 1940 the Cyrillic alphabet was adopted.

Bibliography:

Bidwell, Ch. E., *A Structural Analysis of Uzbek*, Washington D.C. 1955.
Borovkov, A. K., glavnĭi redaktor, *Uzbeksko-russkiĭ slovař*, Moskva 1959.
Gabain, A. von, *Özbekische Grammatik*, Leipzig 1945 (contains a bibliography).
Jarring, G., *Uzbek Texts from Afghan Turkestan with Glossary*, LUÅ-NF 1, 34: 2.
— *The Uzbek Dialect of Qilich (Russian Turkestan)*, ibid., 33: 3.
Kononov, A. N., *Grammatika sovremennogo uzbekskogo literaturnogo yazïka*, Moskva-Leningrad 1960.
Poppe, Nicholas, Jr., *Uzbek Newspaper Reader (with Glossary)*, UAS 10 (1962).
Rešetov, V. V., *Uzbekskiĭ yazïk*, č. 1. Vvedenie, fonetika, Taškent 1959.
Sjoberg, A. F., *Uzbek Structural Grammar*, UAS 30 (1963).
— "The Phonology of Standard Uzbek", *UAS* 13 (1962), pp. 237–61.
Wurm, S., "Das Özbekische", *PhTF*, pp. 489–524.
— "The Uzbek dialect of Qizil Quǰaš", *BSOAS* 12 (1947), pp. 86–105.

1.3242. East Turki.

East Turki which in the Soviet Union is officially called Modern Uighur is spoken by the Turkic population of the Chinese province Sinkiang and by a minority group in the Soviet Union republics of the Kazakhs, Kirghiz, and Uzbeks. The total number of speakers amounts to 3,750,000 of which almost 100,000 live in the three Soviet republics enumerated.

East Turki comprises three groups of dialects: 1. southern dialects, 2. northern dialects, and 3. the Lobnor dialect.

The southern dialects are those spoken in Kashgar-Yarkand, Khotan, and Aksu. The northern dialects are spoken in Karashar, Kucha, Turfan, Khami and Ili. The Lobnor dialect is spoken in the area of the lake Lobnor. It differs strongly from the other dialects and displays some features characteristic of the Kypchak language group, in particular, of Bashkir.

The Ili dialect is spoken in the USSR, all the other dialects being spoken on Chinese territory.

East Turki does not have a uniform literary language. The literary language of the Uighurs in the USSR is based on the Ili dialect and uses the Cyrillic alphabet. Literary East Turki outside the USSR is based on the southern dialect and uses the Arabic alphabet.

Bibliography:

Baskakov, N. A., Nasilov, V. M., *Uĭgursko-russkiĭ slovaŕ*, Moskva 1939.
Borovkov, A. K., *Učebnik uĭgurskogo yazĭka*, Leningrad 1935.
Jarring, G., *Studien zu einer osttürkischen Lautlehre*, Lund 1933.
— *Materials to the Knowledge of Eastern Turki* I, LUÅ-NF 1, 43: 4; II ibid., 44: 7; III ibid., 47: 3; IV ibid., 47: 4.
— *An Eastern Turki-English Dialect Dictionary*, LUÅ – NF 1, 56:4 (1964).
Kaĭdarov, A., *Uĭgurskiĭ yazĭk i literatura, Annotirovannĭĭ bibliografičeskiĭ ukazateĺ*, tom I, Alma-Ata 1962.
Kibirova, S., i Cunvazo, Yu. pod redakcieĭ – ,*Uĭgursko-russkiĭ slovaŕ*, Alma-Ata 1961 (contains a concise grammar).
Malov, S. E., *Uĭgurskiĭ yazĭk*, Moskva-Leningrad 1954.
Menges, K., *Volkskundliche Texte aus Ost-Türkistan aus dem Nachlass von N. Th. Katanov*, Berlin [I] 1933; II Berlin 1943.
— *Glossar zu den Volkskundlichen Texten aus Ost-Türkistan* II AGS Kl. 1954, no. 14.
Nadžip, E. N., *Sovremennĭĭ uĭgurskiĭ yazĭk*, Moskva 1960.
— *Uĭgurskiĭ yazĭk*, Moskva 1954 (dictionary).
Nasilov, V. M., *Grammatika uĭgurskogo yazĭka*, Moskva 1940.
Pritsak, O., "Das Neuuigurische", *PhTF*, pp. 525–563.
Raquette, G., "Eastern Turki Grammar", *MSOS* 15–17 (1912–1914).
— *English-Turki Dictionary Based on the Dialects of Kashgar and Yarkand*, Lund 1927.
Yudaxin, K. K., *Xrestomatiya po uĭgurskomu yazĭku*, Moskva 1947.

1.3243. Salar.

Salar is spoken by a small group in the Chinese province of Kansu. It is close to East Turki and may even be a dialect of the latter. It does not have a script of its own, and those literate use literary East Turki of Sinkiang and the Arabic alphabet.

Bibliography:

Kakuk, S., "Un vocabulaire salar", *AOH* 14: 2 (1962), pp. 173–196.
Poppe, N., "Remarks on the Salar Language", *HJAS* 16: 3–4 (1953), pp. 438–477.
Tenišev, E. R., *Salarskiĭ yazĭk*, Moskva 1962.
— "Sur le folklore et la langue des salars", *AOH* 15: 1–2 (1962), pp. 253–272.
Thomsen, K., "Die Sprache der Gelben Uiguren und das Salarische", *PhTF*, pp. 564–568.

1.325. The Turkmen group.

The Turkmen (or Southern) group comprises Turkmenian, Gagauz, Turkish, and Azerbaijan Turkic.

1.3251. Turkmenian.

Turkmenian *türkmän* is spoken by one million people in the Turkmenian Union Republic of the USSR. It is divided into two groups of dialects. The first group includes Yomud, Göklen, Salïr, Sarïk, and Ersarïn. The second group comprises Nohurlï, Anaulï, Khasarlï, etc., spoken in areas along the frontiers of Iran and Uzbekistan.

The Turkmens used the Arabic script and had a literary language of their own since the XV century. At the present time they use the Cyrillic alphabet (introduced in 1940) and have their own literary language.

Part of the Turkmens left their country east of the Caspian Sea and emigrated to the Northern Caucasus, to be exact, to the Stavropoĺ region. The local Russians call them Trukhmen.

Bibliography:

Alijiv, A., ve Beerijiv, K., *Orъsca-tyrkmence sɵzlik*, Aşhabad 1929 (the best Russian-Turkmen dictionary).
Bazin, L., "Le turkmène", *PhTF*, pp. 308–317.
Baskakov, N. A., "Ob osobennostyax govora severokavkazskix turkmenov (truxmenov)", *Yazïki Severnogo Kavkaza i Dagestana* II, Moskva-Leningrad 1949, pp. 140–182 (contains a bibliography).
Baskakova, N. A., i Xamzaeva, M. Ya., *Russko-turkmenskiĭ slovaŕ*, pod redakcieĭ –, Moskva 1956.
Belyaev, I., *Turkmenskaya grammatika*, Ašxabad 1915.
Benzing, J., "Über die Verbformen in Türkmenischen", *MSOS* 42, Abt. 2 (1939).
Dulling, G. K., *An Introduction to the Turkmen Language*, London 1960.
Karrïeva, B. A., *Turkmensko-russkiĭ slovaŕ*, pod redakcieĭ –, Ašxabad 1943.
Menges, K., "Einige Bemerkungen zur vergleichenden Grammatik des Türkmenischen", *AO* XI (1939).
Nerifi, M., *Nekotorïe voprosï sopostavitelnoĭ grammatiki russkogo i turkmenskogo yazïkov*, Ašxabad 1961.
Poceluevskiĭ, A. P., *Fonetika turkmenskogo yazïka*, Ašxabad 1936.
— *Osnovï sintaksisa turkmenskogo literaturnogo yazïka*, Ašxabad 1943.
— *Dialektï turkmenskogo yazïka*, Ašxabad 1936.

1.3252. Gagauz.

Gagauz is spoken by a Turkic group called Gagauz who live in the Ukraine and in the Moldavian Union Republic (the former Bessarabia), in Romania and Bulgaria. The number of those living in the USSR amounts to 124,000.

Gagauz is not a uniform language but comprises a number of dialects investigated insufficiently.

The Gagauz did not have a system of writing before the XIX century. They now use the Cyrillic alphabet.

Bibliography:

Ceachir, M., *Dicţionar gâgauzo-tiurco-român pentru gagauzii din Basarabia*, Chişinau 1938.
Dmitriev, N. K., "Gagauzskie ètyudï", *Uč. Zap. LGU, Ser. fil. nauk* 20: 1 (1939).
— "Gagausische Lautlehre", I–III, *AO* 4 (1932–33); 5 (1933).
Pokrovskaya, L. A., *Grammatika gagauzskogo yazïka*, Fonetika i morfologiya, Moskva 1964 (With an introduction containing bibliography).

1.3253. Turkish.

Turkish *türk dili*, formerly called Osman Turkish or Osmanli after the name of the Ottoman Empire, is also called Anatolian after the country in Asia Minor where it is spoken. It is the language of almost twenty-five million Turks who are the most important among all the Turkic peoples. Their country is the only independent Turkic nation and belongs to the free world. It also plays an important cultural rôle, having the most developed literature, arts and sciences.

Turkish is divided into a number of dialects which do not differ very much from each other. There are two groups of dialects: 1. the Danube Turkish dialects and 2. the Anatolian dialects.

The literary language is a direct continuation of literary Osman. It was greatly influenced by Arabic and Persian. The Turks used the Arabic alphabet until 1929. Under the founder of the modern Turkish nation, Mustafa Kemal Atatürk, the Latin alphabet was introduced in 1929. The basis of the modern literary language is the dialect of Istanbul and Ankara. The modern literary language is gradually ridding itself of Arabic and Persian elements and introducing a large number of new words created on the national basis. Many modern technical and scientific terms were created on the basis of old Turkish words, e.g., *učak* "airplane", from *uč-* "to fly".

The Turkish alphabet (phonemic transcription is given in / /):

A a	/a/	B b	/b/	C c	/ǰ/	Ç ç	/č/	D d	/d/	E e	/e/
F f	/f/	G g	/g/	ğ	/γ/	H h	/h/	İ i	/i/	I ı	/ï/
J j	/ž/	K k	/k/	L l	/l/	M m	/m/	N n	/n/	O o	/o/
Ö ö	/ö/	P p	/p/	R r	/r/	S s	/s/	Ş ş	/š/	T t	/t/
U u	/u/	Ü ü	/ü/	V v	/v/	Y y	/y/	Z z	/z/		

Bibliography:

Aganin, R. A., *Povtorï i odnorodnïe parnïe sočetaniya v sovremennom tureckom yazike*, Moskva 1959.

Bergsträsser, G., "Zur Phonetik des Türkischen nach gebildeter Konstantinopler Aussprache", *ZDMG* 72 (1918), pp. 233–262.

Caferoğlu, A., "Die anatolischen und rumelischen Dialekte", *PhTF*, pp. 239–260.

Deny, J., *Grammaire de la langue turque*, Paris 1921 (uses the Arabic alphabet).

— "L'Osmanli moderne et le turk de Turquie", *PhTF*, pp. 182–239.

Hony, H. C., *A Turkish-English Dictionary*, Oxford 1947.

Kononov, A. N., *Grammatika sovremennogo tureckogo literaturnogo yazika*, Moskva-Leningrad 1956 (by far the best of all grammars).

Kowalski, T., "Osmanisch-türkische Dialekte", *Enzyklopädie des Islams* IV (1937), pp. 991–1011.

Lees, R. B., *The Phonology of Modern Standard Turkish*, UAS 6 (1961).

— "A Compact Analysis for the Turkish Personal Morphemes", *UAS* 13 (1962), pp. 141–176.

Lotz, T., "Thoughts on Phonology as Applied to Turkish", *ibid.*, pp. 343–351.

Maïzeĺ, S. S., *Izafet v tureckom yazike*, Moskva-Leningrad 1959.

Németh, J., *Turkish Grammar*, English Adaptation of the German Original, by T. Halasi-Kun, New York 1962.
— *Zur Einteilung der türkischen Mundarten Bulgariens*, Sofia 1956.
Räsänen, M., *Chansons populaires turques du Nord-Est de l'Anatolie*, StOF 4: 2 (1932).
— "Eine Sammlung von *māni*-Liedern aus Anatolien", *JSFOu* 41: 2 (1926).
— *Türkische Sprachproben aus Mittel-Anatolien*, I *StOF* 5: 2 (1933); II *StOF* 6: 2 (1935); III *StOF* 8: 2 (1936); IV *StOF* 10: 2 (1942).
Redhouse, J. W., *A Turkish and English Lexicon*, 1890 (uses the Arabic alphabet).
Sevortyan, E. V., *Fonetika tureckogo literaturnogo yazïka*, Moskva 1955.
Swift, L. B., "Some Aspects of Stress and Pitch in Turkish Syntactic Patterns", *UAS* 13, pp. 331–341.
— "A Reference Grammar of Modern Turkish", UAS 19 (1963).
Voegelin, C. F. and Ellinghausen, M. E., "Turkish Structure", *JAOS* 63 (1943), pp. 34–65.

1.3254. Azerbaijan Turkic.

Azerbaijan Turkic or Azerbaijanian, Azerbaijani, (formerly called sometimes incorrectly Aderbaijanian), *azarbayǰan dili* is spoken by three million people in Azerbaijan, a union republic within the USSR, in Transcaucasia. It is divided into five groups of dialects: 1. eastern dialects (on the shore of the Caspian Sea); 2. western dialects (in the north-west); 3. northern dialects (in the northern part of the republic); 4. the southern dialects (in the south); 5. central dialects (in the central area of the republic).

Azerbaijan Turkic is also spoken in Persian Azerbaijan, i.e., in the northern areas of Iran. The total number of speakers may amount there to one million. One of the dialects spoken there is Kashkai *qašqay*.

The Turks of Azerbaijan have had a literary language since the XIV century. The Arabic alphabet was used until 1923 everywhere. In 1923 a romanized alphabet, the so-called *Yanalif* (from *yeni* "new", plus *elifba* "alphabet") was introduced in the Soviet Azerbaijan. *Yanalif* was replaced by the Cyrillic alphabet in 1939.

The Arabic alphabet is still used in the Iranian Azerbaijan.

Bibliography:

Ašmarin, N. I., *Obščiǐ obzor narodnïx tyurkskix govorov gor. Nuxi*, Trudï Obščestva Obsledovaniya i Izučeniya Azerbaĭdžana, Baku 1926.
Azerbaĭdžansko-russkiǐ slovaŕ, Baku 1962.
Caferoğlu, A., und Doerfer, G., "Das Aserbaidschanische", *PhTF*, pp. 280–307.
Foy, K., "Azerbajǧanische Studien I–II", *MSOS*, Abt. 2, 6 (1903), pp. 126–193; 7 (1904), pp. 197–265.
Guseĭnova, G., *Azerbaĭdžansko-russkiǐ slovaŕ*, pod redakcieĭ –, Baku 1939 (uses the romanized alphabet).

Fraenkel, G., "Mutual Intelligibility between Turkish of Turkey and Azerbaijani", *UAS* 13, pp. 71–96.
Ritter, G., "Aserbeidschanische Texte zur nordpersischen Volkskunde", *Der Islam* XI (1921).
Romaskevič, A., "Pěsni kaškaĭcev", *Sbornik Muzeya Antropologii i Ėtnografii*, 5: 2 (1925).
Sevortyan, E. V., *Affiksï glagoloobrazovaniya v azerbaĭdžanskom yazïke, Opït sravniteĺnogo issledovaniya*, Moskva 1962.
Simpson, C. G., *The Turkish Language of Soviet Azerbaijan*, Central Asian Research Centre in association with St. Anthony's College (Oxford), Soviet Affairs Study Group 1957.
Zuĺfugarova, L. S., *Anglo-azerbaĭdžansko-russkiĭ ximičeskiĭ slovaŕ* (English-Azerbaijani-Russian Chemistry Dictionary), Baku 1962.

1.33. The Cyrillic alphabets used by the Chuvash and the Turkic peoples in the USSR.

Table I

The Russian alphabet as it is used to write in Russian, Chuvash, and in all Turkic languages spoken in the USSR. The phonemic value of letters is given in / /.

Letters	Phonemes	Letters	Phonemes	Letters	Phonemes
А а	/a/	К к	/k/	Х х	/x/[2]
Б б	/b/	Л л	/l/	Ц ц	/c/[3]
В в	/v/[1]	М м	/m/	Ч ч	/č/
Г г	/g/	Н н	/n/	Ш ш	/š/
Д д	/d/	О о	/o/	Щ щ	/šč/
Е е	/e, ye/	П п	/p/	Ъ ъ[4]	—
Ё ё	/o, yo/	Р р	/r/	Ы ы	/ï/
Ж ж	/ž/	С с	/s/	Ь ь	'/ (palatalization)
З з	/z/	Т т	/t/	Э э	/e/
И и	/i/	У у	/u/	Ю ю	/yu/
Й й	/y/	Ф ф	/f/	Я я[5]	/ya/

Notes.

1. In most Turkic languages a bilabial fricative /w/.
2. Deep-velar fricative = *kh* in Scottish *lokh*.
3. Affricate *ts*.
4. Denotes in Russian words that the preceding consonant closes the syllable: подъезд *podyezd* "porch".
5. The letters Йй, Цц, Щщ, ъ, ь, Ээ, Юю, Яя are not used for Azerbaijan Turkic.

Phonemes which do not exist in Russian or for which there are no special letters in the Russian alphabet are rendered by special letters given in Table II.
The sign × indicates that the letter in question is used in the alphabet concerned.

1. The Altaic Languages

Table II

Languages	Ă ă /ă/	Гъгъ /ɣ/	Гьгь /h/	Ғ ғ /ɣ/	Б ҕ /ɣ/	Дждж /ǰ/	Дьдь /ǰ/	Ĕ ĕ /ə/	Җ җ /ǰ/	З з /ð/	İ i /ï/ /ə/	J j /ǰ/ /y/
Chuvash	×							×				
Yakut					×		×					
Tuva												
Khakas				×							×	
Kumyk		×	×									
Karachai		×				×						
Balkar		×										
Tatar									×			
Bashkir				×						×		
Nogai												
Kazakh				×							×	
Karakalpak				×								
Kirghiz												
Altai												×
Uzbek				×								
East Turki				×					×			
Turkmenian									×			
Azerbaijani				×								×

Languages	Къкъ /q/	Қ қ /q/	Ҡ ҡ /q/	Ҝ ҝ /ģ/	Нгнг /ŋ/	н /ŋ/	Ньнь /ñ/	Ң ң /ŋ/	ҥ /ŋ/	Оьоь /ö/	Ö ö /ö/	Ө ө /ö/
Chuvash												
Yakut						×	×					×
Tuva							×					×
Khakas					×						×	
Kumyk	×			×					×			
Karachai	×					×						
Balkar	×			×								
Tatar								×				×
Bashkir			×					×				×

1.3. The Chuvash-Turkic Languages

Languages	Letters and Phonemes											
	Къкъ /q/	К к /q/	Ққ /q/	Җк /ǵ/	Нгнг /ŋ/	нъ /ŋ/	Ньнь /ñ/	Ң ң /ŋ/	ҥ /ŋ/	Оьоь /ö/	Ö ö /ö/	Ө ө /ö/
Nogai						×				×		
Kazakh		×						×				×
Karakalpak		×			×							×
Kirghiz								×				×
Altai									×		×	
Uzbek		×			×							
East Turki		×						×				×
Turkmenian								×				×
Azerbaijani				·×								×

Languages	Letters and Phonemes											
	Çç /ϑ/ /ś/	Ў ў /o̩/	ý /w/	Уьуь /ü/	Ÿ ÿ /ü/	Ү ү /ü/	ӿ ӿ /ŏ/	Х х /h/	h h /h/	Ч ч /ǰ/	џ /ǰ/	ә ө /ä/
Chuvash	/ś/			×								
Yakut						×			×			
Tuva						×						
Khakas				×							×	
Kumyk				×								
Karachai		×										
Balkar												
Tatar						×			×			×
Bashkir	/ϑ/					×			×			×
Nogai			×									
Kazakh						×	×		×			×
Karakalpak												
Kirghiz						×						
Altai				×								
Uzbek		×						×				×
East Turki						×			×			×
Turkmenian						×						×
Azerbaijani						×			×	×		×

All Chuvash-Turkic languages do not have the same phonemes. Thus Chuvash does not have /b, d, g, ž/ in native words but only in Russian and other borrowings. It should be also noted that the letters given in the Table I do not always have the same phonemic value in all Turkic languages, e.g., *e* renders /e/ but in other languages only /ye/, e.g., Uighur (East Turki) елип /elip/ "taking", Kazakh етті /ettĭ/ "he made", енді /endĭ/ "now", but Kumyk ep /yer/ "earth".

Whereas letters taken directly from the Russian alphabet display some uniformity, letters specially created for the Turkic languages are rather different. The following phonemes are rendered in quite different manners:

/γ/	Гъ гъ	(Kumyk, Karachai, Balkar);
	Ғ ғ	(Khakas, Bashkir, Kazakh, Karakalpak, Uzbek, East Turki, Azerbaijani);
	ҕ	(Yakut).
/ǰ/	Дж дж	(Karachai);
	Дь дь	(Yakut);
	J j	(= palatalized ǰ) (Altai);
	ҷ	(Khakas);
	ҹ	(Azerbaijani).
/q/	Къ къ	(Kumyk, Karachai, Balkar);
	Ҡ ҡ	(Kazakh, Karakalpak, Uzbek, East Turki);
	Ҡ ҡ	(Bashkir);
/ŋ/	нг	(Kumyk, Balkar, Karakalpak, Uzbek);
	нъ	(Khakas, Karachai, Nogai);
	ң	(Yakut, Tuva, Tatar, Bashkir, Kazakh, Kirghiz, East Turki, Turkmenian).
/y/	(in initial position);	
	j	(Azerbaijani);
	й	(East Turki);
	я = /ya/ and ю = /yu/ in most of the other Turkic languages.	

It is hard to say what the reasons for rendering the same phonemes with so different letters are. They may be lack of coordination of work in this field in the various countries of the USSR or the result of a deliberate policy of making closely related languages and dialects unintelligible to their neighbors.

Thus the words /özi/, in some languages /özü/ "himself", and /köp/ "many" are:

Azerbaijani	ези	—
Kumyk	оьзю	кёп
Karakalpak	ези	көп
Nogai	оьзи	коьп
Kazakh	езi	көп
Altai	—	кöп
Khakas	—	кöп

The word /qara/ "black" is spelled in the following way:

Tatar	кара
Bashkir	ҡара
Kumyk	къара
Karakalpak	қара

These different spellings and use of different letters for the same phonemes represent the Turkic languages spoken in the USSR as much more different than they are in reality.

1.34. Historical periodization of the Turkic languages.

The history of the Turkic languages can be followed back into the times much older than the history of the Mongolian or Manchu-Tungus languages.

1.341. The Language of the Huns.

There is a school of thought which believes that the ancient Turks emerged from the Huns among whom there had been tribes speaking a language which may be regarded as the oldest possible form of Turkic and identified with Proto-Turkic.

There is, however, too little material which could be used as evidence to the fact that the language of the Huns really was Proto-Turkic or a language somehow related to the former.

The Hunnic linguistic material consists first of all of a Hunnic verse in Chinese transcription preserved in a Chinese chronicle, which originated in the IV century A.D. The reading of that verse is rather doubtful and, therefore, the words which occur in it cannot be used for comparative linguistic purposes. Hunnic names recorded in history do not help either because the meanings of the words concerned are unknown.

No less doubtful is also the list of *Tʻo-pa* names which are believed to belong to a Proto-Turkic language. The materials mentioned do not enable the linguist to make any definite statements with regard to Hunnic and its relation to Turkic.

In short, the problem must still be worked on and it is advisable in the present stage to refrain from any categorical statements.

Bibliography:

Bazin, L., "Un texte proto-turc du IV-e siècle; Le distique Hiong-nou du 'Tsin-chou'", *O* 1: 2 (1948), pp. 208–219.
— "Recherches sur les parlers Tʻo-pa", *TP* 39 (1950), pp. 228–329.
Boodberg, P. A., "The Language of the Tʻo-pa Wei", *HJAS* 1 (1936), pp. 167–185.
Gabain, A. von, (Review of Bazin, L., "Un texte proto-turc du IV-e siècle: Le distique Hiong-nou du 'Tsin-chou'"), *Islam* 29: 2, pp. 244–246.
— "Über die Ahnen der Türkvölker", *MIO* 1: 3 (1953), pp. 474–479.
Moravcsik, G., *Byzantinoturcica* I. Die byzantinischen Quellen der Geschichte der Türkvölker; II. Sprachreste der Türkvölker in den byzantinischen Quellen, Berlin 1958.

Pritsak, O., "Bolgaro-Tschuwaschica", *UAJ* 31 (1959), pp. 274–314.
— *Die bulgarische Fürstenliste und die Sprache der Protobulgaren*, Wiesbaden 1955.
— "Ein hunnisches Wort", *ZDMG* 104 (1954), pp. 124–135.
— "Der Titel Attila", *Festschrift Max Vasmer*, Berlin 1956, pp. 404–419.
Shiratori, K., *Über die Sprache der Hiung-nu und der Tunghu-Stämme*, Tokio 1900.
— "Sur l'origine des Hiong-nou", *JA* 202: 2 (1923).

1.342. Volga and Danube Bulgarian.

The Hunnic period in history ends with the VI century A.D., and in the VI century two ethnic groups emerge which theretofore had been unknown, namely the Bulgars in the south of present Russia and in the Volga region, and the Turks in Central Asia. Bulgarian was the ancestor of modern Chuvash or a language closely related to Ancient Chuvash, perhaps a dialect of a language of which the ancestor of Chuvash was another dialect.

The material referring to Bulgarian, both Volga Bulgarian and Danube Bulgarian, is limited but it is sufficient to reconstruct the most characteristic features of that language.

First of all, Bulgarian was a *r*- and *l*- language, like Chuvash: *ǰür* "hundred" = Chuvash *šĕr* id. = Turk. *yüz* id.; *ǰāl* "year" = Ch. *šul* id. = Turk. *yaš* "age".

A large number of words were borrowed from Bulgarian dialects into Hungarian at the time when the Hungarians still lived in the vicinity of the Bulgars and had contact with them. It is known that the Hungarians moved into their present country at the end of the IX century A.D. Such words are:
Hung. *ökör* "ox" = Chuvash *văkăr* id. = Turk. *öküz* id.;
Hung. *borjú* "calf" = Chuvash *păru* id. = Turk. *bïzaγï* id., etc.

Bulgarian was by no means an absolutely uniform language. It had several dialects, one of which had *ǰ*-, the other *y*- and the third *s*- (like Chuvash *š*), cf. the following loan-words in Hungarian:
Hung. *ír*- < **īr*- < **yīr*- "to write" = Chuvash *šĕr*- id. = Ancient Turkic *yaz*- id.;
Hung. *gyúr*- < **ǰoγur*- "to knead" = Chuvash *săr*- id. = Ancient Turkic *yoγur*- id.;
Hung. *szél* < **sēl* "wind" = Chuvash *šil* id. = Ancient Turkic *yel* id.

Bibliography:

Gombocz, Z., *Die bulgarisch-türkischen Lehnwörter in der ungarischen Sprache*, MSFOu 30 (1912).
Ligeti, L., "À propos des éléments 'altaïques' de la langue hongroise", *ALH* 11: 1–2 (1961), pp. 15–42.
Marquart, J., "Die nichtslawischen (altbulgarischen) Ausdrücke in der bulgarischen Fürstenliste", *TP* (1910).
Mikkola, J. J., "Die Chronologie der türkischen Donaubulgaren", *JSFOu* 30: 33 (1913/18), pp. 1–33.

Poppe, N., "On some Altaic Loanwords in Hungarian", *UAS* 1 (1960), pp. 139–147.

Pritsak, O., *Die bulgarische Fürstenliste und die Sprache der Protobulgaren*, Wiesbaden 1955.

— "Bolgaro-Tschuwaschica", *UAJ* 31 (1959), pp. 274–314.

— "Bolgarische Etymologien I–III", *UAJ* 29 (1957), pp. 200–214.

— "Kāšġarī's Angaben über die Sprache der Bolgaren", *ZDMG* 109 (1959), pp. 92–116.

1.343. Ancient Turkic.

The Turks became known, for the first time in history, in the VI century. Even a few words of their ancient language were recorded in Byzantine sources. One of them is the name of the river Ural, in Turkic and in Old Russian Yayik (Turkic *yayïq*), which was for the first time mentioned by Ptolemy and, again, in the VI century, by Menandros Protector. Ptolemy calls it Δάιξ, and Menandros gives Δαίχ. This name is certainly not of Turkic origin but it was used at that time by the Turks, and later on, it became *jayïq* or *yayïq* in different Turkic languages.

Menandros gives also the word *dokhia* (δοχια) "funeral ceremony" which corresponds to *yoγ* of the Orkhon Inscriptions of the VIII century.

Thus, the VI century was the beginning of the ancient period of history of the Turkic languages. It was the beginning of the history of Bulgarian, a *r*-language, and also the beginning of the history of Turkic, a group of *z*-languages, one of which is Ancient Turkic as preserved in the inscriptions in runic script and in manuscripts in Sogdian, Manichean, and Brāhmī scripts, and the oldest manuscripts in reformed Sogdian script, i.e., Uighuric.

The characteristic features of Ancient Turkic are the following:

1. Ancient Turkic was an *adaq*-language: *adaq* "foot", *qadγu* "sorrow", *edgü* "superiority, excellent quality", etc.
2. It was also a *taγ*- and *-ïγ*- language: *taγ* "mountain", *yaγmur* "rain", *baγ* "subdivision, bunch", *ātlïγ* "famous".
3. The direct-object (accusative) form had the suffix *-γ*: *ada-γ* "the danger", *čïγañ-i-γ* "the poor ones".
4. Conditional in *-sar*: *kel-sär* "if he comes", *saqïn-sar* "if you intend".
5. Gerunds in *-tï* (on the negative stem), *-ï*, *-pan*: *saqïn-ma-tï* "not thinking", *bar-ï* "going", *käl-i* "coming", *olur-pan* "having sat down".
6. Past tense in *-dïm* (with *d*) on stems ending in a voiceless consonant but *-tïm* (i.e., with *t*) on stems ending in *n, l, r*: *tik-dim* "I erected", *olur-tïm* "I sat down".
7. The possessive suffix of the third person does not yet comply with the vocalic harmony, thus still preserving the characteristics of the independent pronoun **i* "he": *uluš-i* "his realm", *ada-si* "his danger".

A number of other features characterize Ancient Turkic. Let it be mentioned only that its vocabulary was free from Arabic, Persian, and Mongolian loan-words.

Ancient Turkic was not, however, an absolutely uniform language. First of all, the existence of three dialects has been established on the basis of the correspondence *y/n/ñ*: *ayïγ/anïγ/ añïγ* "evil".

The language of the runic inscriptions is a ñ-dialect: *qoñ* "sheep", *añïγ* "evil". The genitive has there the suffix *-ŋ*. The second person of the past tense is *-tïγ*, *-tïγïz*. The voluntative suffix of the third person is *-sun*. The necessitative has *-sïq*: *alqansïq törü* "the manner of [how] one is to worship". The gerund in *-pan* occurs at least as frequently as that in *-p*. Finally, the dubitative particle is *ärinč*.

The *n*-dialect (*anïγ* "evil") differs from the ñ-dialect in that it has in suffixes and in non-first syllables *a* or *ä* instead of *ï* or *i* respectively. Many Manichean manuscripts and some runic inscriptions are written in the *n*-dialect.

The *y*-dialect is found in many manuscripts in Sogdian and Uighuric script. A special *y*-dialect is that of the manuscripts in Brāhmī script.

To these dialects also the *y*- and *ǰ*-dialects can be added. Thus it is known that the title *yabγu* mentioned in the runic inscriptions corresponds to *ǰabγu* of the Turks of Tokharistan in the VIII century. It is, therefore, possible that as early as in the VIII–IX centuries there existed Ancient Turkic dialects of the type of Kirghiz (*ǰoq* "not") and Anatolian (*yoq* "not").

It can be assumed that Ancient Turkic comprised several dialects or languages: Ancient Oghuz (the language of the runic inscriptions), Ancient Uighur, Ancient Kirghiz, and possibly others.

The Ancient Turkic period lasted from the first mention of the Turks and some words of their language, i.e., from the VI century A.D. to the X century.

1.3431. Runic script.

Ancient Turkic includes the language of the so-called Orkhon-Yenisei monuments written in runic script. These monuments, inscriptions on steles, are found in the area around the upper course of the Yenisei river in East Siberia; in the valley of the Orkhon river in Outer Mongolia and in the area east from Orkhon, including a locality situated not far from Ulan Bator, the capital of the Mongolian People's Republic, to be exact, some 25–30 miles to the east.

The most important runic inscriptions are those in honor of 1. Khan Bilge (died 734 A.D.), 2. his brother, Prince Kül Tegin (died 732 A.D.), and 3. the inscription of 716 in honor of Tonyukuk, the minister of Khan Bilge and, previously, of the latter's father. One of the latest large inscriptions is that on the Selenga stone, a monument discovered by Ramstedt near the river Selenga. This monument dates from 758 or 759 A.D.

Besides inscriptions on steles, a book of divination, some documents, and fragments of Manichean and other manuscripts in runic script have been preserved.

Bibliography:

Aalto, P., "Materialien zu den alttürkischen Inschriften der Mongolei", *JSFOu* 60: 7, pp. 1–91.

Gabain, A. von, *Alttürkische Grammatik*, 2., verbesserte Auflage, Leipzig 1950.

— "Das Alttürkische", *PhTF*, pp. 21–46.

Malov, S. E., *Pamyatniki drevnetyurkskoĭ piśmennosti*, Moskva-Leningrad 1951.

— *Pamyatniki drevnetyurkskoĭ piśmennosti Mongolii i Kirgizii*, Moskva-Leningrad 1959.

— *Eniseĭskaya piśmennosť tyurkov*, Moskva-Leningrad 1952.

1.3. The Chuvash-Turkic Languages

The runic script

Characters	Transcription	Characters	Transcription
ʃ 1 X �český	a, ä	ꜣ	ñ
J	b¹	☺ ⊙ ☻ ☉ ⊗	nt
⚹ ⩙ ⚹	b²	ꜣ	nc
Υ 'I'), ( )(	γ	> ⟩	o, u
Є ʃ	g	ᛗ N ᚻ	ö, ü
⁂ ⁑ ⁂	d¹	1	p
X	d²	4 ꜓	r¹
ⵗ ⵗ ⵗ ⵗ ⵗ	z	↑	r²
Γ ᛓ	ï, i	Y	s¹
D	y¹	I	s²
ꝯ	y²	◊ ⌃	t¹
ꜣ ꜣ ◁ D ↓ ↑	q	h	t²
⅂ ñ ꝩ P B Ƀ	k	⅄ Y	č
J	l¹	¥ Y ꝓ ꜣ ᚻ ⋀	š
Y	l²	⋈	
M	lt		
⚹ ♧	m		
)	n¹		
ⵗ ⵗ ⵗ	n²		
ⵗ ᛓ	ŋ		

Indic Alphabets

Transcription	1.	2.
a		
i		
u		
e		
o		
ā		
ka		
kha		
ga		
gha		
ṅa		
ča		
čha		
ǰa		
ǰha		
ña		
ṭa		
ṭha		
ḍa		
ḍha		
ṇa		
ta		
tha		
da		
dha		
na		
pa		
pha		
ba		
bha		
ma		
ya		
ra		
la		
va		
ša		
ṣa(ša)		
sa		
ha		

Nasilov, V. M., *Yazïk orxono-eniseĭskix pamyatnikov*, Moskva 1960.
Orkun, H. N., *Eski türk yazıtları* I–IV, İstanbul 1936–41.
Ramstedt, G. J., "Zwei uigurische Runeninschriften in der Nord-Mongolei", *JSFOu* 30: 3 (1913), pp. 1–63.
Sprengling, M., "Tonyukuk's Epitaph : An Old Masterpiece", *AmJSL* 56: 1 (1939).
Temir, A., "Die Konjunktionen und Satzeinleitungen im Alttürkischen", *Oriens* 9 (1956), pp. 41–85, 233–280.
Thomsen, V., *Inscriptions de l'Orkhon déchiffrées par* –, MSFOu 5 (1894–96).
— *Turcica*, ibid. 37 (1916).
— "Ein Blatt in türkischer 'Runenschrift' aus Turfan", *SBAW*, Phil. hist. Kl. 15 (1910), pp. 296–306.
— "Dr. M. A. Stein's Manuscripts in Turkish 'Runic' Script from Miran and Tung-Huang", *JRAS* 1912, pp. 181–227.

1.3432. Brāhmī script.

Some Ancient Turkic texts are written in Brāhmī script. The latter originated in India. Its name means "Brahman's" or "of Brahman origin". It was used to write in Sanskrit. Buddhist missionaries introduced it, with some modifications, in Central Asia among the Tokharians, Saka, and Turks. Brāhmī texts are, therefore, Buddhistic in content. Most of them are very fragmentary. The Brāhmī texts probably date from the VIII–IX centuries A.D.

The Brāhmī script as it was used by the Turks in Central Asia is shown in the table on p. 62 (col. 1, col. 2 giving Tokharian).

Bibliography:
Bailey, H. W., "Indo-Turcica", *BSOAS* (1938), pp. 289–302.
— "Turks in Khotanese Texts", *JRAS* (1939), pp. 85–91.
Boyer, A. M., "Note sur le manuscrit sanskrit-ouïgour en brāhmī (Grünwedel)", *Muséon* (1906).
Gabain, A. von, *Alttürkische Grammatik*, 2., verbesserte Auflage, Leipzig 1950, pp. 5–7, 32–41, 267.
— Türkische Turfan-Texte VIII, *ADAW*, Kl. für Spr., Lit., Kunst 1952, 7 (1954).
— "Das Alttürkische", *PhTF*, pp. 21–46.
Lewicki, M., "O tekście sanskrycko-tureckim w piśmie brāhmī, wydanym przez Stönnera", *RO* (1936).
Stönner, H., "Über die kultur- und sprachgeschichtliche Bedeutung der Brāhmītexte in den Turfan-Handschriften", *ZE* (1905), pp. 415–420.

1.3433. The Manichean script.

A number of Ancient Turkic texts are written in the so-called Manichean script.

Ancient Turks who professed the Manichean religion used a script which is called the Manichean script. Other Manichean Turks and also non-Manichean Turks (Buddhists) used the so-called Uighur script which had developed from Sogdian (*vide* 1.3434).

1. The Altaic Languages

The Manichean script goes back to the Palmyran script which is one of the varieties of the Middle Aramaic script. Palmyran is also regarded as the prototype of Syriac from which Estrangelo developed (*vide* 1.3442).

MANICHEAN SCRIPT

Isolated	Finally	Medially	Initially	Transcription	Isolated	Finally	Medially	Initially	Transcription
			א א	a			ﺍ	ﺍ	l
				b	ﻝ	ﻝ	ﻝ	ﻝ	8
				β	ב	ב	ב	ב	88
				g					m
				ɣ		׃ ׃		׃ ׃	n
				d	₈	₈	₈	₈	s
				h					,
				v			₀	₀	p
				ẅ					f
				z	ʓ	ʓ ʓ			č
				ž		ʓ			čy
				h	ʓ	ʓ			čn
6 6	₉ 6	₉ 6	ʓ ʓ	ṭ	₉ ₉	₉			k
				y			⊿	⊿	q
				k	⸱	⸱			r
				x	₃ ₃				š
				q	ʓ	ʓ	ʓ	ʓ	t

Bibliography:

Bang, W., "Manichäische Laien-Beichtenspiegel", *Muséon* 1923, pp. 137–242.
— "Manichäische Hymnen", *ibid.*, 1925, pp. 1–55.
— "Manichäische Erzähler", *ibid.*, 1931, pp. 1–36.
Gabain, A. von und Winter, W., *Türkische Turfantexte IX, Ein Hymnus an den Vater Mani auf "Tocharisch" B mit alttürkischer Übersetzung*, ADAW, Kl. für Spr., Lit., Kunst 1956, 2 (1958).
Le Coq, A. von, "Kurze Einführung in die uigurische Schriftkunde", *MSOS* 22 (1919), Abt. II, West. St., pp. 1–17.
— "Türkische Manichaica aus Chotscho", *APAW* I: 1912; II: 1919; III: 1922.
— "Dr. Stein's Turkish Khuastuanift from Tunhuang, being a Confession-prayer of the Manichaean Auditores", *JRAS* 1911, pp. 277–314.
Lidzbarski, M., "Die Herkunft der manichäischen Schrift", *SBAW*, Phil.-hist. Kl. 50 (1916), pp. 1213–1222.

1.3434. The Sogdian script.

A number of Ancient Turkic texts are written in Sogdian script. The Sogdians were an Iranian people who lived in a country which included the present Tadjikistan (in the USSR) and the adjacent areas of Uzbekistan. The Sogdian script was rarely used by the Turks, and there are only Buddhist manuscripts written in it. Most of the latter probably date from the VIII century.

By far the larger number of Ancient Turkic texts, namely those of later origin (IX–X centuries), are written in the so-called Uighur script. The latter developed from the Sogdian alphabet, to be exact, from what the German scholars call "sogdische Kursivschrift", i.e., Sogdian speedwriting. The Uighur alphabet was, at a later time, probably in the second half of the XII century, transmitted to the Mongols.

Works in Uighur script are mostly Buddhistic, Nestorian, and Manichean in content, although there are also fragments of calendars, astrological works, and specimens of poetry.

The oldest works in Uighur script are fragments of Manichean origin which date from the VIII century A.D., cf. Le Coq, "Türkische Manichaica aus Chotscho" (1.3433) and W. Bang und A. von Gabain (*infra*).

The Buddhist literature in Uighur script reached its acme in the IX–X centuries. The most important works of this kind are the *Maitrisimit*, translated by Prajñarakṣita in the IX century from "Tokharian"; *Altun yaruq*, "The Golden Beam", *Suvarṇaprabhāsa*, translated from Chinese by Singqu Säli Tutung of Bišbalïq some time between 925 and 950 A.D.; and the Uighur version of the *Biography of Hüen-tsang*.

The Sogdian and Uighur alphabets are shown in the table on p. 66.

Bibliography:

Bang, W. und von Gabain, A., "Türkische Turfan-Texte", *SBAW*: I: 1929; II: 1929; III: 1930; IV: 1930; V: 1931.
— "Analytischer Index zu den türkischen Turfan-Texten I–V", *SBAW* 1931.
— und Rachmati, G.R., "Türkische Turfan-Texte VI", *SBAW* 1934.

SOGDIAN				UIGHURIC			
Finally	Medially	Initially	Transcription	Finally	Medially	Initially	Transcription
			a,ä				a,ä
			i,ī				ī,i
			o,ö u,ü				o ö u ü
			γ,q,x				γ,q,x
			g,k				g,k
			i,j				i,j
			r				r
			l				l
			t				t
			d				d
			č				č,ǧ
			s				s
			š				š
			z,ž				z
			n				n
			b,p				b,p
			v				w,f
			w				
			m				m
			h				

Bang, W. und Rachmati, G. R., "Lieder aus Alt-Turfan", *AM* 1933, pp. 129–140.
Gabain, A. von, *Alttürkische Grammatik*, 2. verbesserte Auflage, Leipzig 1950.
— "Das Alttürkische", *PhTF*, pp. 21–46.
Gauthiaut, R., "De l'alphabet sogdien", *JA* 10 sér. 17 (1911), pp. 81–95.
Le Coq, A. von, "Kurze Einführung in die uigurische Schriftkunde", *MSOS* 22 (1919), Abt. II, pp. 1–17.
Malov, S. E., *Pamyatniki drevnetyurkskoǐ piśmennosti*, Moskva-Leningrad 1951.
Müller, F. W. K., "Uigurica", *ABAW* I: 1908; II: 1911; III: 1922; IV: 1931.
Pelliot, P., "La version ouïgoure de l'histoire des princes Kalyāṇamkara et Pāpamkara", *TP* XV (1914), pp. 225–272.
Rachmeti, G. R., "Türkische Turfan-Texte VII", *ABAW* 1937.
— "Zur Heilkunde der Uiguren", *SBAW* I: 1930; II: 1932.
Radlov, V. V. i Malov, S. E., *Suvarṇaprabhāsa (Sutra "Zolotogo Bleska")*, Tekst uĭgurskoĭ redakcii. Izdali –. Bibliotheca Buddhica 17, Sanktpeterburg 1913–1917. Unfinished translation by W. Radloff: *Bibliotheca Buddhica* 27, Leningrad 1930.
Uighur Version of the *Biography of Hüen-tsang*, Facsimile Edition by Wang Chung-min and Ki Sien-lin, Peking 1951. Partly edited and translated by A. von Gabain, *SBAW* 1935, pp. 151–180; 1938, pp. 371–415.

1.344. Middle Turkic.

Middle Turkic is the stage immediately following Ancient Turkic, i.e., that roughly covering the time between the X and the XV centuries A.D.

Middle Turkic was still less uniform than Ancient Turkic and comprised a number of languages much more differing from each other than the Ancient Turkic dialects.

The characteristic features of Middle Turkic are the following:

1°. Some of the languages are *d*-languages, but others are *ð*-languages or *y*-languages: *qaδγu/qaðγu/qayγu* "sorrow", *quδuq/quyu* "well".
   Languages in which all three features occur are Karakhanide and the literary language of the later Uighuric script (XI–XIV centuries).
2°. The development $a > o$ before *u* in disyllabic words: *oltun < altun/altïn* "gold", *xotun < xatun/qatïn* "woman".
3°. The appearance of the accusative suffix *-ni* side by side with the ancient *-γ* still existing.
4°. The appearance of a special ablative suffix *-dïn* in Karakhanide and other languages.
5°. The conditional in *-sa* instead of the older *-sar*.

There are also other features characteristic of individual languages.

Middle Turkic comprises the following languages:

1°. Karakhanide of the XI–XIII centuries;
2°. the written language of manuscripts in Uighuric and Arabic script of the post-Karakhanide period (XII–XIV centuries), which can be called Uighur of the post-Karakhanide period;
3°. the literary language of Khwaresm (XII–XIV centuries) and Chaghatai (XV century);

4°. Kypchak (Kuman) of the XIII–XVI centuries;
5°. Old Anatolian or Osman which appeared in the XIV–XV centuries.

1.3441. Karakhanide.

The literary language in use in the kingdom of the Karakhanides (IX–XIII centuries) in Eastern Turkestan is known under the name of Karakhanide (XI–XIII centuries). Its basis was the language of the tribes Turgesh, Yaghma, and Karluk, which was closely related to the language of literary works written in Uighur script. The Karakhanide language had undergone Iranian and Arabic influences.

The most important works written in Karakhanide are 1. the didactic work *Qutadɣu bilig* by Yūsuf Haṣṣ Hājib of Balasaghun (1069 A.D.), originally written in Arabic script, one copy in Uighur script also existing; 2. the Arabic-Turkic dictionary *Dīvān Luɣāt at-Turk* by Maḥmūd al-Kāšɣarī (1073 A.D.) in which Turkic words, proverbs, and samples of poetry are given in Arabic transcription and translation; and 3. the didactic work *'Ataybat al-Ḥaqā'iq* by Adīb Aḥmad Yuknakli (XI or XII century).

Bibliography:

Arat, R. R., *Kutadgu Bilig* I, Metin, İstanbul 1947.
Atalay, Besim, *Divanü Lûgat-it-Türk tercümesi* I–III, Ankara 1939–40.
— *Divanü Lûgat-it-Türk Dizini "Endeks"*, Ankara 1943.
Balhassan Oglu, N. A., "Un texte ouïgour du XII-e siècle", *KSz* 7 (1906), pp. 257–279.
Bang, W. und Rachmati, G. R., "Die Legende von Oghuz Qaghan", *SBAW* 1932, pp. 683–724.
Brockelmann, C., *Mitteltürkischer Wortschatz nach Maḥmūd al-Kāšɣarīs Dīvān Luɣāt at-Turk*, Budapest-Leipzig 1928.
— "Maḥmūd al-Kāšgharīs Darstellung des türkischen Verbalbaus", *KSz* 18 (1918–19).
Deny, J., "À propos d'un traité de morale turc en écriture ouïgoure", *Revue du Monde Musulman* 1925, pp. 189–234.
Mansuroğlu, M., "Das Karakhanidische", *PhTF*, pp. 87–112.
Pelliot, P., "Sur la légende d'Uɣuz-Khan en écriture ouïgoure", *TP* 27 (1930), pp. 247–358.
Thomsen, V., "Sur le système des consonnes dans la langue ouïgoure", *KSz* 2 (1901), pp. 241–259.
Ščerbak, A. M., *Oguz-nāme; Muxabbat-nāme*, Moskva 1959.
— *Grammatičeskiĭ očerk yazïka tyurkskix tekstov X–XIII vv. iz vostočnogo Turkestana*, Moskva-Leningrad 1961.

1.3442. Post-Karakhanide.

Post-Karakhanide is the immediate continuation of Karakhanide. It served as a literary language during the XIII and XIV centuries. Its basis was still the language of the older literature in Uighur script but it betrays local influences by dialects. It is basically still an *adaq-aðaq* language.

The most important work of the post-Karakhanide period is Rabɣūzī's *Qisas al-anbiya* "Legends of the prophets" (1310–11 A.D.).

1.3. The Chuvash-Turkic Languages

The script used after the XI century was mostly Arabic. However, there is a rather large body of Nestorian Christian inscriptions in Estrangelo, a variant of Syriac script. These inscriptions on tombstones date from the XIII–XIV centuries.

The Arabic alphabet is given in 1.3443. Estrangelo and other Syriac alphabets are given in the table *infra*.

SYRIAC ALPHABETS

Transcription	Estrangelo	Jacobite	Nestorian
ʾ			
b			
g			
d			
h			
w			
z			
x			
ṭ			
y			
k			
l			
m			
n			
s			
ʿ			
p, f			
ṣ			
q			
r			
š			
t			

Bibliography:

Chwolson, D., *Syrisch-nestorianische Grabinschriften aus Semiretschje*. Beilage: W. Radloff, *Über das türkische Sprachmaterial dieser Grabinschriften*, Mémoires de l'Académie des Sciences de S. Pétersbourg 1890, pp. 1–168; *idem* Neue Folge 1897, pp. 1–62.

Grönbech, K., *Rabghuzi*, Monumenta Linguarum Asiae Majoris IV, Kopenhagen 1948.

Malov, S., "Musulmanskie skazaniya o prorokax po Rabguzi", *ZKV* 5 (1930).

Schinkewitsch, J., "Rabγūzī's Syntax", *MSOS* 29 (1926), Abt. II.

1.3443. Khwarezmian and Chaghatai.

Khwarezmian was the literary language of Central Asia since the XIII century, and Chaghatai was the Central Asian literary language which came into existence in the XV century. The basis of both languages which are close to each other was the local dialects joined by elements of Karakhanide.

The most important Khwarezm-Turkic literary work is Qutb's *Xusräw u Šīrīn* (ca. 1342).

Chaghatai is called Ancient Uzbek in Soviet Russian literature. However, Chaghatai served an area much larger than that inhabited by Uzbeks whose predecessors in Central Asia did not even call themselves Uzbek.

The period of highest development of Chaghatai lasted from the second half of the XV century until the middle of the XVI century.

The most important works written in Chaghatai were the works of Lutfī, Mir Ali Shir Nevai (1441–1501), *Babur Name* by the Emperor Babur (1483–1530), and the *History of the Turks* by Abu 'l Ghazi Bahadur (1603–64).

Chaghatai was the literary language of the Turks of Central Asia (Turkmens, Kazakhs, Eastern Turks) and the Golden Horde (Tatars, Bashkirs). It was used, in a modernized form influenced by the local spoken languages, until the revolution in Russia.

Chaghatai used the Arabic script (*vide* p. 71). Regarding the alphabet the following should be noted:

The letters for *v* and *y* are also used as vowel signs: *v* stands for *ü*, *ö*, *u*, *o*; *y* stands for *i*, *ï*.

The letters for $ḥ$, $ṣ$, $ż$, $ẓ$ and $ʿ$ are used only in loan-words of Arabic origin. The letter for $ǰ$ is used for both $č$ and $ǰ$. The Turkic phonemic values are:

$ǰ$ – /ǰ/ and /č/
$ḥ$ – /x/
z – /z/
$ṣ$ – /s/
$ż$ – /z/
$ṭ$ – /t/
$ẓ$ – /z/

Bibliography:

Beveridge, A. S., *The Bábar-Náma, being the Autobiography of the Emperor Bábar*, Facsimile edition, London 1905.

Borovkov, A. K., "*Bada'i al-Luġat*", *Slovaŕ Ṭali' Īmānī Geratskogo k sočineniyam Ališera Navoi*, Moskva 1961.

1.3. The Chuvash-Turkic Languages

THE ARABIC ALPHABET										
LETTERS					LETTERS				
Separately	Final	Medial	Initial	Transcription	Separately	Final	Medial	Initial	Transcription
ا	ﺎ			a	ض	ﺾ	ـﻀـ	ﺿـ	ż
ب	ﺐ	ـﺒـ	ﺑـ	b	ط	ﻂ	ﻂ	ﻃ	ṭ
پ	ﭗ	ـﭙـ	ﭘـ	p	ظ	ﻆ	ﻆ	ﻇ	ẓ
ت	ﺖ	ـﺘـ	ﺗـ	t	ع	ﻊ	ـﻌـ	ﻋـ	ʔ, ʕ
ث	ﺚ	ـﺜـ	ﺛـ	s̱, ÿ	غ	ﻎ	ـﻐـ	ﻏـ	γ
ج	ﺞ	ـﺠـ	ﺟـ	j	ف	ﻒ	ـﻔـ	ﻓـ	f
ح	ﺢ	ـﺤـ	ﺣـ	ḥ	ق	ﻖ	ـﻘـ	ﻗـ	q
خ	ﺦ	ـﺨـ	ﺧـ	x	ك .ك	ﻚ .ﻚ	ـﻜـ	ﻛـ	k, g
چ	ﭻ	ـﭽـ	ﭼـ	č	ل	ﻞ	ـﻠـ	ﻟـ	l
د	ﺪ			d	م	ﻢ	ـﻤـ	ﻣـ	m
ذ	ﺬ			ẕ	ن	ﻦ	ـﻨـ	ﻧـ	n
ر	ﺮ			r	ه	ﻪ	ـﻬـ	ﻫـ	h
ز	ﺰ			z	و	ﻮ			v
ژ	ﮋ			ž	ي	ﻲ	ـﻴـ	ﻳـ	y
س	ﺲ	ـﺴـ	ﺳـ	s					
ش	ﺶ	ـﺸـ	ﺷـ	š					
ص	ﺺ	ـﺼـ	ﺻـ	ṣ					

Brockelmann, C., *Osttürkische Grammatik der islamischen Literatursprachen Mittelasiens*, Leiden 1954.
Budagov, L., *Sravnitelniĭ slovaŕ turecko-tatarskix narěčiĭ*, t. I–II, Sanktpeterburg 1869–71.
Clauson, Sir Gerard, *Muḥammad Mahdī Xan, Sanglax, A Persian Guide to the Turkish Language*, Facsimile Text with an Introduction and Indices, London 1960.
Eckmann, J., *Mirzā Mechdis Darstellung der tschagataischen Sprache*, BOH 5, Budapest 1942–47.
— "Zur Charakteristik der islamischen mittelasiatisch-türkischen Literatursprache", *SA*, Wiesbaden 1957, pp. 51–59.
— "Das Chwarezmtürkische", *PhTF*, pp. 113–137.
— "Das Tschagataische", *PhTF*, pp. 138–160.
Kononov, A. N., *Rodoslovnaya turkmen, Sočinenie Abu-l-Gazi Xivinskogo*, Moskva-Leningrad 1958.
Menges, K., *Das Čayatajische in der persischen Darstellung von Mirzā Mahdī Xān*, AGSKL 1956, nº 9.
Pavet de Courteille, *Dictionnaire turc-oriental*, Paris 1870.
Poppe, N., "Eine viersprachige Zamaxšarī-Handschrift", *ZDMG* 101 (1951), pp. 301–332.
— *Mongolskiĭ slovaŕ Mukaddimat al-Adab* I–III, Moskva-Leningrad 1938–1939.
Velyaminov-Zernov, V., *Slovaŕ džagataĭsko-tureckiĭ*, St. Peterburg 1860.
Zajączkowski, A., *La plus ancienne version turque du Huxräw u Šīrin de Qutb*, Warszawa, vol I, Texte, 1958; vol.. II, Facsimile, 1958; vol. III, Vocabulaire, 1961.

1.3444. Kuman.

Kuman (Polovetsian, called so after the Russian name for Kumans) is also a Middle Turkic language. It was spoken in the XII–XVI centuries by Turkic nomads in Southern Russia, including the Crimea, and parts of Central Asia, and also by turkicized Armenians in the XV–XVIII centuries. Under the pressure of the invading Mongols one part of the Kumans left Southern Russia at the beginning of the XIII century and moved into Hungary. There are no speakers of Kuman at the present time.

Materials on Kuman are abundant. A Latin-Persian-Kuman dictionary was compiled at the end of the XIV century. There are Arabic-Kuman glossaries and even a grammar dating from the XV century.

Bibliography:

Atalay, B., *Ettuhfet-üz-zekiyye fil-lûgat-it-türkiyye*, İstanbul 1945.
Caferoğlu, A., *Abū Ḥaiyān, Kitab al-idrāk il-lisān al-atrāk*, İstanbul 1931.
Deny, J., *L'arméno-coman et les "éphémérides" de Kamieniec (1604–1613)*, Wiesbaden 1957.
Gabain, A. von, "Die Sprache des Codex Cumanicus", *PhTF*, pp. 46–73.
Grønbech, K., *Codex Cumanicus in Faksimile herausgegeben von –*, Kopenhagen 1936.
— *Komanisches Wörterbuch*, Kopenhagen 1942.

Halasi Kun, T., *La langue des kiptchaks d'après un manuscrit arabe d'Istanboul*, Partie II, Budapest 1942.

Houtsma, Th., *Ein türkisch-arabisches Glossar*, Leiden 1894.

Grunin, T., "Pamyatniki poloveckogo yazïka XVI veka", *Akademiku V.A. Gordlevskomu*, Moskva 1953, pp. 90–97.

Kraelitz-Greifenhorst, F., "Sprachprobe eines armenisch-tatarischen Dialektes in Polen", *WZKM* 26 (1912), pp. 307–324.

Lewicki, M., Kohnowa, R., "La version turque-kiptchak du Code des lois des arméniens polonais", *RO* 21 (1957), pp. 153–253.

Pritsak, O., "Das Kiptschakische", *PhTF*, pp. 74–87.

Schütz, E., "On the Transcription of Armeno-Kipchak", *AOH* 12: 1–3 (1961), pp. 139–161.

Telegdi, S., "Eine türkische Grammatik in arabischer Sprache aus dem XV Jahrhundert", *KCsA* 1, Suppl. (1937), pp. 282–326.

Tryjarski, E., "Aus der Arbeit an einem armenisch-kiptschakisch-polnisch-französischen Wörterbuch", *UAJ* 32: 3–4 (1960), pp. 194–213.

Zajączkowski, A., *Słownik arabsko-kipczacki, cz. II, Verba*, Warszawa 1954.

— *Manuel arabe de la langue des Turcs et des Kiptchaks (époque de l'État Mamelouk)*, Warszawa 1938.

1.3445. Old Anatolian.

Old Anatolian (or Old Osman as it is called sometimes) was spoken by those Turks who had come, in the X–XI centuries, from the area of the river Syr Darya into Khwarezm, Iran, Asia Minor, and the Caucasus. It is known that Old Anatolian was spoken as far back as in the XI century A.D. Since the XIV century the language took that shape which became the basis of Osman. Old Anatolian (Osman) used the Arabic script.

Bibliography:

Banguoğlu, T., *Altosmanische Sprachstudien zu Süheyl-ü Nevbahar*, Breslau 1938.

Brockelmann, C., "Ali's Qissa-i Jûsuf, der älteste Vorläufer der osmanischen Literatur", *APAW* 5 (1916–1917).

— "Altosmanische Studien I. Die Sprache Ašyqpāša's und Ahmedī's", *ZDMG* 83 (1919).

Mansuroğlu, M., "Das Altosmanische", *PhTF*, pp. 161–182.

— "The Rise and Development of Written Turkish in Anatolia", *O* 7 (1954), pp. 250–264.

— *Sultan Veled'in Türkçe manzumeleri*, İstanbul 1958.

— *Çarhname*, İstanbul 1956.

— "Drei türkische Gedichte Šayyad Hamza's", *UAJ* 26 (1954), pp. 78–89.

Rossi, E., *Il "Kitāb-i Dede Qorqut"*, Citta del Vaticano 1952.

Zajączkowski, A., *Studia nad językiem staroosmanskim*, Warszawa I: 1934; II: 1937.

1.345. New Turkic.

The new period of history of the Turkic languages begins roughly in the XVI century. All Turkic languages spoken at the present time are in the most recent stage of the modern period.

The Korean alphabet and the systems of transcription

Letter	McCune	Gale	Jung	Letter	McCune	Gale	Jung
ㅏ	a	a	a	ㄱ	K, G, NG	k, g	g
ㅑ	ya, a	ya	ya	ㄴ	N, O, L	n	n
ㅓ	ŏ	ü, ö	o'	ㄷ	T, CH, D, J	t, d,	d
ㅕ	yŏ, ŏ	yü, yö	yo'	ㄹ	N, O, R, L	r, l, n	r, l
ㅗ	o	o	o	ㅁ	M	m	m
ㅛ	yo, o	yo	yo	ㅂ	P, B, M	p, b	b
ㅜ	u	u	u	ㅅ	S, SH, D, T, N	s, t	s, d
ㅠ	yu, u	yu	yu	ㅇ	NG	ng	ng
ㅡ	ŭ, u	eu	u'	ㅈ	CH, J	ch, j	Z, d
ㅣ	i	i	i	ㅊ	CH'	ch'	tch, d
ㅐ	ae	(ai)	e'	ㅋ	K'	k'	k, g
ㅒ	yae	(yai)	ye'	ㅌ	T', CH'	t'	t, d
ㅔ	e	(üi, öi)	e	ㅍ	P'	p'	p, b
ㅖ	ye, e	(yüi, yöi)	ye	ㅎ	H	h	h
ㅚ	oe	(oi)	oe	ㄲ	KK	g	gg, g
ㅟ	wi, i	(ui)	wi	ㄸ	TT	d	dd, d
ㅢ	ŭi, i	(eui)	u'i	ㅃ	PP	b	bb, b
ㅘ	wa	wa	wa	ㅆ	SS	s	ss, d
ㅝ	wŏ	wü, wö	wo'	ㅉ	TCH	j, tj	zz, d
ㅙ	wae	(wai)	we'				
ㅞ	we	(wüi, wöi)	we				

1.4. Korean.

Korean is spoken in Korea by approximately 30 million people (21 million in South Korea and 9 million in North Korea). The relation of Korean to other language groups is still debated. It has been compared to Japanese, Ainu, and Altaic languages. It is structurally close to Japanese and Altaic, and numerous Korean words have been successfully compared with Manchu-Tungus, Mongolian and Turkic. Korean has been strongly influenced by Chinese. The Koreans use two scripts, namely Chinese characters and their own national script introduced in 1443. The latter consists, in its present shape, of 40 letters (p. 74).

Spoken Korean has six dialects: 1. the north-eastern dialect; 2. the north-western dialect; 3. the central dialect; 4. the south-eastern dialect; 5. the south-western dialect, and 6. the dialect spoken on the island of Chejudo.

As for the periodization of Korean, three stages have been established by Korean and Japanese scholars: Ancient Korean, Middle Korean, and New Korean, but there is no unanimity with regard to chronology.

According to the Japanese scholar Kōno, Ancient Korean lasted until the middle of the XV century A.D., when the present Korean alphabet was created (1443 A.D.). Middle Korean existed from 1443 to 1592, the date of the Imjin conflict (the Hideyoshi invasion), and New Korean begins with the latter date. The chronology proposed by the Korean linguist, Ki-Moon Lee, professor at the University of Seoul, differs from the one given above and seems, in the opinion of the author of these lines, to be more correct: Ancient Korean until the X century A.D.; Middle Korean from the X or XI century until the XVI century; and New Korean from the XVI century.

The origin of Korean is represented by Ki-Moon Lee as follows. At the beginning of the Christian era, there existed in Korea and in the adjacent parts of Manchuria two groups of languages assumedly of Altaic origin: 1. a Northern (or Puyę) group which included Puyę, Koguryę, Okję, and Ye, four closely interrelated languages; and 2. a Southern (or Han) group, represented by the so-called "Three Han". In the northern (Puyę) linguistic area the Koguryę kingdom was founded in which the speakers of the languages of the Northern group were united. In the southern area the kingdoms of Silla and Päkje were established. The three kingdoms, Koguryę, Silla, and Päkje, were united in the VII century A.D., Silla having become the dominating group with the capital Kyęngju on the south-eastern coast of Korea. The Silla period lasted until the X century and was replaced by the Koryę kingdom with the capital Käsęng in the center of the peninsula, not very far from present Seoul. The dialect of Käsęng (which included older Koguryę elements) became the language of all Koryę.

Consequently, Ancient Korean included Puyę, Koguryę, Okję, and Ye which were united in the Koguryę kingdom, on the one side, and the dialects of the southern group of the "Three Han" spoken in the Silla and Päkje kingdoms, on the other hand. The unification of all groups mentioned, i.e., Northern and Southern, began in the VII century in the Silla kingdom which lasted until the X century. The Ancient period ended with the succession of the Koryę kingdom (X century) to Silla. Consequently, Middle Korean is based on Silla.

Middle Korean is the language of the Koryę kingdom, and New Korean is its direct continuation.

Materials for the study of Ancient Korean are sparse and fragmentary. They are confined to some names mentioned in Chinese documents, but Middle Korean is represented by *Chi-lin Lei-shih*, a work of Sun Mu, compiled in 1103-4 which comprises about 350 Korean words, and by numerous Korean words in the Korean alphabet, written in the middle of the XV century.

Korean has numerous borrowings from Chinese. More than one half of the vocabulary consists of Chinese words taken, to a large extent, at an ancient time. These borrowings have preserved many ancient features and, therefore, Korean is an important source for the study of the historical phonology of the Chinese language.

The linguistic literature on Korean is rather limited. There are almost no works in European languages on Korean language history.

Bibliography:

Haguenauer, C. A., "Le Coréen", *Les langues du monde*, Nouvelle édition, Paris 1952, pp. 443–446.
Hangil, Hakhoi, *Khin Sajęn*, vol. 1–6, Seoul 1947 (Korean Language Society, *Dictionary of the Korean Language*).
Hyungki, J. Lew, *New Life English-Korean Dictionary*, ed. by – (5th edition), Seoul 1949.
Junker, H. F., *Koreanische Studien*, Berlin 1955.
Konō, R., "Tones of Middle Korean", *Chōsen Gakuhō* (Tenri) I (1951).
— see *An Introduction to the Languages of the World*, edited by S. Ichikawa and S. Hattori, vol. II, Tokyo 1955, pp. 428 ff. (periodization of Korean language history, in Japanese).
Lee, Ki-Moon, *Kugę-sa Käsęl*, Seoul 1961 (an introduction to the history of the Korean language: periodization, pp. 19–23, phonology, grammar, vocabulary of Ancient, Middle, and New Korean, in Korean).
— "Korean Studies in Seoul 1945–1959", *UAJ* 32 (1960), pp. 126–129.
— "On Some Special Stem Alternations in Middle Korean", *Chin-Tan Hak-Po* 23 (1962), pp. 121–153.
Lee, Sung-Nyong, *Čungse Kugę Munpęp*, Seoul 1961 (a Middle Korean grammar, in Korean).
Martin, S. E., "Korean Phonemics", *L* 27: 4 (1951), pp. 519–533.
— *Korean Morphophonemics*, William Dwight Whitney Linguistic Series, Ling. Soc. of America, Baltimore 1954.
Nam, Kwang-U, *Koę Sajęn*, Seoul 1960 (a dictionary of Old Korean).
Ogura, Sh., "Outline of the Korean Dialects", *Memoirs of the Toyo Bunko* 12, Tokyo 1940.
— "A Study on the Dialects in North and South P'yongando", *Bull. of the Faculty of Law and Letters, Misc. Series I*, Keijo 1929.
— "A Study on the Dialects in Hamgyöngnam-do and Hoanghai-do", *ibid.*, 2, Keijo 1930.
Pang, Chong-Hyon, "Kyerim-Yusa Yęngu", *Tong-bang Hak-chi* II (1955) (Studies in the Chi-lin Lei-Shih, in Korean).

1.4. Korean

Ramstedt, G. J., *A Korean Grammar*, MSFOu 82, Helsinki 1939.
— *Studies in Korean Etymology*, MSFOu 95, Helsinki 1949.
Skaličková, A., "The Korean Vowels", *AO* 23: 1–2 (1955), pp. 29–51.
Sunki, Kim, *The Phonetics of Korean*, London 1937.
Sunoo, H.H.W., *A Standard Colloquial Korean Textbook*, Book 1, Seattle 1948.
Yu Hyông-ki, *New Life Korean-English Dictionary*, Seoul 1947.

2. HISTORY OF INVESTIGATION OF THE ALTAIC LANGUAGES

2.0. The general investigation of the Altaic languages has a long history. The first works on individual languages appeared in the XVII century but it would lead the reader too far if an attempt to discuss the history of investigation in detail were made here, not to mention the fact that most of the old writings are obsolete and may be only of historical interest. Therefore, only such works will be discussed here which are still usable and represent milestones along the road which lies behind Altaic linguistics.

2.1 History of Mongolian linguistics.

2.11. Beginnings.

Although the first Mongolian grammar, namely that published by Melchisédech Thévenot appeared in 1672 and was followed by the grammar published by Alexander Bobrovnikov (1835), the beginning of linguistic work on Mongolian on a high level is connected with the name of Isaac Jacob Schmidt (1779–1847), a native of Amsterdam, Netherlands, who lived and worked in Russia and was a member of the Imperial Russian Academy of Sciences in St. Petersburg. Schmidt, his predecessors, and successors studied Written Mongolian, i.e., the language of the Mongolian script. Colloquial Mongolian did not attract their attention, although in some exceptional cases colloquial material had been collected even before: suffice to mention the comparative dictionary of all the languages compiled by order of the Empress Catharine the Great, and edited by Peter Simon Pallas, which includes material from spoken Mongolian languages (1789).

In general, however, mostly literary Altaic languages were studied at the beginning. Therefore, the early history of Mongolian linguistics is that of the investigation of Written Mongolian.

Bibliography:

Aalto, P., "L'esquisse de la grammaire mongole qu'on trouve chez Melchisédech Thévenot", *CAJ* 8 (1963), pp. 151–62 (The grammar is probably based on Ibn al-Muḥannā's work of the XIV century which deals with Middle Mongolian, *vide* 2.38).

Bobrovnikov, Aleksandr, *Grammatika mongolskago yazïka*, St. Peterburg 1835.

Sravnitelnïe slovari vsěx yazïkov i narěčiĭ, sobrannïe desniceyu vsevïsočaĭšeĭ osobï, I–II, St. Peterburg 1787–1789.

Sravnitelnïĭ slovaŕ vsěx yazïkov i narěčiĭ, po azbučnomu poryadku raspoloženniĭ, St. Peterburg 1790–1791.

Thévenot, Essais de la grammaire mongole, 1672.

2.12. Schmidt.

Isaac Jacob Schmidt, of Dutch extraction, published a large number of works on Mongolian and Tibetan, and his most important publication is his edition of the annals of *Saɣaŋ Sečen* (1662) which he also translated into German and supplied with commentaries. There are two linguistic works of his, namely a Written Mongolian grammar and dictionary. Both are obsolete and cannot be recommended to students but they were great achievements at the time of their appearance and during the subsequent decades.

Bibliography:

Babinger, F., "Isaak Jakob Schmidt 1779–1847, Ein Beitrag zur Geschichte der Tibetforschung", *Festschrift für Friedrich Hirth zu seinem 75. Geburtstag, 16. April 1920*, Berlin 1920, pp. 7–21 (Biography).
Schmidt, I. J., *Grammatik der mongolischen Sprache*, St. Petersburg 1831.
— *Grammaire mongole de Schmidt traduite de l'allemand en* 1845, I Partie française, Peiping 1935, II Partie mongole, Peiping 1935 (translation of the previous).
— *Mongolisch-deutsch-russisches Wörterbuch nebst einem deutschen und einem russischen Wortregister*, St. Petersburg 1835.
— *Geschichte der Ost-Mongolen und ihres Fürstenhauses verfasst von Ssanang Ssetsen Chungtaidschi der Ordus*, St. Petersburg 1829.

2.13. Kowalewski.

Schmidt's works were followed by those of Kowalewski. The great Polish scholar Józef (= Joseph) Kowalewski (1801–1878), was a brilliant linguist and philologist. He studied literature and classical philology at the University of Wilna, but because of participation in student disturbances he was exiled by the Russian authorities to Kazań. There he studied Oriental languages and became later on a professor at that university. Kowalewski's publications amount to 72, but his most important works, which made him one of the greatest figures in the history of Oriental studies, are a concise grammar of Written Mongolian which is superior to that published by Schmidt; his Mongolian chrestomathy in two volumes, with a glossary, which contains excellent texts for language study; and his Mongolian-Russian-French dictionary in three volumes which has remained unsurpassed and is still the best dictionary for readers of Mongolian Buddhist literature.

Bibliography:

Kotwicz, Wł., *Józef Kowalewski Orientalista* (1801–1878), Wrocław 1948 (a detailed biography with bibliography).
Kovalevskiĭ, O., *Kratkaya grammatika mongolskago knižnago yazïka*, Kazań 1835.
— *Mongolskaya xrestomatiya*, t. I, Kazań 1836; t. II, Kazań 1837.
Kowalewski, J. E., *Dictionnaire mongol-russe-français*, I, Kasan 1844; II Kasan 1846; III Kasan 1849 (There are new reprint editions).

2.14. Golstunskiĭ.

Kowalewski's Mongolian grammar was superseded by the grammar of Alekseĭ Bobrovnikov which is regarded as a classical work, the best and most reliable grammar of Written Mongolian for almost one hundred years. Kowalewski's dictionary was later on replaced by Golstunskiĭ's Written Mongolian dictionary, not because the latter was better but because Kowalewski's dictionary had been out of print very soon after its appearance, the reason being that a fire had destroyed most of the copies while they were still in the printing shop.

Konstantin Fedorovič Golstunskiĭ (1831–1899), a native of Russia, was a professor of Mongolian at the universities of Kazań and, later on, St. Petersburg. His major work was a lithographed Mongolian-Russian dictionary which contains more words than that of Kowalewski but is inferior from the philological point of view, not to mention the fact that Golstunskiĭ was not a Buddhologist and did not know Sanskrit and Tibetan. The other major works of Golstunskiĭ deal with Oirat. An important work is his edition of the Oirat laws of 1640, accompanied by a Russian translation and notes, and his Russian-Oirat dictionary which appeared soon after Zwick's dictionary but is better than the latter.

Bibliography:

Bobrovnikov, Alekseĭ, *Grammatika mongolsko-kalmĭckago yazĭka*, Kazań 1849.
Golstunskiĭ, K. F., *Mongolsko-russkiĭ slovaŕ*, S. Peterburg, vol. I 1895; vol. II 1894; vol. III 1893. With posthumous addenda et corrigenda by A. Rudnev.
— *Russko-kalmĭckiĭ slovaŕ*, Kazań 1857.
— *Mongolo-oĭratskie zakonĭ 1640 goda, dopolnitelnĭe ukazĭ Galdan-xun-taĭdžiya i zakonĭ, sostavlennĭe dlya volžskix kalmĭkov pri kalmĭckom xanĕ Donduk-Daši*, Sanktpeterburg 1880.
Ivanovskiĭ, A., "Pamyati K. F. Golstunskago", *ZVO* 12 (necrology of Golstunskiĭ).
Zwick, H. A., *Das Handwörterbuch der westmongolischen Sprache*, Donaueschingen 1853.

2.15. Pozdneyev.

A well-known scholar in the Mongolian field was another Russian, Alekseĭ Matveyevich Pozdneyev (1851–1920), professor (1884–99) at the University of Petersburg and, later on, director of the Oriental Institute in Vladivostok. He was a widely travelled explorer of Mongolia, collector of folklore, historian, and linguist. Being reactionary in his political and social views, he was greatly disliked by his fellow-scholars and students, but his scholarly achievements were undeniably great. As far as language study is concerned, the following works of his deserve mentioning. First of all, he published a Mongolian chrestomathy which contains a large number of reading texts, among them very rare and previously unknown works of Mongolian literature. A valuable work is also his Kalmuck (Oirat) chrestomathy which contains a very fine collection of texts in Written Oirat. His Oirat-Russian dictionary is still the best. An outstanding work is also his history of Mongolian literature which unfortunately appeared only as a lithographed edition of his lectures held at the University of St. Petersburg. Its title is misleading, because it is not a history of literature but a collection of old texts both in Uighuric script and ḥP'ags-pa, with Russian translations and philological and linguistic commentaries.

Bibliography:

Pozdněev, A., *Mongolskaya xrestomatiya dlya pervonačalnago prepodavaniya*, St. Peterburg 1900.
— *Obrazcï narodnoĭ literaturï mongolskix plěmen*, vïp. I, Narodnïya pěsni mongolov, Sanktpeterburg 1880.
— *Kalmickaya xrestomatiya dlya čteniya v staršix klassax kalmĭckix narodnïx škol*, Sanktpeterburg (first edition: 1892; second edition: 1907; third edition: 1915).
— *Kalmĭcko-russkiĭ slovaŕ v posobie k izučeniyu russkago yazĭka v kalmĭckix načalnĭx školax*, Sanktpeterburg 1911.
— *Lekcii po istorii mongolskoĭ literaturï*, vol. I–III, St. Peterburg 1895–1908.

2.16. Castrén.

One of the greatest scholars of all times was Alexander Matthew Castrén (1813–1852), a native of Finland. He investigated a number of Uralic (i. e., Finno-Ugric-Samoyed) and Altaic languages and collected, during his travels in Siberia (1845–49), valuable materials on spoken languages theretofore unknown. In addition to being a great mongolist, turcologist, and explorer of Tungus, he also reshaped the Altaic theory and became one of the key figures in the history of Altaic linguistics.

Leaving aside Castrén's achievements in the fields of Finno-Ugric and Samoyed linguistics and anthropology of northern parts of European Russia and Siberia, and speaking of him as an altaicist, it should be pointed out that his greatest merit was his study of spoken languages almost entirely neglected before. He was the first linguist to pay attention to a spoken Mongolian language, namely Buriat. His Buriat grammar is a fine piece of work which remained the only scholarly grammar of that language for more than fifty years. Castrén was fully aware of the fact that Buriat was not a uniform language but consisted of a number of dialects. His grammar makes a clear distinction between the dialects, mainly Nižneudinsk and Selenga, although Khori and some other dialects are also reflected in Castrén's work.

Castrén wrote also an excellent grammar of Karagas and Koibal, two Turkic languages, the second of which is already extinct, and the former is now spoken by a few hundred people. Suffice to mention that this work was one of the first grammars of two spoken Turkic languages in Siberia and became a model for further research. Although Castrén had access to the galleyproofs of Böhtlingk's work on Yakut, which was soon to appear, the Koibal and Karagas grammar had already progressed so far that it was too late to make use of the former. Consequently, it was the result of independent research based only on Castrén's own ideas.

One of the greatest achievements of Castrén was his excellent Tungus

(Evenki) grammar, the first grammar of that language. It remained the only Tungus grammar for more than seventy-five years, until the publication of new grammars of Tungus languages began in the 1920s in the USSR.

All three grammars contain also glossaries and some texts, the first ever published with regard to the languages concerned.

Castrén is equally inportant as one of the prominent protagonists of the Altaic theory. The weakness of all the theories about the affinity of what is now called Altaic languages and other language groups (Caucasian, Dravidian, etc.) had been the lack of any linguistic evidence. Castrén reduced the number of the members of the Altaic group and reshaped the latter in a manner still accepted by some scholars. Not dwelling here on the Altaic theory (*vide* 3.), it should be remarked that Castrén's Buriat grammar determined the further course of history of Mongolian studies. His Tungus grammar laid the foundation for Tungus linguistics.

Most of Castrén's works were prepared for publication by the famous linguist, Anton Schiefner, a member of the Academy of Sciences in St. Petersburg, because Castrén had died soon after his return from his journey. Therefore, the transcription sometimes based on erroneous reading of Castrén's handwriting, and the interpretation of facts found in Castrén's works belong to Schiefner and reflect the latter's views.

Bibliography:

Castrén, Dr. M. A., *Versuch einer burjätischen Sprachlehre nebst kurzem Wörterverzeichnis*, St. Petersburg 1857.
— *Versuch einer koibalischen und karagassischen Sprachlehre nebst Wörterverzeichnissen aus den tatarischen Mundarten des Minussinschen Kreises*, St. Petersburg 1857.
— *Grundzüge einer tungusischen Sprachlehre nebst kurzem Wörterverzeichnis*, St. Petersburg 1856.
Pamyati M. A. Kastrena, K 75-letiyu dnya smerti, Leningrad 1927. (Biography, bibliography, and articles on Castrén as a mongolist, turcologist, etc.)
Setälä, E., "Centenaire de la naissance de Matthias-Alexandre Castrén", *JSFOu* 30: 1b (1913–18). (Commemoration of the 100th anniversary of his birth.)
"The Memory of M. A. Castrén, Speeches Held on the Occasion of the One Hundreth Anniversary of His Death, May 7, 1952", *JSFOu* 56: 2 (1952).

2.17. Ramstedt.

The real founder of modern Mongolian linguistics and Altaic comparative studies was Gustaf John Ramstedt (1873–1950), also a native of Finland. An extraordinarily gifted linguist who spoke fluently at least nine languages (Finnish, Swedish, Hungarian, English, German, French, Russian, Khalkha-Mongolian, and Japanese), he studied Finno-Ugric linguistics and received an excellent training in phonetics and in general and Indo-European comparative linguistics. He possessed a profound knowledge of Germanic languages, Sanskrit, Latin, and Greek and was linguistically as well equipped as none of his predecessors.

Ramstedt became not only a famous mongolist but also an excellent turcologist, he wrote a Korean grammar which is still the best, and published the first scholarly comparative grammar of the Altaic languages.

The scope of Ramstedt's work is so wide that his name will be mentioned time and again as part of the history of Mongolian, Turkic, Korean, and comparative studies. Here only his rôle in the history of Mongolian linguistics will be discussed.

Ramstedt's first major work was his phonetic description of Khalkha-Mongolian. For the first time in the history of Mongolian linguistics, a reliable and precise phonetic transcription was used. Ramstedt established the phonemes and allophones of Khalkha, although he did not use these terms. He introduced, also for the first time in the history of Mongolian studies, the comparative method and established Khalkha equivalents of Written Mongolian graphical representations of phonemes. Last but not least, he was also the first scholar who noticed the importance of ancient glossaries of spoken Mongolian of the XIII century and compared Khalkha forms with both Written Mongolian and colloquial forms of the XIII century given by Kirakos, an Armenian historian of that time.

Thus, Ramstedt's phonetic study of Khalkha-Mongolian laid the foundation for the study of spoken Mongolian languages of which, at the end of the XIX century were known to exist Buriat, Kalmuck, and *Mongolian*, the latter covering a large number of languages and dialects. It also laid the foundation of future historical and comparative Mongolian linguistics and was the first comparative phonology of Khalkha and Written Mongolian (and occasionally Turkic) which was, later on, expanded by Vladimirtsov's voluminous comparative grammar which gives many details lacking in Ramstedt's outline but does not add to the latter much new in principle.

Another important work was Ramstedt's study of Khalkha verb inflection (conjugation) which includes a descriptive and a comparative part. Ramstedt collected a large number of colloquial Khalkha texts such as epics, folktales, songs, and riddles.

Ramstedt undertook several journeys to Outer Mongolia, to the Kalmucks in the Volga region, and to the borderlands of Afghanistan. There he found speakers of Mogol which is spoken in some parts of Afghanistan, and presented the results of his study in a work on Mogol which contains texts in phonetic transcription, a glossary, and an outline of Mogol grammar. Ramstedt's works on Kalmuck include a large Kalmuck-German dictionary which was at the time of its appearance the best dictionary of any Mongolian language. A grammatical outline of spoken Kalmuck is appended to the dictionary. Another valuable work is Ramstedt's collection of Kalmuck folktales in phonetic transcription, with a German translation.

Most of the other works of Ramstedt refer to Altaic comparative linguistics or turcology. Therefore they will be discussed elsewhere.

Ramstedt's importance is hard to exaggerate. It is evident from the fact that most of the mongolists his age and younger at that time and many of the next generation were Ramstedt's pupils either directly or indirectly. They include Kotwicz, Rudnev, Žamtsarano, Vladimirtsov, the author of these lines, Aalto, and others.

Bibliography:

Aalto, P., "Gustaf John Ramstedt", *FUF* 30 (1951), pp. 37–40 (Necrology).
Henrikson, K. E., "Sprachwissenschaftliche Veröffentlichungen von Prof. Dr. G. J. Ramstedt", *StOF* 14: 12 (1950) (Bibliography).
Poppe, N., "Gustaf John Ramstedt", *HJAS* 14 (1951), pp. 315–322 (Necrology).
Poucha, P., "Gustaf John Ramstedt (Ein Nachruf)", *AO* 19: 3–4 (1951), pp. 617–624.
Ramstedt, G. J., "Das Schriftmongolische und die Urgamundart phonetisch verglichen", *JSFOu* 21: 2 (1903).
— Sravnitelnaya fonetika mongolskago pismennago yazïka i xalxasko-urginskago govora, Perevod ... pod redakcieï priv.-doc. A. D. Rudneva s dopolneniyami avtora, S. Peterburg 1908 (Russian translation of the preceding).
— *Über die Konjugation des Khalkha-Mongolischen* MSFOu 19 (1902).
— "Mogholica. Beiträge zur Kenntnis der Moghol-Sprache in Afghanistan", *JSFOu* 23: 4 (1905).
— *Kalmückische Sprachproben I, Kalmückische Märchen*, I MSFOu 27: 1 (1909); II MSFOu 27: 2 (1919).
— *Kalmückisches Wörterbuch*, Helsinki 1935.

2.18. Kotwicz.

The Polish scholar Władysław Kotwicz (1872–1944) was a contemporary of Ramstedt and, to a certain degree, his pupil. Kotwicz studied Chinese, Manchu, and Mongolian at the University of Petersburg and, later on (1900–1922), was professor of Mongolian and Manchu at the same university. Kotwicz left the USSR in 1923 and ever since lived in his native Poland.

When Kotwicz was still very young he became a member of a group of scholars headed by the famous turcologist Radloff. That group was a sort of a learned society, later on known as "Radloff's circle", which held regular meetings in which problems of Turkic, Mongolian, and Manchu linguistics, literature, etc. were discussed and papers read. A frequent visitor of that group was also Ramstedt who came to St. Petersburg to lecture on Mongolian and Altaic subjects. Thus, Kotwicz made Ramstedt's acquaintance and underwent the latter's influence. Kotwicz was definitely Ramstedt's pupil in matters of Mongolian linguistics and comparative Altaic studies.

Kotwicz was a highly erudite scholar and possessed an extraordinary knowledge of Mongolian and Manchu history and literature. He was also a gifted linguist and an excellent teacher.

Kotwicz's most important works in the field of Mongolian linguistics are his manual of Written Mongolian for university students (1902) and his excellent grammar of spoken Kalmuck (first edition 1915), the best and most complete and still unsurpassed work of its kind.

Bibliography:

Kotwicz, Wł., *Lekcii po grammatikě mongolskago yazïka*, St. Peterburg 1902 (lithographed).

— *Opït grammatiki kalmïckago razgovornago yazïka*, Petrograd 1915 (lithographed 1st edition).
— *Opït grammatiki kalmïckago razgovornago yazïka*, Rževnice u Pragi 1929 (lithographed 2nd edition).
— "La déclinaison dans la langue kalmouk moderne", *RO* 2 (1917–1919).
— "La langue mongole, parlée par les Ouïgours Jaunes près de Kan-tcheou, d'après les matériaux recueillis par S. E. Malov et autres voyageurs", *CO* 16 (Wilna 1939); same republished in 1953.

Kotwiczówna, M., "Bibliografia Władysława Kotwicza", *RO* 16 (1953), pp. xxxi–xlvii (Bibliography of Kotwicz's publications).

Lewicki, M., "Władysław Kotwicz", *RO* 16 (1953), pp. xi–xxix (biography).

2.19. Rudnev.

An intimate friend and follower of Ramstedt was Andrew (Andreĭ Dmitrievič) Rudnev (1878–1958). Rudnev was Russian and was born in St. Petersburg. He studied there under Pozdneyev and Golstunskiĭ, but virtually he was a pupil of Ramstedt, being an active member of Radloff's group. Rudnev undertook several journeys to Outer and Inner Mongolia and to the Kalmucks. Rudnev's main interest belonged to the living Mongolian languages, and in his studies he followed Ramstedt's line. Rudnev's greatest merit was that he transmitted Ramstedt's methods to a whole generation of Russian scholars who by the mere fact of living in Russia had the best opportunities of studying and investigating Mongolian languages. It is characteristic of Rudnev that it was he who organized a translation of Ramstedt's *Das Schriftmongolische und die Urga-Mundart* into Russian (*vide* 2.17.).

Rudnev's major works were a study of the Mongolian dialects of Eastern Mongolia (Ujumchin, Gorlos, Durbut-Beise, Ordos, etc. in Inner Mongolia), an excellent work on the Khori-Buriat dialect which was the first work on Buriat written on the basis of modern linguistic methods, and, together with Žamtsarano (vide 2.110.), a lithographed collection of Khalkha-Mongolian texts. Rudnev's lithographed grammar of Written Mongolian was a useful manual for students.

Rudnev was a gifted musician, scholar, and an excellent university teacher. He was a professor at the University of St. Petersburg (1903–1918) and had many students. His pupils were, among others, Vladimirtsov and the writer of these lines. Rudnev had an excellent knowledge of Mongolian and spoke Khalkha-Mongolian fluently.

Rudnev left Russia in 1918, soon after the October revolution, and lived ever since in Finland where he devoted himself to music.

Bibliography:

Poppe, N., "Andrej Rudnev", *CAJ* 4 (1959), pp. 87–89 (Necrology containing a brief biography and bibliography).

Rudnev, A. D., *Materialï po govoram Vostočnoĭ Mongolii, S notami i risunkami v tekstě*, St. Peterburg 1911.

— *Xori-buryatskiĭ govor*, 1–3, St. Peterburg [Petrograd] 1913–1914.

— *Lekcii po grammatikĕ mongolskago pis̀mennago yazïka, čitannïya v 1903–1904 akademičeskom godu*, vïp. 1, St. Peterburg 1905 (lithographed).
— "Melodii mongolskix plĕmen", *ZIRGO po Otd. Ėtn.*, 34 (1909), pp. 395–430.
— "Novïya dannïya po živoĭ mandžurskoĭ rĕči i šamanstvu", *ZVO* 21 (1912), pp. 047–082.
— i Žamcarano, C. Ž., *Obrazcï mongolskoĭ narodnoĭ literaturï*, vïp. I, Xalxaskoe narĕčie, Redaktirovali –, St. Peterburg 1903 (lithographed).

2.110. Žamtsarano.

Tsiben Žamtsarano *Ceben Žamcaranū* was a Buriat, to be exact a Khori-Buriat of the Šarait clan. He was born in 1880 and attended the law school of the University of St. Petersburg, but he was most interested in dialects, folklore, and ancient customs of his native people and other Mongols. He was very close to Kotwicz, Ramstedt, and Rudnev and regarded them as his real teachers. During his numerous journeys in his native country and Mongolia, he collected a large number of epic poems, folktales, songs, riddles, and proverbs. Linguistics was not his speciality, but the material he had collected was extremely valuable to linguists.

Because of his scholarly and literary activities Žamtsarano was accused by the Tsarist authorities of nationalism and exiled to Mongolia. There he started a newspaper and was very active in cultural life of Mongolia. After the revolution of 1917, he was one of the founders of the Mongolian People's Party and became one of the key figures in Mongolian political life. In 1921 he founded the Mongolian Learned Committee (now Academy of Sciences) and, thus, laid the foundation for science in Mongolia. Mongolia owes him very much. He was not only the first Mongolian scholar in history but also a talented writer and one of the founders of the independent Mongolian nation.

Subsequently he fell a victim to Stalinist purges and was imprisoned in 1937 and died, probably, in 1940 in a concentration camp.

Bibliography:

Rupen, R. A., "Cyben Žamcaranovič Žamcarano (1880–?1940)", *HJAS* 19 (1956), pp. 126–145 (Biography and bibliography).
Žamcarano, C. Ž., i Rudnev, A. D., *Obrazcï mongolskoĭ narodnoĭ literaturï*, vïp. I, Xalxaskoe narĕčie (Tekstï v transkripcii), St. Peterburg 1908 (lithographed).
— *Obrazcï narodnoĭ slovesnostï mongolskix plĕmen, Tekstï, Proizvedeniya narodnoĭ slovesnosti buryat*, I Petrograd 1913–1918; II Leningrad 1930.

2.111. Vladimirtsov.

Boris Yakovlevich Vladimirtsov, Russian (1884–1931), studied Mongolian at the University of St. Petersburg under Kotwicz and Rudnev, and some other subjects in Paris. Later on he became professor at the University of Petrograd (Petersburg had already been renamed, to be renamed again to Leningrad in 1924) and lectured from 1915 to 1931. He was an excellently trained philologist and linguist and had a profound knowledge of Tibetan, Sanskrit, and Turkic languages. His teachers were Ščerbatskoĭ (Sanskrit and Tibetan), Barthold (history of Central Asia), Radloff (Turkic), and Antoine Meillet (linguistics, in Paris).

Vladimirtsov undertook several journeys to Mongolia and to the Kalmucks. His main interest in the field of linguistics and anthropology belonged to the Oirats. He collected a large number of materials on Oirat linguistics and folklore. Vladimirtsov's most important works refer to literature and history. His linguistic works deal with the history of the Mongolian language, grammar of Written Mongolian, and comparative linguistics. Of his linguistic works the voluminous comparative grammar of Khalkha and Written Mongolian is best known. Although it does not add much new in principle and method to Ramstedt's *Das Schriftmongolische und die Urga-Mundart*, it gives numerous details and contains comparisons of the two languages mentioned with other Mongolian languages and also Turkic.

Vladimirtsov's greatest merit in the field of Mongolian linguistics was the study of foreign elements in Mongolian, namely old Indo-European (Sogdian, Persian, Sanskrit) and Arabic loan-words. He also published an interesting old Georgian-Mongolian glossary of the XIV century in which colloquial Mongolian of that time is given in Georgian transcription.

During his sixteen years of teaching at the Petrograd-Leningrad University and the Oriental Institute (1920–1931), Vladimirtsov trained a number of younger mongolists, Rinchen (a Mongol, now professor in Ulan Bator), Sanžeyev (a Buriat, now professor in Moscow), the author of these lines, and others who have not survived the purges in the USSR.

Bibliography:

Filologiya i istoriya mongoĺskix narodov, Pamyati akademika Borisa Yakovleviča Vladimircova, Moskva 1958 (a commemorative volume containing, *i.a.*, a biography and appraisal of his linguistic works by N. P. Šastina, "Boris Yakovlevič Vladimircov, 1884–1931", pp. 3–11).

Kotwicz, Wł., "In memoriam", *CO* 2 (1932) (necrology).

Pelliot, P., "Boris Yakovlevič Vladimircov", *TP* 28 (1931), p. 516 (necrology).

Vladimircov, B. Ya., "O časticax otricaniya pri povelitelnom naklonenii v mongoĺskom yazïkě", *IAN* 1916, pp. 349–358.

— "Anonimnïĭ gruzinskiĭ istorik XIV v. o mongoĺskom yazïkě", *IAN* 1917, pp. 1487–1501.

— *Mongoĺskiĭ sbornik razskazov iz Pañcatantra*, Petrograd 1921.

— "O dvux smešannïx yazïkax Zapadnoĭ Mongolii", *YaS* 2 (1923), pp. 32–52.

— "Mongolica I. Ob otnošenii mongoĺskogo yazïka k indo-evropeĭskim yazïkam Sredneĭ Azii", *ZKV* 1 (1925), pp. 305–341.

— *Obrazcï mongoĺskoĭ narodnoĭ slovesnosti* (S.-Z. Mongoliya), Leningrad 1926.

— *Mongolo-Oiratskiĭ geroičeskiĭ épos*, Perevod, vstupitelnaya staťya i primečaniya, Peterburg-Moskva 1923 (Translation of some epics contained in the preceding book).

— "Arabskie slova v mongoĺskom", *ZKV* 5 (1930), pp. 73–82.

— *Sravnitelnaya grammatika mongoĺskogo piśmennogo yazïka i xalxaskogo narečiya*, Vvedenie i fonetika, Leningrad 1929.

2.112. Haenisch.

The German scholar Erich Haenisch (born in 1880) is one of the outstanding contributors to the study of Middle Mongolian, namely, the Mongolian language of the XIV century in Chinese transcription and in ḥP'ags-pa. He studied Chinese, Mongolian, and Manchu under Wilhelm Grube and spent seven years (1904–1911) as a teacher at the military college in Changsha, China. Later on, he was professor in Göttingen, Leipzig, Berlin, and Munich.

His most important works refer to the *Secret History* (Yüan-ch'ao pi-shi), the most ancient narrative text in Mongolian. He published a transcription of the Mongolian text, which is better than that of Pelliot, a German translation, and a dictionary of the language of the text. He also published the Sino-Mongolian collections of texts and glossaries known as the *Hua-i i-yü*. An important work is also his edition of some ḥP'ags-pa texts unknown theretofore.

Bibliography:

"Erich Haenisch, Lebenslauf und Bibliographie", *MS* 5 (1940), pp. 1–5 (Biography and bibliography).

Franke, H., "Erich Haenisch zum 80. Geburtstag", *Studia Sino-Altaica*, Festschrift für Erich Haenisch zum 80. Geburtstag, Wiesbaden 1961, pp. 1–11 (Bibliography giving 134 titles).

Haenisch, E., *Manghol un Niuca Tobca'an (Yüan-ch'ao pi-shi), die Geheime Geschichte der Mongolen*, Aus der chinesischen Transkription im mongolischen Wortlaut wiederhergestellt, Leipzig 1937 (text in transcription).

— *Die Geheime Geschichte der Mongolen*, Aus einer mongolischen Niederschrift des Jahres 1240 von der Insel Kode'e im Keluren-Fluss erstmalig übersetzt und erläutert, (First edition) Leipzig 1940; (Second edition) Leipzig 1948 (German translation of the *Secret History*).

— *Wörterbuch zu Manghol un Niuca Tobca'an (Yüan-ch'ao pi-shi), Geheime Geschichte der Mongolen*, Leipzig 1939 (Dictionary).

— "Sinomongolische Glossare, Das Hua-i ih-yü", *ADAW*, Kl. für Spr., Lit., u. Kunst 1956, 5.

— "Grammatische Besonderheiten in der Sprache des Manghol un Niuca Tobca'an", *StOF* 14: 3 (1950).

— "Steuergerechtsame der chinesischen Klöster unter der Mongolenherrschaft, Eine kulturgeschichtliche Untersuchung mit Beigabe dreier noch unveröffentlichter Phagspa-Inschriften", *Berichte über die Verhandlungen der Sächsischen Akademie der Wissenschaften zu Leipzig, Phil.-histor. Kl.* 92: 2 (1940)

Poppe, N., "Erich Haenisch als Mongolist", *UAJ* 32: 3–4 (1960), pp. 157–160 (Evaluation of works).

2.113. Pelliot.

The French scholar Paul Pelliot (1878–1945) was one of the greatest orientalists. He was mainly a sinologist but he knew also Persian, Turkic, and Mongolian. The scope of his activities was very wide and included the study of history, literature, and religion of peoples of Central Asia, and some works of his are important contributions to Mongolian linguistics. A major work of his is his edition of the *Secret History* with an unfinished French translation. This work was published after his death and, being unfinished, it is slightly inferior to Haenisch's text edition and translation. Pelliot published also a number of articles dealing with a Mongolian glossary in Arabic transcription (*Ḥamd'ullāh Ḳazvini*) and interesting Middle Mongolian forms with initial $h <$ $*p$, etc. Other works of his belong to the field of Turcology.

Bibliography:

Haenisch, E., "Paul Pelliot", *ZDMG* 101 (1951), pp. 9–10 (Necrology).
Pelliot, P., "Les mots à h-initiale, aujourd'hui amuie, dans le mongol des XIII-e et XIV-e siècles", *JA* 1925, pp. 193–263.
— "Les formes turques et mongoles dans la nomenclature zoologique du Nuzhatu'l-Ḳulub", *BSOAS* 6: 3, pp. 3ff.
— *Histoire Secrète des Mongols*, Restitution du texte mongol et traduction française des chapitres I–VI, Paris 1949.
Société Asiatique, *Paul Pelliot*, publié par –, Paris 1946 (speeches at the bier; especially those by L. Hambis on Pelliot's achievements in the field of Mongolian studies, and by J. Deny on his works on Altaic problems).
Ware, J. R., "Paul Pelliot 1878–1945", *HJAS* 9 (1946), pp. 187–188 (Necrology).

2.114. Mostaert.

The Reverend Antoine Mostaert, C.I.C.M., was born in 1881 in Belgium. He is the most outstanding scholar in the field of Mongolian studies. During his many years as a missionary in China (1905–1948), including twenty years among the Mongols, Father Mostaert collected materials on dialects, folklore, and anthropology of the Mongols, which surpass everything ever achieved by any other mongolist. His profound knowledge of Written Mongolian and Chinese has enabled him to publish a number of important works on Mongolian texts of the Yüan period (1270–1368) and make numerous corrections of passages of the *Secret History* which had been misinterpreted by his predecessors. His unrivalled works on the Monguor language (together with the late Father A. de Smedt) and Ordos (Urdus) are excellent from the phonological and phonetic point of view, very precise, and display an unsurpassed knowledge of the spoken languages and the Written Mongolian language.

Bibliography:

"Father Antoine Mostaert, C.I.C.M. (Scheut Society for Foreign Missions)", *MS* 10 (1945), pp. 1–4 (Brief biography and bibliography).
Mostaert, Antoine, C.I.C.M., "Le dialecte des mongols Urdus (Sud), Étude phonétique", *Anthropos* 21 (1926), pp. 851–869; 22 (1927), pp. 160–186; errata 25 (1930), pp. 725–727.
— *Textes oraux ordos, recueillis et publiés avec introduction, notes morphologiques, commentaires et glossaire*, Peip'ing 1937 (contains a concise grammar).
— *Dictionnaire Ordos*, I–III, Peiping 1941–1944.
— *Folklore Ordos*, Traduction des Textes oraux ordos, Peip'ing 1947 (translation of the texts, *vide supra*).

— "The Mongols of Kansu and their Language", *Bull. of the Catholic Univ. of Peking* 8 (1931), pp. 75–89.
Mostaert, A., et A. de Smedt, "Le dialecte monguor parlé par les mongols du Kansu occidental, 1-re partie: Phonétique", *Anthropos* 24 (1929), pp. 145–165, 801–815; 25 (1930), pp. 657–669, 961–971; *errata* 26 (1931), pp. 253–254.
— *Le dialecte monguor parlé par les mongols du Kansu occidental*, III-e partie: Dictionnaire monguor-français, Peip'ing 1933.
Rupen, R. A., "Antoine Mostaert, C.I.C.M. and Comparative Mongolian Folklore", *CAJ* 1 (1954), pp. 1–8 (contains the continuation of the bibliography up to 1954).

2.115. Poppe.

Nicholas Poppe, a native of Russia (born in 1897), a pupil of Kotwicz, Ramstedt, Rudnev, Samoilovich (turcologist), and Vladimirtsov, graduated from the University of Petrograd (now Leningrad) and was subsequently professor at that university (1925–1941). He studied Mongolian, Manchu, Turkic, Tibetan and undertook numerous journeys to the Buriats and Evenki (Tungus) in Eastern Siberia, to the Kalmucks, and travelled in Mongolia. His main fields are the investigation of the spoken Mongolian languages, Middle Mongolian, and comparative linguistics. He published grammars of Written Mongolian (*vide* 1.18), Khalkha (*vide* 1.171), Buriat (*vide* 1.16), and Dagur (*vide* 1.13); a book on Middle Mongolian in rendition with the hP'ags-pa script (*vide* 1.192), and some Arabic-Mongolian and Persian-Mongolian glossaries of the XIII–XIV centuries (*vide* 1.192). Besides, he published a comparative grammar of Mongolian languages, and a number of works referring to Altaic comparative linguistics.

Bibliography:
Krueger, J. R. und Pritsak, O., "Nikolaus Poppe Bibliographie", *SA*, pp. 177–189 (Bibliography of publications up to 1957).
Poppe, N., *Alarskiĭ govor*, čast I, Leningrad 1930; čast II, Leningrad 1931 (Alar Buriat dialect).
— *Praktičeskiĭ učebnik mongolskogo razgovornogo yazïka* (Xalxaskoe narečie), Leningrad 1931 (the first more or less complete Khalkha grammar).
— *Introduction to Mongolian Comparative Studies*, MSFOu 110 (1955).
Pritsak, O., "Nikolaus Poppe zum 60. Geburtstag", *SA*, pp. 7–16 (Biography).

2.116. Lewicki.

The talented Polish scholar Marian Lewicki (1908–1955), a pupil of Kotwicz and Kowalski, worked mostly in the fields of Middle Mongolian and Altaic comparative linguistics. His most important works are devoted to hP'ags-pa script and Sino-Mongolian glossaries of the XIV century. His work on the *Hua-i i-yü* is superior to that of Haenisch. He also edited and published the posthumous works of Kotwicz.

Bibliography:
Lewicki, M., *La langue mongole des transcriptions chinoises du XIV-e siècle, Le Houa-yi yi-yu de 1389*, Wrocław 1949.

— id. vol. II, *Vocabulaire-index*, Wrocław 1959.
— *Les inscriptions mongoles inédites en écriture carrée*, CO 12 (1937).
Pritsak, O., "Marian Lewicki 1908–1955", *UAJ* 29 (1957), pp. 89–93 (Necrology).
Sinor, D., "Marian Lewicki (1908–1955)", *JA* 1958, pp. 467–468 (Necrology).
Zajączkowski, A., "Wspomnienie o Marianie Lewickim", *Przegląd Orientalistyczny* 19 (1956), pp. 291–298 (Necrology).

2.117. Ligeti and his pupils.

Important contributions to Mongolian and Altaic linguistics were made by the Hungarian scholar Louis Ligeti (born in 1902), a sinologist, mongolist, turcologist, and altaicist in general, a pupil of Pelliot, who is presently a professor at the University of Budapest.

Ligeti's most important works in the field of Mongolian linguistics deal with the language of the hP'ags-pa script, the Middle Mongolian as represented in a polyglot Arabic-Persian-Turkic-Mongolian glossary (*vide* 1.192) and Mogol (*vide* 1.14). His other works such as his *Catalogue of the Kanjur*, his report on a journey in Inner Mongolia, etc., do not belong to the category of purely linguistic words and will not be mentioned here, although they are of great importance.

Ligeti's pupils, Bese, Kara, Róna-Tas, and Szabó have published a number of articles on various Mongolian languages.

Bibliography:
Bese, L., "Remarks on a Western Khalkha Dialect", *AOH* 12 (1961), pp. 277–294.
— "Zwillingswörter im Mongolischen", *AOH* 7 (1957), pp. 199–211.
— "Einige Bemerkungen zur partikulären Reduplikation im Mongolischen", *AOH* 11 (1960), pp. 43–49.
— "Ob obnovlenii mongolskogo yazïka", *AOH* 6 (1956), pp. 91–108.
Kara, G., "Sur le dialecte üjümüčin", *AOH* 14 (1962), pp. 145–172.
— "Notes sur les dialectes oïrat de la Mongolie Occidentale", *AOH* 8 (1959), pp. 111–168.
— "Les mots mongols dans une liste de marchandises chez Gmelin (1738)", *AOH* 13 (1961), pp. 175–200.
Róna-Tas, A., "A Study on the Dariganga Phonology", *AOH* 10 (1960), pp. 1–29.
— "A Dariganga Vocabulary", *ibid.*, pp. 147–174.
— "Remarks on the Phonology of the Monguar Language", *AOH* 10 (1960), pp. 263–267.
Szabó, T. M., Kalmük szóképzés; Die Wortbildung im Kalmückischen, Budapest 1943.

2.118. Cleaves.

The American scholar Francis Woodman Cleaves, presently professor at Harvard University, is the author of numerous works in the fields of Chinese and Mongolian studies. His most important works are in the field of Mongolian philology and represent editions of ancient Written Mongolian texts of the Yüan period, with translations, glossaries and grammatical and lexicological commentaries. Although they are not linguistic works, they contain valuable material for the study of the Written Mongolian language of the oldest period of its history.

Bibliography:

Cleaves, F. W., "The Sino-Mongolian Inscription of 1362 in Memory of Prince Hindu", *HJAS* 12 (1949), pp. 1–133.
— "The Sino-Mongolian Inscription of 1335 in Memory of Chang Ying-Jui", *ibid.*, 13 (1950), pp. 1–131.
— "The Sino-Mongolian Inscription of 1338 in Memory of Jigüntei", *ibid.*, 14 (1951), pp. 1–104.
— "The Sino-Mongolian Inscription of 1346", *ibid.*, 15 (1952), pp. 1–123.
— "The Bodistw-a Čari-a Awatar-un Tayilbur of 1312 by Čosgi Odsir", *ibid.*, 17 (1954), pp. 1–129.
— "The Mongolian Documents in the Musée de Téhéran", *ibid.*, 16 (1953), pp. 1–107.
— "An Early Mongolian Version of the Alexander Romance", *ibid.*, 22 (1959), pp. 1–99.

Cleaves has also published a large number of short articles which are found almost in every volume of the *HJAS*, beginning with vol. 10 (1947).

2.119. Mongolian linguistics in Japan.

Linguistic studies of Mongolian are conducted in Japan on a high scholarly level. Most of the works of the Japanese scholars in this field are, unfortunately, published in Japanese and, therefore, inaccessible to altaicists in other countries.

The most well-known scholars in this field are Shirô Hattori, Shinobu Iwamura, Sitiro Murayama, and Masayosi Nomura. Some works of theirs are in English or German but most of them are in Japanese.

Bibliography:

Hattori, Sh., "Phonemic Structure of Mongol (Chakhar Dialect)", *JLSJ* 19–20 (1951), pp. 68–102.
— "The Length of Vowels in Proto-Mongol", *SM* 1: 12 (1959), pp. 1–10.
— "Jemlen in Yüan-ch'ao Mi-shih", *SA* (1957), pp. 69–70.
Iwamura, Sh. and Schurmann, H. F., "Notes on Mongolian Groups in Afghanistan", *Silver Jubilee Volume of the Zinbun-Kagaku-Kenkyusyo, Kyoto University*, Kyoto 1954, pp. 480–517.
Iwamura, Sh. with the collaboration of Natsuki Osada and the late Tadashi Yamasaki, *The Zirni Manuscript, A Persian-Mongolian Dictionary and Grammar*, Kyoto University 1961.
Murayama, S., "Über die Annahme, dass der chinesischen Transkription der Geheimen Geschichte der Mongolen ein Original in hP'ags-pa Schrift zu Grunde liegt", *JLSJ* 24 (1953), pp. 12–47.
— "Sind die Naiman Türken oder Mongolen?", *CAJ* 4: 3 (1959), pp. 188–198.
— "Einige Eigentümlichkeiten der chinesischen Transkription des Mongγolun niuča tobčaān", *XXV Intern. Congr. of Orient.*, Moscow 1960.

Nomura, M., "Remark on the Dipthong /wa/ in the Kharachin Dialect of the Mongol Language", *JLSJ* 16 (1950), pp. 126–142. Suppl. Notes and additions, *ibid.*, 17 (1951), pp. 149–155.
— "On Some Phonological Developments in the Kharachin Dialect", *SA* (1957), pp. 132–136.

2.120. Summary.

The Mongolian languages can be regarded as well-studied. Written Mongolian has been studied very thoroughly. There are detailed grammars and good dictionaries. Influence of dialects on Written Mongolian is the subject of some works by Vladimirtsov and the author of these lines. Middle Mongolian as represented in Arabic-Mongolian and Persian-Mongolian glossaries of the XIII–XIV centuries, in documents in ḫPʻags-pa script, and in *Hua-i i-yü* can also be regarded as studied in detail. The *Secret History*, however, still requires investigation from the linguistic point of view. A complete grammar of the language of the *Secret History*, including the syntax, should be written and detailed studies of its vocabulary are still lacking.

The living Mongolian languages, which one hundred years ago were still unknown, are well-represented in literature. There are fine grammars and dictionaries of Kalmuck, Buriat, Khalkha, Urdus, and Monguor, and there are works on Dagur and Santa, but Mogol is still little studied and there is no more or less complete Mogol grammar or a Mogol dictionary. Some minor Mongolian languages, such as Golok, Shirongol, and Shara Yoghur (all of them near the Tibetan frontier) are practically unexplored. Only brief lists of words collected by non-linguists are available.

The Mongolian language history has been studied intensively by Kotwicz, Lewicki, Ligeti, Pelliot, Vladimirtsov, and the author. A detailed comparative phonology of Khalkha and Written Mongolian and a more or less complete comparative grammar of all Mongolian languages known at the time of research were published by Vladimirtsov and the author respectively. There is also a comparative grammar of Mongolian languages by Sanžeev, which cannot, however, be recommended unreservedly to readers because of numerous errors.

In conclusion, it can be remarked that Mongolian studies are in method superior to Turkic linguistics.

Bibliography:

Poppe, N., "Geserica, Untersuchung der sprachlichen Eigentümlichkeiten der mongolischen Version des Gesserkhan", *AM* 3 (1926), pp. 1–32, 167–193.
— *Introduction to Mongolian Comparative Studies*, MSFOu 110 (1955).
Potanin, G. N., *Tangutsko-tibetskaya okraina Kitaya i Centralnaya Mongoliya*, St. Peterburg 1893 (Contains glossaries of Shirongol, Shera Yogur and some other dialects or languages on pp. 410–437).
Sanžeev, G., *Sravnitelnaya grammatika mongolskix yazïkov*, I, Moskva-Leningrad 1953; *Sravnitel'naya grammatika mongol'skix yazïkov*, Glagol, Moskva 1963 (Better than vol. I).
Vladimircov, B. Ya., *Mongolskiĭ sbornik razskazov iz Pañcatantra*, Petrograd 1921.

— *Sravnitelnaya grammatika mongolskogo pisʹmennogo yazïka i xalxaskogo narečiya*, Vvedenie i fonetika, Leningrad 1929.

2.2. History of Manchu-Tungus linguistics.

2.21. Beginnings.

The first language of the Manchu-Tungus group to be studied was Manchu which played an important rôle as the official language in diplomatic relations between the Chinese Empire, under the Manchu dynasty (1644–1911), and Europe.

Manchu was studied much in Europe in the XVIII century because most of the historical works on China and descriptions of China in Chinese were available in Manchu translations and, Manchu being much easier than Chinese, the translations in question attracted attention. The first Manchu grammar ever written in a European language is that by Ferdinand Verbiest, completed in 1668 and published by Melchisédech Thévenot between 1681 and 1692 under the title *Elementa Linguae Tartaricae*. The grammar appeared without mention of the name of its author, and therefore it was commonly ascribed to the famous Jesuit scholar Gerbillon.

Another old work is *Alphabet tartare-mantchou* (Paris 1787) and *Alphabet mantchou rédigé d'après le syllabaire et le dictionnaire universel de cette langue*, Paris 1807 (3rd edition) by Louis Mathieu Langlès (1763–1824). These and some other old grammars are only of historical interest. The same can be said of Joseph Amyot's *Dictionnaire tartare-mantchou-français* (Paris 1789–90).

Still usable are, however, the Manchu Grammar by Gabelentz (1807–1874), one of the most brilliant orientalists, and another grammar by Lucien Adam (1833–1918).

Gabelentz published (1864) also a still usable Manchu-German dictionary.

There cannot by any doubts about the significance of the works mentioned. However, notwithstanding their importance, they are obsolete. On the other hand, Hans Conon von der Gabelentz published only an outline of Manchu grammar. A more or less complete Manchu grammar and better dictionaries appeared at a later time.

Bibliography:

Adam, L., *Grammaire de la langue mandchou*, Paris 1873.
Gabelentz, H. C. von der, *Éléments de la grammaire mandchoue*, Altenbourg 1832.
— "Sse-schu, Schu-king, Schi-king in mandschuischer Übersetzung mit einem mandschu-deutschen Wörterbuch", *Abhandlungen für die Kunde des Morgenlandes* 3 (1864).
de Jaegher, P. Karel, "Le Père Verbiest, auteur de la première grammaire mandchou", *TP* 22 (1923), pp. 189–192.
Pelliot, P., "Le véritable auteur des Elementa Linguae Tartaricae", *TP* 21 (1922), pp. 367–386.

2.22. Zakharov.

The Russian scholar Ivan Ilʹyič Zaxarov (1817–1885) who had spent many years in China and, later on, become a professor at the University of St. Petersburg was the author of the most complete and best grammar of Manchu. He published also a complete Manchu-Russian dictionary which remained the best until Hauer's dictionary appeared, but even now it supplements Hauer's dictionary. Very useful additions to Zakharov's dictionary were made by von Zach.

Zakharov was the first author of works on Manchu who devoted himself entirely and solely to Manchu studies.

Bibliography:

Zach, E. von –, "Einige Ergänzungen zu Sacharow's Mandžursko-Russki Slowarj", *Mitteilungen der Deutschen Gesellschaft für Natur- und Völkerkunde Ostasiens* 14 (1911–13), pp. 1–25, 255–267; *AM* 5 (1930), pp. 489–519.

Zaxarov, I., *Grammatika mańčžurskago yazika*, Sanktpeterburg 1879.

— *Polnii mańčžursko-russkii slovar'*, Sanktpeterburg 1875 (reprinted at H. Vetch's Publ. house in Peking, China, in 1939).

2.23. Grube.

The German scholar Wilhelm Grube (1855–1908) who had been born in St. Petersburg, Russia, studied Chinese, Manchu, and Mongolian at the University of St. Petersburg. Later on, he moved to Germany and became professor at the University of Berlin. Grube was a brilliant scholar and became famous in the field of Altaic studies thanks to two works of his which are still of great importance. The first of them is his glossary of Nanai (Goldi) compiled on the basis of materials collected by Maximowicz in the Amur region (1855–60), with the addition of some materials collected by Schrenck's expedition. The other work deals with the Juchen language. This is a transcription of Juchen texts rendered with Chinese characters, and contains a brief grammar and a glossary. It is still the principal source of our knowledge of Juchen.

Grube was not only an outstanding scholar but also a prominent university professor. One of his pupils is the well-known sinologist, mongolist, and manchuist, Professor Haenisch, whose Manchu grammar is the best in Europe.

Bibliography:

Grube, W., "Goldisch-deutsches Wörterverzeichnis mit vergleichender Berücksichtigung der übrigen tungusischen Dialekte": L. Schrenck, *Reisen und Forschungen im Amur-Lande*, III, St. Petersburg 1900.

— *Die Sprache und Schrift der Jučen*, Leipzig 1896 (Reprinted in 1941 in Tientsin).

2.24. Hauer.

The German scholar Erich Hauer (1878–1936) started his career as a diplomat in China and became a prominent scholar in the fields of sinology and studies of Manchu. Later on he became a professor of Chinese and Manchu at the University of Berlin.

Hauer's most important work is his Manchu-German dictionary in three volumes, this being, however, an abridged version of the original which was lost. He published also several articles on Manchu.

Bibliography:

Haenisch, E., "Erich Hauer (1878–1936)", *ZDMG* 107 (1957), pp. 1–6 (Necrology with a bibliography).

Hauer, E., "Das San-tzĕ-king in dreisprachigem Texte, Mit einem chinesischen, mandschurischen und mongolischen Wörterverzeichnis samt einer deutschen Übertragung", *MSOS*, Abt. I, 26–27 (1921), pp. 61–128.

— "Ein Thesaurus der Mandschusprache", *AM* 7 (1931), pp. 629–641.

— *Handwörterbuch der Mandschusprache*, Wiesbaden 1952–1955.

2.25. Sinor.

Denis Sinor, Hungarian by birth, a pupil of Pelliot, professor at the Cambridge University in Great Britain, and presently professor at Indiana University, is the author of a number of important contributions to Manchu studies: an article on transcription of Written Manchu, a study of the Manchu verbal system, an introduction to Manchu studies, and a general article on Manchu and Tungus.

Bibliography:

Sinor, D., "Le verbe mandjou", *Bulletin de la Société Linguistique de Paris* 45 (1949), pp. 146–156.

— "La transcription du mandjou", *JA* 1949, pp. 261–272.

— "Langues toungouzes", *Les langues du monde*, Paris 1952, pp. 385–402.

— "Introduction aux études mandjoues", *TP* 42, pp. 70–100.

— *Introduction à l'étude de l'Eurasie Centrale*, Wiesbaden 1963. (One of the best bibliographies).

2.26. Tsintsius.

Vera Ivanovna Tsintsius, a native of Russia, is the most outstanding scholar in the field of Tungus studies. She graduated from the Leningrad Geographic Institute and Leningrad University, after several years of study under the well-known scholars Leo Sternberg and Vladimir Bogoraz. She undertook a number of expeditions to the Tungus, mainly to the Lamut (Even), and wrote a large number of works on Tungus and Lamut. She is at the present time a professor at the Leningrad University and a leading scholar in the field. To evaluate the significance of the works of Tsintsius, it is necessary to describe, in short, the situation before the beginning of her activities.

The only scholarly work on Tungus had been for a long time Castrén's Tungus grammar written on the basis of the Nerchinsk dialect spoken in Transbaikalia, in the region of Nerchinsk (vide 2.16.). The only works which appeared more or less soon after Castrén's grammar were some glossaries collected by non-linguists. They are rather unreliable and may be of historical interest only. Therefore they will not be mentioned here. Readers interested in them can use the bibliographic data given in Grube's Goldi (Nanai) glossary (vide 2.23.).

The first serious work after Castrén's grammar was a book on the Barguzin dialect of the Evenki language, published by the author of these lines in 1927. A few years later, a work on the Solon language by the same author appeared.

The materials on Barguzin Evenki were used by Gortsevskaya who wrote a more or less complete grammar of that dialect.

Due to extremely unhappy circumstances in the USSR during a whole decade (from 1930 to 1940), Tsintsius was unable to publish anything of importance at that time, and most of her remarkable and highly reliable works appeared after World War II, and particulary in the period of de-Stalinization.

The most important work of Tsintsius is her comparative phonology of the Manchu-Tungus languages, written on the basis of a vast knowledge of material and modern methods of comparative linguistics. She is also the author of two excellent Lamut grammars, and published, together with Lydia Rishes, a large Russian-Lamut dictionary. Although Lamut seems to be her special field, Tsintsius is also known as the author of works on Orochi, Negidal, etc.

Tsintsius is not only a prolific scholar but also a successful university teacher. Together with Vasilevich, she has trained several excellent linguists in the Manchu-Tungus field. These are, to enumerate them in alphabetic order, Avrorin, Boitsova, Gortsevskaya, Konstantinova, Lebedeva, Novikova, Rishes, and Sunik.

Bibliography:

Cincius, V. I., *Očerk grammatiki ėvenskogo (lamutskogo) yazïka*, Leningrad 1947.
Cincius, V. I. i Rišes, L. D., *Russko-ėvenskiĭ slovaŕ*, Moskva 1952 (With a grammar by Cincius).
Cincius, V. I., "Očerk morfologii oročskogo yazïka", *Uč. Zap. LGU* 98: 1 (1949).
— "Množestvennoe čislo imeni v tunguso-mańčžurskix yazïkax", *ibid.*, 69: 10 (1946).
— *Sravnitelnaya fonetika tunguso-mańčžurskix yazïkov*, Leningrad 1949.
Gorcevskaya, V. A., *Xarakteristika govora barguzinskix ėvenkov*, Leningrad 1936.
— *Formï otricaniya v ėvenkiĭskom yazïke*, Leningrad 1936.
— *Očerk istorii izučeniya tunguso-mańčžurskix yazïkov*, Leningrad 1959 (A very good outline of history of study of Manchu-Tungus with bibliographical data).
Poppe, N., *Materialï dlya issledovaniya tungusskogo yazïka*, Narečie barguzinskix tungusov, Leningrad 1927.
— *Materialï po solonskomu yazïku*, Leningrad 1931.

2.27. Vasilevich.

Glafira Makarievna Vasilevich (born in 1895), a native of Russia, is also a well-known scholar in the field of Tungus linguistics. Very active and energetic, a prolific author of numerous works on Tungus, she has made important contributions to Tungus linguistics, although she lacks the profundity, precision, and carefulness of Cincius. Vasilevich graduated from the same schools as Cincius and was also a pupil of Sternberg and Bogoraz. She made numerous expeditions to various Tungus tribes and published a large number of works. She is also a successful university teacher.

Bibliography:

Vasilevič, G. M., *Učebnik ėvenkiĭskogo (tungusskogo) yazïka*, Leningrad 1934.

— *Očerk grammatiki ėvenkiĭskogo (tungusskogo) yazïka*, Leningrad 1940.
— *Očerki dialektov ėvenkiĭskogo (tungusskogo) yazïka*, Leningrad 1948.
— *Ėvenkiĭsko-russkiĭ slovaŕ*, Moskva 1958 (With a concise grammar).
— "K voprosu o klassifikacii tunguso-mańčžurskix yazïkov", *VoYa* 2 (1960).

2.28. Petrova.

Taisiya Ivanovna Petrova, a native of Russia, is an excellent scholar of the same generation as Tsintsius and Vasilevich. She was very active, together with Tsintsius and Vasilevich, in the research division of the Leningrad Institute of Arctic Peoples and taught at the Hertzen Institute. She is now at the Leningrad University.

Petrova has published a number of works on Goldi (Nanai), Ulcha, and Oroki. All her works are written on the basis of carefully verified materials and are absolutely reliable.

Bibliography:

Petrova, T.I., *Kratkiĭ nanaĭsko-russkiĭ slovaŕ s priloženiem grammatičeskogo očerka*, Leningrad 1935.
— *Ulĉskiĭ dialekt nanaĭskogo yazïka*, Leningrad 1936.
— *Nanaĭsko-russkiĭ slovaŕ*, Leningrad 1960.

2.29. The pupils of Tsintsius.

Tsintsius, Vasilevich, and Petrova trained a number of younger scholars. Although the latter had the benefit of studying under a number of recognized scholars of high standing, they owe most of their knowledge to Tsintsius. The pupils of Tsintsius include Avrorin, Boitsova, Gortsevskaya, Konstantinova, Lebedeva, Novikova, Rishes, and Sunik.

Avrorin's specialty is Goldi (Nanai). His most important works are a Nanai grammar in two volumes and a book on the Nanai syntax.

Boitsova has not published much. Her principal work is a book on the category of person in Evenki. Gortsevskaya's works were mentioned above (*vide* 2.26).

Olga Konstantinova and Elena Lebedeva have published some minor works on Evenki.

Novikova is the author of a number of excellent works on Lamut, and Sunik has been very active in the field of comparative Manchu-Tungus linguistics.

Bibliography:

Avrorin, V.A., *Grammatika nanaĭskogo yazïka*, I–II, Moskva-Leningrad 1959–61. (With bibliography).
— *Očerki po sintaksisu nanaĭskogo yazïka*, Leningrad 1948.
Boĭcova, A.F., *Kategoriya lica v ėvenkiĭskom yazïke*, Leningrad 1940.
Konstantinova, O.A., i Lebedeva, E.P., *Ėvenkiĭskiĭ yazïk*, Učebnoe posobie dlya pedučilišč, Leningrad 1953.
Lebedeva, E.P., "Govorï Bolŝogo Poroga i Agatï, Iz ėkspedicionnïx zapiseĭ", *Učenïe Zapiski Leningradskogo Gosudarstvennogo Pedagogičeskogo Instituta im. A.I. Gercena* 167 (1960).

Novikova, K.A., *Očerki dialektov évenskogo yazïka*, Olskiĭ govor, č. I, Moskva-Leningrad 1960.
— *Proekt edinoĭ fonetičeskoĭ transkripcii dlya tunguso-mańčžurskix yazïkov*, Moskva-Leningrad 1961.
Sunik, O.P., *Glagol v tunguso-mańčžurskix yazïkax*, Moskva-Leningrad 1962. (With bibliography).

2.230. Manchu-Tungus Linguistics in Japan.

The Manchu-Tungus languages have also been studied by Japanese scholars. Most of their works are written in Japanese and, therefore, accessible to very few readers outside Japan.

Manchu was studied by Ikegami, Okada, and Yamamoto. Of the spoken minor languages Oroki was investigated by Ikegami. Of larger works in Japanese, the publication of the Manchu text of the "Secret Chronicles of the Manchu Dynasty" should be mentioned. Although it is by no means a linguistic work and the translations and footnotes are in Japanese, it deserves mention because it is the newest edition of a large text of the XVII century which presents interesting material for language study.

Bibliography:

Ikegami, Jirô, "The Substantive Inflection of Orok", *JLSJ* 30 (1956), pp. 79–96.
— "Orok Texts", *Mem. of the Res. Dep. of the Toyo Bunko* 17 (1958), pp. 85–95.
— "The Verb Inflection of Orok", *Kokugo Kenkyu* 9 (1959), pp. 34–73.
— "Über die Herkunft einiger unregelmäßiger Imperativformen der mandschurischen Verben", *SA*, pp. 88–94.
Kanda, N., Shimada, J., Matsumura, J., Okamoto, K., Honda, M., Okada, H., *Tongki Fuka Sindaha Hergen i Dangse*, vol. I–VII, Tokyo 1955–1963.
Okada, Hidehiro, "Color-Names in Manchu", *ASAL* 1962, pp. 225–228.
Yamamoto, K., "On the Suffix *-ri* in Some Tungus and Mongolian Languages", *JLSJ* 14 (1949), pp. 49–62.
— "On the Suffix *-mbihe* in Some Manchurian Texts", *ibid.* 16 (1950), pp. 59–79.
— "On the Verb Form in *-cina* in Script Manchu", *Memoirs of the Research Department of the Toyo Bunko* 14, pp. 155–167.

2.3. History of Chuvash and Turkic linguistics.

2.31. The beginnings.

Turkish was one of the first Oriental languages to be studied in Europe. The first grammar of Turkish appeared at the beginning of the XVII century because Turkey played at that time an important rôle. It was a constant military menace to the Habsburg Empire and was regarded as one of the most powerful nations. Relations with Turkey required a better knowledge of that country and, of course, language.

The first Turkish grammars and those which followed them in the subsequent decades are only of historical interest. With the exception of the grammar and dictionary by Meninski, they are not usable at the present time. In the subsequent periods, Turkic studies were developing mainly in Russia, although important results were also achieved in other countries, including Turkey. The largest centers of Turkic linguistic studies are Russia (USSR), Denmark, Germany, Finland, Sweden, France, Poland, and Hungary. The development of Turkic studies in individual countries will be discussed in this order. One of the largest centers of turcology is, of course, Turkey.

Bibliography:

Hieronymus Megiser, *Institutionum Linguae Turcicae Liber Primus seu Sagoges Grammaticae Turcicae* [Leipzig 1612].
Franciscus a Mesgnien Meninski, *Thesaurus Linguarum Orientalium, Turcicae, Arabicae, Persicae Institutiones seu Grammatica Turcica*, Vienna 1680.
— *Complementum Thesauri* etc., Vienna 1687.

2.32. Böhtlingk.

The foundation for Turkic linguistics was laid with the appearance of Böhtlingk's famous work on Yakut. Otto Böhtlingk (1815–1904), a Dutch citizen of German extraction, was born in St. Petersburg, Russia, and became a Russian citizen at an advanced age. He owed his world-wide reputation to his works on Sanskrit, his principal work being his famous Sanskrit-German dictionary which he had compiled on behalf of the Russian Academy of Sciences. He became a full member of the academy. Later he left Russia and lived in Germany.

It was the Academy of Sciences which commissioned Böhtlingk to write his work on Yakut, a grammar, edition of texts, with a German translation, and a dictionary. The academy had put at Böhtlingk's disposal some material gathered by the Siberian expedition of A. Th. von Middendorff. Böhtlingk used, however, his own material which he had collected with his native informant, Uvarovskiï who had been born in the Yakut region.

Böhtlingk established the phonological system of Yakut and all the morphophonemic alternations and sound changes. He also formulated the rules with reference to inflection, word formation, word classes, phrase and clause structure. The characteristic features of his work are phonetic reliability, precision of description, and the introduction of the comparative method to Turkic studies. He was the first who established the existence of primary long vowels in Yakut (e.g., *āt* "name" versus *at* "horse"), the developments *$*a\gamma > ia$, *$*äg > iä$, etc. Thus, his unsurpassed work on Yakut has served for a long time as a model for description of other Turkic languages and was the first comparative linguistic work in the Turkic field.

Böhtlingk's work is still one of the principal sources of information about the Yakut language. Its author can be regarded as the founder of Turkic linguistics.

Bibliography:

Böhtlingk, O., *Über die Sprache der Yakuten*, St. Petersburg 1851.
Windisch, E., "Zu Böhtlingks 100. Geburtstag am 11. Juni 1915", *Indogermanisches Jahrbuch* 3 (1915), pp. 176–187.

2.33. Radloff.

Wilhelm Radloff (1837–1918), who had been born in Germany and studied Indo-European linguistics at the University of Berlin, went as a young man to Russia, stayed there for his remaining life, and became a Russian citizen. Radloff spent many years in the city of Barnaul, in the Altai region. There he taught German and Latin at the local mining school. During his stay there, Radloff studied local Turkic languages and undertook numerous trips to various Turkic tribes in Siberia. Later on, he went to Kazan and studied Tatar, Bashkir, and Kazakh. Radloff himself was an enthusiastic collector of linguistic material, folklore, and anthropological data. He transmitted his enthusiasm to several natives and made them collect material for his studies. Such natives inspired by Radloff's work were the Teleut Chuvalkov and, later on, the Sagai Turk, Katanov, who himself became an internationally recognized outstanding linguist in the Turkic field.

The material collected by Radloff and his few assistants was enormous. After he had moved, in 1883, to St. Petersburg and joined the Academy of Sciences, he began the preparation of his materials for publication. The most outstanding works of Radloff which have fully preserved their significance up to now and remained unsurpassed and are justly regarded as the rock on which modern Turkic linguistics are standing, are his four-volume (Turkic-German-Russian) dictionary of the Turkic languages and dialects, and his specimens of oral poetry of various Turkic tribes with translations (mostly into German, a few volumes in Russian). These specimens include texts in Altai, Teleut, Lebed Tatar, Shor, Soyot, Abakan dialects (Sagai, Koibal), Kızıl, Chulīm, Baraba, Tara, Tobol Tatar, Tumen Tatar, Kazakh, Kirghiz, Crimean dialects, Gagauz, dialects of Turkey, and East Turki.

This vast material is invaluable because most of the dialects have changed during the years which passed after their investigation, and some of them have disappeared, not to mention the fact that the folklore collected by Radloff could not be collected now because most of it has been thoroughly forgotten.

Radloff undertook also an archeological expedition to Mongolia with the purpose of photographing the Ancient Turkic monuments, the so-called Orkhon Inscriptions. He published the texts of the inscriptions in his *Atlas der Altertümer der Mongolei*. Unfortunately, Radloff had his photographs retouched and the rubbings overpainted each time the text was not making sense to him. Therefore, they cannot be used for scholarly research. After the great Danish scholar, Vilhelm Thomsen, had deciphered the Turkic runic alphabet, Radloff transcribed and translated the most important inscriptions and investigated them from the linguistic point of view. The fact that Radloff had not waited until Thomsen's translation appeared, but had published his own translation soon after the appearance of Thomsen's preliminary report on the decipherment, made Radloff very unpopular with the European scholars. Radloff's works on the Orkhon inscriptions are, however, much inferior to Thomsen's interpretation of the runic inscriptions, and at the present time cannot be taken into consideration. Radloff published also a large number of texts in Uighur script, transcribed and translated them. These works of his cannot be recommended either because the basic idea of Radloff that ancient Uighur texts should be read in accordance with the phonological system of modern Altai dialects was wrong. It was again Thomsen who established the correct reading of Karakhanide.

In general, Radloff's works on old Turkic languages (Ancient Turkic, Middle Turkic – Karakhanide, Kuman) cannot be used at the present time. Likewise, his *Phonetik der nördlichen Türksprachen* (Leipzig 1882) and his comparative linguistic works (e.g., *Die jakutische Sprache in ihrem Verhältnis zu den Türksprachen*) are only of historical interest.

However, Radloff is to be regarded as the greatest turcologist. He owes his reputation to his *Dictionary* and the specimens.

Radloff did not teach at any university and worked only as a full member of the Russian Academy of Sciences.

Bibliography:

Bartoĺd, V. V., "Pamyati V. V. Radlova 1837–1918", *IRGO* 54 (1918), pp. 164–189 (Necrology).

Ko dnyu semidesyatilětiya Vasiliya Vasiĺyeviča Radlova 5 yanvarya 1907 goda, St. Peterburg 1907 (Anniversary volume with a biography and bibliography).

Pritsak, O., "Vorwort zum Nachdruck" (phot. reprint of the dictionary, vol. I, pp. V–XXVII).

Radloff, W., *Versuch eines Wörterbuches der Türk-Dialekte*, I–IV, St. Petersburg 1893, 1899, 1905, 1911. A new photogr. reprint: s'Gravenhage 1960; another photogr. reprint has been published in the USSR.

— *Narěčiya tyurkskix plěmen, živuščix v Yužnoǐ Sibiri i Dzungarskoǐ stepi, I Otdělenie: Obrazcï narodnoǐ literaturï*, Část I, St. Peterburg 1866; II (1868); III (1870); IV (1872); V (1885); VI (1886); VII (1896); VIII (1899); IX (1907); X (1904). (Texts in various dialects, the vol. VIII–X containing those collected by Kúnos, Katanov, and Moshkov).

— *Proben der Volksliteratur der türkischen Stämme Süd-Sibiriens*, I Theil, St. Petersburg 1866; II (1868); III (1870); IV (1872); V (1885); VI (1886) (German translation of the texts).

— *Aus Sibirien*, Lose Blätter aus dem Tagebuche eines reisenden Linguisten I–II, Leipzig 1884 (Radloff's diary.) Its Turkish translation by Dr. Ahmet Temir, W. Radloff, *Sibiryadan*, contains (in the first volume, İstanbul 1954) an excellent biography and a complete bibliography of Radloff's works.

2.34. Iĺminskiǐ.

When Radloff came to Barnaul (1859) and started his study of the Altai dialects, the Russian missionary Nikolaǐ Ivanovič Iĺminskiǐ (1822–1891) had already become known as a turcologist. Iĺminskiǐ had graduated from the theological academy in Kazan, had studied Turkic and Arabic and made a journey to Cairo. After his return from there, he became a member of the academy mentioned and played an important rôle as an organizer of mission work among the natives of the Volga region, such as Tatars, Bashkirs, Chuvash, and Finno-Ugrians (Mari, Udmurt, etc.). He and his assistants composed alphabets for the natives who did not have a script of their own, and published grammars. Only a few works of Iĺminskiǐ are of real scholarly value. One of them is his edition of the *History of Prophets* by Rabɣūzī in Middle Turkic. Another important work is his publication of the Kazakh epic *Er Targïn*, and the most outstanding work is a grammar of the Altai dialect published anonymously by the members of the "Altai Mission". Its main author was probably Iĺminskiĭ.

Iĺminskiĭ sponsored also works of other authors. The most important of them is the Altai and Shor (called by its author Aladag) dictionary by V. Verbitskiĭ (1827–1890), also a missionary, who had been working under Iĺminskiĭ's guidance.

Bibliography:

Iĺminskiĭ, N. I., "Vstupiteĺnoe čtenie v kurs tyurksko-tatarskix yazïkov", *Uč. Zap. Kaz. Un-ta* 1862, 59 pp.
— "Materialï k izučeniyu kirgizskago yazïka", *ibid.*, 1860, No. 3, pp. 107–159; No. 4, pp. 53–165; 1861, No. 1, pp. 130–162 (According to the terminology used at that time, this was Kazakh).
Iĺminskiĭ, N. I., *Istoriya prorokov Rabguzi na džagataĭskom narěčii*, Kazań 1859 (To be correct, this is Post-Karakhanide).
— "Über die Sprache der Turkmenen", *Mél. As.* 4 (1860), pp. 63–74.
— *Ir-Targïn*, Kirgizskaya pověst, Kazań 1861 (This is a Kazakh story).
— *Grammatika altaĭskago yazïka*, Izdannaya trudami Altaĭskoĭ Missii, Kazań 1869.
Verbickiĭ, V., *Slovaŕ altaĭskago i aladagskago narěčii tyurkskago yazïka*, Kazań 1884.

2.35. Katanov.

Nikolaĭ Fedorovič Katanov (1862–1922), a Sagai Turk by birth (his father was Sagai, his mother was a Kacha woman), was one of the most outstanding turcologists. A member of an illiterate tribe, born in a primitive settlement in the Abakan region, he was lucky enough first to get elementary education and, later on, graduate from high school and the University of St. Petersburg. There he studied Arabic, Persian, and Turkic and, being unusually gifted, he drew the attention of his professors and did graduate work. While in high school, he made the acquaintance of Verbitskii and Il'minskiĭ who played important rôles in Katanov's life as his first teachers and sponsors. In Petersburg, Katanov became a close associate of Radloff and remained under the latter's influence until Radloff's death. Radloff sponsored Katanov's extensive travels in Siberia and Eastern Turkestan. Later on (in 1894), he became professor of Turkic languages at the University of Kazan.

Katanov's works are numerous. The most important of them is his description of the Uryankhai (Soyot or Tuva) language which contains a descriptive and comparative (with other Turkic languages) grammar of Uryankhai, and texts with translations. Other important works are his collection of texts in various Siberian Turkic languages, and his samples of East Turki.

Bibliography:

Ivanov, S. N., *Nikolaĭ Fedorovič Katanov 1862–1962, Očerk žizni i deyateĺnosti*, Moskva-Leningrad 1962 (Biography and complete bibliography).

Katanov, N. F., *Opït izslĕdovaniya uryanxaĭskago yazïka s ukazaniem glavnĕĭšix rodstvennïx otnošeniĭ ego k drugim yazïkam tyurkskago kornya*, Kazań 1903.
— *Narĕčiya uryanxaĭcev, abakanskix tatar i karagasov*, Obrazcï narodnoĭ literaturï tyurkskix plĕmen IX, t. I–II, St. Peterburg 1907 (*vide* V. V. Radloff *Obrazcï* and *Proben*).
Menges, K. H., *Volkskundliche Texte aus Ost-Türkistan aus dem Nachlass von N. Th. Katanov*, [I] SBAW 1933, pp. 1173–1293; II Berlin 1943, 185 pp.

2.36. Piekarski.

Edward Piekarski (1858–1934), a Pole born in Russia, was an outstanding scholar in the field of Yakut linguistics. He became a scholar by accident. He had studied veterinary medicine but, having been involved in anti-government activities, was exiled, in 1881, to the city of Yakutsk in the Yakut area, and spent there 24 years during which he had enormous opportunities of studying Yakut. His most important work is his Yakut-Russian dictionary and a collection of texts (*vide* 1.321).

Bibliography:

Ėduard Karlovič Pekarskiĭ (K 100-letiyu so dnya roždeniya), Yakutskiĭ filial Akademii Nauk SSSR, Yakutsk 1958, 55 pp.
Poppe, N., "Eduard Piekarski", *UJ* 7 (1928), pp. 338–340 (Article on the occasion of the 45th anniversary of the beginning of his work on the dictionary. Brief biography).

2.37. Ashmarin.

The Russian Nikolaĭ Ivanovič Ašmarin (1870–1933) was the most outstanding scholar in the Chuvash field. He had studied Turkic and other languages at the Oriental Institute in Moscow and worked as a high school teacher and, since 1925, as a professor of Turkic linguistics at the University of Baku, Azerbaijan.

Ashmarin was the first scholar to devote all his time to Chuvash. What Piekarski was doing in the Yakut field, Ashmarin was doing in the Chuvash field.

His most important works are the first complete Chuvash grammar including the syntax, and a Chuvash-Russian dictionary in 17 volumes. He also published a work on the dialects spoken in the city of Nukha in Azerbaijan.

Bibliography:

Ašmarin, N. I., *Materialï dlya izslĕdovaniya čuvašskago yazïka*, Kazań 1898 (Grammar).
— *Opït izslĕdovaniya čuvašskago sintaksisa* I, Kazań 1903 (Syntax, vol. I).
— *Opït issledovaniya čuvašskogo sintaksisa* II, Simbirsk 1923 (Syntax, vol. II).
— *Slovař čuvašskogo yazïka* I–XVII, Čeboksarï 1928–1950.
— *Obščiĭ obzor tyurkskix govorov goroda Nuxi*, Baku 1926.
Egorov, V. G., *N. I. Ašmarin kak issledovateľ čuvašskogo yazïka*, K 75-letiyu so dnya roždeniya, Čeboksarï 1948 (Biography and bibliography).

2.38. Melioranskii.

The Russian scholar Platon Mixaĭlovič Melioranskiĭ (1868–1906) had studied Turkic, Arabic, and Persian. He became professor at the University of St. Petersburg and was associated with Radloff. Unfortunately, he died very young. He was a gifted and broad-minded scholar equally interested in ancient and new Turkic languages. He was one of the first turcologists who recognized the importance of ancient linguistic works by Moslem scholars, and published a work on Turkic of the XIV century as represented by Ibn Muḥannā. The latter had also left a work on Mongolian which consists of some grammatical rules and a glossary. Melioranskii's work was the first work on an Arabic source of Middle Mongolian. His Kazakh grammar in two volumes was the first scholarly representation of that language and, at that time, one of the very few scholarly grammars of any Turkic language. Melioranskii was deeply interested in Ancient Turkic. His book on the inscription in honor of Kül Tegin and its language was a considerable step forward in comparison to Radloff's work on the same subject. Melioranskii was also an excellent comparativist. His work on the Turkic elements in the language of the ancient Russian Igor Song of the XII century was one of the few works on Oriental elements in Old Russian.

Bibliography:

Melioranskiĭ, P. M., *Kratkaya grammatika Kazak-Kirgizskago yazïka*, I–II, Sanktpeterburg 1894–97.
— "Ob orxonskix i eniseĭskix nadgrobnïx pamyatnikax s nadpisyami", *ŽMNP* 317: 2 (1898), pp. 203–292.
— *Pamyatnik v čest́ Kyul̂-tegina*, St. Peterburg 1899.
— *Arab-filolog o tureckom yazïkě*, Sanktpeterburg 1900.
— *Arab-filolog o mongol̂skom yazïkě*, Sanktpeterburg 1903.
— "Tureckie elementï v yazïkě slova o Polku Igorevě", *IORYaS* 7: 2 (1902); 10 : 2 (1905).
Samoĭlovič, A., "Pamyati P. M. Melioranskago", *ZVO* 1907.

2.39. Malov.

Sergeĭ Efimovič Malov (1880–1957), a Russian and the son of a professor at the theological academy in Kazan, studied Turkic and Arabic at the same academy and at the Kazan University. His teacher was Katanov. Later on, Malov studied the same languages at the University of St. Petersburg. There his official teacher was V. D. Smirnov, professor of Turkish, but he owed most of his training to Radloff. Radloff taught him the Turkic languages spoken in Siberia, Ancient Turkic of the Orkhon Inscriptions, and Uighur. Malov undertook a number of expeditions, the most important ones being those conducted in 1909–11 and 1913–14 during which he collected valuable material on the languages of the Yellow Uighurs and East Turki. He found also many precious Uighur manuscripts, among them the famous *Altun Yaruq*, i.e., the *Golden Beam*, Sanskrit *Suvarṇaprabhāsa*. Malov was not only Radloff's pupil but also his faithful helper. He was assisting Radloff in his work. Malov was a professor in Kazan (1917–1922) and Leningrad (1922–1938). He was elected a corresponding member of the Academy of Sciences of the USSR. He published, together with Radloff, the text of the *Golden Beam Sūtra*. Other outstanding works of his are his books on the language of the Yellow Uighurs and East Turki (Modern Uighur).

Bibliography:

Malov, S. E., *Pamyatniki drevnetyurkskoĭ piśmennosti*, Tekstï i issledovaniya, Moskva-Leningrad 1951.
— *Pamyatniki drevnetyurkskoĭ piśmennosti Mongolii i Kirgizii*, Moskva-Leningrad 1959.
— *Eniseĭskaya piśmennosť tyurkov*, Tekstï i perevodï, Moskva-Leningrad 1952.
— *Yazïk želtïx uĭgurov*, Slovaŕ i grammatika, Alma-Ata 1957.
— *Lobnorskiĭ yazïk*, Tekstï, perevodï, slovaŕ, Frunze 1956.
— *Uĭgurskiĭ yazïk*, Xamiĭskoe narečie, Tekstï, perevodï i slovaŕ, Moskva-Leningrad 1954.
— *Uĭgurskĭe narečiya Sińczyana*, Tekstï, perevodï, slovaŕ, Moskva 1961.
Ubryatova, E. T., "O naučnoĭ i obščestvennoĭ deyatelnosti Sergeya Efimoviča Malova", *Tyurkologičeskiĭ sbornik* I, Moskva-Leningrad 1951, pp. 5–30 (Biography and bibliography up to 1951).
— "Sergeĭ Efimovič Malov", *IAN-OLYa* 16: 6 (1957), pp. 574–578 (Necrology).

2.310. Samoilovich.

Aleksandr (Alexander) Nikolayevič Samoĭlovič (1880–1938), of Ukrainian ancestry, had studied Turkic, Arabic, and Persian at the University of St. Petersburg. His teachers were P. M. Melioranskii and V. D. Smirnov but he was also associated with Radloff. Samoilovich was a gifted linguist and spoke Turkish, Turkmenian, Uzbek, and some other Turkic languages better than any of his teachers. He travelled much in Turkey, Crimea, and Turkestan, and was the first turcologist engaged in studies of Turkmenian. Samoilovich was more interested in literature, folklore, cultural history, and ethnography than in linguistics. Therefore, his linguistic works are few as compared to more than 300 works on various other subjects.

Samoilovich's most brilliant work is his *Classification of the Turkic Languages* which, with some minor changes, is the basis for present-day classification. Excellent works are also his study of the Turkic numerals, and a study of Turkic names of the days. He is also the author of a good grammar of Crimean Tatar and a Turkish grammar. Important works are also his articles on some Ancient Turkic inscriptions in Runic script.

Samoilovich was not old when he suddenly disappeared from the stage. He was imprisoned in 1937 and died in 1938 in a concentration camp in Russian Central Asia.

Bibliography:

Menzel, Th., "Über die Werke des russischen Turkologen A. Samojlovič", *AO* 1 (1929), pp. 209–234.
Samoĭlovič, A. N., *Nekotorïe dopolneniya k klassifikacii tureckix yazïkov*, Petrograd 1922.

— "Tureckie čislitelnïe količestvennïe i obzor popïtok ix tolkovaniya", *Yazïkovednïe problemï po čislitelnïm I*. Sbornik stateǐ, Leningrad 1927, pp. 135–156.
— "Ne 'idol' a 'plemya'", *Sov. Ėtn.* 1935, no. 6, pp. 44–46.
— "Ne 'turki' a 'carica'", *Sov. Ėtn.* 1936, no..2, pp. 255–256.
— "Novïe tyurkskie runï iz Mongolii I–II", *IAN OON* 1934, pp. 631–634, 657–659.
— "Bogatïǐ i bednïǐ v tyurkskix yazïkax", *ibid.* 1936, no. 4, pp. 21–66.
— *Opït kratkoǐ krïmskotatarskoǐ grammatiki*, Petrograd 1916.
— *Kratkaya učebnaya grammatika sovremennogo osmanskotureckogo yazïka*, Leningrad 1925.
Samoïlovitch, A. et Kotwicz, Wł., "Le monument turc d'Ikhékhuchotu en Mongolie centrale", *RO* 4 (1928).

2.311. Dmitriev.

The Russian turcologist Nikolai Konstantinovich Dmitriev (1898–1954) was professor of Turkish at the University of Leningrad (1926–1941) and that of Moscow (1941–1954). He was a linguist excellently trained and familiar with modern methods of linguistic research, his works making a clear distinction between phonemes and their allophones. He was an excellent phonetician and a careful collector of grammatical facts.

Dmitriev made frequent journeys to the Bashkirs, Tatars, Kumyks in Daghestan, Turks of Azerbaijan, Turkmens, Chuvash, etc., and trained a number of young native linguists, this being one of his greatest achievements in his capacity of a university professor.

Dmitriev published more than one hundred books and articles, many of them referring to Bashkir, among them a Bashkir grammar, a Kumyk grammar, a survey of Chuvash, and articles on phonology, on various problems of Turkic grammar, and Turkic comparative linguistics. His most important achievements are, however, in the field of study of Bashkir.

Bibliography:

Dmitriev, N. K., "Étude sur la phonétique bachkire", *JA* 210 (1927), pp. 193–252.
— *Grammatika baškirskogo yazïka*, Moskva-Leningrad 1948.
— *Russko-baškirskiǐ slovaŕ*, pod redakcieǐ N. K. Dmitrieva, K. Z. Axmerova, T. G. Baiševa, Moskva 1948 (With a concise Bashkir grammar by Dmitriev).
Dmitriev, N. K., Gorskiǐ, S. P., "Kratkiǐ grammatičeskiǐ očerk čuvašskogo yazïka", *Russko-čuvašskiǐ slovaŕ* pod redakcieǐ N. K. Dmitrieva, Moskva 1951 (Concise Chuvash grammar).
Dmitriev, N. K., *Grammatika kumïkskogo yazïka*, Moskva-Leningrad 1940.
— *Stroǐ tureckogo yazïka*, Leningrad 1939.
— *Tureckiǐ yazïk*, Moskva 1960.
Dmitriev, N. K. i Isxakov, F. G., *Voprosï izučeniya xakasskogo yazïka i ego dialektov* (Materialï dlya naučnoǐ grammatiki), Abakan 1948.
Dmitriev, N. K., *Issledovaniya po sravnitelnoǐ grammatike tyurkskix yazïkov* I,

Moskva 1955, II Moskva 1956, III Moskva 1961, IV Moskva 1962. (This work edited by Dmitriev contains a number of articles in the field of Turkic comparative studies, twenty of them written by Dmitriev).

Dmitriev, N. K., *Stroï tureckix yazïkov*, Moskva 1962 (Posthumous volume containing reprints of some selected works published in his lifetime).

Voprosï baškirskoĭ filologii, Moskva 1959 (Contains a brief biography and bibliography of Dmitriev's works on Bashkir, pp. 7–16).

Pritsak, O., "Nikolaj Konstantinovič Dmitriev (1898–1954)", *UAJ* 27 (1955), pp. 237–241 (Necrology).

Voprosï xakasskogo yazïka i literaturï, Abakan 1955 (Biography and bibliography, pp. 5–12).

2.312. Dyrenkova.

Nadežda Petrovna Dïrenkova, a native of Russia (1904–1942), graduated from the Ethnography Department of the Leningrad Geographic Institute. Her main field was anthropology (or ethnography as it is called in the USSR). She studied under the well-known ethnographers Leo Sternberg and Vladimir Bogoraz. Her teachers of Turkic languages were Samoilovich and Malov.

Dyrenkova investigated a number of Turkic tribes in Siberia, collected folklore texts, and published a remarkable collection of various texts in Turkic dialects of the Altai region and an excellent collection of Shor materials. She is also the author of three grammars, namely an Oirot (i.e., Altai), a Shor, and an unfinished (only the first volume) Khakas grammar. Dyrenkova died at a young age in Leningrad besieged by the Germans. The premature death of this talented scholar was a great loss.

Bibliography:

Dïrenkova, N. P., *Grammatika oĭrotskogo yazïka*, Moskva-Leningrad 1940.
— *Grammatika šorskogo yazïka*, Moskva-Leningrad 1941.
— *Grammatika xakasskogo yazïka*, Fonetika i morfologiya, Abakan 1948 (Posthumously published).
— *Šorskiĭ folklor*, Zapisi, perevod, vstupitelnaya statya, Moskva-Leningrad 1940.
— "Kul̆t ognya u altaĭcev i teleutov", *Sbornik Muzeya Antropologii i Ėtnografii*, 6 (1927), pp. 63–78.
— "Materialï po šamanstvu u teleutov", *ibid.* 10 (1949), pp. 107–190.
— "Oxotnič'i legendï kumandincev", *ibid.* 11 (1949), pp. 110–132.
— "Perežitki materinskogo roda u altaĭskix tyurkov", *Sov. Ėtn.* 1937, no. 4, pp. 18–45.
— "Kumandinskie pesni tapqaq", *Sovetskiĭ Folklor* 7 (1941), pp. 82–90.

2.313. Borovkov.

Aleksandr (Alexander) Konstantinovich Borovkov (1900–1962), Russian, corresponding member of the Academy of Sciences of the USSR, investigated Karachai-Balkar, Uzbek and East Turki (Modern Uighur). He published valuable material on Chaghatai and Middle Turkic of the older period. A large Uzbek-Russian dictionary was published under his supervision.

Bibliography:

Borovkov, A. K., "Karačaevo-balkarskiĭ yazïk", *YaS* 7 (1932), pp. 37–55.
— "Očerki karačaevo-balkarskoĭ grammatiki", *Yazïki Severnogo Kavkaza i Dagestana* I, Moskva-Leningrad 1935, pp. 11–40.
— "Ob edinoĭ karačaevo-balkarskoĭ orfografii", *IAN* 1935, pp. 501–518.
— *Uzbekskiĭ literaturnïĭ yazïk v period 1905–1917 gg.*, Taškent 1940.
— *Učebnik uĭgurskogo yazïka*, Leningrad 1935.
— "Očerki istorii uzbekskogo yazïka" I: *SV* 5 (1948), pp. 229–250; II: *ibid.* 6 (1949), pp. 24–51; III: *UZIV* 16 (1958), pp. 138–219.
— "Iz materialov dlya istorii uzbekskogo yazïka", *Tyurkologičeskiĭ Sbornik* I (Moskva-Leningrad 1951), pp. 73–79.
— "Ališer Navoi kak osnovopoložnik uzbekskogo literaturnogo yazïka", *Ališer Navoi*, Sbornik Stateĭ, Moskva-Leningrad 1946, pp. 92–120.
— "*Badā'i 'al-luġat*", *Slovaŕ Ṭāli' Imānī Geratskogo k sočineniyamAlišera Navoi*, Moskva 1961.
— (glavn. redaktor) *Uzbeksko-russkiĭ slovaŕ*, Moskva 1959.
— *Leksika sredneaziatskogo tefsira XII–XIII vv.*, Moskva 1963.

2.314. Kononov.

The Russian scholar Andrei Nikolayevich Kononov, a pupil of Samoilovich, is a professor at the University of Leningrad and a corresponding member of the Academy of Sciences of the USSR. He has been working mainly in the fields of modern Turkish and Uzbek language and is the author of two detailed grammars of these languages, which give complete bibliographies of works on some individual problems. His are the best grammars of the languages concerned. He published also two important Chaghatai texts.

Bibliography:

Kononov, A. N., *Grammatika sovremennogo tureckogo literaturnogo yazïka*, Moskva-Leningrad 1956.
— *Grammatika sovremennogo uzbekskogo literaturnogo yazïka*, Moskva-Leningrad 1960.
— *Rodoslovnaya Turkmen*, Sočinenie Abu-l-Gazi Xana, Moskva-Leningrad 1958.

2.315. Baskakov.

The Russian turcologist, Nikolai Aleksandrovich Baskakov (born 1905), is the author of several grammars and dictionaries of various Turkic languages. He has worked so far mostly in the field of descriptive linguistics. His major subject is the Karakalpak language which is a dialect of Kazakh, which was, for political reasons, declared an independent language. Baskakov was the first scholar to pay attention to Karakalpak and can be regarded as the founder of this special field of Turkic linguistics. His most important works on Karakalpak are his two-volume grammar, a Russian-Karakalpak dictionary, and a Karakalpak-Russian dictionary. He published also a grammar and dictionary of Oirot (i.e., Altai and Teleut), a book on the Altai dialect, a Nogai grammar, a grammar of East Turki, and a grammar and dictionary of Khakas (artificial name for the Abakan dialects). He is a prolific writer and possesses a good knowledge of many Turkic languages. He is also known as the author of a general survey of Turkic languages and an introduction to Turkic linguistics.

Bibliography:

Baskakov, N. A., "Očerk grammatiki oĭrotskogo yazïka": Baskakov, N. A. i Toščakova, T. M., *Oĭrotsko-russkiĭ slovaŕ*, Moskva 1947.
— *Altaĭskiĭ yazïk* (Vvedenie v izučenie altaĭskogo yazïka i ego dialektov), Moskva 1958.
— *Zalogi v karakalpakskom yazïke*, Taškent 1951.
— *Karakalpakskiĭ yazïk* I. Materialï po dialektologii (Tekstï i slovaŕ), Moskva 1951; II. Fonetika i morfologiya, část I, (Časti reči i slovoobrazovanie), Moskva 1952.
— *Russko-karakalpakskiĭ slovaŕ*, sostavili Baskakov, N. A., S. B. Beknazarov i U. N. Kožurov, pod redakcieĭ N. A. Baskakova, Moskva 1947.
— *Karakalpaksko-russkiĭ slovaŕ*, pod redakcieĭ prof. N. A. Baskakova, S priloženiem grammatičeskogo očerka karakalpakskogo yazïka, sostavlennogo N. A. Baskakovïm, Moskva 1958.
— *Nogaĭskiĭ yazïk i ego dialektï*. Grammatika, tekstï i slovaŕ, Moskva-Leningrad 1940.
— "Xakasskiĭ yazïk": Baskakov, N. A. i Inkižekova-Grekul, A. I., *Xakassko-russkiĭ slovaŕ*, Moskva 1953.
— *Tyurkskie yazïki*, Moskva 1960.
— *Vvedenie v izučenie tyurkskix yazïkov*, Moskva 1962.

2.316. Thomsen.

The existence in Mongolia and adjacent parts of Siberia of inscriptions made in an unknown script on stone steles had been known since the XVIII century, and the first reproduction of such a stone was published in 1730 by Strahlenberg. Many speculations about their authors and their language had been made. The first archaeological expeditions with the purpose of investigation of the inscriptions were undertaken only in the last quarter of the XIX century.

The first archaeological expeditions were conducted by the Finnish scholars J. R. Aspelin (in 1887 and 1889) and A. O. Heikel (in 1890). Simultaneously with Aspelin's second expedition conducted in the Yenisei area, the Russian scholar N. M. Yadrintsev discovered, in 1889, the famous Orkhon inscriptions. A larger expedition was sent by the Russian Academy of Sciences in 1891. This expedition was headed by Radloff. The material collected by him and his companions was published in 1892.

The key to the decipherment of the alphabet was found by Vilhelm Thomsen who published his decipherment of the alphabet in 1893. The language of the inscriptions proved to be Turkic, i.e., Ancient Turkic of the VIII century, thus confirming Klaproth's hypothesis (1823) that the language of the inscriptions might be Turkic. On the basis of Thomsen's decipherment, Radloff made, in 1894, a transcription and translation of one of the inscriptions and published it, not waiting for Thomsen's transcription. Thomsen published his transcription and translation in 1896. His work was much superior to that of Radloff. Thomsen is universally regarded as the decipherer of these inscriptions called the Orkhon-Yenisei or Ancient Turkic inscriptions. The alphabet is known as the runic alphabet. Thomsen established also the phonemic system of Middle-Turkic texts which had been misread by Radloff who believed that the texts in question should be read in accordance with the pronunciation of Altai and Teleut Turkic.

Vilhelm Thomsen (1842–1927) was a Dane. He was one of the greatest linguists. His principal field was the comparative and historical study of Indo-European languages, contacts between the Baltic-Finnic and Balto-Slavic languages, etc.

Bibliography:

Brondal, V., "L'oeuvre de Vilhelm Thomsen", *Acta Philologica Scandinavica* 1927, pp. 289–318.
Pamyati V. Tomsena, K godovščine so dnya smerti, Leningrad 1928 (Articles about Thomsen and his significance for turcology, Germanic, Slavic studies, etc. On Thomsen's significance in the history of Turkic linguistics *vide* A. N. Samoilovič's article "Vilgelm Tomsen i turgologiya", pp. 14–34).
Schaeder, H. H., "Vilhelm Thomsen", *ZDMG* 81 (1927), pp. 278–283 (Necrology).
— "Alttürkische Inschriften aus der Mongolei in Übersetzung und mit Einleitung von Vilhelm Thomsen", *ZDMG* 78 (1924–25), pp. 121–175.
Thomsen, V., "Déchiffrement des inscriptions de l'Orkhon et de l'Iénissé, Notice préliminaire", *Bulletin de l'Académie Royale de Danemark* 1893, pp. 285–299.
— *Inscriptions de l'Orkhon déchiffrées par* –, MSFOu 5 (1894–96).
— *Turcica*, Études concernant l'interprétation des inscriptions turques de la Mongolie et de la Sibérie, MSFOu 37 (1916).
— "Sur le système des consonnes dans la langue ouïgoure", *KSz* 2 (1901), pp. 241–259.
— *Samlede Afhandlinger*, vol. III, København, Gyldendal, 1922, pp. 1–353.

2.317. Grønbech.

The Danish turcologist Kaare Grønbech (1901–1957) was one of the finest scholars in his field. Son of a scholar, he studied turcology and made several study trips to Turkey. In 1938, he went as a member of the Danish Central Asian Expedition to Mongolia. There he acquired a good knowledge of Mongolian and collected a large number of valuable manuscripts which now belong to the Danish Royal Library in Kopenhagen. Grønbech's first large work was his doctoral dissertation, a fundamental work on the Turkic language structure, a work still unsurpassed. His other important work was the edition of the text of the Codex Cumanicus, and a Kuman-German dictionary which replaced Radloff's obsolete work on Kuman.

Grønbech published also a number of articles, the one on accent in Turkic and Mongolian deserving much attention.

Bibliography:

Grønbech, K., *Der türkische Sprachbau* I, Kopenhagen 1936.
— *Monumenta Linguarum Asiae Maioris* I, *Codex Cumanicus*. Cod. Marc. Lat.

DXLIX, In Faksimile herausgegeben, Mit einer Einleitung von –, Kopenhagen 1936.
— *Monumenta Linguarum Asiae Maioris. Subsidia I, Komanisches Wörterbuch*, Türkischer Wortindex zu Codex Cumanicus, København 1942.
— *Monumenta Linguarum Asiae Maioris IV, Rabghuzi Narrationes de Prophetis*. Cod. Mus. Brit. Add. 7851, Reproduced in Facsimile, with an Introduction by –, København 1942.
— "Der Akzent im Türkischen und Mongolischen", *ZDMG* 94 (1940), pp. 375–390.
Krueger, J. R., "In Memoriam Kaare Grønbech 1901–1957", *CAJ* 3 (1957), pp. 3–5 (Necrology).
— "Bibliography of the Works of Professor Kaare Grønbech 1901–1957, edited by – from a compilation by Mogen Schou (Copenhagen), *ibid.*, pp. 13–18.
Pritsak, O., "Kaare Grønbech 1901–1957", *UAJ* 29 (1957), pp. 81–87 (Necrology).

2.318. F.W.K. Müller.

A chair of Turkic studies was founded in Germany in 1890. It became part of the "Seminar für orientalische Sprachen" of the Berlin University, and its first head was Professor Karl Foy (1856–1907) who published several works on Azerbaijan Turkic. He introduced F.W.K. Müller to Turkic studies.

Friedrich Wilhelm Karl Müller, mostly referred to as F.W.K. Müller (1863–1930), was one of the greatest scholars ever known in the history of Oriental studies. He knew most of the important languages of Asia. He was an anthropologist, historian of religions, and was well-versed in literatures of many Oriental peoples. He deciphered a number of documents written in languages that had been unknown theretofore, brought by the German expeditions from Turfan. Among the documents deciphered there were writings in Manichean and Sogdic script. He was the first scholar to decipher these two scripts. Thanks to his vast knowledge of Buddhism and Buddhist literature in Chinese and Sanskrit, and also the Manichean literature, he was in a position to do philological work on the basis of Uighur texts. F.W.K. Müller is the founder of Uighur philology.

Bibliography:

Lessing, F., "F.W.K. Müller zum Gedächtnis", *OZ* 6 (16): 3–4 (1930), pp. 141–144.
Müller, F.W.K., "Uigurica I" *ABAW* 1908; II: *ABAW* 1910; III: *ABAW* 1922; IV(ed. by A. von Gabain): *SBAW* 1931, pp. 675–727.
— "Zwei Pfahlinschriften aus den Turfanfunden", *ABAW* 1915.
— "Uigurische Glossen", *OZ* 1920, pp. 310–324.
Trautz, F. M., "Professor Dr. F.W.K. Müllers Veröffentlichungen von 1889–1924", *AM* 2: 1 (1925), pp. XI–XVI.
Weller, Fr. u. Schindler, B., "F.W.K. Müller", *AM* 2: 1 (1925), pp. VII–X.

2.319. Von Le Coq.

Albert von Le Coq (1860–1930) was the head of three German expeditions in Central Asia, known as the Turfan Expeditions (1904–5, 1905–7, 1913–14). He discovered and brought a large number of manuscripts such as Manichean writings of the VIII–IX centuries A.D. and objects of arts, and made also extensive studies of Turkic dialects spoken in the Turfan region. Le Coq possessed an unsurpassed knowledge of Uighur paleography. Most of the editions of Uighur texts are based on his readings and transcriptions.

Bibliography:

Von Le Coq, A., "Kurze Einführung in die uigurische Schriftkunde", *MSOS*, Abt. II, 1919, pp. 93–109.
— "Sprichwörter und Lieder aus der Gegend von Turfan mit einer dort aufgenommenen Wörterliste", *Baessler-Archiv*, Beiheft I (1911), IV.
"Verzeichnis der Schriften von Albert von Le Coq", *Baessler-Archiv*, Beiheft I (s. a. 1930?).

2.320. Bang-Kaup.

Willy Bang-Kaup (1869–1934) was a pupil of the well-known Belgian scholar Ch. de Harlez and had studied Iranian and Ural-Altaic languages. Prior to 1914, he was professor of English philology at the University of Louvain, being mainly engaged in study and publication of Old English drama.

One of his greatest achievements was the creation of new criteria for publication of documents such as *Codex Cumanicus*. Here he used his vast experience accumulated in the process of preparing critical editions of literary documents in European languages. His ensuing polemics with Radloff were very fruitful.

In 1920 Bang moved to Berlin. His arrival there opened a new chapter in the history of Turkic studies in that city.

During the fourteen years of his stay in Berlin, Bang was doing research and teaching. All the outstanding European scholars, including those in Turkey, who received their education before 1934, were either his pupils or somehow connected with his name: A. von Gabain (2.322), Jarring (2.326), Menges (2.323), Räsänen (2.325), Jakob Schinkewitsch, and Zajączkowski (2.329). Bang was also the teacher of the Turkisch scholars Saadet Is'haki Çagatai and Reşid Rahmeti Arat, the leading turcologist in Turkey, engaged in publication of Uighur and Karakhanide texts and investigation of morphology of Turkic languages. Arat died in 1964. His death is a great loss to Turkic studies.

Bibliography:

Bang, W., *Zur Kritik des Codex Cumanicus*, Louvain 1910.
— "Komanische Texte", *Bull. de l'Acad. Royale de Belgique, Cl. des lettres* 1911, pp. 459–473.
— "Vom Köktürkischen zum Osmanischen" I: *ABAW* 1917; II–III: *ABAW* 1919; IV: *ABAW* 1921.
— *Turkologische Epikrisen*, Heidelberg 1910.
— *Monographien zur türkischen Sprachgeschichte*, Heidelberg 1918.

— "Studien zur vergleichenden Grammatik der Türksprachen" I: *SBAW* 1916, pp. 522–535; II: *ibid.*, pp. 910–928; III: *ibid.*, pp. 1236–1254.
— "Turkologische Briefe aus dem Berliner Ungarischen Institut", I: *UJ* 5 (1925), pp. 41–48; II: *ibid.*, pp. 231–251; III: *ibid.*, pp. 392–410; IV: *ibid.* 7 (1927), pp. 36–45; V: *ibid.* 10 (1930), pp. 16–26; VI: *ibid.* 12 (1932), pp. 90–104; VII: *ibid.* 14 (1934), pp. 193–214.
Gabain, A. von, "W. Bang-Kaup 1869–1934", *UJ* 14 (1934), pp. 335–340 (Necrology).
Gabain, A. von und Rachmati, G. R., "Bibliographie der Arbeiten von Professor W. Bang-Kaup – Uralaltaische Sprachforschung, Iranistik", *UJ* 9 (1929), pp. 192–195.
Is'haki Schakir, Saadet, *Denominale Verbbildung in den Türksprachen*, Roma 1933.
Rachmatullin [Rahmeti Arat], G. R., "Die Hilfsverben und Verbaladverbia im Altaischen", *UJ* 8 (1928), pp. 1–24, 309–343.
Schinkewitsch, J., "Rabɣuzi's Syntax", *MSOS*, Abt. II (1927).

2.321. Brockelmann.

The well-known arabicist, Carl Brockelmann (1868–1956) made great efforts to make Arabic sources on Turkic accessible to the turcologists. A kind of synthesis of Islamic sources on Turkic is his grammar of literary Turkic languages in Central Asia. His works on Old Osman are particularly valuable. Several important works of his are devoted to Maḥmūd al-Kāšɣarī's treatise on Middle Turkic.

Brockelmann is regarded as a great scholar, but his works in the Turkic field suffer from many defects. He worked very fast, obviously wishing to be the first scholar to publish such sources as Kāšɣarī's *Dīvān luɣāt at-turk*. Such an attitude resulted in numerous *lacunae*, inaccuracies in quotations, inadequate methodological approach to problems, which is so obvious in his edition of *Dīvān luɣāt at-turk*. All this lowers considerably the value of his works. Nevertheless, his works give an idea of the rich Islamic sources on Turkic. It would be incorrect to write them off.

Bibliography:
Brockelmann, C., "Zur Grammatik des Osmanisch-Türkischen", *ZDMG* 70 (1916), pp. 185–215.
— *'Alī's Qiṣṣa'i Jūsuf, der älteste Vorläufer der osmanischen Literatur*, ABAW 1917.
— "Altosmanische Studien I", *ZDMG* 73 (1919), pp. 1–29.
— "Ein türkisches Imperativ-Prekativsuffix", *KSz* 18 (1919), pp. 149–150.
— "Turkologische Studien", *ZDMG* 74 (1920), pp. 212–215.
— "Maḥmūd al-Kāšghārīs Darstellung des türkischen Verbalbaus", *KSz* 18 (1919), pp. 24–49.
— "Maḥmūd al-Kāšghārī über die Sprachen und Stämme der Türken im 11. Jahrhundert", *KCsA* 1: 1 (1921), pp. 26–40.
— "Altturkestanische Volksweisheit", *OZ* 8 (1920), pp. 49–73.
— "Altturkestanische Volkspoesie I", *AM* (Probeband 1923), pp. 3–24; II: *AM* I (1924), pp. 24–44.

— "Volkskundliches aus Altturkestan", *AM* II (1925), pp. 116–124.
— "Naturlaute im Mittelturkischen", *UJ* 8 (1928), pp. 257–265.
— "Die Hofsprache in Alt-Turkestan", *Donum Natalicium Schrijnen*, Nijmegen-Utrecht 1929, pp. 222–227.
— *Mitteltürkischer Wortschatz nach Maḥmūd al-Kāšyarīs Dīvān luγāt at-turk*, Budapest-Leipzig 1928.
— *Ostturkische Grammatik der islamischen Literatursprachen Mittelasiens*, Leiden 1954.

Fuck, J., "Carl Brockelmann (1868–1956)", *ZDMG* 108 (1958), pp. 1–13 (Necrology).

Pritsak, O., "Carl Brockelmann 1868–1956", *UAJ* 28 (1956), pp. 54–56 (Necrology).

2.322. Von Gabain.

The German scholar Annemarie von Gabain (born in 1901) began her career as a student of Chinese under Professor Haenisch (*vide* 2.112) and presented a doctoral dissertation on a sinologic subject. She studied also Turkic under W. Bang-Kaup *vide* 2.320 at the University of Berlin. She taught subsequently at the University of Berlin, worked at the Academy of Sciences in Berlin, and is now a professor at the University of Hamburg.

Professor von Gabain has not done much work on spoken Turkic languages and her only work in this field is her Uzbek grammar, the first grammar of that language ever written and published outside the USSR. It is rather a grammar of spoken than modern literary Uzbek and does not use the current Cyrillic alphabet. Being an interdialectal grammar, it does not reflect any particular dialect, such as the Iranized dialects on which the official literary language in Soviet Uzbekistan is based. Professor von Gabain's grammar is a useful contribution to Turkic linguistics. It contains also a bibliography, some texts and a glossary.

Von Gabain has never done field work, although she travelled in Turkey. She did not collect materials on dialects or spoken languages. She devoted herself mainly to the study of Ancient Turkic, mostly Turkic in Uighur, Brāhmī, and Manichean script, thus continuing the tradition brilliantly established in Germany by F.W.K. Müller.

Von Gabain's largest work in the field of study of Ancient Turkic is her Ancient Turkic grammar which is the only work of this kind outside the USSR. It contains specimens of scripts and texts, a grammatical outline, a bibliography, and glossary.

Her other major works are large articles mostly published in the *Abhandlungen* of the Academy of Sciences in Berlin. One of them deals with an Uighur translation of Hiuen-tsang's biography, and other articles are devoted to Turkic fragments from Turfan, which were brought from there by the three German expeditions in Central Asia at the beginning of this century. These works, together with those of F.W.K. Müller, Le Coq, Bang-Kaup, Rahmeti-Arat, and other scholars, are the basis for future research on Ancient Turkic in the scripts mentioned.

The scope of von Gabain's interests is wide and includes history and cultural history. She is, however, predominantly a philologist rather than a linguist.

Bibliography:

Gabain, A. von, *Özbekische Grammatik*, Mit Bibliographie, Lesestücken und Wörterverzeichnis, Leipzig und Wien 1945.
— *Alttürkische Grammatik*, Mit Bibliographie, Lesestücken und Wörterverzeichnis, auch Neutürkisch, 2., verbesserte Auflage, Leipzig 1950.
— "Die uigurische Übersetzung der Biographie Hüen-tsangs, V. Kap.", *SBAW* 1935, pp. 151–180.
— "Briefe der uigurischen Hüen-tsang Biographie", *SBAW* 1938, pp. 371–415.
— *Türkische Turfantexte VIII*, ADAW 1952, no. 7.
— *Türkische Turfantexte IX. Ein Hymnus an den Vater Mani auf "Tocharisch" B mit alttürkischer Übersetzung*, ADAW 1956, no. 2 (in collaboration with W. Winter).
— *Türkische Turfantexte X. Das Avadāna des Dämons Ātavaka*, ADAW 1958, no. 1 (in collaboration with T. Kowalski).
— *Türkische Turfantexte I: Bruchstücke eines Wahrsagebuches*, SBAW 1929, pp. 1–30; II: *Manichaica*, ibid., 1929, pp. 411–430; III: *Der große Hymnus auf Mani*, ibid.,1930, pp. 183–211; IV: *Ein neues uigurisches Sündenbekenntnis*, ibid., 1930, pp. 432–450; V: *Aus buddhistischen Schriften*, ibid., 1931, pp. 323–356; VI: *Das buddhistische Sūtra Säkiz Yükmäk*, ibid., pp. 93–192 (all in collaboration with W. Bang; VI in collaboration with W. Bang and G. R. Rachmati).
— *Maitrisimit I*. Facsimile der alttürkischen Version eines Werkes der buddhistischen Vaibhāṣika-Schule, Einleitung von H. Scheel, Wiesbaden 1957; II, Geleitwort von R. Hartmann, Berlin 1961.
— "Das Alttürkische", *PhTF*, pp. 21–45.
— "Die Sprache des Codex Cumanicus", *ibid.*, pp. 46–73.
"Schriftenverzeichnis Annemarie von Gabain 1928–1961", *UAJ* 33 (1961), pp. 5–11 (Bibliography up to 1961).

2.323. Menges.

Karl Heinrich Menges (born 1908), German by birth, is one of the outstanding turcologists and altaicists. He studied Slavic linguistics under Max Vasmer (1886–1962) and Turkic under Bang-Kaup (*vide* 2.320), and made several journeys with the purpose of carrying out linguistic field work in Russian Turkestan, Turkey, and Iran.

His works can be divided into two main groups. Some of them deal with Turkic, other works of his are devoted to problems revolving around the relations between the Altaic and other languages.

Menges has published a large number of books and articles. Among them, the Karakalpak phonology is one of the most important contributions to Turkic linguistics. It is the first work on Karakalpak outside the USSR and contains a phonetic description of Karakalpak, followed by a comparative phonetic study. Menges has correctly stated that Karakalpak is a dialect of Kazakh but not an independent language as the Soviet scholars believe.

Another important work is his edition of Katanov's East Turki texts which were translated by Menges. He published also a glossary.

Menges investigated also the Chaghatai material as represented by the Iranian scholar Mīrzā Mahdī Xān (XVII century), and published a number of articles on Uzbek spoken in the northern parts of Afghanistan, on Turkic dialects spoken in Iran, on Sagai, Oirot (Altai and Teleut), South-Siberian Turkic dialects, Kazakh, Nogai, Kypchak-Uzbek, Kirghiz, Soyot, Karagas, etc.

To these works his contributions to the study of Altaic elements in Indo-European languages and Indo-European influences on Altaic should be added. A particularly important work is his research on the Oriental, mostly Turkic, borrowings in the language of the Russian Igoŕ Song (1182 A.D.).

Bibliography:

Menges, K. H., *Qaraqalpaq Grammar*, Part One: Phonology, New York 1947.
— *Volkskundliche Texte aus Ost-Türkistan. I., Aus dem Nachlaß von N. Th. Katanov*, Berlin 1933; II. Berlin 1943 (the second volume was published without mentioning Menges' name, this being due to political conditions in Germany at that time).
— *Glossar zu den volkskundlichen Texten aus Ost-Türkistan II*, Abh. d. Geistes- und Soz. Kl. Jhg. 1954, no. 14, Wiesbaden 1955.
— "Zum Özbekischen von Nord-Afghanistan", *Anthropos* XLI/XLIV (1946–49), pp. 673–710.
— "Research in the Turkic Dialects of Iran (Preliminary Report on a Trip to Persia)", *O* 4 (1951), pp. 273–279.
— "Some Remarks on Oyrot Morphology", *BSOAS* 21 (1958), pp. 491–521.
— "Zum Stammesnamen der Sagaj", *CAJ* 6 (1961), pp. 110–115.
— "The South-Siberian Turkic Languages I", *CAJ* 1 (1955), pp. 107–136; II: *CAJ* 2 (1956), pp. 161–175.
— "Die Aralo-Kaspische Gruppe (Kasakisch, Karakalpakisch, Nogaisch, Kiptschak-Özbekisch, Kirgisisch)", *PhTF*, pp. 434–488.
— "Das Sojonische und Karagassische", *ibid.*, pp. 640–670.
— "Altaic Elements in the Proto-Bulgarian Inscriptions", *Byzantion* 21 (1951) pp. 85–118.
— "Altaic Loanwords in Slavonic", *Language* 20 (1944), pp. 66–72.
— "Altajische Kulturwörter im Slavischen", *UAJ* 33 (1961), pp. 107–116.
— "Altajische Lehnwörter im Slavischen", *ZSPh* 23 (1955), pp. 327–334.
— "On Some Loanwords from or via Turkic in Old-Russian", *Mélanges Fuad Köprülü*, İstanbul 1953, pp. 369–90.
— "Etymological Notes on Some Non-Altaic Oriental Words in the Old-Russian Igoŕ Song", *O* 9 (1956), pp. 86–94.
— *The Oriental Elements in the Vocabulary of the Oldest Russian Epos, The Igoŕ Tale*, Suppl. to Word, Journal of the Linguistic Circle of New York, Monograph No. 1, 1951.
— "Indo-European Influences on Ural-Altaic Languages", *Word* 1 (1945).
— "Zwei alt-mesopotamische Lehnwörter im Altajischen", *UAJ* 25 (1953), pp. 299–304.
— *Morphologische Probleme I, Zum Genetiv und Accusativ*, UAB 9 (1960).

2.324. Pritsak.

Omelian Pritsak (born in 1919), Ukrainian by birth, studied Turkic languages, Islamic and Iranian philology in Lwów, Kiev, Berlin, and Göttingen and became a professor at the University of Hamburg and, briefly at the University of Washington, Seattle, Washington, and since 1964, at the Harvard University.

Pritsak is a many-sided scholar, an expert on history of Central Asia, Southern Russia, and Eastern Europe, and a gifted linguist working in the fields of Turkic and Altaic studies. Possessing a thorough knowledge of Turkic, Mongolian, Manchu, Korean, he is well equipped for work on Altaic languages. Besides, he knows some Finno-Ugric languages, not to mention his knowledge of numerous other languages which serve as tools for his research.

Pritsak's main linguistic works are devoted to ancient Danube Bulgarian, mutual relations of Chuvash and Bulgarian, and Hunnic. He is also the author of a work on Turkmenian, and articles on Kypchak, Karai, Karachai-Balkar, East Turki, Ancient Turkic, and the Turkic dialects spoken in the Abakan area. Some works of his deal with Mongolian languages.

Bibliography:

Pritsak, O., *Die bulgarische Fürstenliste und die Sprache der Protobulgaren*, Wiesbaden 1955.
— "Ein hunnisches Wort", *ZDMG* 104 (1954), pp. 124–135.
— "Bolgaro-Tschuwaschica", *UAJ* 31 (1959), pp. 274–314.
— "Bolgarische Etymologien I–III", *UAJ* 29 (1957), pp. 200–214.
— "Kāšġarīs Angaben über die Sprache der Bolgaren", *ZDMG* 109 (1959), pp. 92–116.
— "Die Herkunft des tschuwaschischen Futurums", *WZKM* 56 (1960), pp. 141–153.
— "Tschuwaschische Pluralsuffixe", *SA* (1957), pp. 137–155.
— "Die ursprünglichen türkischen Vokallängen im Balkarischen", *Deny Armağanı* (1958), pp. 203–207.
— "Die Oberstufenzählung im Tungusischen und Jakutischen", *ZDMG* 105 (1955), pp. 184–191.
— "Die Herkunft der Allophone und Allomorphe im Türkischen", *UAJ* 33 (1961), pp. 142–145.
— "Der Titel Attila", *Festschrift Max Vasmer*, Berlin 1956, pp. 404–419.
— "Kultur und Sprache der Hunnen", *Čyževśkyj-Festschrift*, Berlin 1954, pp. 238–249.
— "Orientierung und Farbsymbolik, Zu den Farbenbezeichnungen in den altaischen Völkernamen", *Saeculum* 5: 4 (1954), pp. 376–383.
— "Stammesnamen und Titulaturen der altaischen Völker (I Teil)", *UAJ* 24: 1–2 (1952), pp. 49–104.
— "Das Kiptschakische", *PhTF*, pp. 74–87.
— "Das Karaimische", *ibid.*, pp. 318–340.
— "Das Karatschaische und Balkarische", *ibid.*, pp. 340–368.
— "Das Neuuigurische", *ibid.*, pp. 525–563.
— "Das Altaitürkische", *ibid.*, pp. 568–597.

— "Das Abakan- und Čulymtürkische und das Schorische", *ibid.*, pp. 598–639.
— "Das Mogholische", *HO* 5, 2. Abschnitt (1964), pp. 158–84.

2.325. Räsänen.

The Finnish finno-ugricist and turcologist Martti Räsänen (born in 1893), a pupil of Ramstedt and Bang, has been working on Chuvash, Tatar, Anatolian Turkish, and problems of Turkic comparative linguistics. His early works are devoted to Chuvash and Tatar loanwords in Mari (or Cheremis, a Finno-Ugric language). He traveled in Anatolia and collected a large number of texts in various Anatolian dialects. The texts published by him are the result of fine field work. They are phonetically exact and precise. A major field of Räsänen is the comparative grammar. He published a comparative phonology of Turkic languages in which he had established all the principal laws of sound correspondence. It is the first and so far the only more or less complete comparative phonology of Turkic languages. It was followed by a comparative morphology. It is a useful survey of morphological correspondences in all the Turkic languages, such as declension, pronouns, conjugation, etc.

Räsänen is also the author of a number of articles on various problems of Turkic linguistics.

Bibliography:

Gabain, A. von, Pritsak, O., "Zum 60. Geburtstag Martti Räsänens", *UAJ* 26 (1954), pp. 124–125.
Räsänen, M., *Die tschuwassischen Lehnwörter im Tscheremissischen*, MSFOu 48 (1920).
— *Die tatarischen Lehnwörter im Tscheremissischen*, MSFOu 50 (1923).
— "Eine Sammlung von *māni*-Liedern aus Anatolien", *JSFOu* 41: 2 (1926).
Türkische Sprachproben aus Mittel-Anatolien I. Sivas vil., StOF 5: 2 (1933); II. *Jazgat vil.*, StOF 6: 2 (1935); III. *Ankara, Kaiseri, Kirşehir, Čankiri, Afion vil.*, StOF 8: 2 (1936); IV. *Konja vil.*, StOF 10: 2 (1942).
— *Materialien zur Lautgeschichte der türkischen Sprachen*, StOF 15 (1949).
— *Materialien zur Morphologie der türkischen Sprachen*, StOF 21 (1957).
Jyrkänkallio, P., "Die sprachwissenschaftlichen Veröffentlichungen von Prof. Dr. Martti Räsänen", *StOF* 21: 13 (1954), pp. 1–14 (Bibliography).

2.326. Jarring.

Gunnar Jarring, a Swede, is one of the most distinguished linguists in the Turkic field. A pupil of Gustav Raquette, a well-known scholar in the field of East Turki, and Wilhelm Bang, Jarring made the little-studied Turkic dialects of Chinese Turkestan and Afghanistan the object of his studies. His works deal with East Turki and Uzbek. An important work is his phonology of East Turki. It is an excellent phonetic description of the dialects and is also an important contribution to Turkic comparative linguistics.

Jarring travelled much in Chinese and Afghan Turkestan. There he collected a large number of texts published in a very fine, precise transcription with English translation. Most of the texts were collected in Khotan, Yarkand, Kashgar, Kucha, and Guma (all in Chinese Turkestan). The Uzbek texts were obtained from native speakers, refugees from the Russian Turkestan, and represent the dialects of Qilich and Andkhui. As a matter of fact, there are very few collections of Uzbek and East Turki texts in phonetic transcription. Therefore, Jarring's texts are important materials for the study of both Uzbek and East Turki. A most important work is his dictionary of dialects of East Turki.

Bibliography:

Jarring, G., *Studien zu einer osttürkischen Lautlehre*, Lund 1933.
— *Materials to the Knowledge of Eastern Turki*, I. Lund 1946; II. Lund 1948; III. Lund 1951; IV. Lund 1951.
— *The Uzbek Dialect of Qilich (Russian Turkestan)*, Lund 1937.
— *The Contest of the Fruits, An Eastern Turki Allegory*, Lund 1936.
— *Uzbek Texts from Afghan Turkestan with Glossary*, Lund 1938.
— *An Eastern Turki-English Dialect Dictionary*, Lund 1964.

2.327. Deny and French turcology.

Paris is one of the oldest centers of Turkic studies. A chair of Turkic studies was established in 1795 at the École spéciale des langues orientales vivantes. Main attention was given to Osman Turkish philology, the first professors being Pierre-Amédé Jaubert (1779–1847) and Casimir-Adrien Barbier de Meynard (1827–1908), and Chaghatai philology (Marc Étienne Quatremère, 1782–1857).

Jean Deny (born in 1879), Professor of Turkish language and literature at the mentioned School of Oriental languages in Paris (retired in 1948), started his career in the French diplomatic service and spent many years in Turkey. He is the author of an excellent Turkish grammar (in which the Arabic script is used), a fundamental work which has remained in many aspects unsurpassed. It can be regarded as his most valuable contribution to Turkic linguistics. Two other works of his go in line with it, namely, a book on Turkish structure and another one giving the fundamentals of Turkish.

A scholar with interests of wide range, Deny did not confine himself to the study of Turkish (Osmanli, Turkish spoken in Turkey) but he investigated also some important sources on Kypchak, one of them referring to Armeno-Kuman. Deny is also known as the author of general reference articles and numerous smaller items on various problems of Turkish linguistics. The total number of his publications amounts to more than 140.

Deny's pupil and successor at the School of Oriental languages is Louis Bazin (born in 1920) whose main fields are Ancient Turkic and the languages of the Turkmen group.

Bibliography:

Bazin, L., "Recherches sur les parlers Tʻo-pa", *TP* 39, pp. 228–327.
— "Structures et tendences communes des langues turques (Sprachbau)", *PhTF*, pp. 11–19.
— "Le Turkmène", *ibid.*, pp. 308–317.

Deny, J., *Grammaire de la langue turque* (dialecte osmanli), Paris 1921.
— *Principes de grammaire turque* ("Turk" de Turquie), Paris 1955.
— "Structure de la langue turque", *Conférences de l'Institut de Linguistique de l'Université de Paris* 9 (1949), pp. 17–51.
— "Au sujet de textes inédits en turk Kiptchak ou Kiptchak-Coman", *JA* 18 (1921), pp. 134–135.
— "L'osmanli moderne et le 'Turk' de Turquie", *PhTF*, pp. 182–239.
— *L'arméno-coman et les "Ephémérides" de Kamieniec (1604–1613)*, Wiesbaden 1957.
— "Langues turques, langues mongoles et langues tongouzes", *Langues du Monde*, Paris 1924, pp. 185–243.
— "Langues turques, langues mongoles et langues tongouzes", *Langues du Monde*, 2nd edition, Paris 1952, pp. 319–368.
Eckmann, J., "Jean Deny'nin eserleri 1909–1957", *Jean Deny Armağanı, Mélanges Jean Deny*, Ankara 1958, pp. 7–18 (Bibliography).
Roux, J.-P., "Jean Deny", *ibid.*, pp. 1–4 (Biography).

2.328. Kowalski.

The Polish scholar Tadeusz Kowalski (1889–1948) was professor at the Kraków University since 1919. His special field was Islamic philology, mainly Arabic studies. He became interested in Turkic languages at an early stage of his scholarly activities, the result being that almost one half of his works totalling 210 was devoted to problems of turcology.

Kowalski's favorite fields were the dialects of the Turkish language and the language of the Karai. He is generally regarded as the founder of Karai studies. Several valuable works of his are devoted to Turkish popular literature.

Kowalski endeavoured in his Islamic studies to give a synthesis of Islamic culture. The same method was applied by him to problems of turcology.

Bibliography:

Kowalski, T., "Język karaimski", *Myśl Karaimska* I (Wilna 1926).
— *Karaimische Texte im Dialect von Troki*, Kraków 1929.
— "Próba charakterystyki języków tureckich", *Myśl Karaimska* N. S., I (Wrocław 1946), pp. 35–73.
— *Zur semantischen Funktion des Pluralsuffixes -lar, -lär in den Türksprachen*, Kraków 1936.
— "De la nature du causatif et du passif dans les langues turques", *RO* 15 (1949), pp. 430–438.
— "Osmanisch-türkische Dialekte", *Enzyklopädie des Islams*, IV (Leiden 1931), pp. 991–1011.
— *Ze studiów nad formą poezii ludów tureckich*, Kraków 1922.
Zajączkowski, A., "Tadeusz Kowalski i jego prace orientalisticzne", *RO* 17 (1953), pp. IX–XVI.
— "Bibliografija Tadeusza Kowalskiego", *ibid.*, pp. XVII–XXXVI.

2.329. Zajączkowski.

The Polish scholar Ananiasz Zajączkowski (born in 1903), professor at the Warsaw University and a full member of the Polish Academy of Sciences, is one of the greatest authorities in the field of Old Osman and the languages of the Kypchak group. A pupil of T. Kowalski and W. Bang-Kaup, he is the author of nearly 200 works. His main merit is the publication of a number of texts with excellent glossaries and outlines of grammar.

Bibliography:

Zajączkowski, A., *Sufiksy imienne i czasownikowe w języku zachodnio-karaimskim. Przyczynek do morfologii języków tureckich* (Les suffixes nominaux et verbaux dans la langue des Karaimes occidentaux. Contribution à la morfologie des langues turques), Kraków 1932.
— *Études sur la langue vieille-osmanli* I, Kraków 1934; II, Kraków 1937.
— *Manuel arabe de la langue des turcs et kiptchaks. Époque de l'état Mamelouk*, I, Warszawa 1938; II, Warszawa 1954.
— *Ze studiów nad zagadnicniem chazarskim. Études sur le problème des Khazars*, Kraków 1947.
— *Związki językowe połowiecko-słowjańskie*, Wrocław 1949.
— *Najstarsza wersja turecka Husrev-u-Širin Qutba. La plus ancienne version turque du Husrev-u-Širin de Qutb*, vol. I, Texte, Warszawa 1958; vol. II, Facsimile, Warszawa 1958; vol. III, Vocabulaire, Warszawa 1961.
— *Le traité arabe Mukaddima d'Abou-l-lait as-Samarkandi en version Mamelouk-Kiptchak*, Warszawa 1962.

2.330. Németh and Hungarian turcology.

A chair of Turkic studies was established in Budapest in 1864 for Vámbéry Ármin (1831–1913), the well-known traveler in Turkestan. His works on Chaghatai, Ancient Turkic, and Osman Turkish are now completely obsolete and cannot be used any longer.

Vámbéry's successor, Joszef Thury (1861–1906), gave turcology valuable works in the field of Chaghatai philology but, due to the fact that he wrote in Hungarian, they had little influence on turcology outside Hungary.

An outstanding scholar was Ignácz Kúnos (1861–1941) whose field was Osman studies. Of all his compatriots Gyula (Julius) Németh (born in 1890) became the first internationally known representative of Hungarian turcology. He became professor in 1918. His fields are the Ancient Turkic inscriptions, problems revolving around the Pecheneg, the language of the *Codex Cumanicus*, problems of Hungarian culture, Osman philology and linguistics, and the Turkic languages spoken in the Caucasus. His works referring to Altaic studies are mentioned in 3.10. The bibliography (publ. in 1961) of his works lists 258 titles.

Németh is the teacher of numerous turcologists who work mainly in the fields of Kypchak language (T. Halasi-Kun, S. Telegdi), Chaghatai (J. Eckmann), dialects of the Turkish language (G. Hazai), and Turkic lexicography (Hasan Eren).

Bibliography:

Eckmann, J., "Gyula Németh", *Türk Dili, Belletin*, ser. III, 14–15 (1951), pp. 81–95.
Hazai, G., "Les dialectes turcs du Rhodope", *AOH* 9 (1959), pp. 205–229.
— "Textes turcs du Rhodope", *AOH* 10 (1960), pp. 185–229.
Uray, G., "A bibliography of the works of Prof. J. Németh", *AOH* 11: 1–3 (1961), pp. 11–28.

3. THE ALTAIC THEORY

3.1. The first hypotheses with regard to the relations between the Altaic and some other languages date from the first half of the XVIII century. The first scholar who noticed certain similarities existing between Turkic, Mongolian, and Manchu-Tungus was Johann von Strahlenberg (Tabbert), a Swedish officer, who had been taken prisoner of war during the battle of Poltava, one of the decisive battles of the Great Northern War. Von Strahlenberg spent many years in various parts of Eastern Russia and investigated some Finno-Ugric, Turkic, Mongolian, and other languages. One of his achievements was the compilation of the first dictionary of the Kalmuck language. He was the first to notice similarities in the structures of a large number of languages which he called "the Tatar languages" classified by him in six groups .These six groups of speakers of the languages in question are: 1. the Uighurs as he calls the Finno-Ugric peoples, the Baraba Tatars, and the Huns; 2. the Turco-Tatar peoples; 3. the Samoyeds; 4. the Mongols and Manchu; 5. the Tungus; and 6. "the tribes living between the Black and Caspian sea". This classification cannot be accepted at the present time because it is inconsistent and contains errors: the Finno-Ugric peoples do not belong to the same group as the Baraba who are a Turkic tribe, and the tribes living between the seas mentioned include Turks, Iranians, and Caucasians who have nothing in common. However, von Strahlenberg's classification deserves mentioning as the first attempt at classification of a large number of languages some of which are Altaic.

Bibliography:

von Strahlenberg, Phillip Johann, *Das nord- und östliche Theil von Europa und Asia, insoweit das gantze Russische Reich mit Sibirien und grossen Tatarei in sich begreiffet*, etc., Stockholm 1730.

3.2. The problem of the affinity of the Altaic languages was treated again, one hundred years after von Strahlenberg, by the famous Danish linguist Rasmus Rask. He renamed the "Tatar languages" and gave them the name of "the Scythian languages", having added to them also the languages spoken in Greenland, North America, all of Northern Asia and Europe, and in the Caucasus. He also included in the Scythian group the non-Indo-European language spoken in Spain (Basque). Consequently, the Scythian group included Mongolian, Manchu-Tungus, Turkic, Finno-Ugric (or even Uralic), Eskimo, the Palaeo-Asiatic languages, the Caucasian languages, and the languages of the ancient, non-Indo-European inhabitants of Europe.

Bibliography:

Rask, R. K., "Den skytiske Sproget", *Sammlede tilldels forhen utrykte Afhandlingen* I, København 1834.

3.3 In the middle of the XIX century linguistics were in such an advanced stage that comparative language studies could be conducted on a relatively solid foundation, once the Indo-European comparative linguistics had been established. One of the criteria for establishing language affinity was the morphological structure. The inflective structure being characteristic of the Indo-European languages, the agglutinative grammatical structure of the Altaic and a vast number of other languages was elevated to the main principle for judging what languages should be regarded as related. On the basis of the agglutinative features of a large number of languages, Max Müller included in the groups postulated by von Strahlenberg and Rask also Siamese, Tibetan, Dravidian, and Malayan. This expanded group was given the name of "the Turanian languages", because the center of the thus established linguistic area was Turan, i.e., part of Inner Asia, the hypothetic homeland of the Turks.

The Turanian hypothesis added little to Rask's Scythian hypothesis. It only involved a still larger number of languages.

Occupying a vast territory, the Turanian languages could impossibly be regarded as possessing features as clearly and distinctly defined as those of the Indo-European or Semitic languages. Therefore, Max Müller believed that different methods should be applied in research in the Turanian languages. Whereas the Indo-European and Semitic languages were *political languages*, as Max Müller defined them, the Turanian languages were only *nomadic* languages. He felt that the ties uniting the latter could not be as strong as those between the "political languages", and therefore, he rarely used the term *language family* with regard to the „nomadic languages" and preferred the term "language group".

In general, the problems set by Max Müller were never solved, and his own statements with regard to the languages concerned were rather vague.

Bibliography:

Müller, Max, *Essays* I, Leipzig 1869.
— *The Languages of the Seat of War in the East*, With a Survey of Three Families of Languages, Semitic, Arian, and Turanian, London-Edinburgh-Leipzig 1855.

3.4. A new period began with Castrén's appearance on the stage. Castrén was the first to apply *linguistic criteria* to languages supposed to belong to the same family. He was not satisfied with conglomerating vast numbers of languages almost unknown or very little investigated. The agglutinative grammatical structure alone was insufficient, in his opinion, to prove the affinity of languages, and he believed that identity of morphemes was essential. Castrén included in one group only the Finno-Ugric, Samoyed, Turkic, Mongolian, and Manchu-Tungus languages, and he excluded from that group all the other languages. Castrén demonstrated the identity of the personal suffixes in the languages mentioned but he formulated his findings in a cautious manner. His opinion was that one could not find in the Altaic languages as much similarity as within the Indo-European family. However, whether the similarities are as significant as to enable the linguists to assign all the languages concerned to one family was, in his opinion, a question which could be answered only in the future.

The languages called Altaic by Castrén are now called Ural-Altaic languages comprising two groups: the Uralic (Finno-Ugric-Samoyed) whose affinity was proven long ago, and the Altaic languages (Turkic, Mongolian, Manchu-Tungus, and Korean) whose mutual relations are still debated. What was called Altaic by Castrén and is still called so are two different things: in Castrén's writings Altaic means Ural-Altaic. At the present time only Turkic, Mongolian, Manchu-Tungus, and, with certain reservations and even reluctance, Korean are counted among the Altaic languages.

Bibliography:

Castrén, M. A., "Über die Personalaffixe in den altaischen Sprachen", *Kleinere Schriften*, St. Petersburg 1862.
— *Reiseberichte und Briefe aus den Jahren 1845–49*, St. Petersburg 1856.

3.5. Since Castrén the Ural-Altaic theory has been uniting, in general, four language families, namely, Uralic (comprising Samoyed and Finno-Ugric), Mongolian, Manchu-Tungus, and Turkic. However, relapses into the previous stages occurred from time to time for a long period. Thus, several unsuccessful attempts at including Japanese were made. On the other hand, some extinct ancient languages were declared as belonging to the Ural-Altaic group, and even the name of Turanian reappeared for brief periods.

Bibliography:

Boller, "Die Wurzelsuffixe in den ural-altaischen Sprachen", *SWAW* 22: 1 (1856), pp. 91–180.
— *Nachweis, daß das Japanische zum ural-altaischen Stamme gehört*, Wien 1857.
Lenormant, Fr., *La magie chez les chaldéens et les origines accadiennes*, Paris 1874.
— *La langue primitive de la Chaldée et les idiomes touraniens*, Paris 1875.
Pröhle, W., "Studien zur Vergleichung des Japanischen mit den uralischen und altaischen Sprachen", *KSz* 17, pp. 147ff.
Winkler, H., *Der ural-altaische Sprachenstamm, das Finnische und das Japanische*, Berlin 1909.

3.6. Serious investigation of the Ural-Altaic languages and their mutual relations on the basis of comparative linguistic studies began with the appearance of Schott's works.

Whereas most of his predecessors and contemporaries, with the exception of Castrén, had confined themselves to general observations and conclusions drawn from structural resemblances of the Ural-Altaic languages, Schott based his observations on correspondences in vocabulary, not neglecting, however, morphology. Schott limited his investigations to the Chudic (his term for Finno-Ugric) and Tatar (his term for Turkic, Mongolian, and Manchu-Tungus) languages and called this large group the Altaic or Chudic-Tatar group.

Like Castrén, Schott believed that the affinity of the different branches of the Ural-Altaic (in his terminology, Chudic-Tatar) languages varied in degree. The languages related to each other in the closest manner are, in his opinion, Samoyed and Finno-Ugric. This family was called by him "Finnic" or "Chudic". As for the remaining languages, i.e., the "Tatar" languages, Schott did not attempt at defining their mutual relations in a precise manner.

Schott was not only a ural-altaicist but he paid also much attention to the mutual relations of the Turkic, Mongolian, and Tungus languages. He also established many correspondences between Chuvash and Turkic and made the correct observation that Chuvash is closest to the Turkic languages. He was the first scholar who integrated the Chuvash language into Altaic comparative studies.

Bibliography:

Schott, W., *Über das altaische oder finnisch-tatarische Sprachengeschlecht*, Berlin 1849.
— *Das Zahlwort in der tschudischen Sprachenklasse, wie auch im Türkischen, Tungusischen und Mongolischen*, Berlin 1853.
— *Altaische Studien oder Untersuchungen auf dem Gebiete der Altai-Sprachen*, Berlin 1860.
— *De lingua tschuwaschorum*, Berolini (s. a.).

3.7. After Schott, attention was paid chiefly to the mutual relations of languages either within the Uralic or Altaic group. The linguists became more interested in phonetic and morphologic correspondences in Finno-Ugric-Samoyed or Mongolian-Tungus-Turkic groups, and comparative studies on Uralic and Altaic became less popular. However, Ural-Altaic comparative studies have never ceased completely.

Before proceeding to the Altaic theory, a brief outline of history of the Ural-Altaic theory after Schott will be given.

Ural-Altaic studies were continued by the German scholar Winkler. He also proposed his own division of the languages in question into two groups, one of them comprising Finno-Ugric, Samoyed, and Tungus, and the other one including Mongolian and Turkic. As for Manchu, Winkler believed it to be a link between Japanese and the Finno-Ugric-Samoyed languages. Winkler's classification did not find support among other linguists and, at the present time, only Finno-Ugric-Samoyed and Altaic are recognized.

One of the most serious works in the field of Ural-Altaic comparative studies is the book of the French linguist Sauvageot. He pointed out as the main weakness of most of the previous works in this field the indiscriminate comparison of words which somehow resembled each other. Sauvageot states that only such comparisons count which permit of establishing regular sound correspondences. However, such words being very few, the results of his own work are unconvincing.

Sauvageot's views were criticized by the Russian anthropologist Shirokogoroff who rejected Sauvageot's conclusions based on Ramstedt's theory with regard to Manchu initial $f = x$, h, and $\emptyset$ (i.e., Zero) in other languages. Shirokogoroff believed that h ($>x$) was a secondary "aspiration" with a subsequent "labialization" ($x > f$), this interpretation being, however, utterly wrong.

The well-known Finnish turcologist Martti Räsänen supports the Ural-Altaic theory and gives in his book on the historical phonology of Turkic languages a number of reasons in favour of Uralic and Altaic affinity. Professor Menges is also an adherent of the Ural-Altaic theory.

The Ural-Altaic theory is regarded by many scholars as unproven, to say the least. The Swedish scholar Björn Collinder is right, however, when he warns against exaggerated scepticism and points out that Proto-Uralic, Proto-Turkic, Proto-Mongolian, Proto-Tungus, and Korean might have existed in a prehistoric period as related but already separate languages, no Proto-Altaic having ever existed. This would lead to the conclusion that there has never been a Common Ural-Altaic language. Other alternatives are no less possible, e.g., a Uralic-Turkic unity and Proto-Mongolian-Tungus side by side with Korean, etc. Collinder's conclusion is that Ural-Altaic sound correspondences should be established which would then permit drawing of conclusions.

Collinder feels that it is premature to reject the Ural-Altaic hypothesis just as it is premature to draw conclusions from similarities already observed. It should be pointed out, however, that the most outstanding altaicist in the history of Altaic comparative studies and the real founder of the latter, Ramstedt, was sceptical about the affinity of Uralic and Altaic and confined his research to the Altaic languages.

The Ural-Altaic theory is accepted by very few scholars. On the other hand, a number of linguists believe that the Uralic languages are somehow related to the Indo-European languages.

As for the attitude of the author of these lines it is strictly negative as far as the hypothesis about Indo-European and Altaic affinity is concerned, whereas the Indo-European and Uralic affinity is regarded as possible although not yet proven. The same can be said about the Ural-Altaic theory: the Uralic and Altaic languages may be distant relatives but their affinity must yet be proven.

Bibliography:

Buge, E., *Über die Stellung des Tungusischen zum Mongolisch-Türkischen*, Halle 1887.

Collinder, B., "Ural-Altaisch", *UAJ* 24 (1952), pp. 1–26 (Gives not only his own ideas but also a brief history and bibliography).

— *Finno-Ugric Vocabulary*, An Etymological Dictionary of the Uralic Languages, Stockholm 1955, pp. 142–149.

Menges, K. H., "Indo-European Influences on Ural-Altaic Languages", *Word* 1: 2 (1945).

— *Morphologische Probleme I, Zum Genitiv und Accusativ*, UAB 9 (1960).

Räsänen, M., *Zur Lautgeschichte der türkischen Sprachen*, Helsinki 1949, pp. 9–19.

Sauvageot, A., *Recherches sur le vocabulaire des langues ouralo-altaïques*, Paris 1930.

Shirokogoroff, S. M., *Ethnological and Linguistical Aspects of the Ural-Altaic Hypothesis*, Peiping 1931.

Winkler, H., *Uralaltaische Völker und Sprachen*, Berlin 1884.
— *Das Uralaltaische und seine Gruppen*, Berlin 1886.
— "Tungusisch und Finno-Ugrisch I", *JSFOu* 30: 9; II: *JSFOu* 39: 1.

3.8. Proceeding to the Altaic theory, i.e., the theory about the affinity of Chuvash-Turkic, Mongolian, Manchu-Tungus, and possibly Korean, it should be remarked that by the end of the XIX century the study of Chuvash-Turkic, Mongolian, and Manchu-Tungus had achieved such results that comparative linguistic studies on a limited basis became possible, such as establishing of individual sound-correspondences or studies in morphology, e.g., declension, conjugation, verb or noun derivation, etc. The field was, however, still too little prepared for general works of the type of comparative grammars. Therefore, the comparative grammar by Grunzel was premature and, as Ramstedt said, presented a deterrent example.

Bibliography:

Grunzel, J., *Entwurf einer vergleichenden Grammatik der altaischen Sprachen nebst einem vergleichenden Wörterbuch*, Leipzig 1895.

3.9. The beginning of Altaic comparative linguistics is associated with the name of Ramstedt, the founder of modern Mongolian linguistics and a prominent turcologist.

Ramstedt started as a finno-ugricist but in 1898 he went to Outer Mongolia, in order to collect material on spoken Mongolian dialects. Later on, he spent a long time in studying Kalmuck and investigated the Mogol language. A finno-ugricist by university training and a brilliant mongolist and turcologist, Ramstedt knew the Finno-Ugric and several Altaic languages not only theoretically but he spoke Finnish (his native language), Cheremis (which he had studied on the spot), Hungarian (which he had studied at the university), and Khalkha-Mongolian and Kalmuck (which he had studied during his field work). Consequently, his negative attitude towards the Ural-Altaic theory was not the result of inadequate knowledge of the languages in question, limited to what one could find in grammars and dictionaries which at that time were rather incomplete, but it sprang up from a profound first-hand knowledge of the material.

Like many scholars, Ramstedt underwent evolution as far as his views were concerned. At the beginning, he was sceptical about protolanguages such as Common Altaic (Proto-Altaic) and he believed that the common elements in Mongolian and Turkic were the results of cross borrowing which had been taking place through centuries (*vide*: *Über die Konjugation des Khalkha-Mongolischen*, p. VII; "Über die Zahlwörter der altaischen Sprachen", p. 1). Later on, however, he renounced this view and came to the conclusion that Mongolian, Turkic, and Manchu-Tungus were genetically related to each other and had originated from one common source, i.e., Common Altaic (*vide* "Ein anlautender stimmloser Labial in der mongolisch-türkischen Ursprache", p. 1.).

Ramstedt established a number of sound correspondences in the Altaic languages. He was the first to notice the correspondence of Mongolian r to Turkic z, and Mongolian l to Turkic $š$ (*Über die Konjugation des Khalkha-Mongolischen*) analogous to Chuvash r and l = Turkic z and $š$ respectively which latter correspondences had been known since Schott. At the beginning, Ramstedt, like his predecessors, believed that Mongolian r had originated from *z, and Mongolian l < *$š$ but later he came to the conclusion that Mongolian and Chuvash r and l were older than Turkic z and $š$, the latter having developed from *r and *l respectively (*vide* "Zur Frage nach der Stellung des Tschuwassischen", p. 29). At the present time this latter view is shared by most of the altaicists, and only a few scholars still adhere to the old concept. He also found that the Mongolian initial n, d, $ǰ$, y corresponded to Chuvash $š$ and Turkic *y in which the former four consonants had converged. Ramstedt established the correspondence Turk. -p-, -b- = Written Mongolian $γ$ on the one side, and Turk. Ø (zero) = Middle Mongolian h- = Manchu f-, Goldi (Nanai) p-, Evenki and Lamut h- on the other hand.

Ramstedt did not confine himself to phonetic correspondences but he studied also a number of problems of morphology. Although his work on Khalkha conjugation is now to be regarded as obsolete, many sections of it are still valid. His comparative study of verb formation in Mongolian and Turkic is still one of the most important works in the Altaic field. In addition, Ramstedt published a large number of articles dealing with individual problems of Altaic comparative studies, such as the deverbal noun in -i, the deverbal noun in -m, etc.

A work summarizing all the observations made by him in the field of Altaic comparative linguistics is Ramstedt's comparative grammar consisting of a comparative phonology and morphology of Mongolian, Manchu-Tungus, Korean, and Turkic. Leaving aside Ramstedt's works on Korean and the latter's relation to Mongolian, Manchu-Tungus, and Turkic languages, and not going into a discussion of what Ramstedt says about Korean in his comparative grammar, it should be stated that his comparative grammar is the basis on which all future work will be conducted. As for Ramstedt's Korean comparative studies, they will be dealt with *infra*, in connection with the history of the Korean problem.

In conclusion, it should be remarked that Ramstedt has left a rich heritage: firmly established sound-correspondences, numerous works on morphology, and a well-corroborated theory about the mutual genetic affinity of the Altaic languages.

According to his latest, posthumous work, namely the comparative grammar, Common Altaic included at least four dialects, namely Proto-Korean, Proto-Turkic, Proto-Mongolian, and Proto-Manchu-Tungus. Proto-Korean and Proto-Turkic (we would say, Proto-Chuvash-Turkic) probably occupied the southern part of the original linguistic area, whereas Proto-Mongolian and Proto-Manchu-Tungus occupied the northern part. At the same time, Proto-Manchu-Tungus and Proto-Korean occupied the eastern portion, and Proto-Turkic (Proto-Chuvash-Turkic) and Proto-Mongolian occupied the western portion of the area. Of course, this is only a hypothesis which cannot be proven easily, but it is one of those working hypotheses which are useful as a starting point for future research.

Bibliography:

Ramstedt, G. J., *Über die Konjugation des Khalkha-Mongolischen*, Helsinki 1902.
— "Über mongolische Pronomina", *JSFOu* 23: 3 (1904).
— "Zur Geschichte des labialen Spiranten im Mongolischen", *Festschrift Vilhelm Thomsen*, Leipzig 1912, pp. 182–187.
— "Zur Verbstammbildungslehre der mongolisch-türkischen Sprachen", *JSFOu* 28: 3 (1912).
— "Ein anlautender stimmloser Labial in der mongolisch-türkischen Ursprache", *JSFOu* 32: 2 (1916).
— "Zur Frage nach der Stellung des Tschuwassischen", *JSFOu* 38: 1 (1922).
— "Über den Ursprung der türkischen Sprache", *SBFAW* 1935, pp. 81–91.
— "Das deverbale Nomen auf -*i* in den altaischen Sprachen", *StOF* 11: 6 (1945).
— "Das deverbale Nomen auf -*m* in den altaischen Sprachen", *MSFOu* 98 (1950), pp. 255–264.
— *Einführung in die altaische Sprachwissenschaft* I, Lautlehre, Bearbeitet und herausgegeben von Pentti Aalto, MSFOu 104: 1 (1957).
— id., II, Formenlehre, Bearbeitet und herausgegeben von Pentti Aalto, MSFOu 104: 2 (1952).

For a complete bibliography of Ramstedt's works *vide*: Karl-Erik Henrikson, "Sprachwissenschaftliche Veröffentlichungen von Prof. Dr. G. J. Ramstedt", *StOF* 14: 12 (1950), pp. 1–14.

3.10. Ramstedt's ideas fell upon a fertile soil. The first scholars to respond to and develop them were the mongolists in Russia. The Polish mongolist, Władysław Kotwicz who at that time, i.e., before 1923, was working at the University of St. Petersburg (now Leningrad), Rudnev, and Vladimirtsov became interested in Ramstedt's work and accepted his method and most of his etymologies as well as the phonetic correspondences established by him.

Ramstedt found also adepts outside Russia. Although the well-known Hungarian turcologist Julius Németh had been rather sceptical at first about the affinity of Turkic and Mongolian ("Die türkisch-mongolische Hypothese"), he too, came to the conclusion that they are related to each other. According to Németh's scheme greatly differing from that of Ramstedt, four stages could be established in the history of the Altaic languages: 1. primitive unity, i.e., genetic affinity; 2. the period of Chuvash-Mongolian mutual influences; 3. the period of Turkic-Mongolian mutual influences; and 4. the period of Yakut borrowings from Mongolian ("Über den Ursprung des Wortes 'Schaman' und einige Bemerkungen zur türkisch-mongolischen Lautgeschichte"). Németh's scheme cannot now be accepted because it is known that there has never been a Chuvash-Mongolian common stage.

Another Hungarian scholar, Gombocz, continued Ramstedt's work. An important work of his is devoted to the correspondences of Manchu-Tungus, Mongolian, and Chuvash *r*, *l* to Turkic *z*, *š* respectively, and Manchu-Tungus and Mongolian initial *d*, *n* to Turkic initial *y*. Another work of great importance is Gombocz's book on the Volga Bulgarian loan-words in Hungarian.

Gombocz's views differ from those of Ramstedt in that he regards Turkic *z* and *š* as original, whereas Ramstedt regards them as having developed from *r and *l respectively. According to Ramstedt, Chuvash *văkăr* "ox" < *ökür > Turkic *öküz* "ox", but Gombocz regards Chuv. *văkăr* as having developed from *öküz > Turk. *öküz*. Otherwise Ramstedt's and Gombocz's work supplement each other.

Bibliography:

Gombocz, Z., *Die bulgarisch-türkischen Lehnwörter in der ungarischen Sprache*, MSFOu 30 (1912).
— "Zur Lautgeschichte der altaischen Sprachen", *KSz* 13 (1912), pp. 1–37.
Németh, J., "Die türkisch-mongolische Hypothese", *ZDMG* 66 (1912), pp. 549–576.
— "Über den Ursprung des Wortes 'Schaman' und einige Bemerkungen zur türkisch-mongolischen Lautgeschichte", *KSz* 14 (1914), pp. 240–249.

3.11. To return to the St. Petersburg school of altaicists, it should be remarked that it accepted Ramstedt's methods, etymologies, and observations with regard to sound correspondences with only a few reservations.

The first generation of scholars engaged in Altaic comparative studies based on Ramstedt's works comprised Kotwicz and Vladimirtsov. Both of them accepted the phonetic correspondences established by Ramstedt. They also accepted his etymologies and rejected only those of them which were doubtful or obviously erroneous.

As far as the common origin of many words and suffixes is concerned, Kotwicz fully shared Ramstedt's views. He was, however, more reserved in his statements with regard to the genetic affinity of the Altaic languages, i.e., their origin from one common language, namely Common Altaic or Proto-Altaic. Details referring to the latter and discussion of the mutual relations of the members of the Altaic group will be given below, but it should be mentioned here that in later stages of his scholarly activities Ramstedt believed in the existence of a Common Altaic or Proto-Altaic language, the ancestor of all Altaic languages spoken at the present time. Vladimirtsov was of Ramstedt's opinion in most matters, including the problems of Common Altaic. One could add that Vladimirtsov was actually unoriginal as far as the Altaic theory is concerned and accepted everything Ramstedt had to say with regard to problems involving the mutual relations of the Altaic languages. This statement is not meant to minimize Vladimirtsov's achievements, and its purpose is to stress out that Vladimirtsov did not have any doubts about the genetic affinity of Mongolian, Turkic, and Manchu-Tungus.

Kotwicz, however, was less categorical in his statements. He accepted Ramstedt's thesis that the Altaic languages possess a large body of common elements (grammatical structure, suffixes of common origin, words, regular sound correspondences) and he established a number of ancient forms reconstructed on the basis of comparative study, but he conceded that genetic affinity is by no means the only possible explanation of resemblances or even identity of those common elements. From this point of view his posthumous major work

Studies on Altaic Languages (in Polish) is particularly important. It is unfortunate that this work is not available in translation into English but there is a somewhat incomplete Russian translation. The relations of the Altaic languages are represented by Kotwicz in the following manner.

At the beginning of the Christian era, there existed three groups of languages structurally very close to each other, namely Turkic, Tungus, and Mongolian, or as we should say, the predecessors of Turkic, predecessors of Tungus, and predecessors of Mongolian. Turkic, in Kotwicz's opinion, may have exercized a strong influence upon Mongolian, and the latter influenced Tungus. Geographically seen, these three language groups may have represented three concentric circles.

The similarities observed in the languages in question may be the result of contacts and influences, in addition to an original structural resemblance. These contacts may have extended as far as to involve Korean. Consequently, Kotwicz's theory differs from that of Ramstedt only as far as the conclusions are concerned. Ramstedt concluded from the similarities and identities that the languages in question were genetically kindred, whereas Kotwicz was more inclined to explain the similarities as results of contacts.

Vladimirtsov who was Kotwicz's pupil, a member of Radloff's circle, and a regular attendant of Ramstedt's lectures and talks on Altaic subjects, was at the beginning of his career rather reserved in his opinions about Altaic affinity.

At the beginning, Vladimirtsov felt that the existence of the Altaic language family, i.e., a family of genetically related languages, had by no means been proven. Vladimirtsov interpreted many common elements as cross borrowings, i.e., as words borrowed from Turkic into Mongolian and, *vice versa*, from Mongolian into Turkic. This attitude of Vladimirtsov towards similarities between Mongolian and Turkic is characteristic of his article on the Turkic elements in Mongolian which appeared in 1911. Later on, after having worked on the problems revolving around the mutual relations between Mongolian, Turkic, and Manchu-Tungus for another fifteen years, Vladimirtsov became much less reserved in his opinions about the Altaic problem. In his latest work in the field of Altaic comparative studies, in his *Comparative Grammar* (in Russian) Vladimirtsov unequivocally appears as an adherent of the theory about the genetic affinity of Mongolian, Turkic, and Manchu-Tungus. There he says that Mongolian belongs to the Altaic language family which includes also Turkic and Manchu-Tungus. Mongolian is related to the latter two because all three languages came into existence as a result of different developments of the same language which had been spoken some time ago. Mongolian, Turkic, and Manchu-Tungus have a common ancestor which can be conventionally called "the Altaic language". Mongolian is an Altaic language because it is one of the forms of development of that Altaic language (*Comparative Grammar*, p. 45). These quotations demonstrate that Vladimirtsov was in the later stages of his research an outspoken supporter of the Altaic theory based on the assumption of genetic affinity.

Bibliography:

Kotwicz, Wł., "Contributions aux études altaïques I. (Notice préliminaire);

II. (Les noms de nombre); III. (Les noms de couleurs)", *RO* 7 (1931), pp. 130–234.

Kotwicz, Wł., "Contributions aux études altaïques IV. (Sons intercalaires); V. (*n* nominal)", *RO* 12 (1936), pp. 122–142.

— "Contributions aux études altaïques, A. Les termes concernant le service des relais postaux; B. Les titres princiers: turc *bäg*, mo. *begi* et ma. *beile*", *RO* 16 (1953), pp. 327–368.

— *Les pronouns dans les langues altaïques*, Mémoires de la commission orientaliste 24, Kraków 1936.

— *Studia nad językami altajskimi*, wydał Marian Lewicki, RO 16 (1953), pp. 1–318. The same in an abbridged Russian translation (omitting quotations from authors who are *personae non gratae* in the USSR): *Issledovanie po altaĭskim yazïkam*, Moskva 1962.

Kotwiczówna, M., "Bibliografia Władysława Kotwicza", *RO* 16 (1953), pp. XXXI–XLVIII (a complete bibliography of Kotwicz's publications).

Vladimircov, B. Ya., "Tureckie elementï v mongolskom yazïke", *ZVO* 20 (1911), pp. 153–184.

— *Sravnitelnaya grammatika mongolskogo piśmennogo yazïka i xalxaskogo narečiya*, Vvedenie i fonetika, Leningrad 1929.

Vladimircov, B. Ya. i Poppe, N. N., "Iz oblasti vokalizma mongolo-tureckogo prayazïka", *DRAN* 1924, pp. 33–35.

3.12. The Altaic theory is also recognized by some Soviet scholars. An outspoken representative of the Altaic theory as formulated by Vladimirtsov is the turcologist Baskakov. "The most ancient period in the development of Turkic languages ... is the Altaic period in which Turkic was little differentiated from Mongolian and the latter from Manchu-Tungus", says Baskakov in his book *Tyurkskie yazïki* (p. 28). Although his ideas referring to certain phonetic correspondences differ from those of Ramstedt and Vladimirtsov, he agrees in essence with their statements with regard to the Altaic affinity.

An interesting contribution to Altaic comparative linguistics was published by the Soviet scholar, Illich- Svitych.

Another Soviet altaicist, Sanžeyev expresses himself rather vaguely. In his article dedicated to Vladimirtsov's linguistic theories and achievements, Sanžeyev says that it is premature to insist on the concept of Common Altaic and, consequently, on the genetic affinity of the languages in question, as being more than a hypothesis. In quoting Ligeti who believes that the genetic affinity of the Altaic languages has not yet been proven, Sanžeyev (p. 17) says that the idea of affinity is no more than a hypothesis (p. 25). In his article on "Modern Mongolian" (in Russian), however, Sanžeyev states that the Mongolian languages are regarded as closely related to Turkic, having *genetically* originated from a common Mongolian-Turkic language (p. 7). It is difficult to say why he floats between two theories in articles which appeared one year apart. The only explanation one can find is that in the article "Modern Mongolian" Sanžeyev meant to say that Mongolian and Turkic are commonly regarded as closely related and having originated from one ancestor *but he, Sanžeyev, did not believe it*. His position would have become much more definite if he had added it. Anyway, as he fails to give an unequivocal formulation of his position, he should be excluded from discussion of adherents or opponents of the Altaic theory.

An opponent of the Altaic theory is, however, the Soviet linguist Serebrennikov in whose opinion the "formulae established by the altaicists" such as $r > z$; d-, n-, $ǰ$-, y- $> y$; $l > š$ have not yet been proven.

Bibliography:

Baskakov, N. A., *Tyurkskie yazïki*, Moskva 1960, pp. 21–32.
— "Predislovie", G. I. Ramstedt, *Vvedenie v altaĭskoe yazïkoznanie*, Morfologiya, Obrabotano i izdano Pentti Aalto, Perevod s nemeckogo L. S. Slonim, Pod redakcieĭ i s predisloviem N. A. Baskakova, Moskva 1957, pp. 5–20. (Preface to the Russian translation of Ramstedt's *Einführung in die altaische Sprachwissenschaft*).
Illič-Svitič, V. M., "Altaĭskie dentalnïe: $t, d, δ$", *Voprosï Yazïkoznaniya* 6 (1963), pp. 37–56.
Sanžeev, G. D., "B. Ya. Vladimircov – issledovatel mongolskix yazïkov", *Filologiya i istoriya mongolskix narodov, Pamyati akademika Borisa Yakovleviča Vladimircova*, Moskva 1958, pp. 12–40.
— *Sovremennïĭ mongolskiĭ yazïk*, Moskva 1959.
Serebrennikov, B. A., "O nekotorïx spornïx voprosax sravnitelnoistoričeskoĭ fonetiki tyurkskix yazïkov", *Voprosï yazïkoznaniya* 4 (1960), pp. 62–72.

3.13. A follower of Ramstedt is his pupil, the Finnish scholar Pentti Aalto. He edited and published Ramstedt's comparative grammar after the death of its author. Aalto has accepted the phonetic correspondences and the common suffixes established by Ramstedt. As far as the interrelationship of the Altaic languages is concerned, Aalto is an adherent of the affinity theory. He believes that the Altaic languages are genetically related to one another and regards the fact that the author of these lines accepted Ramstedt's theory about the genetic affinity of the Altaic languages as a positive achievement. Whereas the author of these lines had been somewhat uncertain about Korean and hesitated between original genetic affinity (in German, "Urverwandtschaft") and an Altaic substratum in Korean, Aalto refused to see any difference between the two possibilities and stated that it is hard to distinguish between "Urverwandtschaft" and a substratum (*vide* his review of the author's comparative grammar, p. 9). This demonstrates that Aalto accepts the Altaic theory without reservations. Moreover, he does not reject the possibility of primitive ties connecting the Altaic and Uralic languages, although he does not believe that the admission of such a remote affinity might be of value at the present time (*ibid.*, pp. 9–10). He is more cautious in this aspect than the Finnish turcologist Martti Räsänen, also a pupil of Ramstedt, who is an adherent of both the Altaic and Ural-Altaic theories.

Aalto published a number of articles in which he presented his views on the mutual affinity of the Altaic languages, including Korean, e.g., an article on the Altaic initial *p.

Another follower of Ramstedt's theories is Pritsak whose views expressed in his works on Chuvash and Bulgar are particularly close to the opinions of the author of these lines. Pritsak has also been, since 1958, the editor-in-chief of the journal *Ural-Altaische Jahrbücher*.

Bibliography:

Aalto, P. [Review of] N. Poppe, Vergleichende Grammatik der altaischen Sprachen, Teil I, Vergleichende Lautlehre: *StOF* 25: 4 (1960), pp. 8–11.
— "On the Altaic Initial *p-", *CAJ* 1 (1955), pp. 9–16.
Pritsak, O., "Die sogenannte Bulgarische Fürstenliste und die Sprache der Protobulgaren", *UAJ* 26: 1–2 (1954), pp. 61–77.
— *Die Bulgarische Fürstenliste und die Sprache der Protobulgaren*, UAB, Wiesbaden 1955.
— "Bolgaro-Tschuwaschica", *UAJ* 31 (1959), pp. 274–314.

3.14. Before proceeding to further discussion of the Altaic theory, it is necessary to define the place of Korean among the Altaic (or *other* Altaic) languages.

The Korean language, its dialects and history, are still insufficiently investigated. Therefore its relation to other languages is less clear than that of Mongolian, Turkic, or Manchu-Tungus. In general, there are the following theories and hypotheses with regard to affinity of Korean: 1. affinity with Japanese; 2. affinity with Dravidian; 3. with Chinese; 4. with the Indo-European languages; 5. with the Altaic languages.

1. The theory about Korean and Japanese affinity is based on the fact that both languages are agglutinative and possess a number of stems resembling one another, partly due to the fact that many of them are borrowings from Korean into Japanese or *vice versa* or borrowings in both languages from Chinese. There are, however, words which are not borrowings, their similarities having not yet been explained in a satisfactory manner, the result being that some scholars believe that both Korean and Japanese belong to the Altaic group. The Korean-Japanese affinity is postulated by Aston, Kanazawa, and some other scholars.

2. The Dravidian languages are spoken in India. They include Tamil, Telugu, and a number of other languages. Possessing an agglutinative grammatical structure, they were regarded as akin to the Ural-Altaic languages. The theory about the affinity of Korean and Dravidian was established by Hulbert.

3. Korean has numerous borrowings from Chinese and is practically flooded with Chinese elements. It owes most of its vocabulary to Chinese and is an important source for the study of Ancient Chinese, because Korean has preserved many features of the former and particularly the ancient pronunciation of words borrowed from Ancient Chinese.

Edkins was the first to discuss Sino-Korean correspondences, dealing at the same time with Mongolian and Chinese, and Korean and Mongolian correspondences.

4. The primitive affinity of the Altaic and Indo-European languages has also found supporters, one of them being the well-known turcologist Karl H. Menges.

The best-known supporters of the Korean-Indo-European theory are Jensen, Koppelmann, and Junker.

5. As for the Altaic origin of Korean, this is corroborated better than any other theory or hypothesis established so far.

It was established by first-rate linguists, such as Polivanov and Ramstedt who did not confine themselves to general statements but corroborated their views with numerous convincing etymologies. It should be also pointed out that Vladimirtsov was quite enthusiastic about the affinity of Korean and Altaic. Although he had not published his observations, he quoted orally such correspondences as Kor. *nal* "day" and Mongolian *nara* "sun"; Kor. *tol* "stone" = Mong. *čilaγun* < Com. Alt. *$t_i\bar{a}la$-$g\bar{u}n$ "stone" = Chuvash *čul* < *$t_i\bar{a}l$ "stone" = Turk. *tāš* "stone", etc.

Much more important are Ramstedt's works on Korean and its relation to the Altaic languages. Ramstedt believed that Korean is an Altaic language and has originated from Common Altaic, like Mongolian, Manchu-Tungus, and Chuvash-Turkic. The same opinion is shared by Aalto.

Some Korean scholars also believe that Korean is an Altaic language. The following scheme demonstrating the origin of Korean has been suggested by Ki-Moon Lee, professor at the University of Seoul:

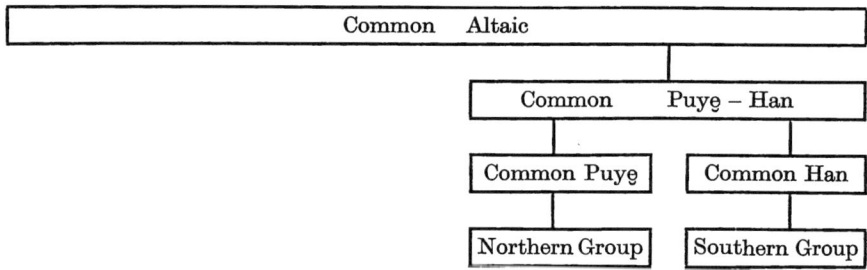

Middle Korean was based on Silla which belonged to the Southern group, and began with the appearance of Koryę which played the rôle of a κοινή and had absorbed elements of Koguryę which belonged to the Northern group.

At the present time, the Altaic origin of Korean is regarded as more likely than the affinity with Dravidian, Chinese, Ainu, or Indo-European, although some scholars have doubts about the Altaic origin of Korean. But then, as it will be demonstrated *infra*, some scholars even reject the whole Altaic theory.

Bibliography:

Aalto, P., [Review of] N. Poppe, Vergleichende Grammatik der altaischen Sprachen, Teil I: "De novis libris judicia", *StFO* 25: 4 (1960), pp. 8–11.

Aston, W.C., "A Comparative Study of the Japanese and Korean Languages", *JRAS* n. s. 11 (1879), pp. 317–364.

Hattori, Sh., "The Relationship of Japanese to the Ryu Kyu, Korean, and Altaic Languages", Delivered before the Linguistic Group of the Asiatic Society, January 8, 1948.

Hulbert, H. B., *A Comparative Grammar of the Korean Language and the Dravidian Dialects in India*, Seoul 1905.

Jensen, H., "Indogermanisch und Koreanisch", *Germanen und Indogermanen* II, Heidelberg 1936.

Junker, H.F., *Koreanische Studien*, Berlin 1955.

Kanazawa, S., *The Common Origin of the Japanese and Korean Languages*, Tokyo 1910.
— *Über die Kultur Japans und Koreas in alten Zeiten vom Standpunkt der Sprachvergleichung aus betrachtet*, Tokyo 1913.
Koppelmann, D. H., *Die Verwandtschaft des Koreanischen und der Ainu-Sprache mit den indogermanischen Sprachen*, Wien 1928.
— *Die eurasische Sprachfamilie – Indogermanisch, Koreanisch und Verwandtes*, Heidelberg 1933.
Polivanov, E. D., "K voprosu o rodstvennïx otnošeniyax koreĭskogo i 'altaĭskix' yazïkov", *IAN SSSR* 1927.
Rahder, J., *Etymological Vocabulary of Chinese, Japanese, Korean, and Ainu*, I Tokyo 1956; II–III New Haven, Conn., 1959; IV 1960; V 1962.
Ramstedt, G. J., "Remarks on the Korean Language", *MSFOu* 58 (1928), pp. 441–453.
— "Koreanisch kęs 'Ding, Stück'", *JSFOu* 48: 4 (1937).
— *Studies in Korean Etymology*, MSFOu 95 (1949).
— *Einführung in die altaische Sprachwissenschaft* I: Lautlehre, MSFOu 104: 1 (1957); II: Formenlehre, MSFOu 104: 2 (1952).
— "Additional Korean Etymologies" by –, Collected and edited by Pentti Aalto, *JSFOu* 57: 3 (1954).

3.15. The comparative grammars of the Altaic languages available at the present time, namely Ramstedt's *Einführung in die altaische Sprachwissenschaft* (two volumes) and that of the author of these lines (*Vergleichende Grammatik der altaischen Sprachen*, Teil I) are based on a large descriptive literature and comparative grammars of the individual language groups. At the present time, there are comparative grammars of the languages belonging to the Mongolian, Turkic, and Manchu-Tungus groups.

The oldest comparative grammar of the Mongolian languages is that by Vladimirtsov (1929). It is both incomplete and obsolete, containing formulations and etymologies which cannot be accepted at the present time. It is basically a comparative grammar of Khalkha and Written Mongolian, i.e., an enlarged version of Ramstedt's *Das Schriftmongolische und die Urgamundart phonetisch verglichen* but includes some data on dialects spoken in Inner Mongolia, on Oirat, Buriat, Middle Mongolian (the language of the ḥP'ags-pa script), but also Manchu, Tungus, and Turkic. It does not contain any data on Ordos, Monguor, and Dagur because these languages had not yet been studied, and ḥP'ags-pa forms are in Vladimirtsov's book misspelled, because at that time the correct readings had not been established, e.g., *daḥul-ya-yuė* (p. 214) "proclaiming" (instead of *du'ulqaquė*), *bolyan* "city" (p. 147), a form artificially and erroneously reconstructed (the original gives *bolqaqun* "those who will do" which was misunderstood as *bolqadun* "of the cities"); *moŋk'a / moŋk'e* (p. 167) "eternal" (instead of *moŋk'a / moŋk'e*), etc.

A number of equations is wrong in Vladimirtsov's book, e.g., Mong. *dabusun* "salt" = Yakut *tūs* id., Chuvash *tăvăr* id. (p. 258), because *tūs* goes back to *tūz < *tūr > Chuv. *tăvăr*, whereas Mongolian *dabusun* goes back to *dabur-sun* which would have yielded Turkic *yabuz > Turkish *yavuz* but not *duz*; Mong. *čimügen* "bone, marrow" = Turkic *süŋük* "bone" (p. 251), because Mong. č does not correspond to Turk *s*; Mong. *uγu-*, Khalkha *ū-* "to drink" = Manchu *omi-* id. (p. 211), because *omi-* corresponds to Mong. *umdan* "a drink", *umdayas-* "to become thirsty"; Mong. *bisil-* "to be industrious" = Turk. *baš* "head" (p. 145), because Turk. *š* corresponds to Mongolian *l* but not *s*, etc.

Leaving aside Vladimirtsov's incorrect statements with regard to Mongolian, Manchu-Tungus, and Turkic correspondences, and proceeding to his observations on Mongolian languages, one should remark that there, too, are numerous inadequacies. Thus, contrary to Vladimirtsov's statement, there has never been **ȯ* as a phoneme distinct from **ö*, nor a phoneme **u̇* as different from **ü* (pp. 166–167). The development of **i > o* before **u* cannot be explained in the manner Vladimirtsov explains (p. 181). As a matter of fact, Khalkha *ǰolō* "reins" has *o* in the first syllable because the original form **ǰilugā* developed first into **ǰiloyā > ǰilo'ā* and then into *ǰilō > ǰolō* but not because of the initial *ǰ* (vide p. 185). As for **ugā*, it does not result in *ā* (p. 197) but in *ō*, cf. **čupàkur > *čußāqur > *čo'āqur >* Khalkha *cōxor* "motley".

There are many other statements which cannot now be accepted. Therefore, one has to be cautious when using Vladimirtsov's comparative grammar. This should not be interpreted, however, as a negative verdict on his work. One should bear in his mind that Vladimirtsov's book was written more than thirty years ago, at a time when of all the Mongolian languages only Khalkha, Kalmuck, and one Buriat dialect (namely, Khori) were known, at a time when Middle Mongolian had not been studied. Vladimirtsov's book was an achievement at the time of its publication and it is not its author's fault that it is now obsolete. One should remember that Ordos (Urdus), Monguor, Dagur, and Buriat as a whole were investigated after the appearance of the book under discussion. The *Secret History*, the documents in *ḥP'ags-pa* script, and sources like *Muqaddimat al-Adab* were also published many years after Vladimirtsov's work.

A comparative grammar of Mongolian languages was also published by the author of these lines (1955). Whereas Vladimirtsov's grammar gives only a comparative phonology, this one gives a phonology and morphology. It avoids comparison with other Altaic languages and includes, instead, Written Mongolian, Middle Mongolian (the language of the *Secret History*, *Hua-i i-yü*, *ḥP'ags-pa* script, Moslem sources of the XIII–XIV centuries), Buriat, Khalkha, Ordos (Urdus), Dagur, Monguor, and Oirat. It is still the most complete and reliable comparative grammar and needs correction only as far as two problems of historical and comparative phonology are concerned. First of all, it should include a statement to the effect that certain consonants (e.g., *g*, *b*, *η*, *y*) have disappeared only in *weak position*, i.e., before a long (originally, i.e., Common Altaic accented) vowel, e.g., Khalkha *ūl* "mountain" *< *ayūla < *agùla*. The same consonants in *strong position*, i.e., before a short (originally unaccented) vowel have not disappeared, e.g., CA **bága* "small" > Common Mongolian **baga >* Khalkha *baga* id.

Second, Proto-Mongolian had primary long vowels there where Dagur and Monguor have long vowels corresponding to short vowels in other Mongolian languages, e.g., Monguor *tāwęn* "five", Dagur *tāyṇ* id. *< *tābun >* Written Mongolian *tabun*, Khalkha *taw* id. In the comparative grammar, however, these long vowels were treated as secondary long vowels, their length being due to position. This was corrected in an article by Hattori and in the author's *Vergleichende Grammatik der altaischen Sprachen*.

A comparative grammar of Mongolian languages was also published by the Soviet mongolist Sanžeyev. It was written at the peak of the cult of Stalin and contains numerous quotations from Stalin's speeches and political writings, praise of Stalin, etc. This alone has added a very peculiar flavor to the book as a whole, the latter being a hybrid of linguistics and political propaganda, something that is unique in the history of Altaic studies. Apart from this, it contains numerous errors. It was unanimously rejected by the scholarly world and had several most critical reviews. Therefore, it cannot be recommended. A few years later, a second volume appeared which deals with the verbal system of the Mongolian languages. It is much better and can be regarded as quite acceptable.

To proceed to comparative studies of Turkic languages, the comparative phonology of the northern Turkic languages by Radloff should be mentioned in the first place, because it is the oldest work of this kind (1882). It is by no means a comparative phonology in the modern sense, because it discusses sounds but not phonemes of each individual Turkic language, almost not establishing any correspondences or developments of older forms into newer forms. It is a collection of articles each one devoted to a particular Turkic language, in which the vowels and consonants of that language are enumerated. It is nothing but an inventory of sounds found in various Turkic languages. It is also incomplete, contains errors, and is obsolete in method. It can hardly be used any longer.

An excellent comparative grammar of the Turkic languages is that by the Finnish scholar Martti Räsänen. The first volume contains a comparative phonology, the second volume is devoted to morphology. This work is written along the lines of modern comparative linguistics. As any work, this too has its defects, the main one consisting in that in some cases only constatations but no explanations of facts are given, e.g., "t- > d-. The sound shift is sporadic and frequent in the South-Western languages and Karakalpak, appearing, however, from time to time in other languages, too" (p. 158). In other words, in some instances this work does not add much to what was known long ago, and some problems have remained as obscure as before. Another defect is the vagueness of expression, e.g., "In Uighur there is occasional fluctuation (Gabain, ATG 54): t/d: *kitär / kidär* 'to remove'" (p. 159), etc. These remarks should not be regarded as criticism, and what is meant is that Räsänen's comparative grammar has not solved all problems of Turkic comparative linguistics, which will have to be studied in the future, in order to find an answer, because lack of answer does not mean that there cannot be an answer. There is an answer but it has not yet been found. Otherwise Räsänen's work is excellent and one can hardly expect anything better in the present stage. It is a valuable summary of everything firmly established in the field of Turkic comparative studies, and the gaps occurring in it will serve the purpose by drawing the attention of linguists to problems still unsolved.

A comparative linguistic work on Turkic languages was also published in the USSR. It comprises four volumes, the first one containing a number of articles on phonetics both descriptive and comparative, the second volume presenting a selection of essays on morphology, the third volume discussing problems of syntax, and the fourth volume dealing with lexicology. This work is not really a comparative grammar but a collection of studies in comparative phonetics, morphology, syntax, and lexicology. It discusses a number of problems but leaves aside as many other problems. The articles are written by a number of scholars and edited by the late Dmitriev, a scholar of high standing. The quality of the articles is rather uneven, and no article exhausts its subject. The title of the whole work is "Materials for a comparative grammar of Turkic languages", and it really contains only materials. It is by no means a comparative grammar.

To leave the Turkic field and proceed to Manchu-Tungus, one may remark that there is an excellent comparative phonology of the Tungus languages by Tsintsius. Her work deals with all Manchu-Tungus languages and is written carefully, containing a large amount of material and giving exhaustive information. It contains also comparative charts of declensions, conjugations, and derivational suffixes, thus exceeding the framework of a comparative phonology. It is written in Russian and is unfortunately out of print. Only a few libraries outside the Soviet Union possess it.

There is also a brief comparative grammar of the Manchu-Tungus languages written in German by Benzing. Its author owes much to the grammar of Tsintsius (he makes reference to it) and is by no means original. His grammar is by far inferior to that of Tsintsius.

Bibliography:

Benzing, J., *Die tungusischen Sprachen*, Wiesbaden 1956.
Cincius, V. I., *Sravnitelnaya fonetika tunguso-mańčžurskix yazïkov*, Leningrad 1949.
Dmitriev, N. K., *Issledovaniya po sravnitelnoĭ grammatike tyurkskix yazïkov*, Pod obščeĭ redakcieĭ člena-korrespondenta AN SSSR –, č. I, Fonetika, Moskva 1955; č. II, Morfologiya, Moskva 1956; č. III, Sintaksis, Moskva 1961; č. IV, Leksika, Moskva 1962.
Hattori, Sh., "The Length of Vowels in Proto-Mongol", *SM* 1: 12 (Ulaanbaatar 1959).
Poppe, N., *Introduction to Mongolian Comparative Studies*, MSFOu 110 (1955).
— *Vergleichende Grammatik der altaischen Sprachen*, Teil I, Vergleichende Lautlehre, Wiesbaden 1960.
— "The Primary long Vowels in Mongolian", *JSFOu* 63: 2 (1962).
Radloff, W., *Phonetik der nördlichen Türksprachen*, Leipzig 1882.
Ramstedt, G. J., *Einführung in die altaische Sprachwissenschaft* I: Lautlehre, Bearbeitet und herausgegeben von Pentti Aalto, MSFOu 104: 1 (1957); II: Formenlehre, Bearbeitet und herausgegeben von Pentti Aalto, MSFOu 104: 2 (1952).
Räsänen, M., *Materialien zur Lautgeschichte der türkischen Sprachen*, StOF 15 (1949).
— *Materialien zur Morphologie der türkischen Sprachen*, StOF 21 (1957).
Sanžeev, G. D., *Sravnitelnaya grammatika mongolskix yazïkov*, t. I, Moskva 1953; *Sravnitelnaya grammatika mongolskix yazïkov, Glagol*, Moskva 1963.

Ubryatova, E. I., Otvetstvennïĭ redaktor, *Istoričeskoe razvitie leksiki tyurkskix yazïkov*, Moskva 1961.

Vladimircov, B. Ya., *Sravnitelnaya grammatika mongolskogo pismennogo yazïka i xalxaskogo narečiya*, Vvedenie i fonetika, Leningrad 1929.

3.16. On the basis of the comparative studies on individual language families, Turkic, Mongolian, and Manchu-Tungus, and comparisons of Turkic with Mongolian and Manchu-Tungus, the mutual relations of the latter are believed by various scholars to be as follows.

At the beginning, Ramstedt himself was sceptical about the parent language from which Mongolian and Turkic had originated, but as soon as in 1916 he mentioned Common Mongolian-Turkic ("die mongolisch-türkische Ursprache"). It is hard to say whether Ramstedt believed in the former existence of a Mongolian-Turkic language unity as an intermediate stage following the dissolution of the Altaic language unity or whether he believed that Mongolian-Turkic had been identical with the Altaic unity. In other words, Ramstedt's "mongolisch-türkische Ursprache" may have been another name for Common Altaic. To make the question clearer, the following diagrams are given:

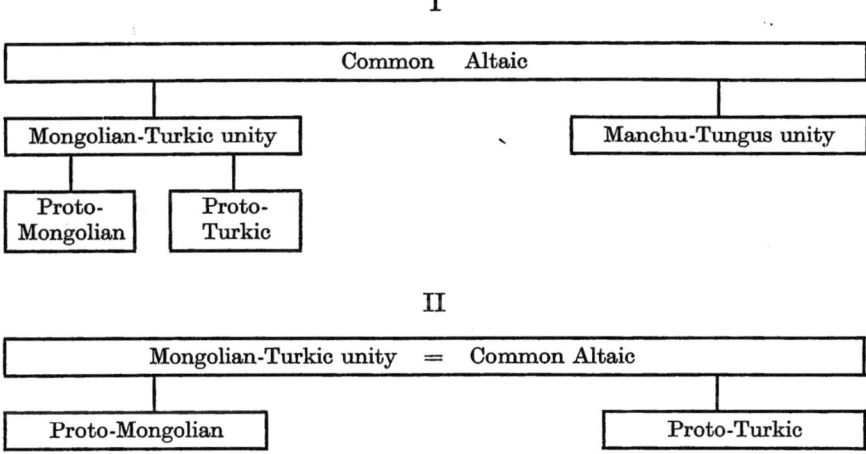

Ramstedt did not then give a clear answer to this question but it looks as if the first scheme is more applicable to his theory, because he reconstructed the initial *p on the basis of correspondences in Manchu-Tungus which could not be accomodated under the second scheme.

A much clearer formulation was given in 1929 by Vladimirtsov who illustrated his views with the following scheme (see page 144).

Vladimirtsov was clearly in favor of the first scheme, i. e., he did not identify Common Mongolian-Turkic with Common Altaic but assumed the existence of a Mongolian-Turkic unity as an intermediate stage between Common Altaic and Common-Mongolian (and Common Turkic). In other words, Common Al-

144   3. The Altaic Theory

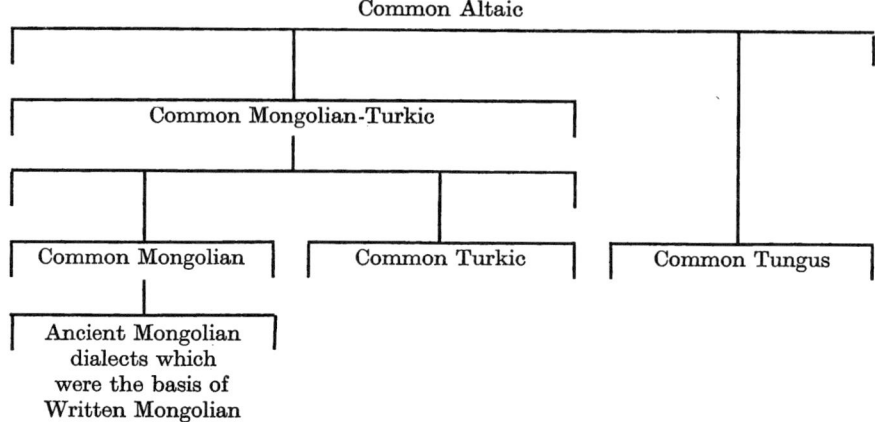

taic, says Vladimirtsov, split into Common Mongolian-Turkic and Common-Tungus. The former split, later on, into Common Mongolian and Common Turkic. Consequently, if Ramstedt had been in favor of the first scheme given above, Vladimirtsov's scheme should be regarded as identical with Ramstedt's views. This is unlikely, however.

Vladimirtsov's scheme was repeated by Baskakov without any additions or changes.

Ramstedt returned to the problems revolving around the mutual relations of Turkic (including Chuvash which is classified by him as a Turkic language), Mongolian, Manchu-Tungus (and Korean) in his comparative grammar. There he says that the original homeland of the Altaic languages may have been in and around the Khingan mountain range in Manchuria. The Khingan mountains may have served as a frontier between two groups: west of the range there lived the ancestors of the Mongols and Turks, and east of the range there was the domicile of the ancestors of the Manchu-Tungus and Koreans:

```
                          N
Ancestors of the Mongols  |  Ancestors of the Manchu-Tungus
Ancestors of the Turks    |  Ancestors of the Koreans
                          S
```

Ramstedt preferred, however, the following, modified scheme:

```
            Ancestors of the Manchu-Tungus
Ancestors of              Ancestors of
the Mongols               the Koreans
            Ancestors of the Turks
```

He based the latter scheme on the fact that the isoglosses connected 1. Turkic with Korean, 2. Mongolian with Manchu-Tungus, 3. Mongolian with Turkic, and 4. Korean with Tungus. When the isoglosses are drawn the following picture appears:

3. The Altaic Theory

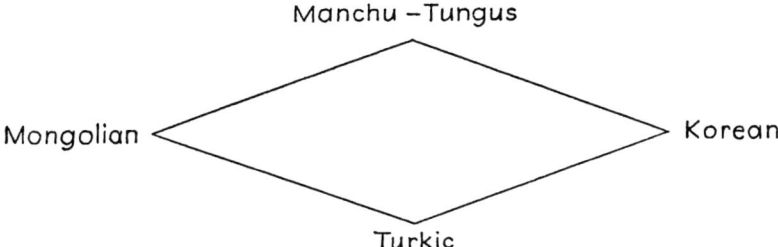

From this scheme the conclusion can be drawn that obviously there has never existed a Mongolian-Korean or a Manchu-Tungus-Turkic unity.

Ramstedt does not extablish any intermediate stages between Common Altaic and the four language families existing at the present time. According to him the division took place in the following manner:

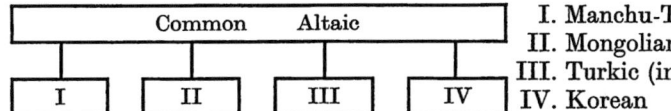

I. Manchu-Tungus
II. Mongolian
III. Turkic (including Chuvash)
IV. Korean

The same can be represented as a circle:

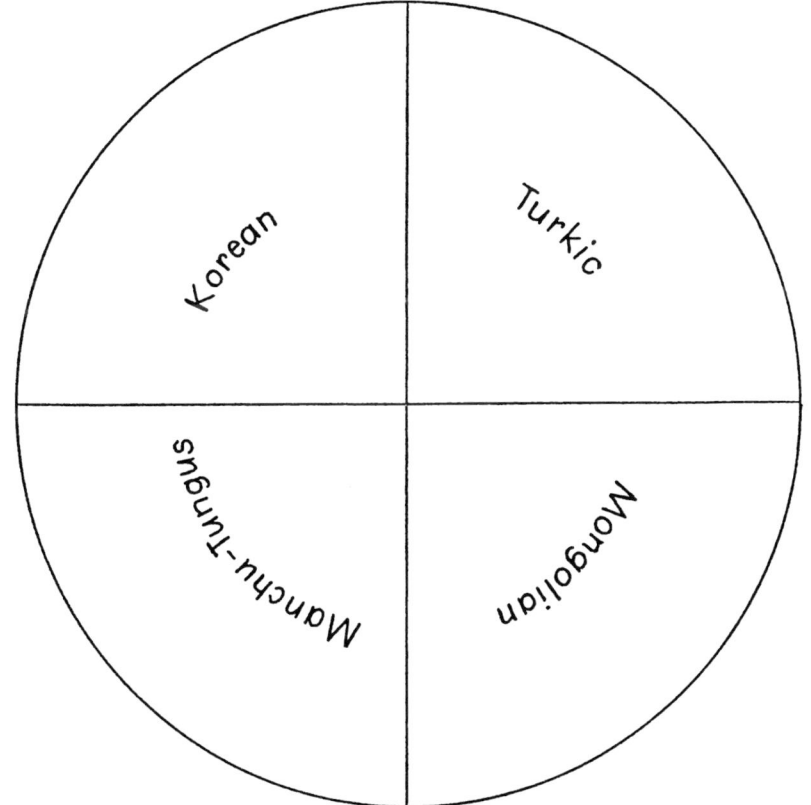

A dissolution of the unity into four branches which took place at the same time is, however, improbable. As a matter of fact, Mongolian has more in common with Manchu-Tungus than with any other branch. Therefore, a Mongolian-Manchu-Tungus unity is to be assumed. On the other hand, Turkic has more in common with Mongolian-Manchu-Tungus than with Korean. Consequently, it is to be assumed that Proto-Korean emerged when the Mongolian-Manchu-Tungus-Turkic unity still existed. Finally, when Proto-Chuvash-Turkic emerged, the latter became the parent language of Proto-Chuvash (a *r*-language: *tăxxăr* "nine") and Proto-Turkic (a *z*-language: *toquz* "nine").

The author of these lines represented the mutual relations of the languages in question as follows (see page 147).

The same can be represented as s system of concentric circles:

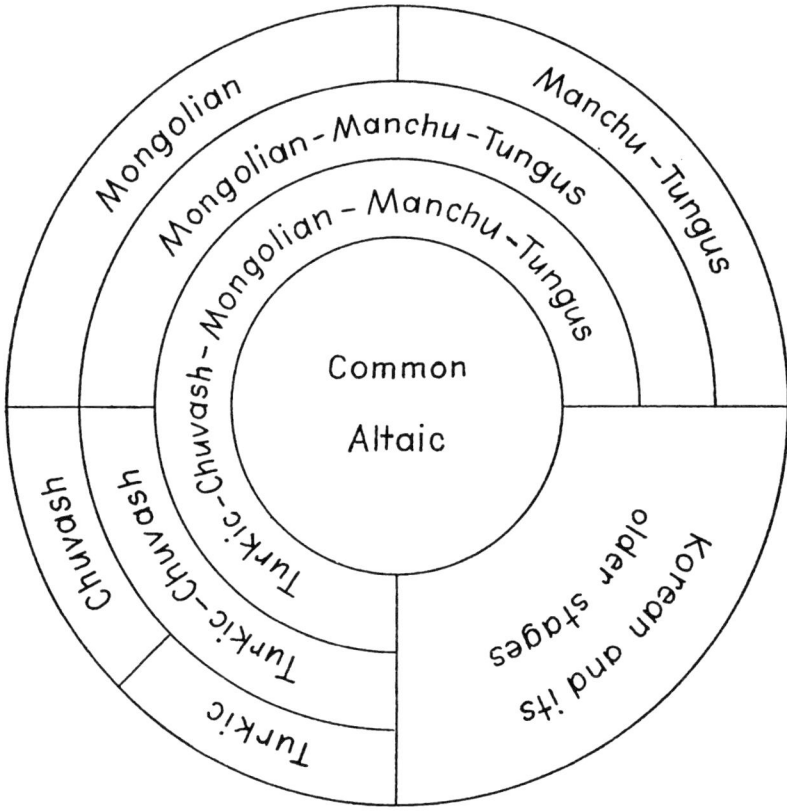

The latter scheme is closer to the situation in the Altaic language world. A doubtful link is still Korean. Therefore, Street has suggested the following scheme, which, under the present conditions, might be closest to the truth.

Street postulates a hypothetic Proto-North Asiatic language which split into Proto-Altaic and another, unspecified proto-language. The latter split, in its

3. The Altaic Theory

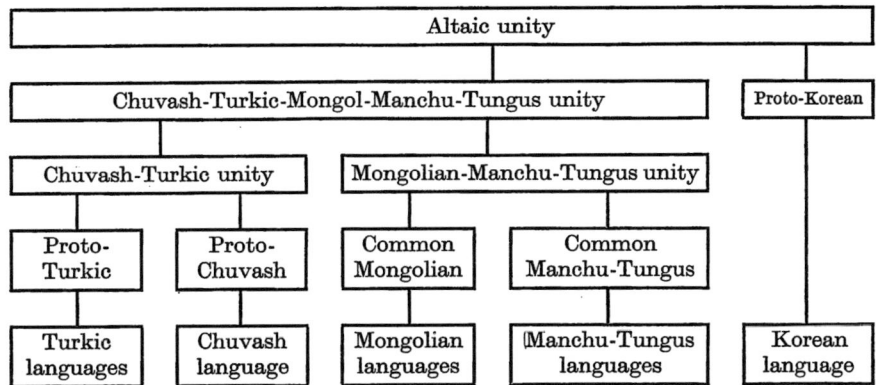

turn, into Korean, Japanese, and Ainu. As for Proto-Altaic, it split, according to Street, into Proto-West Altaic (which is the ancestor of Proto-Turkic and the older stage of Chuvash). Proto-East Altaic was the ancestor of Proto-Mongolian and Proto-Tungusic.

Street suggests the following scheme:

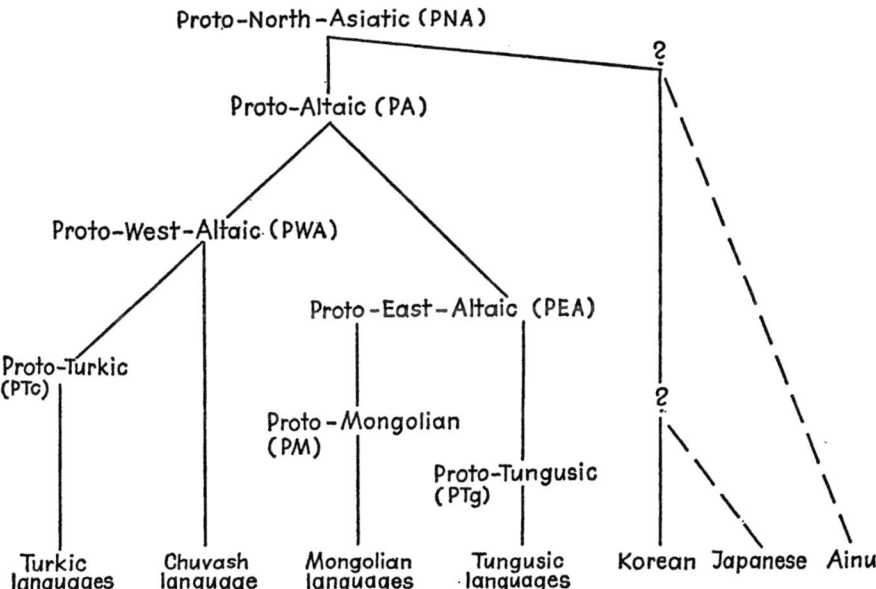

The difference between Street's and the author's schemes concerns mainly the position of Korean. Whereas Poppe applies the term Common Altaic to the hypothetical parent language of Turkic-Mongolian-Manchu-Tungus-Korean, Street believes that Korean developed from a hypothetical language which had branched off from a language in a stage still older than Common (Proto-) Altaic. As for the relations between Turkic, Chuvash, Mongolian, and Manchu-

Tungus, Street's scheme is almost identical with that of the author of these lines. This is an encouraging result, because it demonstrates that there are no differences in views with regard to Chuvash-Turkic, Mongolian, and Manchu-Tungus.

The schemes given above should not be taken literally. They are only schemes and their purpose is to demonstrate the relative chronology of developments (of sounds, grammatical forms, and vocabulary) in the four branches. The scheme of the author of these lines and that of Street coincide in that Korean, according to them, acquired certain characteristics before the other languages. The latter remained little differentiated for a while, when Korean already had acquired its characteristic features. The same can be said, *mutatis mutandis*, about the other Altaic languages.

In conclusion, it should be remarked that close affinity of the languages under discussion is also defended by Martin who is a general linguist and, in addition, both koreanist and mongolist.

Bibliography:

Baskakov, N. A., *Tyurkskie yazïki*, Moskva 1960, pp. 28–32.

Poppe, N., *Vergleichende Grammatik der altaischen Sprachen*, Teil I, Vergleichende Lautlehre, Wiesbaden 1960, pp. 1–8.

Ramstedt, G. J., "Zur Verbstammbildungslehre der mongolisch-türkischen Sprachen", *JSFOu* 28: 3 (1912).

— "Zur mongolisch-türkischen Lautgeschichte" I: Mongolisch-türkisches č; II: Mongolisches ǰ und seine Vertretungen im Türkischen", *KSz* 15 (1914), pp. 134–150; III: Der y-Laut und damit zusammenhängende Fragen, *ibid.*, 16 (1915), pp. 66–84.

— *Einführung in die altaische Sprachwissenschaft* I, Lautlehre, Bearbeitet und herausgegeben von Pentti Aalto, MSFOu 104: 1 (1957), pp. 13–16.

Street, J. C., [Review of] Poppe, *op. cit.*, *Language* 38 (1962), pp. 92–98.

Vladimircov, B. Ya., *Sravnitel'naya grammatika mongol'skogo pis'mennogo yazïka i xalxaskogo narečiya*, Vvedenie i fonetika, Leningrad 1929, pp. 44–47.

3.17. The Altaic theory, i.e., the theory about the affinity of Turkic, Mongolian, and Manchu-Tungus, including or excluding Korean, is not accepted by all scholars. The position of Korean is, indeed, rather unclear. The author of these lines admits of several possibilities with regard to the position of Korean: 1. Korean may be related to the other Altaic languages just as Manchu-Tungus and Turkic are related to one another; 2. Proto-Korean may have branched off before the Altaic unity had come into existence; 3. Korean may have nothing but an Altaic substratum, originally being an un-Altaic language which absorbed an ancient Altaic language or was imposed upon a medium which had been speaking an Altaic language. Therefore, Korean will be left out of further discussion, and only the mutual affinity of Manchu-Tungus, Mongolian, and Turkic will be dealt with. And it is the latter, i.e., the Manchu-Tungus-Mongolian-Chuvash-Turkic affinity which raises objections on the side of some scholars.

Ramstedt himself was at the beginning of his Altaic studies rather undecided or even sceptical about the *genetic* affinity of Mongolian, Manchu-Tungus, and Turkic (he did not then discuss Chuvash). In one of his first works, *Über die Konjugation des Khalkha-Mongolischen* (1903), Ramstedt stated that he was sceptical about proto-languages in general (Ursprachen) and primitive unity (Urgemeinschaft). He was not sure whether the common elements in Mongolian, Manchu-Tungus, and Turkic were old borrowings or proof of genetic affinity. – "Is there a common 'proto-language' if the Central Asiatic nomads who cannot be separated from each other by stable frontiers, definite settled areas, etc., have lived together and fought each other for millenia and, meanwhile, let us say, 99 per cent of borrowings were taken from time to time by their languages?", asked he and added that Mongolian and Turkic should be regarded as closer to each other because of their conjugations which display numerous common elements. As for the relations between Tungus and Manchu, they were unclear to Ramstedt at that time. However, he regarded the common elements in Manchu and Mongolian mostly as borrowings from Mongolian into Manchu.

Later on, in 1907, Ramstedt pointed out in his article on the numerals in the Altaic languages that Turkic, Mongolian, and Tungus displayed only structural similarities and common elements in vocabulary and grammar, and he asked: "Are these similarities ... only borrowings or do they point in the direction of an older unity? The affinity of the Altaic languages is still, in the opinion of most of the investigators, only a vague hypothesis, as long as one is unable to explain in some manner why the numerals in these languages have so little, almost nothing in common ... The Altaic question is still open exactly because it is impossible to deduce the Mongolian and Turkic numerals from common 'proto-words'". After these remarks, Ramstedt said that the value of numerals is only a relative one, because languages may still be related languages in spite of the fact that etymological ties between numerals cannot be established.

In his later works, Ramstedt concentrated his attention on etymologies and phonetic correspondences, and finally came to the conclusion that the Altaic languages are genetically related to each other. But the doubts which he had had at the beginning remained in the minds of many scholars.

The scholars who do not accept the Altaic theory can be divided roughly into two groups.

The first group includes scholars who believe that the Altaic theory is premature and the affinity of the languages in question still needs further proof. The scholars concerned do not reject the Altaic theory but believe that the evidence presented so far is insufficient. They do not say that the Altaic theory is wrong and how could they? To say so, they would be obliged to present evidence against the Altaic theory, but there is no such evidence. Therefore, the scholars concerned do not object but demand additional proof.

This point of view is expressed by, among others, the late Grønbech and his pupil Krueger: "The supposed genetic affiliation of these groups (i.e., Manchu-Tungus, Mongolian, and Turkic, *N.P.*) has never been proved, but the practical utilization of the term 'Altaic languages' lies in the presence of common traits in the syntax, general structure, and vocabularies of the three language families" (*Introduction to Classical Mongolian*, p. 13).

A similar idea underlies Ligeti's remark that "the affinity of the so-called

Altaic languages is *a very probable hypothesis* (italicized by N. P.) *accepted by all of us*, but it is only a hypothesis which has not yet been proved scientifically" (*Voprosï yazïkoznaniya*, p. 134). Ligeti is right in that he regards the Altaic theory as less corroborated than the mutual affinity of the Finno-Ugric languages or the affinity of the latter and Samoyed. And yet he insists that comparative study of Altaic languages should be continued because only the comparative method could help to solve the most important problems revolving around the Altaic theory.

Neither Grønbech nor Ligeti reject the Altaic theory. Their position is absolutely clear: while they admit the possibility of affinity, they believe that the evidence available is insufficient to prove it. Therefore, it is premature, in their opinions, to draw conclusions.

A similar position is taken by Benzing. Whereas he believes the Ural-Altaic unity to be highly disputable, he regards the mutual affinity of the Altaic languages, in view of numerous common features, as not improbable although not yet proven (*Die tungusischen Sprachen*, p. 7). Benzing arrived at this conclusion after a period of a rather negative attitude towards the Altaic theory, rooted in his rejection of the Ural-Altaic theory. It has been demonstrated *supra* that the Ural-Altaic theory is now accepted by very few scholars. However, rejection of the theory about the mutual affinity of the Uralic and Altaic languages does not automatically eliminate the theory about the mutual affinity of the Altaic languages. To do this would be tantamount, to a certain degree, to rejection of the affinity of the Indo-European languages as a sequel of rejection of the theory about the Indo-European and Semitic affinity which is postulated by some scholars: Indo-European and Semitic may have never been related language families but this does not mean that Indo-European is not a family of related languages. This remark should not be construed as the author's belief that the mutual relations of the Altaic languages have been established as firmly as those of the Indo-European languages. The author is very far from such a naivety.

In his *Introduction to Altaic Studies* written in German, Benzing does not draw a line between Altaic and Ural-Altaic and discusses the theories revolving around both groups, the narrower and wider one, indiscriminately, the reason being that some scholars in the past, e.g., Castrén, Winkler, and others used the term "Altaic" in the sense of Ural-Altaic, and included the Finno-Ugric and Samoyed languages in one group called by them "Altaic". Although Benzing's book under discussion includes the chapters "The older period of Altaic studies" (pp. 4–11) and "The Altaic hypothesis at the beginning of the XX century" (pp. 11–15), these chapters do not discuss problems of *Altaic studies* but contain criticism of the Ural-Altaic theory or hypothesis, criticism to which most scholars subscribe. As for the Altaic theory, Benzing's strongest point is the absence of numerals of common origin, i.e., the same objection which Ramstedt had in mind in his early years, when he regarded the lack of common numeral adjectives as a weakness of the Altaic theory ("Über die Zahlwörter der altaischen Sprachen", pp. 1–2). Thus, Benzing's rejection of the Altaic theory was not, at that time, a result of independent research but a repetition of doubts expressed by Ramstedt long ago. Nevertheless, Benzing acknowledges in his *Introduction* the fact that there have been established absolutely irreproachable sound correspondences, and adds that what remains to be done is the interpretation of the correspondences (p. 62). Benzing's rejection of the Altaic theory in his earlier works and his hesitation to accept it fully in his later works are based, to a large extent, on numerous doubtful and often erroneous etymologies found in the works of the altaicists, including Ramstedt who became rather careless in his latest works. Thus, Ramstedt often quoted examples from his memory, compared words which were borrowings from Chinese or Tibetan, etc. Of course, Benzing's doubts based on such defects are absolutely legitimate, and his latest statement with regard to the probability of the theory about the mutual affinity of the Altaic languages shows that he does not really reject the Altaic theory but is merely waiting for more proof.

Whereas Benzing had taken a rather negative attitude towards the Altaic theory at the beginning but, later on, regarded the affinity of the languages concerned as not improbable, Sinor moved exactly in the opposite direction. In his earlier works he appeared as a follower of the Ural-Altaic theory, i.e., more than the theory postulating the Altaic affinity. Thus, in his article "Ouralo-Altaïque – Indo-Européen", Sinor states that the Ural-Altaic theory is dear to him (p. 227), he accepts the Common Altaic *p- (p. 228), gives a number of etymologies such as Turk. öŋ "front" ... ~ Mong. *ekin* "head" ~ Manchu *fexi* "brain" (p. 229); Turk. *äski* "ancient" ~ Mong. *esin* "origin, beginning" (p. 232), etc., and represents the developments of *p- in various languages in the following diagram (p. 235):

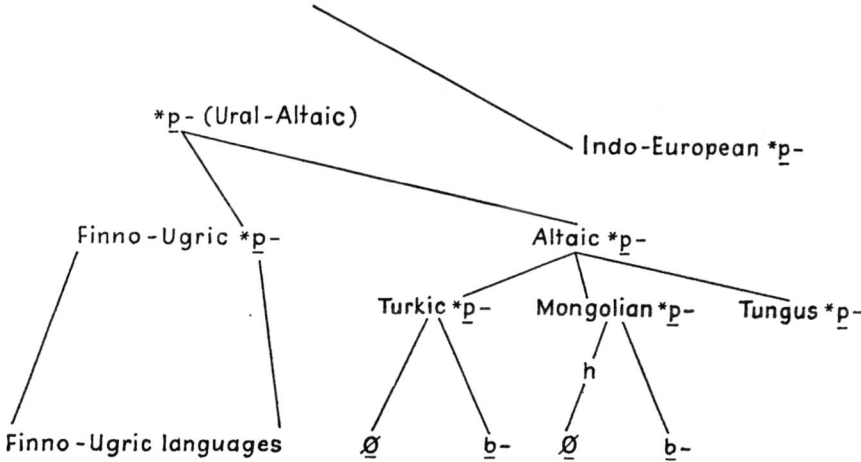

From this diagram representing a kind of genealogical tree of phonemes going back to *p- only the conclusion can be drawn that the languages concerned or, at least, the Altaic languages, are genetically related to each other. Indeed, Sinor even uses the term *primitive people*, meaning the Proto-Altaic people, i.e., the original speakers of the Proto-Altaic language.

Speaking of the relationship that existed between Ural-Altaic and Indo-European, and the Altaic and Indo-European comparative studies (p. 243),

Sinor mentions the two primitive peoples (one of which is Altaic) in the following context: "I do not wish to speak about affinity (of Altaic and Indo-European, *N.P.*), but from the historical and geographical point of view – I beg to forgive me this heresy – it amounts almost to the same whether the *two primitive peoples in question* (italicized by *N.P.*), beyond the geographical neighborhood were related to each other or not" (p. 244). It is important to note that Sinor speaks about two primitive peoples one of which is the Proto-Altaic people. And it goes without saying that the language spoken by that proto-people was Proto-Altaic. From this the conclusion can be drawn that the Altaic languages, according to Sinor, must have been genetically related to each other.

Later on, a change occurred in Sinor's views, and he became more reserved with regard to concepts as genetic affinity, proto-people, proto-language, etc. In 1952, Sinor published an article on the Ural-Altaic plural suffixes. Although he stated that, as far as the plural suffixes are concerned, the close relation existing between the Ural-Altaic languages cannot be denied (p. 229), he does not trace them back to original, primitive forms, and expresses the hope that his article may set an example for further studies and ultimatley lead to a reconsideration of the whole Ural-Altaic hypothesis (p. 203). However, he does not say anything about the affinity of the Altaic languages.

Finally, in an article on a directive suffix in Ural-Altaic (1961), Sinor discusses a suffix identical in Finno-Ugric, Tungus, and Mongolian but lacking in Turkic, and regards the latter circumstance as another breach made in the theory postulating the Altaic "Ursprache" (p. 178). In his latest pronouncements made on this subject, Sinor denies the existence of a common vocabulary in Altaic languages, and explains the common elements as a result of contacts.

The same ideas underlie Sir Gerard Clauson's attitude towards the Altaic theory. He goes further than Grønbech and some other scholars in that he not only regards the genetic affinity of the Altaic languages as not proved but undertakes to prove the opposite, i.e., that they do not possess a common ancestor. The proof that there has never been a common ancestor of the Altaic languages is found, in Sir Gerard's opinion, in the fact that the languages concerned lack a common vocabulary, i.e., common numerals and words for "to say, to give, to take, to go, food, horse, good, bad," etc. His article "The Case against the Altaic Theory" is based on these statements (p. 182), and what ancient words common to the Turkic and Mongolian vocabulary do exist are regarded by him as ancient borrowings from Turkic into Mongolian, e.g., Mongolian *dayin* < Proto-Turkic *$\delta ay\ddot{\imath}$ "enemy" > Ancient Turkic *yay\"i*; Mong. *nidurga* < PTu. *$\check{n}odruq$ "fist" > Turk. *yudruq* ("The Earliest Turkish Loan Words in Mongolian", p. 185). Thus, Sir Gerard Clauson is actually the only scholar who has made an attempt to prove that the Altaic languages are not related, whereas his predecessors in this field confined themselves to expressing doubts and conclusions drawn from the fact that some Altaic languages lack what other Altaic languages possess.

An ouptspoken opponent of the Altaic theory is Doerfer. He rejects it completely and regards all the common elements as old borrowings from one language into another. His main work in this field is his book on the Turkic and

3. The Altaic Theory

Mongolian elements in Modern Persian, which contains a rather long treatise (*Bemerkungen zur Verwandtschaft der sog. altaischen Sprachen*, pp. 51–105) aimed at the refutation of the Altaic theory, a treatise not connected with the main subject of the book and which one would hardly expect to find in a work dealing with Mongolian words which occur in Persian literature.

Doerfer's attitude is characterized by two main features. First of all, he regards all words common to Mongolian and Turkic as loan-words. Second, he regards Mongolian as the borrowing language and Turkic as the lending language. It is to be noted that the Mongolian forms are always deduced from reconstructed Proto-Turkic forms which, curiously enough and quite surprisingly are almost in all cases identical with Mongolian forms. Doerfer's reconstructed Proto-Turkic forms are in most instances identical with Written Mongolian forms, and yet he regards the Written Mongolian (and other Mongolian) forms as borrowings from Turkic which, at the time of borrowing, supposedly displayed almost the same forms as Mongolian. Thus, he reconstructs a Proto-Turkic *d- which is now represented by y- (and its developments) in Turkic and by d- in Mongolian, e.g., *dayïz "brown" > Mong. *dayïr > dayir and Ancient Turkic yayïz id. (p. 98). However, Doerfer disregards the fact that Turkic has only y- (ǰ and other developments). There is no such Turkic language, either modern or ancient, which has an initial *d. On the basis of the existing Turkic languages only *y- can be reconstructed. Therefore, Mongolian *dayïr cannot be deduced from Proto-Turkic *dayïz because there has never been such Proto-Turkic or Turkic forms. Proto-Turkic had *yayïz. The same can be said about Mongolian *daqu* "fur coat, pelt" and Ancient Turkic *yaqu* id.: Proto-Turkic had *yaqu and, if borrowed into Mongolian, this would have yielded *yaqu in Mongolian (cf. Mong. *yara* "wound" < Turk. *yara* id., Mong. *yašil* "purple, also name of a plant" < Turk. *yašïl* "green", etc.). What Doerfer reconstructs as Proto-Turkic is actually much older than Proto-Turkic. It is nothing but Common Altaic: Ancient Turkic y- < Proto-Turkic *y- < Common-Altaic *d- > Proto-Mongolian *d- > Mongolian d-. The point is that Doerfer does not give any evidence to prove the following theses of his:

1. Why cannot *yaqu be a Proto-Turkic form? Why must the Proto-Turkic form be *daqu? What Turkic language (ancient or modern) enables us to reconstruct an initial *d?

2. Why must Mongolian *daqu* be a borrowing from Turkic? If Proto-Turkic was *yaqu (and only such a Proto-Turkic form can be reconstructed on the basis of Turkic evidence) how could the Mongols "transform" initial y into d? Can such a substitution of d for Turkic y be proven?

3. How would Doerfer prove that Turkic could not have borrowed *yaqu* from Mongolian? If the Mongolian form is more ancient than the Turkic form, why must Mongolian be a borrowing from Turkic? Why not *vice versa*?

4. What speaks against the development of Turkic *yaqu* and Mongolian *daqu* from a Common source? Why is such a development impossible: Proto-Turkic *yaqu < *daqu > Proto-Mongolian *daqu? If it is possible, why, then, call *daqu Proto-Turkic? Why cannot it be Common or Proto-Altaic?

These questions cannot be answered if one insists on Proto-Turkic having had *daqu.

To conclude this discussion, it should be also stated that Doerfer's remark to the effect that he regards most of the previous comparisons of words as doubtful (p. 99) does not refute anything. Anyone who has doubts should express them but, then, he should also give his reasons.

In conclusion, it should be remarked that the defenders of the Altaic theory are still in a more advantageous position. They base their views on firmly established etymologies and on phonetic laws corroborated by numerous examples. The opponents, however, have to prove that the elements common to the Altaic languages are borrowings. They have also to prove that Proto-Turkic really had all those consonants in initial position which can be only reconstructed on the basis of Mongolian data.

Bibliography:

Benzing, J., *Einführung in das Studium der altaischen Philologie und der Turkologie*, Wiesbaden 1953, pp. 1–15, 62–63.
— *Die tungusischen Sprachen*, Versuch einer vergleichenden Grammatik, Ak. d. Wiss. u. d. Lit., Abh. d. Geistes- u. Sozialwiss. Kl., Jg. 1955, no. 11, Wiesbaden 1956.
Clauson, Sir Gerard, "The Case against the Altaic Theory", *CAJ* 2 (1956), pp. 181–187.
— "The Earliest Turkish Loan Words in Mongolian", *CAJ* 4 (1959), pp. 174–187.
— "Turk, Mongol, Tungus", *AM* New Ser. 8 (1960), pp. 105–123.
— "The Turkish Elements in 14th Century Mongolian", *CAJ* 5 (1960), pp. 301–316.
— *Turkish and Mongolian Studies*, London 1962, pp. 210–247.
Doerfer, Gerhard, *Türkische und mongolische Elemente im Neupersischen*, Bd. I: Mongolische Elemente im Neupersischen, Wiesbaden 1963.
Grønbech, K. and J.R. Krueger, *An Introduction to Classical Mongolian*, Wiesbaden 1955, p. 13.
Ligeti, L., [Review in Russian of G. D. Sanžeev, Sravnitelnaya grammatika mongolskix yazïkov], *Voprosï Yazïkoznaniya* 5 (1955), pp. 133–140.
Ramstedt, G. J., *Über die Konjugation des Khalkha-Mongolischen*, MSFOu 19 (1903), pp. III–IV.
— "Über die Zahlwörter der altaischen Sprachen", *JSFOu* 24: 1 (1907).
Sinor, D., "Ouralo-Altaïque – Indo-Européen", *TP* 37 (1943), pp. 226–244.
— "On Some Ural-Altaic Plural Suffixes", *AM* New Ser. 2 (1952), pp. 203–230.
— "Observations on a new comparative Altaic phonology", *BSOAS* 26: 1 (1963), pp. 133–144.

3.18. The present situation with regard to the Altaic theory can be summarized as follows. One group of scholars believes that the Altaic languages – all of them or excluding Korean – represent a group of genetically related languages. The proof is found by them in firmly established laws of sound correspondences, in numerous common suffixes, in the identical structure of personal pronouns, and in similarities in syntax (e.g., Ramstedt). Other scholars hesitate to accept the genetic affinity as a definitely proved fact, the lack of common numerals playing the decisive role in their reluctant attitude (e.g., Benzing). Other scholars display a clearly pronounced negative attitude, rejecting the genetic affinity, and refuting the Altaic theory (e.g., Sir Gerard Clauson).

Ramstedt had been the first to see the weakness of the Altaic theory in the lack of numerals common to all languages concerned. Later on, the numerous sound correspondences became more important to him than the lack of numerals. Indeed, it should be emphasized that what is lacking is less important than what is there. Thus, the lack of a declension system of the Latin, Greek, or Sanskrit type in English does not render the latter unrelated to other Indo-European languages. It is the elements common to English and other Indo-European languages that make them related. Therefore, the lack of numerals common to all Altaic languages is not a decisive factor.

This refers equally to Benzing's and Sir Gerard Clauson's objections based on the lack of numerals and basic words common to all Altaic languages. As for the basic words, it is extremely difficult to define which words are basic and which are not. Sir Clauson gives a few examples such as "to say, to give, to take, to go, food, horse, good, bad", etc. However, correspondences to the words "say, take, horse, good, bad" are not even found in all Indo-European languages. Therefore, the absence of an equivalent of Turkish *eyi* "good" from Mongolian does not have a greater significance than the absence of Latin *bonus* "good" from Germanic or Slavic. On the other hand, it happens that some of the words listed above are common to Turkic, Mongolian, and Tungus:

1. "food" : Turkic *yä-* "to eat" = Mongolian *je-me* "carrion, animal killed and partly devoured by a wolf" = Tungus *ǰe-* "to eat";
2. "horse" : Turkic *at* "horse" = Mo. *ata* < *aɣta* "gelding";
3. "good" : Turkic *aya* = Mong. *aya* "decency, suitability", *ayatai* "suitable, good" = Tungus *aya* "good";
4. "to say" : Ancient Turk. *ay-* = Mong. *ayi-bu-r-či* "loquacious, chatterbox";
5. "to take" : Turkic *al-* "to take" = Mong. *ali* "give!" = Manchu *ali-* "to take".

Thus, these and many other basic words are by no means absent from the vocabularies of the individual Altaic languages.

Much more important is Sir Gerard Clauson's theory that most of the common elements are borrowings, namely borrowings from Turkic into Mongolian. In his article "The Earliest Turkish Loan Words in Mongolian" (*CAJ* 4, pp. 174–187) and in the book *Turkish and Mongolian Studies* (pp. 211 ff.) he undertakes to prove that the following words are typical examples of Turkic loanwords in Mongolian (p. 185): Mongolian *dayin* < Proto-Turkic *$\delta a\gamma\ddot{\imath}$ "enemy"; Mong. *nidurga* < Proto-Turkic *ñodruq* "fist" (his transcription) > Turkic of the VIII century *yuðruq*; Proto-Turkic *ñaz* "summer" > Turkic *yaz*.

If proved correct, this interpretation of the origin of the Mongolian words in question would refute the Altaic theory completely. However, the weakness of this attempt at refutation lies in that the forms *$\delta a\gamma\ddot{\imath}$, and *ñodruq, are not Proto-Turkic. To arrive at true Proto-Turkic forms, one should remember that the latter can be reconstructed only on the basis of evidence presented by the

Turkic languages. The Turkic languages give for *ðaγï only yaγï, yaṷ, or ǰaṷ "enemy, war". There is no Turkic language which has d or ð in this word. Likewise, no Turkic language can give evidence to what words with initial y (ǰ, etc.) had *n or *ñ at their onset. Thus, it is impossible to make any conclusion about the original consonant in initial position in yoq "not", yol "road", yüz "face", yaz- "to write", etc., as long as one confines himself to the evidence presented by the Turkic languages. The forms common to all Turkic languages and, therefore, called Common-Turkic or Proto-Turkic forms of the words given here are *yoq, *yol, *yüz, *yaz-. No Turkic language presents any evidence that these words might have originated from *doq (or *noq), *dol (or *nol), *düz (or *nüz), *daz- (or *naz-). In order to establish the oldest forms of the words mentioned, one has to go farther than the evidence presented by the Turkic languages. One has to expand one's research and include Mongolian and Manchu-Tungus material. But it would be incorrect to call the forms established on the basis of such a broader research "Proto-Turkic". Just as forms established on the basis of comparative study of Slavic and Baltic languages are older than Proto-Slavic forms and are generally regarded as Balto-Slavic, just as forms established on the basis of comparative studies of Latin and Greek are not Ancient Italic or Proto-Italic but Graeco-Italic, forms reconstructed on the basis of Turkic and Mongolian data are not Proto-Turkic but Turco-Mongolian, i.e., Common Altaic or Proto-Altaic. In order to prove that Mongolian dayin "enemy" is a borrowing from Turkic, one must show that there was the Proto-Turkic form *ðaγï, and to do this, one must find a Turkic language which unmistakably points in the direction of a *ð- or *n- respectively. Danube Bulgarian evidence should be used very cautiously because it has not been proved yet that it was a *Turkic* language. It was certainly an Altaic language but unmistakably points in the direction of a *d- or *n- respectively. Danube-Bulgarian evidence should be used cautiously because it is so sparse and we do not actually know what *dilom* quoted by the linguists is. It might have been "snake" but it might also have been something else. Besides, it is not known what d stands there for: *dilom* may have been /dilom/ or /d̆ilom = ǰilom/.

As long as the original sounds can be reconstructed only on the basis of Mongolian (and Manchu-Tungus) the sounds in question cannot be labelled as Proto-Turkic. No linguist engaged in comparative studies of Indo-European languages will ever agree to call Proto-Germanic such forms which are reconstructed on the basis of Greek, Latin, or Vedic forms.

To conclude this section, one may remark that the genetic affinity of the Altaic languages may not have been definitely proved, as some scholars believe, but no one has yet advanced reasons against it which might be acceptable to a linguist. No one has proved linguistically that Mongolian nirai "fresh, new, newborn" and Manchu ńarxun "green" are borrowings from Turkic. Neither has it ever been proved that Turkic ever had such forms as *ńār "summer" or *ti̯āl "stone".

4. MUTUAL INFLUENCES WITHIN THE ALTAIC GROUP

4.0. The Altaic languages possess a large number of elements common to all or most of them, which cannot be explained, in a satisfactory manner, as mutual borrowings or borrowings from one language into another. These elements are regarded by Ramstedt's school of altaicists as an evidence of genetic affinity of the Altaic languages.

Side by side with these elements, there are also obvious loan-words which were taken, let us say, by the Mongolian languages from Turkic or by Turkic languages from Mongolian.

How can borrowings be distinguished from common elements, i.e., from elements inherited by the Altaic languages from the parent language? There is only one criterion, namely, sound correspondences. This idea can be illustrated with the following examples.

It is known that Turkic *z* corresponds to Chuvash and Mongolian *r*, e.g., Turkic *uzun* "long" and *uzaq* "long lasting" = Chuvash *vărăm* < **urun* "long" = Mongolian *urtu* "long"; Turk. *bïzayï* "calf" = Chuv. *păru* "calf" = Mong. *birayu* "calf"; Turk. *sez-* "to feel" = Mong. *seri-* "to be awake, to be fresh, to be cool", etc.

In view of the correspondence Turk. *z* = Chuv. and Mong. *r*, Mong. *boyos* "pregnant" (of animals) is a borrowing, cf. Turk. *buyaz* "pregnant", with *z* substituted for by *s*, because Mongolian does not have *z*. Likewise, Mongolian *semǰi* "fat layer around the intestines" is also a borrowing from Turkic, cf. Turk. *semiz* "fat, grease" = Chuv. *samăr* "fat, grease". Cf. also Khalkha *šāʒgai̯* "magpie" < Turk. *sayïzyan* "magpie". The words discussed are borrowings from Turkic because they display Turkic features, namely, consonants which are substitutes for Turkic *z* which is in regular correspondences represented by *r* in Mongolian. The borrowings enumerated are borrowings from Turkic into Mongolian because legitimate Mongolian forms should be **boyor* "pregnant", **semir* or **semiri* "fat", and **sayariyai* > Khalkha **sārgai̯* "magpie".

Another regular correspondence is Turkic *š* = Chuvash and Mongolian *l*, e.g., Turk. *köšäk* "young animal" = Mong. *gölige* "welp"; Turk. *tāš* "stone" = Chuv. *čul* < **ti̯āl* "stone" = Mong. *čilayun* < **tilagūn* < **ti̯ālagūn* "stone" = Korean *tol* "stone".

In view of the latter correspondence, Mongolian *tušaya*, Khalkha *tušā* "hobble, fetters for the feet of a horse" is a borrowing from Turkic, cf. Turk. *tušay* "hobbles" = Chuv. *tălă* id. A regular Mongolian correspondence would be Mong. **tulaya* or **tuliya*.

There are, of course, Mongolian borrowings in Turkic which can also be recognized. Thus, in view of the correspondence Turk. *sez-* "to feel" = Mong. *seri-* "to be awake, to be fresh", Turkic *sergäk* "vigilant" must be a borrowing from Mongolian, cf. Mong. *sergeg* "vigilant", because a genuine Turkic form should be **sezgäk*.

4. Mutual Influences within the Altaic Group

4.1. Altaic borrowings in Mongolian.

Mongolian has Turkic and Manchu-Tungus borrowings.

4.11. Turkic loan-words in Mongolian.

Mongolian has numerous Turkic loan-words. There are Turkic borrowings in Written Mongolian and in the languages spoken at the present time. Some Turkic loan-words are probably very old and date from the Ancient Turkic period, i.e., the period ending with the X century A.D. when Mongolia was inhabited by Turks, and the Mongols lived in Transbaikalia and North-Western Manchuria.

Ancient Turkic (AT) borrowings which had penetrated into Ancient Mongolian and were inherited, later on, by the Mongolian languages that had originated from Middle Mongolian dialects are, *inter alia*, the following:

Ancient Turkic *ada* "danger, misfortune, obstacle" > Mongolian *ada* "misfortune" (pre-classical Written language), "evil spirit" (classical Written language), Buriat *ada* "kind of a female vampire sucking out the blood from infants".

AT *amraq* "beloved" > Mong. *amarag* same, Khalkha, Buriat *amrag* same.

AT *aŋ* "wild animal" > Mong., Kh., Bur. *aŋ* id.

AT *aral* "wilderness, island" > Mong., Kh., Bur. *aral* "island".

AT *arpa* "barley" > Mong., Kh., Bur. *arbai̯* same.

AT *arqaγ* "hem, border of a cloth" > Mong. *arqag* same.

AT *artaq* "spoiled, evil, bad" > Mong. *ardag* "stubborn, disobedient" (horse).

AT *asïγ* "profit, benefit" > Mong. *ašig*, Kh. *ašig* same.

AT *ayaq* "bowl, cup" > Mong. *ayaga*, Kh. *ayag* same.

AT *basa* "then" from *bas-* "to step on" > Mong. *basa* "again", Kh. *bas* same, Bur. *bahā*, Kalm. *bas* same.

AT *bars* "tiger" > Mong. *bars*, Kh. *baras* or *bar* same.

AT *bas-* "to step on, to oppress" > Mong. *bas-u-* "to oppress".

AT *belgü* "sign, mark" > Mong. *belge* same, etc.

There are many more Ancient Turkic loan-words in Mongolian. In many instances it is impossible, however, to determine whether a word was borrowed from Ancient Turkic into Ancient Mongolian or at a later time, because the oldest Written Mongolian documents date from the XIII century, and the oldest specimens of Colloquial Mongolian (Middle Mongolian) date from the XIII and XIV centuries.

There is a large body of words borrowed by Written Mongolian from Uighur (Uig.) at the time when the Mongols were receiving their Buddhist literature from the Uighurs and translating Buddhist writings from Uighur. Such Uighur borrowings in Written Mongolian attested in the oldest documents dating from the XIV century are, *inter alia*, the following:

Uig. *bilig* "knowledge, wisdom" > Mong. *bilig* same.

Uig. *bire* "mile" > Mong. *bere* same.

Uig. *bošuγ* "salvation, rescue" > Mong. *bošug* "prophecy".

Uig. *bölüg* "part, chapter" > Mong. *bölüg* "chapter".
Uig. *iši* "lady" > Mong. *eši* in *eši qatun* "empress".
Uig. *qilinč* "deed, action" > Mong. *qilinča* (precl.), *kilinče* (class.) "sin, evil deed".
Uig. *quvraɣ* "clergy" > Mong. *quvaraɣ* same.
Uig. *taɣ* "mountain" > Mong. *taɣ* same.
Uig. *tetrü* "on the contrary" > Mong. *tedrü* same.
Uig. *ters* "wrong" > Mong. *ters* "heretic".
Uig. *tültaɣ* "cause, reason for" > Mong. *šiltaɣ* "subterfuge".
Uig. *tusu* "profit" > Mong. *tusa*, Bur. *tuha* same.
Uig. *tayaq* "support, prop" > Mong. *tayaɣ* "staff, walking stick".

These and many other loan-words taken from or through Uighur are found in Buddhist *sūtras* (i.e., sacred books containing Buddha's sermons) of the XIV century.

As mentioned above, the Turkic borrowings in Middle Mongolian are particularly numerous. The *Secret History*, the *Hua-yi yi-yü*, the documents in ḥP'ags-pa script, the Moslem (Arabic and Persian) sources on Mongolian contain a large body of Turkic loan-words.

There are also Turkic words borrowed from modern Turkic languages directly into modern Mongolian. Such borrowings are found in Mongolian languages spoken on territories adjacent to Turkic areas, e.g., in Kalmuck (and in Oirat, in general). In Kalmuck there are numerous Tatar loan-words, such as Kalm. *ayū* "bear" < Tat. *ayu*; Kalm. *burɒntɒg* "a leather rein or leash of a camel" < Turk. *burunduq* same from *burun* "nose"; Kalm. *aršɪm* "arshin, a measure of length (= 24 inches)" < Turk. *aršım* same > Russian *aršin*; Kalm. *bi* "scorpion" < Turk. *bi* "tarantula", etc.

The problems revolving around Turkic loan-words in Mongolian are numerous, but they have been studied very little. The older works are at the present time of little use because they do not distinguish between borrowings and words of common origin, i.e., words inherited from Common Altaic.

Therefore, Németh's and Vladimirtsov's articles on this subject cannot be recommended, being only of historical interest.

The Turkic loan-words deserve, however, much attention because they are the most numerous among all words of foreign origin in Mongolian. It would not be an exaggeration to say that about twenty-five per cent of the Mongolian vocabulary is of Turkic origin.

Bibliography:

Németh, J., "Die türkisch-mongolische Hypothese", *ZDMG* 66 (1912), pp. 549–576.

Poppe, N., "The Turkic Loan-Words in Middle Mongolian", *CAJ* 1 (1955), pp. 36–42.

Vladimircov, B., "Tureckie èlementï v mongoĺskom yazïkĕ", *ZVO* 20 (1911), pp. 153–184.

4.12. Manchu-Tungus loan-words in Mongolian.

Besides Turkic loan-words, there are also Manchu-Tungus borrowings in Mongolian.

Manchu influenced Mongolian very little and gave the latter a few terms referring to administration, and some titles which penetrated into Mongolian at the end of the XVII and in the XVIII century, e.g., Mong. *amban*, Khalkha *ambas* "governor" < Manchu *amban* same; Bur. *šüleŋge* an official rank < Ma. *šuleŋge*; Mong. *qaban*, Kh. *xawan* "officer" < Ma. *xafan* same, etc.

Manchu borrowings other than titles and administrative terms are also found in colloquial Mongolian languages. Dagur has particularly numerous loan-words, due to the fact that the Dagurs until recently used only Manchu (or Chinese) as their literary language. Such borrowings are, e.g., Dag. *jorgon-bē* "the twelfth month of the year" < Ma. *jorɣon biya* same; Dag. *xabil* "turtle" < Ma. *qayilan* same; Dag. *jŭrŭ* "pair" < Ma. *juru* same; Dag. *aidān* "boar" < Ma. *ayidaɣan* same; Dag. *faful-* "to forbid" < Ma. *fafula-* same, etc.

Tungus borrowings occur also in Mongolian. It is unknown whether Written Mongolian has Tungus borrowings, although Mong. *seleme*, Bur. *heleme* "sabre, sword" is very likely to be a Tungus borrowing, because Tungus *seleme* "of iron" is an adjective (with the suff. *-me*) derived from *sele* "iron". Mongolian has neither *sele* "iron" nor the adjective (forming adjectives from nouns) suff. *-ma/-me*. There are, however, some Tungus loan-words in such Mongolian languages which are spoken in areas adjacent to Tungus territories. There is quite a large number of Tungus, to be exact Solon, borrowings in Dagur, e.g., Dag. *giskę* "wolf" < Sol. *gusxę̄* same; Dag. *kękę* "cat" < Sol. *xęxę* same; Dag. *kęŋgęr* "breast, chest" < Sol. *kęŋgęr*, Manchu *kęŋgeri* same; Dag. *kurimultu* "eyelid" < Sol. *xurmultę* "eye lashes"; Dag. *męrgę̄-* "to be sad" < Sol., Evenki *męrgę̄-* same; Dag. *subi* "side" < Sol. *suvęȳ* "short ribs"; Dag. *sarmilta* "eyebrows" < Sol. *sarmilta* same, etc.

The Manchu-Tungus borrowings in Mongolian have not yet been studied.

4.2. Altaic borrowings in Manchu-Tungus.

Manchu-Tungus has some Turkic and numerous Mongolian loan-words.

4.21. Turkic loan-words in Manchu-Tungus.

The Turkic loan-words in Manchu were probably borrowed through Mongolian because most of the words concerned occur also in the latter. Consequently, the words in question are actually Mongolian loan-words in Manchu, although they had been borrowed by the Mongols from the Turks. This is not surprising because Manchu had no immediate contacts with Turkic in historical times.

The Turkic loan-words in Manchu were investigated by Bang.

Spoken Tungus languages, mainly Evenki and Lamut have numerous Turkic loan-words which can be easily recognized as borrowings from Yakut, the only Turkic language now spoken in an area adjacent to Tungus territories, not to mention the fact that in many places Yakuts and Tungus live together.

The Turkic loan-words in Tungus have not yet been studied.

Bibliography:

Bang, W., "Türkisches Lehngut im Mandschurischen", *UJ* 4 (1924), pp. 15–19.

4.22. Mongolian loan-words in Manchu-Tungus.

Manchu has a large number of Mongolian loan-words. No less than twenty-five or thirty per cent of the entire Manchu vocabulary are words of Mongolian origin. This is to be expected because the Mongols were at the time of the oldest contacts on a higher cultural level than the Manchu. The latter took also the Mongolian script and adapted it to their language.

The Mongolian influence on Manchu is so strong that a good knowledge of Mongolian is a prerequisite for successful study of Manchu.

The Mongolian elements in Manchu were investigated by Sanžeyev.

As for the Mongolian loan-words in spoken Tungus languages, they are very numerous but have not been studied. Mongolian loan-words are found in all Tungus languages, including Lamut which is now far away from the Mongolian linguistic area. In Lamut they must be a result of older contacts.

The Mongolian loan-words in Tungus are important for the study of Mongolian language history. Some words were borrowed by the Tungus from Ancient Mongolian, preserving Ancient Mongolian features, e.g., Solon *imayān* "goat" < AMo. *imayān, Written Mongolian *imayan*, Khalkha *yamā* same. Other words go back to Middle Mongolian, e.g., Evenki of Barguzin *hokor sōl* "sacrum" < MMo. *hoqar* "short" + *se'ül* "tail"; Ev. *hükür* "ox" < MMo. *hüker* same.

These borrowings are very useful for reconstruction of older Mongolian forms.

There are, of course, numerous loan-words taken from Modern Mongolian.

Bibliography:

Sanžeev, G. D., "Mańčžuro-mongoĺskie yazïkovïe paralleli", *IAN SSSR* 1930, pp. 601–626, 673–708.

4.3. Altaic borrowings in Chuvash-Turkic languages.

4.31. Mongolian borrowings in Turkic.

Most Turkic languages have no loan-words taken from other Altaic languages but Mongolian. An exception is Yakut which does have some Tungus (Evenki and Lamut) borrowings.

The Mongolian loan-words in Turkic are numerous. They are found in modern and older Turkic languages.

Speaking of older borrowings from Mongolian, one should mention in the first place the Mongolian loan-words in Kuman of the XIV century. All Turkic languages possess Mongolian words which constitute up to thirty-forty per cent of the vocabulary of some Turkic languages. The languages with the highest percentage of Mongolian words are Yakut (no less than twenty-five per cent), Soyot (Tuvinian, with about thirty per cent of borrowings), Karagas and Sagai (no less than twenty-five per cent), Altai and Teleut (about twenty or twenty-five per cent), etc. Such languages as Volga Tatar, Bashkir, Kirghiz, Kazakh, Uzbek, and Chaghatai have also Mongolian words.

The vocabularies of Anatolian, Osman Turkish, and Azerbaijan Turkic are not free from Mongolian elements either.

The Mongolian elements in Turkic vocabulary have been studied very little. There is a study on Mongolian loan-words in Yakut and another one on borrowings in Kuman.

The Mongolian elements in Turkic are important for the study of the Mongolian language history because some Mongolian words were borrowed from Ancient Mongolian, e.g., Kazakh *köbögön* "boy" < AMo. *köbegün* same. Other words were borrowed from Middle Mongolian, e.g., Azerbaijan Turkic *höndür* "high" < MMo. *höndür* same. These and other, similar forms are of great value for the Mongolian historical phonology. They also refute the opinion of some scholars that intervocalic *γ* or *g* in Written Mongolian was only an orthographic feature, standing for the length of the vowel.

Mongolian has also transmitted some suffixes to the Turkic languages, e.g., Yakut *-āččï* < Mo. *-γači*, Kh. *-āči* of the deverbal noun of the actor (Yak. *bïhāččï* "mower, cutter, harvester" from *bïs-* "to cut"); Tuvinian *-qči* < Mo. *-gči*, Kh. *-gči* of the deverbal noun of the actor, e.g., *aliqči* "receiver" from *al-* "to take, receive"; Tatar *-mta* < Mo. *-mta* of deverbal nouns, e.g., *əlǝmtä* "connection, communication" from *əl-*, etc.

Bibliography:

Kałużyński, S., *Mongolische Elemente in der jakutischen Sprache*, Warszawa 1961.

Poppe, N., "Die mongolischen Lehnwörter im Komanischen", *Németh Armağanı*, Ankara 1962.

— "Jakutische Etymologien", *UAJ* 33: 1–2 (1961), pp. 136–141.

4.32. Turkic borrowings in Chuvash.

Chuvash has a large number of borrowings from Turkic, chiefly from Tatar. The Tatar loan-words in Chuvash are easily recognized because they preserve the Tatar features, e.g., Chuv. *čap* "fame" < Tat. *čap* (*č* > Chuv. *ś*, *a* mostly > *u*); Chuv. *čakma* "flint" < Tat. *čaqma*; Chuv. *kapkăn* "trap, iron" (*q* > Chuv. *x*, *a* mostly > *u*) < Tat. *qapqan*; Chuv. *yăpar* "skunk" < Tat. *yïpar* "musk" (*j-* > Chuv. *ś*), etc.

The Tatar loan-words in Chuvash were studied by Poppe.

Bibliography:

Poppe, N., "Die türkischen Lehnwörter im Tschuwassischen", *UJ* 7 (1927), pp. 151–167.

4.33. Mutual borrowings in Turkic.

Mutual borrowings in Turkic are numerous. There are in all Turkic languages borrowings from other Turkic languages. In many cases, the borrowings are recognized easily, because they preserve the features of the original language. To give only a few examples, let it be remarked that in *ayaq*-languages, forms taken from *adaq*-languages are found, and *vice versa*, in *adaq*-languages forms taken from *ayaq*-languages occur, e.g., Tatar *izgə* "sacred",

Kazakh *ezgi* same (both are *ayaq*-languages) = Uig. *edgü*, Tatar of Crimea *eyi* "good"; East Turki *öt* "time" < Uighur *öd* same (East Turki is an *ayaq*-language, and the to be expected form should be *öy*, like in Teleut); Altai, Teleut, etc. *yuduruq* "fist", Kazakh *juduruq* same < *adaq*-language, cf. Tuva *čuduruq*, Yakut *suturuk*, Middle Turkic *yuðruq* "fist", etc.

There are numerous borrowings from Turkish into Azerbaijan Turkic, Tatar, Uzbek, etc.

The problem of loan-words taken by one Turkic language from another has not been studied.

4.4. Altaic borrowings in Korean.

Korean is too little investigated from the historical and comparative linguistic point of view to permit of conclusions in this stage of research. *A priori*, one would not expect to find Turkic loan-words in Korean, but Manchu-Tungus, especially Manchu borrowings, and Middle-Mongolian loan-words have been found in Korean. Some Korean words, indeed, are of Manchu origin, e.g., Kor. *kalbi* "ribs" < Ma. *qalbi/qalbin* "fleshy sides on both sides of the abdomen", Evenki *kalbin* "subcutaneous layer of fat". A number of Mongolion loan-words is found in Middle Korean.

Bibliography:

Lee, Ki-Moon, "Mongolian Loan-Words in Middle Korean" *UAJ* 35, fasc. B (1964), pp. 188–97.

5. CONTACTS OF ALTAIC LANGUAGES WITH OTHER LANGUAGES

5.0. The Altaic languages underwent influences by numerous languages: Chinese, Ancient Semitic languages, Arabic, Sanskrit, Tokharian, Sogdian, Ancient, Middle, and New Persian, Tibetan, and modern Indo-European languages, including English and Russian.

These influences affected some Altaic languages to a higher, other languages to a lower degree. Besides, some Altaic languages experienced direct influence, whereas other Altaic languages were affected only indirectly.

5.1. Chinese elements in Altaic languages.

The Chinese elements in Altaic languages are numerous. A direct Chinese influence is found in Ancient and Middle Turkic, namely Uighur which transmitted some Chinese elements, later on, to Written Mongolian in the XIII–XIV centuries. Modern Chinese influence is noticeable in East Turki.

Direct Chinese influence is also found in Middle Mongolian and in most spoken Mongolian languages (in Outer and Inner Mongolia, Manchuria, Ch'inhai, and Kansu) and in Juchen, Manchu, Goldi, and some other Manchu-Tungus languages.

Chinese has influenced Korean in a particularly strong manner so that the greater portion of the Korean vocabulary is Chinese.

5.11. Chinese elements in Turkic.

The oldest Chinese loan-words were taken by the Turks from Ancient Chinese (ACh.). They have preserved the ancient features in many cases, e.g., Ancient Turkic (AT) *tuγ* "banner" < ACh. **tuk* same; AT *kög* "tune, music" < ACh. **g'og* "tune"; AT *baqšï* "Buddhist monk, teacher" < ACh. **pāk-si*; AT *bir* "brush" < ACh. **pi̯ĕt* same; AT *biti-* "to write" < ACh. **pi̯ĕt* "brush"; AT *luŋ/luu* "dragon" < ACh. *luŋ* same; AT *qunčuy* "princess" < Chinese *kung-chu* same; AT *quŋqïu* "harp" < Chin. *k'ung-hou* same; Uig. *tavčaŋ* "throne" < Chin. *tao-ch'ang* "sacred place"; Uig. *toyïn* "monk" < Chin. *tao-jên* same, etc.

Uighur transmitted many of these loan-words to Mongolian. Consequently, these words are actually Uighur loan-words in Mongolian, because they were taken from Uighur and felt as Uighur words by the Mongols, e.g., Mo. (Written Mongolian) *tuγ* "banner" < Uig. *tuγ* < ACh. **tuk*; Mo. *kög* "tune, music" < Uig. *kög* < ACh. **g'og*; Mo. *bir* "brush" < Uig. *bir* same; Mo. *luu* "dragon" < Uig. *luu* same; Mo. *toyin* "monk of noble descent" < Uig. *toyin* "monk" < Chin. *tao-jên*.

The Chinese elements in Turkic have not been studied.

5.12. Chinese elements in Mongolian.

It would be incorrect to say that the Mongols did not borrow directly from Chinese. They did. One of the oldest borrowings is Mo. *dabčaŋ* "throne" < Chin. *tao-chʻang* "sacred place". It is not a borrowing through Uighur, because Uighur did not have the consonant *d* in initial position, i.e., at the beginning of words, and substituted *t* for the Chinese unaspirated *t*. The Uighur form is *tavčaŋ*, and the Mongols would have borrowed it from Uighur as *tabčaŋ*. Another ancient borrowing is Mo. *noyan* "lord, prince" < Chin. *lao-ye* "lord".

Numerous Chinese words occur in the documents in ḥPʻags-pa script, and still more are found in modern Mongolian languages. It is interesting that one and the same word was borrowed several times and occurs in different forms, e.g., Khalkha *lā* "candle" < Chin. *la* same, and Mo. *lab* "wax" < ACh. *lab* same > Chinese *la*.

The Chinese elements in Mongolian have not been studied.

5.13. Chinese elements in Manchu-Tungus.

More than twenty per cent of the Manchu vocabulary is of Chinese origin. There are also some Chinese loan-words in Goldi, Ulcha, Orochi, Oroki, and Udehe.

The Chinese loan-words in Manchu were studied by Schmidt.

Bibliography:

Schmidt, P., "Chinesische Elemente im Mandschu", *AM* 7 (1931), pp. 573–628.

5.14. Chinese elements in Korean.

A language influenced by Chinese more than any other Altaic language is Korean. More than fifty per cent of Korean vocabulary is Chinese. Korean borrowed from Ancient Chinese and preserved most of the ancient features of the borrowings concerned. The Chinese elements in Korean have been studied thoroughly because of their importance for reconstruction of the Ancient Chinese forms. Sino-Korean is an important field in Chinese historical linguistics. Sinologists have been working on Sino-Korean since the appearance of Karlgren's monumental works.

Unfortunately, the Ancient Chinese elements in Korean have not been taken into consideration by the altaicists. It is known when Ancient Chinese was spoken and ancient loan-words penetrated into Korean. Comparing the modern Korean forms of the words concerned with their Ancient Chinese equivalents, the altaicists could establish a number of sound developments which also might apply to the Altaic stratum in the Korean vocabulary. However, this work has not even been started. This is partly responsible for the fact that the relation of Korean to other Altaic languages raises more doubts than the mutual relations of Turkic, Mongolian, and Manchu-Tungus.

Bibliography:

Karlgren, B., *Études sur la phonologie chinoise*, Stockholm-Leyden 1915–26.
— *Analytic Dictionary of Chinese and Sino-Japanese*, Paris 1923.
— "Grammata Serica", *BMFEA* 12 (1940).

— "Grammata Serica Recensa", *BMFEA* 29 (1957).
— "A Compendium of Phonetics in Ancient and Archaic Chinese", *BMFEA* 26 (1954).
Koreĭskiĭ yazïk, Sbornik stateĭ, Moskva 1961.
Voprosï koreĭskogo i kitaĭskogo yazïkoznaniya, Leningrad 1958.

5.2. Tibetan elements in the Altaic languages.

Tibetan loan-words occur in Mongolian. They appeared as a consequence of the spread of Buddhism which was accomplished in the XVI–XVII centuries and resulted in the foundation of numerous monasteries in which Tibetan was the only language of worship and learning.

Numerous Tibetan words, not only religious terms, are found in Monguor and Santa. Mongolian spoken in the Mongolian People's Republic and in Inner Mongolia, Buriat, and Oirat (including Kalmuck) have Tibetan religious terms, proper names, some numerals, names of the days, and names of objects which are used in monasteries, e. g., Khalkha *biamba* "Saturday" < Tib. *spen-pa*; Kh. *donir* "a rank in Buddhist monasteries" < Tib. *mgron-gñer*; Kh. *dewājin* "paradise" < Tib. *bde-ba-can*; Kh. *xorlō* "prayer wheel" < Tib. *ḫkor-lo*; Kh. *güŋgerwā* "shrine" < Tib. *kun-dgaḫ-ra-ba*; Kh. *jiwā* "ten million" < Tib. *bye-ba*; Kh. *diŋwa* "carpet" < Tib. *gtiŋ-ba*; Kh. *migma* "chess" < Tib. *mig-dmag*, etc.

From these and other Tibetan loan-words the conclusion can be drawn that the Mongolian forms do not reflect the Tibetan orthography but the spoken pronunciation, to be exact, the pronunciation of Tibetan as spoken in Mongolian monasteries.

There are no works on Tibetan elements in Mongolian.

5.3. Ancient Indo-European elements in Altaic languages.

The ancient Indo-European languages which exercised a relatively strong influence upon the Altaic languages are Sanskrit, Tokharian, Sogdian (and some other Iranian languages). Loan-words from these languages are found in Ancient Turkic and Mongolian.

Bibliography:
Menges, K. H., "Indo-European Influences on Ural-Altaic Languages", *Word* 1: 2 (1945).

5.31. Sanskrit, Tokharian, Saka, and Sogdian elements in Turkic.

Buddhism came to the Ancient Turks in the VIII century and brought Buddhist religious works translated into Ancient Turkic. The script was either Uighur or Brāhmī. The language of the original Buddhist works was Sanskrit (Skr.), but it is doubtful that many books were translated into Turkic directly from Sanskrit. Many books were translated from Tokharian (an Indo-European *centum*-language spoken in the first centuries A.D. in some parts of Turkestan and extinct since) or Sogdian, an Eastern Iranian language presently extinct, which was close to Yaghnobi and Ossetian and was spoken in what is now Tadjikistan and the adjacent areas of Uzbekistan, USSR. Therefore, many Sanskrit words penetrated into Turkic through Tokharian or Sogdian, displaying Tokharian or Sogdian features respectively.

Here are a few examples of words probably borrowed directly from Sanskrit into Turkic: *amṛta* "immortal" < Skr. *amṛta*; *kušal* "meritorious" < Skr. *kuśala*; *maytrī* "love, kindness" < Skr. *maitrī*; *višnu* "name of a god" < Skr. *viṣṇu*; *sadu* "good" < Skr. *sadhu*; *batïr* "bowl of a mendicant" < Skr. *pātra*, etc.

The following Sanskrit words were, however, borrowed through Tokharian-A: *čadik* "tale about one of the former lives of Buddha" < Tokh.-A *jātak* < Skr. *jātaka*; *dyan* "meditation" < Tokh.-A *dhyāṃ* < Skr. *dhyāna*; *kinari* "a legendary creature, half-man and half-horse" < Tokh.-A *kinnare* < Skr. *kiṃnara*; *klp* < Tokh.-A *kalp* < Skr. *kalpa* "eon, Buddha period"; *kšan* "moment" < Tokh.-A < Skr. *kṣaṇa*; *nirvan* "nirvana" < Tokh.-A *nervāṃ* < Skr. *nirvāṇa*; *madar* < Tokh.-A *mātār* < Skr. *makara* "a sea monster", etc.

There are Sanskrit loan-words borrowed through Tokharian-B, otherwise called also Kuchan, e.g., *asanki* "innumerable" < Kuch. *asaṃkhyai* < Skr. *asaṃkhyeya*; *avyakirt* < Kuch. < Skr. *avyākṛta* "unexplained", etc.

Ancient Turkic had also Tokharian borrowings which were not of Sanskrit origin, e.g., *nayvaziki* "benevolent spirits" < Tokh.-A *naivāsik*.

A few borrowings from Saka (an Iranian language which existed until the end of the first millenium A.D.) are also known, e.g., *ton* "garment" < Sak. *thauna*.

Numerous Sanskrit words were borrowed through Sogdian (Sogd.), an Eastern Iranian language, e.g., *vrxar* "monastery" < Sogd. *βarxār* < Skr. *vihāra*; *nizvanï* "lust, attachment" < Sogd. *nizβān*, a corruption of a Sanskrit word; *arzi / irži* "anahoret" < Sogd. *risay* (rz'y) < Skr. *ṛṣi*; *čaqšaput / čaqšapat* "prescription, commandment" < Sogd. *čixsāpaδ* < Skr. *śikṣāpada*, etc.

Side by side, other Sogdian words, not only words of Sanskrit origin, were also transmitted. These borrowings include original Sogdian words and words of foreign origin. Such Sogdian words are: *ažun* "life, existence" < Sogd. *āžun*; *možak* "teacher" < Sogd. *mōčak* "archbishop"; *tamu* "hell" < Sogd. *tamu*; *känt* "city" < Sogd. *kanth*; *xormuzta* "Indra" (a god) < Sgd. *xormuzda*; *moγuč* "the Magi" (Christian) < Sgd. *moγoč*; *satir* "stater" (a weight) < Sgd. *satīr* < Greek *statḗr*; *nom* "doctrine, religion, dharma" < Sgd. *nom* < Greek *nómos* "law"; *niγošak* "disciple" < Sgd. *niγōšak*, etc.

Ancient Turkic, including the older Uighur language of the VIII–X centuries, possessed also some loan-words taken from Middle Iranian, i.e., Parthian (which existed until the end of the first millenium A.D.) and Middle Persian (or Pahlavi in the III–X centuries A.D.), e.g., *amvrdšn* "collection" < Parth.; *amari* "some, innumerable" < MIr. *ahmāra, cf. Saka *ahumara*; *šäkär* "sugar" < MIr. *šakar*; *rošn* "light" < MIr.; *ančmn* "crowd" < MPers. *hnzmn*; *az* "greed" < MPers. *āz*; *maxistak* "presbyter" < MPers. *mahistag*, etc.

5.32. Iranian elements in Modern Turkic languages.

The Iranian influence is particularly strong in Turkish, Azerbaijan Turkic, Turkmenian, Uzbek, East Turki, and is also felt in Kumyk, Karachai-Balkar, Tatar, and Bashkir.

5.3. Ancient Indo-European Elements in Altaic Languages

The Iranian vocabulary has greatly influenced the Turkic vocabulary. Turkish, Azerbaijan Turkic, Uzbek, etc. have hundreds of Persian words. Individual Persian words have reached as far as Altai Turkic, e.g., Altai and Teleut *qudai* "God" < Pers. *xudai / xudā*.

Persian has also greatly influenced the phonemic system of some Turkic languages. Under Persian influence, such phonemes as /ž, h/ appeared in all Turkic languages mentioned above. Moreover, the phonological vowel system completely changed in most dialects of the Uzbek language. The "Iranized" dialects of Uzbek have even lost the original vowel harmony.

Equally strong is Iranian influence in morphology and syntax. Osman Turkish, Azerbaijan Turkic, Uzbek, etc. have taken the Persian *izafet*-construction, i.e., constructions of the type *ämri ma'rūf* "the commandment of the decency".

Many Turkic languages borrowed the Persian subordinative conjunction *ki* "that", e.g., Turkish *yaziyor ki* "he writes that ...", the result being that compound clauses appeared which are identical with certain types of Persian compound clauses.

The Iranian influence has resulted in great structural changes of a number of Turkic languages which, in consequence, acquired some "non-Altaic" featrues.

Speaking of Iranian influence, numerous Ossetian loan-words in Karachai-Balkar should be mentioned.

5.33. Of the languages closest to the Turkic languages Chuvash also underwent Iranian influence. However, the Iranian influence upon Chuvash did not affect phonology, the grammatical structure, and syntax, but manifested itself only in vocabulary.

Chuvash has a number of Iranian loan-words, e.g., *ärnä* < **aðina* "week" < Pers. *āðina*; *sărnay* "flute" < Pers. *surnāy*; *sănčăr* "chain" < Pers. *zenǰir*, etc. Some of the Iranian loan-words were taken directly from Persian, e.g., *ärnä* "week". Others may have been obtained through Turkic.

5.34. Ancient Indo-European loan-words in Mongolian.

Mongolian has a number of words of Indo-European origin. In the first place, there are Sanskrit (Skr.) words, e.g., Mo. (Written Mongolian) *rasiyan*, Khalkha *aršān* "nectar, holy water, medicinal water, curative spring" < Skr. *rasāyana*; Mo. *adiya* "sun, Sunday" < Skr. *adya*; Mo. *ariya* "noble, sublime, pure, holy" < Skr. *ārya*; Mo. *badir*, Kh. *badar* "mendicant's bowl" < Skr. *pātra*, etc.

Some of these words may have been taken from Tibetan translations of Sanskrit originals, because sometimes Sanskrit words are given in transcription in Tibetan translations, but many of them were certainly taken through Uighur.

This is evident from the fact that in many cases Sanskrit words in Mongolian display Uighur forms, e.g., Mo. *badir* "mendicant's bowl" < Uig. *batïr* < Skr. *pātra*; Mo. *erdeni / erdini* "jewel" < Uig. *erdini* < Skr. *ratna*; Mo. *nayud* "limitless" < Uig. *nayut* < Skr. *nayuta*; Mo. *ǰandan*, Kh. *ʒandan* "sandal wood" < Uig. *čintan* < Skr. *candana*; Mo. *čindamani* "a jewel which fulfills all desires" < Uig. *čintamani* < Skr. *cintāmaṇi*, etc.

Therefore, these and many other Sanskrit words are borrowings in Mongolian from Turkic, in other words, indirect borrowings from Sanskrit.

Likewise, the Tokharian, Sogdian, and possibly other ancient Indo-European loan-words in Mongolian are borrowings from Uighur, e.g., Mo. *nom* "doctrine, dharma, book" < Uig. *nom* id. < Sogd. *nom* id. < Greek *nómos* "law"; Mo. *kinari* "half-man half-horse, a mythical creature, kind of centaur" < Uig. *kinari* < Tokh. *kinnare* < Skr. *kiṃnara*; Mo. *čedig* "tale about Buddha's previous rebirths" < Uig. *čadik* < Tokh.-A *jātak* < Skr. *jātaka*; Mo. *gšan*, Kh. *agšan* "moment, instant" < Uig. *kšan* < Tokh.-A < Skr. *kṣana*; Mo. *diyan*, Kh. *dayān* "meditation" < Uig. *dyan* < Tokh.-A *dhyāṃ* < Skr. *dhyāna*; Mo. *tamu* "hell" < Uig. *tamu* < Sogd. *tamu*; MMo. *bor* "wine" < Uig. *bor* < MPers. *bhor*; Mo. *jada* "rain stone" < Uig. *yadu*, Chag., Osm. *yada* < Pers. *jādū* "magic"; MMo. *tana* "pearl" < Middle Turkic *tana* < Pers. *dāna* "grain, pearl"; Mo. *čačir* "tent" < MTurk. *čačir / čatir* < MPers. *čādar* "tent, pavillion", etc.

There are probably few words which penetrated into Mongolian directly from Persian, bypassing Turkic. Therefore, the socalled ancient Indo-European loan-words in Mongolian are actually borrowings from Turkic, and in the latter they are direct borrowings from Sogdian, Tokharian, etc.

Bibliography:

Ramstedt, G. J., "The Relation of the Altaic Languages to Other Language Groups", *JSFOu* 53: 1 (1947), pp. 15–26.

Vladimircov, B. Ya., "Mongolica I, Ob otnošenii mongoĺskogo yazïka k indoevropeĭskim yazïkam Sredneĭ Azii", *ZKV* 1 (1925), pp. 305–341.

5.4. Semitic influences upon Altaic.

There are a few very ancient Semitic loan-words in Altaic languages. It is possible that they were borrowed by Common Altaic from one of the ancient Semitic languages.

One of such words is Manchu *folxo* "hammer", Middle Mongolian *haluqa* < Common Mongolian **paluqa* < Babylonian-Assyrian *pilaqqu*, Sumerian *balag* "ax".

It is hardly possible that Common Altaic or any most ancient Altaic language might ever have been a neighbor of Akkadian or Babylonian, not to mention the fact that direct borrowing was hardly possible for reasons of chronology. Therefore, it is to be assumed that this word penetrated into Altaic through an intermedium which, in the present stage of research, cannot be determined.

There are numerous relatively new Arabic loan-words in most of the Turkic languages and particularly in Turkish, Azerbaijan Turkic, Turkmenian, Uzbek, East Turki, Kumyk, and Tatar. Arabic loan-words were even more numerous in Osman Turkish, because Modern Turkish rid itself of many Arabic borrowings after the reforms carried out in the 1930s.

Not only Arabic loan-words penetrated into various Turkic languages but also some Arabic grammatical forms found their way into Turkish, Azerbaijan

Turkic, etc. The Arabic elements in Turkic are even stronger than the Persian elements. Arabic words and grammatical forms penetrated into Turkic after the X century, when Islam was beginning to spread among some Turkic peoples. First, they invaded the Turkic languages of the Turkmen group (i.e., Turkish, Azerbaijan Turkic, and Turkmenian) and those spoken in Turkestan, and from there they were carried to the Tatars and other Turkic peoples.

Some Arabic words found their way to the Mongols. There are a few words of Arabic origin in Mongolian, mostly in Written Mongolian. They were not borrowed directly from Arabic but through Turkic. Therefore, such words as Written Mongolian (Mo.) *iblis* "evil spirit" < Ar. *iblis*; Mo. *araki* "liquor, alcoholic beverage made of milk" < Turk. *araqï* < Ar. *'araq* "wine", etc. are not exactly Arabic words in Mongolian but rather Turkic borrowings of Arabic origin.

There are also Hebrew borrowings in Karai, because the Karai Turks profess a modified Jewish religion and use, in their religious literature, the Hebrew alphabet.

Bibliography:

Menges, K. H., "Zwei alt-mesopotamische Lehnwörter im Altajischen", *UAJ* 25 (1953), pp. 299–304.

Poppe, N., "Ein altes Kulturwort in den altaischen Sprachen", *StOF* 19: 5 (1953), pp. 23–25.

Vladimircov, B. Ya., "Arabskie slova v mongoĺskom", *ZKV* 5 (1930), pp. 73–82.

5.5 Modern European influences upon Altaic.

Loan-words taken from European languages occur in all Altaic languages.

There are numerous English, German, French, and Italian borrowings in Turkish. English, French, and Latin words (the latter penetrated through English) occur in Korean. Words of English, French, Italian, Latin, and Greek penetrated through Russian into all Turkic languages spoken in the USSR, into some Mongolian languages (Buriat, Kalmuck, Khalkha), and into the Manchu-Tungus languages (Evenki, Lamut, Nanai).

The Slavonic languages, in the first place, Russian, have influenced the Altaic languages enormously. Thus, Polish words were borrowed by Karai, numerous Russian words have virtually invaded all Turkic languages spoken in the USSR, Mongolian (mainly Kalmuck and Buriat, to a lesser degree Khalkha), and all Manchu-Tungus languages with the exception of Manchu, of course. Not only Russian words like *sovet* or Russianized western words like *revolúciya* "revolution" or *organizaciya* "organization" but numerous calques from Russian have appeared, e.g., Khalkha *xereg dēr* "in reality" (lit. "on the deed" < Russ. *na dele*), Buriat *ńūr* "person, legal person" (lit. "face" < Russ. *ličnostʹ* "person, individual" from *lico* "face"), Tatar *yörən-* "to go for a walk" (a reflexive verb derived from *yör-* "to walk", lit. "to walk oneself" after Russian *proxaživatśa* or *progulivatśa*), etc.

In recent translations from Russian, influence of Russian syntax upon Buriat, Kalmuck, Tatar, Bashkir, and many other languages is felt rather strongly.

6. ALTAIC INFLUENCES UPON OTHER LANGUAGES

6.1. Altaic elements in Indo-European languages.

The Altaic languages were influenced by ancient and new Indo-European languages, but they also influenced, in their turn, some Indo-European languages.

There are some Turkic and Mongolian loan-words in Persian, and occasionally Turkish or Mongolian words are found even in English, French, and German, e.g., Engl. *koumiss* "fermented liquor of mare's milk" < Turk.; Fr. *chabraque* "saddle cover" < Turk.; Germ. *Jurte* "yurt, a nomad dwelling" < Turk. However, such words are few and they have not become an integral part of the vocabulary of the languages concerned, being felt as foreign words and occurring mostly in special literature, in scholarly works or novels dealing with Turkey or Mongolia respectively. The main bulk of the population does not even know them. To give an example, one would hardly expect an average Londoner or New Yorker to know what *koumiss* or *yataghan* is.

A very strong influence, however, was exercized by some Altaic languages upon Slavonic. Some scholars as Menges believe that the ancient Slavs and some Altaic peoples might have been neighbors as early as in the first century A.D. This is possible, because there are very ancient Altaic borrowings in Slavonic languages.

There are numerous Altaic words in Slavonic languages, but Menges ascribes to Altaic influence also some features in Slavonic phonology and morphology. However, as said above, it is the Slavonic vocabulary which underwent the strongest Altaic influence.

One area of vocabulary of most of the languages is particularly open to foreign influence. This is the official terminology, referring to titles and ranks. Menges investigated the Proto-Bulgarian inscriptions discovered in the region of Shumen and Novi Pazar, which go back to the first half of the IX century A.D. In these inscriptions, he found non-Slavonic titles which he identified with Turkic titles. In the same inscriptions non-Slavonic tribal and proper names also occur.

Some ancient words of Altaic origin still occur in Russian and Ukrainian, e.g., Russ. *gaĭ*, Ukr. *haĭ* "coppice" < Middle Mongolian *hoi* "coppice"; Russ. *turʹma* "prison" < Turk. *türmä*; Russ. *kirpič* "brick" < Turk. *kerpič*, etc. They were investigated by Menges.

Menges' works on Slavonic and Altaic relations are the most recent in this field. There exists, however, an extensive literature on Altaic, mainly Turkic loan-words in Slavonic languages and, in particular, in Russian.

Russian has hundreds of Turkic loan-words. Some of them occurred in Old Russian, other borrowings appeared in later periods. The oldest Turkic loan-words in Russian are of Kuman (Cuman, Polovetzian) origin. Other loan-words were taken from Old Tatar, the main language of the Golden Horde. There are loan-words of Crimean, Turkish, modern Tatar, Kazakh, and even Yakut origin. Many Russians living in areas with predominantly Turkic population speak the local Turkic languages fluently. There are numerous Russians who speak Tatar, Uzbek, Kazakh, or Yakut, depending on the area.

A general work on Turkic loan-words in Slavonic languages is that by Miklosich. It is obsolete and contains errors but it is the only general work on this subject. The Turkic origin of many Russian words is indicated in the etymological dictionaries of the Russian language by Preobraženskiĭ and Vasmer. Of these two, Vasmer's work is the most reliable collection of Turkic words in Russian, but it is incomplete and gives the Turkic or Mongolian origin only of such words which were included in the dictionary, whereas numerous other words have not been included. Therefore, a complete dictionary of Turkic loan-words in Russian (including Old and Modern Russian, both the literary language and the dialects) is one of the most urgent tasks.

One work of old Russian literature has been studied very thoroughly from the point of view of lexical borrowings. This is the *Slovo o polku Igoreve*, the so-called Igor Song, compiled in 1182, a poem written in Old Russian. The text contains a relatively large number of Altaic (Avar, Turkic), Persian, and Arabic loan-words which became the subject of special research carried out by Melioranskiĭ, Korš, Prince, Malov, and Menges, the latest and the most up to date work being that by Menges.

Speaking of Mongolian loan-words in Russian, it should be pointed out that they are not numerous and have not been studied. Most of them are recent borrowings, e.g., from Buriat into the local Russian dialects or from Khalkha into the speech of Russians living in Mongolia, e.g., *kačerik* "a two-year old heifer" < Bur. *xaširig*; *xalzanka* "a horse which has a white spot on the head" < Bur. *xalzan* "blaze"; *tarïk* "kind of sour milk" < Bur. *tarag* id.; *na zaxadïre* "on the market" < Khalkha *zaxa dēr* "on the edge" (i.e., "on the edge of the city"), etc.

There are also some Tungus loan-words in the local Russian dialects.

It was mentioned above that the Iranian languages had exercized a strong influence upon the Altaic languages. On the other hand, there are numerous Mongolian and Turkic elements in Iranian. The Mongolian elements in Modern Persian were studied by Doerfer. His book is useful as a collection of material but its defect is that no distinction is made between Mongolian loan-words in Persian and Mongolian words which occur in Persian literature but are not integral part of the Persian vocabulary, and, second, it does not deal with the phonetic treatment of the words borrowed from Mongolian into Persian.

Bibliography:

Dmitriev, N. K., "O tyurkskix élementax russkogo yazïka", *Leksikografičeskiĭ sbornik* III, Moskva 1958, pp. 3–47.

Doerfer, Gerhard, *Türkische und mongolische Elemente im Neupersischen*, Band I: Mongolische Elemente im Neupersischen, Wiesbaden 1963.

Korš, F., "Tureckie élementï v yazïkě Slova o polku Igorevě", *IORYaS* 8: 4 (1904), pp. 1–58.

— "Po povodu vtoroĭ staťyi prof. Melioranskago o tureckix élementax v yazïkě Slova o polku Igorevě", *ibid.*, 11: 1 (1906), pp. 259–315.

Kraelitz-Greifenhorst, F. von, "Corollarien zu Miklosich 'Die türkischen Elemente in den südost- und osteuropäischen Sprachen'", *SWAW* 166: 4 (1911), pp. 1–65.
Malov, S. E., "Tyurkizmï v yazïke Slova o Polku Igoreve", *IAN SSSR* 5: 2 (1947), pp. 129–139.
Melioranskiĭ, P. M., "Tureckie èlementï v yazïkě Slova o polku Igorevě", *IORYaS* 7: 2 (1902), pp. 273–302.
— "Vtoraya staťya o tureckix èlementax v yazïkě Slova o polku Igorevě", *ibid.*, 10: 2 (1905), pp. 66–92.
Menges, K. H., "Influences altaïques en Slave", *Bull. de la Classe des lettres et des sciences morales et politiques* 5-e sér., t. 44 (1958), pp. 518–541.
— "Altaic Elements in the Proto-Bulgarian Inscriptions", *Byzantion* 21 (1951), pp. 85–118.
— "Altaic Loanwords in Slavonic", *Language* 20 (1944), pp. 66–72.
— "Altajische Kulturwörter im Slavischen", *UAJ* 33 (1961), pp. 107–116.
— "On Some Loanwords from or via Turkic in Old Russian", *Mélanges Fuad Köprülü*, İstanbul 1953, pp. 369–390.
— "Altajische Lehnwörter im Slavischen", *ZSPh* 23 (1955), pp. 327–334.
— *The Oriental Elements in the Vocabulary of the Oldest Russian Epos, The Igoŕ Tale*, Suppl. to Word, vol. 7 (1951), Monogr. No. 1.
Miklosich, Fr., *Die Fremdwörter in den slavischen Sprachen*, DWAW (Philologisch-historische Klasse), 15 (1867).
— *Die türkischen Elemente in den südost- und osteuropäischen Sprachen*, DWAW (Ph.-hist. Kl.), 34 (1884), 35 (1885); Nachtrag: *ibid.* 37 (1889), 38 (1890).
Peisker, J., Die älteren Beziehungen der Slawen zu Turkotataren und Germanen, *Vierteljahrschrift für Sozial- und Wirtschaftsgeschichte* 3 (1905).
Prince, J. D., "Tatar Material in Old Russian", *Proceedings of the American Philosophical Society* 58 (1919), pp. 74–88.
Vasmer, M., *Russisches etymologisches Wörterbuch*, I–III, Heidelberg 1953, 1955, 1958.

6.2. Altaic elements in Georgian.

There are Turkic and Middle Mongolian loan-words in Georgian. Dr. D. M. Farquhar has made a list of such words but it has not yet been published.

6.3. Altaic elements in Uralic.

Some Uralic languages have a considerable number of Altaic, mostly Turkic loan-words.

6.31. Altaic elements in Samoyed.

An excellent study of Altaic elements in Sayan Samoyed is Joki's book. Southern Samoyed (Kamass) has a considerable number of Altaic, namely Turkic and Mongolian loan-words. An old loan-word is Kam. *šili* < Common Altaic **kili* > Turk. *kiš* "sable". New borrowings from Turkic and Mongolian through Turkic are very numerous.

Bibliography:
Joki, A., *Die Lehnwörter des Sajansamojedischen*, Helsinki 1952.

6.32. Altaic elements in Hungarian.

Hungarian possesses a large body of Altaic loan-words. Some of them were taken from an Altaic r- and l- language close to ancient Volga Bulgarian and Chuvash. A careful analysis of these words leads to the conclusion that they were taken from several dialects closely related to Bulgarian and Ancient Chuvash (the latter may have been identical with Bulgarian). Other loan-words are of younger date and were taken from Turkish. There are no Mongolian loan-words in Hungarian.

Bibliography:

Gombocz, Z., *Die bulgarisch-türkischen Lehnwörter in der ungarischen Sprache*, Helsinki 1912.

Ligeti, L., "A propos des éléments 'altaïques' de la langue hongroise", *ALH* 11: 1–2 (1961), pp. 15–42.

Poppe, N., "On Some Altaic Loanwords in Hungarian", *UAS* 1 (1960), pp. 139–147.

6.33. Chuvash elements in Finno-Ugric.

Chuvash has influenced the Volga Finnic (i.e., Mordvan and Mari) and the Permian (i.e., Udmurt and Komi) languages. The loan-words in question were studied by Räsänen and Wichmann.

Bibliography:

Räsänen, M., *Die tschuwassischen Lehnwörter im Tscheremissischen*, Helsinki 1920.

Raun, A., "The Chuvash Borrowings in Zyrian", *JAOS* 77: 1 (1957), pp. 40–45.

Wichmann, Y., *Die tschuwassischen Lehnwörter in den permischen Sprachen*, Helsinki 1903.

6.34. Turkic elements in Finno-Ugric.

A number of Turkic loan-words is found in Finno-Ugric languages. There are Tatar words in Mari, Mordvan, and in Permian languages. Borrowings from Turkic languages of Siberia are found in Ob Ugric, i.e., Vogul (Mansi) and Ostiak (i.e., Khanty).

Bibliography:

Kannisto, A., "Die tatarischen Lehnwörter im Wogulischen", *FUF* 17, pp. 1ff.

Paasonen, H., "Die türkischen Lehnwörter im Mordwinischen", *JSFOu* 15: 2 (1897).

— "Über die türkischen Lehnwörter im Ostjakischen", *FUF* 2 (1902), pp. 81–137.

Räsänen, M., *Die tatarischen Lehnwörter im Tscheremissischen*, Helsinki 1923.

— "Türkische Lehnwörter in den permischen Sprachen und im Tscheremissischen", *FUF* 23 (1935), pp. 103–107.

Wichmann, Y., "Die türkischen Lehnwörter im Tscheremissischen", *FUF* 16 A, pp. 32ff.

7. CHARACTERISTIC STRUCTURAL FEATURES OF THE ALTAIC LANGUAGES

7.0. The Altaic languages have many features in common which distinguish them from many other languages (e.g., Indo-European, Semitic, Sino-Tibetan, etc.) and render them close to each other. Common features are found in the fields of phonemics, morphophonemics, inflection and word-formation, and syntax. The following characteristic general features of the Altaic languages will be discussed:
1. Opposition of long vowels *versus* short vowels;
2. Stress and pitch;
3. Vowel and consonant harmony;
4. Internal sandhi;
5. Word-structure:
    A. Agglutination
    B. The stem
    C. The suffixes
6. Word categories.

7.1. Long vowels.

Long vowels occur in all Altaic languages. Length is a phonemic feature, i.e., long and short vowels are different phonemes.

There are two kinds of long vowels, namely, primary and secondary long vowels. The primary long vowels were long vowels even in the oldest stage of the languages in question, as far as it can be reconstructed. It is possible, however, that the length is due to a particular type of accent. The secondary long vowels have, however, developed from combinations of VC (i.e., vowel and consonant) or VCV (i.e., vowel and consonant and vowel).

7.11. Long vowels in Turkic.

The primary long vowels are still preserved as long vowels (or diphthongs) in Turkmenian and Yakut, e.g., Trkm. *āt* "name" = Yak. *āt*; Trkm. *āč* "hungry" = Yak. *ās*; Trkm. *bār* "is" = Yak. *bār* "present"; Trkm. *gāz* "goose" = Yak. *xās*; Trkm. *yāz* "spring" = Yak. *sās*; Trkm. *ōt* "fire" = Yak. *uot*; Trkm. *güök* "blue" = Yak. *küöx*; Trkm. *düört* "four" = Yak. *tüört*, etc. These long vowels were inherited from Ancient Turkic (cf. Uig. *oot* "fire"). They have been preserved in many loan-words in Hungarian, taken from Ancient Bulgarian or another ancient language close to the latter, e.g., Hung. *nyár* "summer" < *ńār* > Common Turkic *yāz* > Trkm. *yāz* "spring".

In most of the Turkic languages the primary long vowels became short and converged with the short vowels. But traces are still found. Thus, in Turkish an original voiceless consonant following a primary long vowel is voiced, e.g., *od* < **ōt* "fire" but *ot* "hay"; *oda* < **ōtaγ* "room", etc. In some Turkic languages original long vowels have resulted in short vowels but of another quality, e.g., Sagai *ut* < **ōt* "fire", *ül* < **ȫl* "wet, damp", etc.

The secondary long vowels have developed from VC or VCV. Ancient and Middle Turkic did not have these long vowels. The latter appeared in Modern Turkic languages, e.g., Ancient Turkic *oγul* "son" > Tuvinian, Sagai, Shor *ōl*, Altai, Kirghiz *ūl*, Yakut *uol*; AT *aγïz* "mouth" > Tuv., Sag., Shor *ās*, Alt. *ōs*, Kirg. *ōz*, Yak. *uos*; AT *taγ* "mountain" > Alt. *tū*, Kirg. *tō*, etc.

It is to be noted that of languages still preserving the primary long vowels Turkmenian does not have secondary long vowels, but Yakut does have both primary and secondary long vowels, in few instances the primary and secondary long vowels being represented in a different manner: **āč* > Yak. *ās* "hungry" but **taγ* > Yak. *tïa* (but not *tā*). In most instances the primary and secondary long vowels have converged: **yōq* > Yak. *suox* "not" and **yoγan* > Yak. *suon* "thick"; **tȫrt* > Yak. *tüört* "four" and **ögrän-* > Yak. *üörän-* "to study", etc.

Bibliography:

Dmitriev, N. K., "Dolgie glasnïe v turkmenskom yazïke", *Issledovaniya po sravnitelnoi grammatike tyurkskix yazïkov*, I, Fonetika, Moskva 1955, pp. 182–191.
— "Dolgie glasnïe v yakutskom yazïke", *ibid.*, pp. 192–197.
— "Vtoričnïe dolgotï v tyurkskix yazïkax", *ibid.*, pp. 198–202.
— "Dolgie glasnïe v gagauzskom yazïke", *ibid.*, pp. 203–207.
Isxakov, F. G., "Dolgie glasnïe v tyurkskix yazïkax", *ibid.*, pp. 160–174.
Palmbax, A. A., "Dolgie i poludolgie glasnïe tuvinskogo yazïka", *ibid.*, pp. 175–181.
Räsänen, M., *Zur Lautgeschichte der türkischen Sprachen*, Helsinki 1949, pp. 64–73, 80–95, 111–135.
— "Türkische Miszellen", *StOF* 25: 1 (1960), pp. 3–19.

7.12. Long vowels in Chuvash.

The primary long vowels are in most cases undistinguishable from short vowels, e.g., Chuv. *xur* < **qār* "goose" = Yak. *xās*, Trkm. *gāz*; Chuv. *ut* < **at* "horse" = Yak., Trkm. *at*. However, in some instances traces of primary long vowels can be found, e.g., *ō* > *ăva*, *ē* > **iä* > *ya*: Chuv. *kăvak* < **kȫk* "blue" = Yak. *küöx*, Trkm. *güök*; Chuv. *tăvattă* < **tȫrt* "four" = Yak. *tüört*, Trkm. *düört*; Chuv. *yal* < **ial* < **iäl* < **ēl* "village".

Chuvash does not have secondary long vowels.

Bibliography:

Ramstedt, G. J., "Zur Frage nach der Stellung des Tschuwassischen", *JSFOu* 38: 1 (1922), pp. 12–13.

7.13. The long vowels in Mongolian.

The long and short vowels are in phonemic opposition to each other, e.g., Khalkha *dēl* "coat, robe" and *del* "mane"; *yāsan* "what kind of" and *yasan* "osseous, made of bone"; *tōs* "dust" and *tos* "fat, grease, butter", etc.

7.1. Long Vowels

The primary long vowels are still found in Dagur and Monguor, e.g., Dag. *tāųn* "five", Mng. *tāwęn* < **tābun* = Kh. *tawa*, Mo. (Written Mongolian) *tabun*; Mng. *dālī* < **dālū* "shoulder" = Kh. *dal*, Mo. *dalu* (= Trkm. *yāl* < **dāl* "mane", Yak. *sāl* < **čāl* < **ǰāl* < **dāl* "the fat-layer under the mane"); Dag. *mōd* < **mōdun* "tree", Mng. *mōdi* "wood" = Kh. *mod*, Mo. *modun* (cf. Evenki *mō*, Manchu *moo* < **mō* "tree"), etc.

The secondary long vowels occur only in modern Mongolian languages. They are the result of the development of VCV, the second vowel having been stressed, e.g., Kh. *tāl-* < **tapàla-* "to love, to caress" (cf. AT *tapla-* "to love"); Kh. *sā-*, Mo. *saγa-* < **sagà-* "to milk" (cf. Middle Turkic *saγ-*); Kh. *tōno* "the round frame of the smoke opening in the roof of a yurt", Mo. *toγori-* < **togàri-* "to rotate, encircle" (cf. Chaghatai *toγalaq* "round"); Buriat *bōrlo-* < **bogàrla-* "to torment", Mo. *boγorla-* "to cut the throat" (cf. Turkish *boγaz* "throat", *boγazla-* "to cut the throat"); Bur. *burū* < **bīragù* "calf", Mo. *biraγu* (cf. Chuv. *păru*, Turkish *bīzaγï*), etc.

Bibliography:

Hattori, Sh., "The Length of Vowels in Proto-Mongol", *SM* 1: 12 (1959), pp. 3–10.

Poppe, N., *Introduction to Mongolian Comparative Studies*, Helsinki 1955, pp. 59–76.

— "The Primary Long Vowels in Mongolian", *JSFOu* 63: 2 (1962), pp. 1–19.

7.14. The Manchu-Tungus languages also have long vowels. The long and short vowels are in phonemic opposition: Evenki *illę* "they start entering" – *illę* "body"; *ęlę̄* "here" – *ęlę* "only"; *ūrę* "they scrape" – *urę* "mountain", etc.

There are primary and secondary long vowels.

Primary long vowels are found in the following examples: Evenki, Solon, Negidal, Orochi, Udehe, Oroki, Ulcha, Goldi *sā-*, Lamut *hā-* "to know" (= Turkmen *sān* "number", *sāy-* "to count", Yakut *āx-* < **sāq-* "to count", Ancient Turkic *sa-*, probably *sā-* "to count"); Ev., Lam., Sol., Neg., Orochi, Oroki, Ud., Ulcha, Goldi *mō* "tree", Manchu *moo* (= Monguor *mōdi*, Dagur *mōd* "tree"), etc.

The secondary vowels are a result of contraction of two vowels, e.g., *ē* < **ia* < **ya*: Ev. *ēkun* "who, what", Orochi *yaw*, Goldi *xay-* < **yay*, Lam. *yak* (= Mo. *yaγun*, Middle Mongolian *yan*); Ev., Neg. *sēn* < **sian* < **syan* < **siyan* "ear", Goldi *seā*, Ma. *šan* < **siyan*; Ev. *mēwan* < **miawan* < **miyawan* "heart", Goldi *meawā*, Ma. *niyaman* < **miyawan*, etc.

Other long vowels are a result of contraction of two vowels, subsequent to the disappearance of a consonant in intervocalic position, e.g., Ev., Neg., Oroki *nī-* < **ney-* < **neye-* "to open", Ma. *neye-* (cf. Khalkha *nē-* < **neyē-* < **neyè-* "to open"); Lam. *helūn* "spit, broach" < **silapun* < **sirapun*, Ev. *silawun*, Oroki *silapu* (= Mo. *sira-* "to roast, to fry", Kh. *šar-*); Orochi *xoo* "parietal bones, the top of the head" < **poron*, Ev. *horon* "top", Ulcha *poroni* "summit", Goldi *porõ* "top" (= Middle Mongolian *horai* < **porai* "top of the head"); Ud. *ǰū-* "to transport" < **ǰugū-*, Ev. *ǰugū-* (= Mo. *ǰüge-*, Kh. *ʒȫ* <

ǰüge- "to transport" = Ancient Turkic yük "load" from yü-); Ev. mīrę "shoulder", Oroki muyrę < *möyrę, Goldi meyrę (= Mo. mörü); Ud. bā- "to find", Ev. baka- < *baka-; Oroki bō "country, locality", Ev. buγa < *buga; Ud. gā "branch", Ev., Sol., Oroki gara "branch, twig"; Ev. ǰū "house, dwelling", Sol., ǰuγ, Oroki duku < *ǰuku; Ev., Lam. mū "water", Ulcha muę, Ma. muke < *möke; Ud. ō "thigh, shank", Ev. oγo; Orochi too "fire", Ud. tō < *togo, Ev. toγo < *togo, etc.

Bibliography:

Cincius, V. I., *Sravnitelnaya fonetika tunguso-mańčžurskix yazїkov*, Leningrad 1949, pp. 95–123.

7.15. The opposition of long versus short vowels is also present in Korean, e.g., pāl "an arm's length" – pal "foot"; nūn "snow" – nun "eye"; māl "speech" – mal "horse", etc.

In many cases the long vowels are secondary in origin, e.g., mām (in dialects mayąm) "mind"; ōm < *ohom < *osom "scab, scabies" (cf. Ev. osi- "to scratch", Mo. osqur "abrasion", Chaghatai osul- "to abrade"); kīm (in dialects kiim, kisim) "weeds"; hōn (North Korean habun) "single"; ōn (North Korean obun) "whole", etc.

In other instances the long vowels may be primary in origin, e.g., kōl "reeds" (cf. Mo. qulusun < *kulusun); kōl "valley, street" (cf. Mo. gool < *gōl "river, valley, centre", AT qol < *gōl "river basin").

Bibliography:

Ramstedt, G. J., *A Korean Grammar*, Helsinki 1939, pp. 23–25.

7.2. Stress and pitch.

The expiratory, dynamic stress is in all Altaic languages bound to the same syllable. It is fixed and, therefore, non-phonemic. Side by side with the dynamic stress there is also a musical tone.

7.21. In most Turkic languages, e.g., Turkish, Uzbek, Shor, Sagai, Yakut, etc., the expiratory stress falls on the first syllable. Being fixed, it is phonologically speaking irrelevant, because there are no such contrasting pairs as in Russian, e.g., múka "torment, suffering" and muká "flour", or English (a) pérmit (noun) and (to) permít (verb).

The musical tone is independent of the stress and falls on the last syllable, e.g., Turkish áyàq "foot", áyaγîm "my foot".

7.22. In Mongolian the dynamic, expiratory stress is usually on the first syllable. When one of the non-first syllables is long, the stress rests on it, e.g., Kh. írsen "one who has come", irlḗ "he came".

The musical tone is on the last syllable in di- and trisyllabic words, e.g., Kh. irsèn "one who has come", irsendèn "when he came". In words of more than three syllables each second syllable has a weak rising of the musical tone: bárildasàn "they wrestled".

7.23. Tungus has a dynamic stress and a musical tone. The first falls on the first syllable, the latter is on the second syllable. When a monosyllabic suffix is added the musical tone shifts upon the latter, e.g., Udehe *tádà* "arrow" but *tádajì* "by means of an arrow". When a disyllabic suffix is added, the musical tone is on the second and the last syllable, the dynamic stress disappearing, e.g., *tadàtigì*.

The Udehe stress and tone pattern probably reflects the most ancient conditions.

7.24. In Korean there is an expiratory stress which is on the first syllable. The pitch is high on a vowel immediately following a word-initial emphatic consonant (i.e., *kk, tt, pp, čč, ss*) and the intonation falls at the end of the syllable. In all the other cases the first syllable has a low accent, i.e., starts low and gradually rises. Thus, there are two tone scales on the first syllable: a high and falling tone and a low and rising tone. The second syllable is as a rule lower than the first but without a noticeably falling pitch.

Bibliography:

Cincius, V. I., *Sravnitelnaya fonetika tunguso-mańčžurskix yazïkov*, Leningrad 1949, pp. 124–125.

Poppe, N., *Vergleichende Grammatik der altaischen Sprachen*, Wiesbaden 1960, pp. 143–147.

Ramstedt, G. J., *A Korean Grammar*, Helsinki 1939, pp. 30–31.

Räsänen, M., *Zur Lautgeschichte der türkischen Sprachen*, Helsinki 1949, pp. 32–49.

7.3. Vowel harmony.

7.31. Vowel harmony in Turkic.

The vowel harmony is a feature common to all Altaic languages. It is not easy to give a general definition of what vowel harmony is, which could be applied to all Altaic languages without any exceptions. In the simplest cases, the vowel harmony manifests itself in that in one word there may occur either only back vowels or only front vowels. This type of vowel harmony occurs in such Turkic languages as Tatar: *at-lar* "horses", *ət-lär* "dogs"; *etti* "he gained", *üttə* "he passed by". In Tatar the plural suffix is *-lar* on stems of back vowels, and *-lär* on stems of front vowels. Likewise, the form of the 3rd person of the past tense is *-tï* on stems of back vowels, and *-tə* on stems of front vowels. (There are also the allophomorphs *-dï/-də* but the alternation *d/t* has nothing in common with the vowel harmony and is irrelevant here). In other Turkic languages the vowel harmony is complicated by the fact that after rounded vowels only rounded vowels may occur, the basic rule concerning the opposition of back and front vowels remaining in force. Whereas in Tatar the vowels are, under the vowel harmony rules, divided only into back versus front, in some other languages, e.g., in Bashkir, the middle vowels, i.e., *ï* and *ə*, are subject to the influence of the rounded vowel of the preceding syllable, and, consequently, there is the opposition of back versus front, and rounded versus unrounded. This is illustrated with the following two tables:

	Tatar		
Front	ä	ə	ö
Back	a	ï	ө

Bashkir

	Beyond opposition of rounded versus unrounded:	Opposition of rounded versus unrounded:	
		unrounded	rounded
Front	ä	ə	ö
Back	a	ï	ө

The following examples will illustrate this: Tatar: *kəttə* "he went away"; *öttə* "he sang"; *čïqtï* "he went out"; *ötti* "he gained". Bashkir: *kəttə* "he went away", but *öttö* "he sang"; *sïqtï* "he went out", but *өttө* "he gained".

There is a third type of vowel harmony, namely one manifesting itself in that all vowels are divided into back versus front, and rounded versus unrounded. Such a language is Yakut.

	Unrounded		Rounded	
Front	ä	i	ö	ü
Back	a	ï	o	u

As examples may serve such suffixes of nouns from verbs as *-laŋ* and *-bïl*: *battalaŋ* "suppression" from *battā-*, *kistäläŋ* "secret" from *kistä-*, *soboloŋ* "compensation" from *sobō-*; *sattabïl* "know-how" from *sattā-*, *kätäbil* "waiting, expectation" from *kätä-*, *toxtobul* "waiting" from *toxtō-*.

No matter how different the vowel harmony is in various Turkic languages, one feature is present in all of them, namely, the opposition of back versus front vowels. However, in some Turkic languages there is no phoneme *ï*, this resulting in that *i* occurs in words of front and back vowels, e.g., East Turki. The vowel *i* < **ï* has changed the vowel **a* of the preceding syllable into *e*, e.g., *eliš* "the taking" from *al-* "to take". However, the vowel of a syllable following a syllable with *i* < **ï* remains unchanged, e.g., *elin-* "to be taken" (stem) from *al-* "to take" (stem), and *elinmaq* "to be taken" (verbal noun). The result is that East Turki does not have the same type of vowel harmony as Tatar, because certain vowels, namely, *e* and *i* are not subject to vowel harmony. They are, from the point of view of vowel harmony, neutral.

Before proceding to further discussion, let it be remarked that the vowel harmony of the Tatar type is actually palatal harmony, i.e., it manifests itself in that one word may have either front (palatal) or back (velar) vowels. The dependence of middle (or high) vowels on the rounded or unrounded vowels of the preceding syllable is called the labial harmony, e.g., Bashkir *kəttə* "he went away" and *öttö* "he sang". The vowel harmony in Yakut includes also the dependence of the low (wide) vowels on the rounded or unrounded vowel of the preceding syllable. This kind of vowel harmony is called labial attraction, e.g., *ayalar* "the fathers" but *oyolor* "the children".

7.3. Vowel Harmony

In some Turkic languages only palatal harmony occurs (e.g., in Turkmenian, Kazakh, Nogai, Tatar). In these languages suffixes occur only with the vowels *ä/a* or *ə/ï* (i.e., the suffix of the plural *-lar* occurs only in the forms *-lär/-lar*; likewise the possessive suffix of the 3rd person is always either *-ə* or *-ï* but never *-ü* or *-u*).

In other Turkic languages only palatal harmony complicated by labial harmony occurs (e.g., Turkish, Azerbaijan Turkic, Tuvinian, Kumyk). Here the vowels of the plural suffix are only *ä/a*, but the possessive suffix of the 3rd person is there *-i/-ï/-ü/-u*.

In the third group of Turkic languages palatal harmony, labial harmony and labial attraction occur: the plural suffix is there *-lär/-lar/-lör/-lor* and the possessive suffix of the 3rd person is *-i/-ï/-ü/-u*.

There is a fourth group which has palatal harmony and labial attraction but no labial harmony, e.g., Altai: cf. *qoldor* "arms" but *qolï* (not *qolu*!) "his arm".

Finally, there are languages in which *e* and *i* are neutral with regard to vowel harmony in that *e* followed by *i* (and only in this position) may be followed by *a* in the third syllable. It is important to state that *e* cannot be followed by *a* immediately but only by *a* in the third syllable provided that the vowel of the second syllable is *i*. In other words, the only exception from the rules of palatal harmony are words of the type *e-i-a* (*e* in the 1st syllable, *i* in the second, and *a* in the third). This one exception from the basic rule of vowel harmony, namely, the palatal harmony, shows that the usual definition of vowel harmony as the dependence of vowels of the non-first syllables on the character of the vowel of the first syllable does not cover all the cases.

It will be seen *infra* that there are more exceptions from this basic rule and, therefore, the most general formulation of what vowel harmony is should be worded as follows: vowel harmony is a morphophonemic feature the essence of which is that only certain vowels may occur in one word.

Bibliography:

Isxakov, F. G., "Garmoniya glasnïx v tyurkskix yazïkax", *Issledovaniya po sravnitelnoĭ grammatike tyurkskix yazikov* I, Fonetika, Moskva 1955, pp. 122–159.

Menges, K. H., *Qaraqalpaq Grammar*, Part One: Phonology, New York 1947, pp. 54–56, 59–64.

Poppe, N., *Vergleichende Grammatik der altaischen Sprachen*, Wiesbaden 1960, pp. 147–152.

Räsänen, M., *Zur Lautgeschichte der türkischen Sprachen*, Helsinki 1949, pp. 96–106.

7.32. Vowel harmony in Chuvash.

Vowel harmony in Chuvash is only palatal harmony, i.e., only the back or front character of a vowel is relevant. However, there are numerous exceptions which concern certain suffixes which are, in origin, ancient independent words, e.g., *urasem* "legs" from *ura* "leg" + *sem* < **sayïn* "every". There are also other exceptions but, in general, suffixes on stems of back vowels have back vowels, and suffixes on stems of front vowels have front vowels: *arman* 'mill', gen. *arman-ăn*, dat.-acc. *arman-a*, loc. *arman-ta*, etc., but *tir* "skin", gen. *tir-ĕn*, dat.-acc. *tir-e*, loc. *tir-te*, etc.

7.33. Vowel harmony in Mongolian.

In proceeding to vowel harmony in Mongolian languages, it should be remarked that the simplest type, namely, back versus front vowels, is represented by the vowel harmony in Written Mongolian and Kalmuck. Here, in one word only *a, o, u* or *e, ö, ü* may occur, the vowel *i* being neutral. Kalmuck has developed a few vowel phonemes which are lacking in Written Mongolian, namely the short vowel *ä* < **a* followed by **i* in the subsequent syllable, e.g., *ämṇ* < **amin* "life". The groups **ayi, *oyi*, etc. and the diphthongs **ai, *oi* have resulted in long front vowels: *ǟ* < **ayi* and **ai*, *ȫ* < **oyi* and *oi*, etc. The result of this is that numerous stems of back vowels have become stems of front vowels, e.g., *ǟ-* < **ayi-* "to be afraid", *ȫ* < **oi* < **hoi* < **poi* "forest". They take suffixes with front vowels: *ǟγǟd* "having been afraid", *ȫγǟs* "from the forest".

As for *i*, it is neutral in all Mongolian languages. However, monosyllabic stems with *i*, or stems having the vowel *i* in all syllables take only suffixes with front vowels, e.g., Kalm. *nis-* "to fly" – *nisēd* "having flown"; Khalkha *bičig* "writing, letter" – *bičigēs* "from a letter".

In most of the Mongolian languages the vowel harmony includes also the labial attraction, e.g., Khalkha *gar-* "to go out" – *garād* "having gone out" but *or-* "to enter" – *orōd* "having entered"; *xür-* "to arrive" – *xürēd* "having arrived" but *ög-* "to give" – *ögȫd* "having given".

In the western dialects of Buriat the groups **ayi, *oyi*, etc. and the diphthongs **ai, *oi* have resulted in long front vowels as in Kalmuck: Alar *ǟl* < **ayil* "yurt", *ȫ* < **oi* "forest". However, whereas in Kalmuck *ǟ* and *ȫ* require front vowels in subsequent syllables, they function as back vowels in Buriat: Alar *ǟlār* "through a yurt", *ȫγōr* "through a forest". Consequently, from the point of view of their behaviour under the rules of vowel harmony, *ǟ* and *ȫ* are front vowels in Kalmuck, but they are back vowels in Buriat.

Bibliography:

Poppe, N., *Introduction to Mongolian Comparative Studies*, Helsinki 1955, pp. 84–94.

7.34. Vowel harmony in Manchu-Tungus.

Vowel harmony is also characteristic of the Manchu-Tungus languages. Tungus vowel harmony is complicated by the fact that Tungus does not have *ö* and *ü*, because **ö* has developed into *u*, converging with **u*, whereas **ü* has become *i*, converging with **i* and **ï*. Besides, *ya* has resulted in *ē*. Consequently, *ē* functions under the vowel harmony rules as a back vowel: *sēn* "ear" – *sēnma* accusative. As for the vowels *u* and *i*, they are neutral: *urīkal* (**uri-*) "pull out!" but *urīkęl* (**öri-*) "remain!"; *ulikal* "row!" but *ulikęl* "feed!"; *silan* "barbecued meat" but *silę* "soup"; *sikkal* "sweep!" but *sikęl* "extinguish!".

There is limited labial attraction in Tungus: after *o* no *a/ā* may occur but only *o/ō*; however after *ō* only *a* and *ā* occur but no *o/ō*: *oŋolo* "woodpecker", *dokolōk* "lame" but *ōmakta* "new", *dōlā* "inside, within". In conclusion, it should be pointed out that after *ā* no *a* may occur but only *ę*: *ākęl* "fall asleep!" (but *afkal* "wash!").

Tungus has very strict rules of vowel harmony but it is very different from Turkic harmony. Tungus does not have the opposition of back versus front vowels. Instead, some back vowels are followed by certain back or even front vowels but are never followed by certain other back vowels.

Bibliography:

Avrorin, V. A., *Grammatika nanaĭskogo yazïka*, t. I, Moskva-Leningrad 1959, pp. 40–46.

Cincius, V. I., *Sravnitelnaya fonetika tunguso-mańčžurskix yazïkov*, Leningrad 1949, pp. 116–124.

7.35. Vowel harmony in Korean.

Traces of vowel harmony are also found in Korean.

In Korean the suffix vowels are subject to vowel harmony. The following vowels alternate: *a/ę*, *ai/ęi* (*ä/e*), *o/u*. Stems with *a* or *o* take suffixes with *a*, *ai* (*ä*), *o*; stems with other vowels take suffixes with *ę*, *ęi* (*e*), *u*.

Bibliography:

Ramstedt, G. J., *A Korean Grammar*, Helsinki 1939, pp. 25–28.

7.36. Consonant harmony.

In some Altaic languages all consonants do not occur in words of front vowels. In Turkic *k* and *g* occur only in words of front vowels, but *q* and *ġ* (or *γ*) occur only in words of back vowels. Therefore, suffixes with *k* or *g* occur as *-kä*, *-gä*, *-qa*, *-γa*, e.g., Ancient Turkic *sü-g* "the army" (acc.) but *at-ï-γ* "the horse" (acc.); *il-gärü* "forwards" but *qurï-γaru* "backwards, to the west"; *ödkä* "to the time" but *taluyqa* "to the sea".

This dependence of deep-velar or post-palatal consonants on the back or front character of vowels is called the consonant harmony.

In Yakut, however, *x* (there is no *q*) and *k* do not depend on the back or front character of the vowels but on their low and high character: *x* occurs before *a* and *o* (back vowels) and after *ä*, *ö*, *a*, *o* (low); *k* occurs before *e*, *i*, *ö*, *ü* (front) and *ï*, *u* (back) and also after *i*, *ï*, *ü*, *u* (high).

In some Mongolian languages *g* and *k* occur only in words of front vowels. In stems of back vowels only *q* (*χ*) and *ġ* (*γ*) occur.

Korean and the Tungus languages do not have deep velar consonants, and *k*, *g*, *x* occur there independently of the vocalism. In Manchu script the situation is, however, like in Mongolian, because the alphabet is of Mongolian origin and the orthography is based on Mongolian rules. Korean and Tungus have preserved the most ancient, original features. The consonant harmony in Turkic and Mongolian is a later product.

Bibliography:

Menges, K. H., *Qaraqalpaq Grammar*, Part One: Phonology, New York 1947, pp. 59 ff.

7.37. Summary.

To summarize the observations made with regard to vowel harmony, it should be remarked that the palatal harmony, i.e., the one based on the opposition of back and front vowels, is ancient and common to all Altaic languages. The labial harmony and labial attraction are, however, new and have appeared in languages belonging to one family (e.g., Turkic, Mongolian) independently. There was no labial harmony and labial attraction in Ancient Turkic. Middle Turkic already had labial harmony but no labial attraction. Neither Ancient nor Middle Mongolian had labial attraction.

That labial harmony and labial attraction are new can be seen in Yakut: whereas *o* can be followed only by either *o* or *u*, the diphthong *uo* < *ō is followed by *a*, as in Tungus. This proves that at the time when *uo* had not yet developed from *ō and the latter still existed as *ō, Yakut did not have labial attraction, the latter having appeared only after *ō had developed into *uo*. This explains why the labial attraction has affected *o* but not *ō: when labial attraction appeared, *ō had already resulted in *uo* but *u* does not exercise labializing influence.

7.4. Internal sandhi.

Internal sandhi manifests itself in assimilation of adjacent consonants. The opposite, i.e., dissimilation also takes place.

Internal sandhi occurs both within a morpheme and in cases when two morphemes join. The latter case is of particular importance because it concerns the mutual influence of stem-final and suffix-initial consonants.

7.41. Instances of internal sandhi in Turkic are numerous. In Ancient Turkic there were only a few cases of assimilation of consonants belonging to two adjacent morphemes.

First of all, there was no assimilation in voicing: *öd-kä* "to the time", *ärsän-kä* "to the Arsans", *qapuɣ-qa* "to the gate" (consequently, the dative suffix occurred only with a voiceless consonant at the onset); *toɣsiq-da* "in the east", *yiš-da* "on a forested mountain range", *qontuq-da* "when they spent a night" (the locative suffix has only *d* at the onset); *ät-dim* "I made", *qobart-dim* "I raised", *sözläš-dimiz* "we talked" (the past tense suffix has only *d* at the onset); *bertük-gärü* "towards the giving" (the directive suffix has only a voiced consonant at the onset), etc.

The conclusion which can be drawn from this is that the assimilation in voicing is a feature alien to Ancient Turkic and appeared in Turkic languages at a later date.

There was, however, one interesting case of a phoneme having two allophones. Whereas in all positions with the exception of that following *l, r, n* one allophone of /d/ occurs, in the clusters /ld, rd, nd/ another allophone of /d/ occurs. The former was probably dental and spirantized (i.e., /ð/), the latter was alveolar (i.e., /d/). It is interesting, however, that the locative, ablative, and some other suffixes in Chuvash have each two allomorphs: -*ra* (loc.), -*ran* (abl.), -*răm* (1st p. of the past) after all consonants in stem-final position with the exception of *l, r, n*, whereas the same suffixes are -*ta*, -*tan*, -*tăm* respectively after the stem-final *l, r, n*.

7.4. Internal Sandhi

In the modern Turkic languages there is not only assimilation in voicing, e.g., Turkish *ev-de* "in the house" but *bulaq-ta* "in the spring", but also other kinds of assimilation. To give only a few examples the plural suffix *-lar* will be mentioned.

The plural suffix *-lar* has in most of the Turkic languages and in all positions the consonant *l* at the onset, e.g., Turkish *oda-lar* "rooms", *ay-lar* "months", *at-lar* "horses", *gün-ler* "days", etc.

In Kazakh, however, the suffix occurs with the consonant *l* only after stem-final vowels, *r*, *u̯* and *y*: *qala-lar* "cities", *kiši-ler* "people", *žer-ler* "lands", *tau̯-lar* "mountains", *qoy-lar* "sheep". After *l*, *m*, *n*, *ŋ* the consonant is, however, *d*; and after all the other consonants it is *t*, e.g., *ayıl-dar* "villages", *köl-der* "lakes", *kün-der* "days", *esik-ter* "doors", *at-tar* "horses", etc.

A partly different picture appears in Bashkir and Yakut. To demonstrate similarities and divergences, the following chart is given:

Stem-final phoneme	Kazakh	Bashkir	Yakut
Vowel	-lar	-lar	-lar
y, u̯	-lar	-ðar	-dar
r	-lar	-ðar	-dar
ð	—	-ðar	—
z	-dar	—	—
l	-dar	-dar	-lar
m	-dar	-dar	-nar
n	-dar	-dar	-nar
ŋ	-dar	-dar	-nar
ž	-dar	-dar	—
Other phonemes	-tar	-tar	-tar

The assimilation (and dissimilation: Kaz., Bash. *ayıl-dar* "villages") are partly identical, e.g., *-lar* > *-tar* in all three languages in the same positions; *-dar* occurs in Kazakh and Bashkir after *l*, *m*, *n*, *ŋ*, *ž* (and after *z* in Kazakh). The phoneme *ð* does not occur in Kazakh or Yakut, and in Yakut *d* corresponds after the stem final *y* (but Kazakh has *l*). Only Yakut has *-nar* after nasals, whereas Kazakh and Bashkir have *-dar*.

It is hard to say what the reasons for these assimilations are. Are they purely physiological? Certainly, they are, but some other reasons should also be taken into consideration. As a matter of fact, Bashkir has verbs derived from nouns by adding the suffix *-la-*. The consonant at the onset of the suffix is always and only *l*, e.g., *baš-la-* "to begin" (cf. *baš-tar* "heads"), *aŋ-la-* "to understand" (cf. *aŋ-dar* "concepts, ideas"). If Bashkir could not have *l* after *š* in *baš*, and *l* in *-lar* had by all means to become *-tar* in the plural form *baš-tar*, it should also have become *t* in *baš-la-* "to begin" but it has not. Consequently, the different suffix-initial consonants in *baš-tar* and *baš-la-* prove that the reason of the morphophonemic alternation in *šl* > *št* in *baštar* and absence of it in *bašla* is not of physiological nature.

There are two kinds of assimilation. In some instances the second consonant is assimilated by the preceding consonant. An example of this kind of assimilation is Kazakh *attar* "horses" < *at* + *-lar*. The reverse case is assimilation of the preceding consonant by the following one. Such an example is Yakut *akka* "to the horse" < *at* + *-ka* (dat.), *ekke* "to the meat" < *et* + *-ke* (dat.); *iččit* "dog keeper" < *it* "dog" + *-čit* (professional noun-suffix); *appït* "our horse" < *at* + *-bït* (possessive suffix). The latter example, i.e., *appït* is particularly interesting, because the possessive suffix is *-bït* which was first assimilated in voicing by the final *t* in *at*, but after that assimilated *t*.

Assimilations of consonants occur in many Turkic languages but not in all of them.

Bibliography:

Dmitriev, N. K., "Assimilyaciya i dissimilyaciya soglasnïx v kumïkskom yazïke", *Issledovaniya po sravn. gram. tyurkskix yazïkov* I, Fonetika, Moskva 1955, pp. 298–302.
— "Assimilyaciya i dissimilyaciya soglasnïx v baškirskom yazïke", *ibid.*, pp. 303–306.
Isxakov, F. G., "Yavleniya složnoĭ assimilyacii soglasnïx, voznikayuščie pri vïpadenii beglïx glasnïx v tuvinskom i yakutskom yazïkax", *ibid.*, pp. 314–319.
Malov, S. E., *Pamyatniki drevnetyurkskoĭ piśmennosti*, Tekstï i issledovaniya, Moskva-Leningrad 1951, pp. 45–47.
Räsänen, M., *Zur Lautgeschichte der türkischen Sprachen*, Helsinki 1949, pp. 215–238.
Sevortyan, E. V., "Assimilyaciya i dissimilyaciya soglasnïx v južnïx tyurkskix yazïkax", *Issledovaniya* etc., pp. 307–316.

7.42. Assimilation of consonants occurs also in Mongolian. In Mongolian the suffix consonant *d* is replaced by *t* after any stem-final consonant other than *l, m, n, ŋ*, e.g., Khalkha *gal-da* "in the fire" but *gar-ta* "in the hand", *ulas-ta* "in the nation", etc. Likewise, the suffix consonant *ǰ* is replaced by *č* after any stem-final consonant other than *l*, e.g., *bol-ǰi* "becoming" but *ög-či* "giving".

The consonant *g* is replaced by *k* (*x*) in the same positions after any consonant other than *l, r*, e.g., *bol-go-* "to make", *gar-ga-* "to make come out" but *bos-xo-* "to erect".

These assimilations in voicing are of different age.

The alternation *ǰ/č* already occurs in Middle Mongolian, e.g., *bolǰu* "becoming" but *duradču* "commemorating". The alternations *d/t* and *g/k* are however younger because in Middle Mongolian there still occur forms like *daruqasda* "to the chieftains".

Modern Dagur has still *d* in the dative-locative after all consonants, e.g., *gaǰirda* "on the earth".

These are assimilations in voicing. But there are also assimilations in quality, the preceding consonant being assimilated to the succeeding one, e.g., Dag. *yau̯ōššin* "when thou goest" (cf. *yau̯ōsmin* "when I go", *yau̯ōs* "when he goes"). Cf. also the Alar Buriat form *garakka* < *gargxa* < *gargaxa* "to take out": first *x* was assimilated to *g* (*x*, a fricative, became a voiceless stop) and, then, *k* (< *x*) assimilated *g*.

A case of regressive assimilation is also Khalkha *irex-beddē* "he will certainly come": *irex* + *biȝ* + *dē*.

In general, however, assimilation of consonants is less frequent in the Mongolian languages than in Turkic.

It should be pointed out that consonant clusters belonging to the stem and clusters of consonants of which one belongs to the stem and the other one to the suffix are different in Mongolian. Thus, whereas there are clusters *gd*, *rd* in stems, the dative-locative suffix on stems ending in *g* or *r* has *t*: Mo. *bogda*, Kh. *bogdo* "holy", Mo. *erdem*, Kh. *erdem* "virtue" but Mo. *bog-tur*, Kh. *bogto* "to the dirt", Mo. *ger-tegen*, Kh. *gertē* "in one's own house".

7.43. Assimilation of consonants in Manchu-Tungus is as frequent as in Turkic.

In Manchu-Tungus **s* after *l* is assimilated in various ways: Oroki *-lasa* > *-*lsa* > Ulcha, Goldi *-lta*, Lamut *-lda* (/*-l^{d}ra*/*-lra*/), Evenki *-lla* (full assimilation). Likewise *-*nsa* > *-nta, -nda, -nna*; *-*msa* > *-mda, -mna*.

In Solon numerous reverse cases of assimilation of the first consonant to the second occur, e.g., Sol. *dakkur* < *dapkur* "layer"; *natči* < *napči* "leaf"; *batta-* < *bakta-* "to have enough space, to fit into", etc.

Bibliography:
Cincius, *op. cit.*, pp. 195–203.
Poppe, N.N., *Materialï po solonskomu yaziku*, Leningrad 1931, pp. 105–106.

7.44. In Korean some stem final stops are assimilated to the following suffix consonant, e.g., *-t*: *pat-ta* "to receive", *pannan* "receiving", *pakko* "in receiving", *passe* "may receive".

Korean has three series of consonants in word initial position: unaspirated or weak *k, t, p, č*; aspirated or strong *kh, th, ph, čh* (or *k', t', p', č'*); and long, emphatical unaspirated *kk, tt, pp, čč*. The latter have originated from assimilation of an initial consonant to the following consonant, after the disappearance of the vowel of the original first syllable: *kkịl* < **kökül* "hair" (cf. Mo. *kökül* "tuft of hair"), *ppul* < Ancient Korean *spur* "horn", etc.

Bibliography:
Ramstedt, G.J., *A Korean Grammar*, Helsinki 1939, pp. 5–6.
— *Studies in Korean Etymology*, Helsinki 1949.

7.5. Word structure.

The Altaic languages have many common features in grammatical structure.

7.51. Agglutination.

All Altaic languages are agglutinative in structure. Agglutinative means that inflection and word formation take place by adding of suffixes to stems. This definition is not exhaustive, however, because suffixes, endings, etc. are also mechanically added in many languages which are not agglutinative, e.g.,

English *father's* or *the soldiers*: in both instances the ending is added to a stem. The point is, however, that in English forms like *soldiers* are not the only ones and there are also such forms as *men* versus *man* or *drove* versus *drive*. In the agglutinative languages no sets of forms such as *sink, sank, sunk* or *sing, sang, sung* occur. To this one more detail should be added: the suffixes are monofunctional contrary to the polyfunctional endings of the inflectional Indo-European languages. As an example the Latin forms *hominem praeclarum* may serve. The ending *-em* in *hominem* has two functions: it serves to denote the direct object and the singular number. The ending *-um* in *praeclarum* denotes the direct object, the singular number, and the masculine gender. Likewise, in *hominibus* the ending conveys the meaning of a dative (or ablative) and that of the plural. The endings (suffixes) in the Altaic languages are quite different in this respect, in that each of them has only one function. Thus the Turkish suffix *-e* in *eve* "to the house" is only a dative suffix. It does not denote any number. To form a plural, the word *ev* "house" requires the suffix *-ler*: *evler* "houses". The latter takes the suffix *-e*, and the form *evlere* "to the houses" appears which consists of three morphemes: *ev* (stem) "house", *-ler* plural suffix, and *-e* dative suffix.

The same can be said about Mongolian, Manchu-Tungus, and Korean, e.g., Khalkha *gernūdte* "to the houses": *ger* "house" + *-nūd* plural suffix + *-te* dative-locative suffix; Evenki *ǰūldu* "to the houses": *ǰū* "house" + *-l* plural suffix + *-du* dative suffix; Korean *čiptilgē* "in the houses": *čip* "house" + *-tịl* plural + *-gē* locative suffix.

Consequently, the agglutinative character of the Altaic word inflection manifests itself in adding suffixes, each one having only one function.

When a suffix is added, the stem does not undergo any internal changes, i.e., the vowel of the stem does not disappear and is not replaced by another vowel as it happens in inflectional (or inflected) languages. One could say that the suffixes are added mechanically, if one disregards the assimilation or dissimilation of the stem-final and suffix-initial consonant or even the disappearance of a consonant. However, there are Altaic languages in which the suffixes are really added mechanically to the stem or to other suffixes.

7.52. The stem.

The minimum form of a word is the stem. In all Altaic languages stems are real forms, i.e., they are used in speech without any suffixes. Thus the Tatar verbal stems *kil-* "to come", *kit-* "to go away", *qal-* "to remain", etc. are not abstractions but function also as imperative forms of the 2nd p. sing.: *kil* "come!", *kit* "go away!", *qal* "remain!". Cf. also Ancient Turkic *ešid* "hear!", *tiŋla* "listen!" which are also stems to which tense suffixes are added.

Likewise, Khalkha *ir-* "to come", *yaw-* "to go", *sū-* "to sit" are also imperative forms: *ir* "come!", *yaw* "go!", *sū* "sit down!".

The stem of the noun is also the subject form, i.e., corresponds in function to the nominative, e.g., Turkish *at* "horse", *ev* "house", etc. to which all suffixes are added: *atïn* "of the horse", *attan* "from the horse", *evin* "of the house", *evden* "from the house", etc.

In Mongolian, Manchu-Tungus, and Korean the pattern is the same: Khalkha *ger* "house", *gerte* "in the house", *gerēs* "from the house", etc.; Evenki *ǰū* "house", *ǰūlā* "in the house", *ǰūduk* "from the house", etc.; Korean *saram* "man", *saramiige* "to the man", *saramiro* "by the man", etc.

There are primary stems and secondary (even tertiary, etc.) stems. Primary stems are Turkish *ev* "house", *at* "horse"; Khalkha *ger* "house", *gar* "hand"; Evenki *ǰū* "house", *ŋālę* "hand"; Korean *mul* "water", *čip* "house". These and many other stems cannot be divided into smaller units, i.e., they consist of one morpheme.

The secondary stems are formed by adding word-forming suffixes to primary stems, e.g., Turkish *evle-* "to marry" (< "to make a house"), *demirǰi* "ironsmith" (< *demir* "iron" + *-ǰi* suffix of names of professions); Khalkha *gerle-* "to marry" (< "to make a house"), etc.

7.53. The suffixes.

The suffixes, both inflectional and derivational, are added mechanically (with reservations made above in 7.51) to the stem. The suffixes are subject to vowel harmony. Thus, the Turkish suffix of the ablative is *-den* on stems of front vowels, and *-dan* on stems of back vowels: *evden* "from the house", *odadan* "from the room". In languages having labial attraction and labial harmony, the suffixes are subject to them, e.g., Yakut *aγalar* "fathers", *ǰiälär* "houses", *oγolor* "children", *kötördör* "birds" (*-dör* < *-lör* after *r*); Kirghiz *atï* "his horse", *qulunu* "his foal", etc.

Cf. also Buriat *garhā* "from the hand", *gerhē* "from the house", *modonhō* "from the forest"; Evenki *nannawa* "the hide, skin" (accusative), *bęyęwę* "the man" (acc.), *toγowo* "the fire" (acc.).

The consonant at the onset of a suffix is assimilated to the stem-final consonant in voicing or articulation or both, e.g., Turkish *evden* "from the house" but *attan* "from the horse". In some languages the suffix consonant assimilates the stem-final consonant, e.g., Yakut *akka* < *at* + *-ka* "to the horse", *ïččit* < *ït* + *-čit* "dog keeper".

Some suffixes have developed from original independent words, e.g., the Turkish possessive suffix of the 3rd person *-i* in *atï* "his horse", *evi* "his house": cf. Manchu *i* "he", *ini* genitive, *inde* dative-locative; the Written Mongolian reflexive possessive suffix *-bēn* "own" in *ečigebēn* "his own father", cf. Evenki *mēn* "self"; Chuvash *-sem* plural suffix in *utsem* "horses", which developed from **sayïn*, cf. Chaghatai *sayïn* "every", etc.

However, most suffixes probably go back to suffixes. It is impossible to prove that formerly they were independent words. It should be added that it is even improbable that there might ever have been a time when no suffixes or endings existed and all words were unchanging. The Altaic languages have never been amorphous.

7.531. The possessive suffixes.

A characteristic feature of most Altaic languages are the so-called possessive suffixes which serve to express the same idea as the possessive pronouns in English, e.g., Turkish *evim* "my house" from *ev* "house".

In Chuvash, Turkic, Mongolian, and Manchu-Tungus the person of the owner of an object is indicated by special suffixes: AT *oγlan-ïm* "my sons", *budun-ïm* "my people"; *üläsik-iŋ* "thy part, part of thee"; *bäglär-i* "their princes", *budun-i* "their people"; Buriat *axa-mni* "my elder brother", *axa-šni* "thy elder brother", *axa-ń* "his elder brother"; Ev. *ǰū-w* "my house", *ǰū-s* "thy house", *ǰū-n* "his house"; Goldi *ogda-i* "my boat", *ogda-si* "thy boat", *ogda-ni* "his boat".

The Manchu-Tungus languages have two possessive suffixes of the 1st p. pl., namely an exclusive and inclusive form, e.g., ev. *ǰū-t* "our (incl.) house" and *ǰū-wun* "our (excl.) house". It should be remarked that both Manchu-Tungus and Mongolian have two pronouns of the 1st p. pl.: Ev. *mit* "we" (incl.) and *bū* "we" (excl.); Mo. *bida* "we" (incl.) and *ba* "we" (excl.). The opposition of *incl.* versus *excl.* is found only in few Turkic languages, e.g., in the Khiva dialect of Uzbek: *bizlär* "we" (incl.) and *biz* "we" (excl.).

Mongolian and Tungus has also reflexive-possessive suffixes which express the ownership by oneself ("own", i.e., the actor): Khalkha *axā* or *axāŋ* "one's own elder brother" (direct object), Mo. *aqaban* < **aqa* + **bēn* "self"; Ev. *ǰūwi* "one's own house", *ǰūlwar* "houses which belong to oneself", *-wi* and *-war* going back to **bēn* > *męn* "self".

As for the personal possessive suffixes, they go back to personal pronouns: Ev. *ǰūw* < **ǰū* "house" + *-w* < *bi* "I"; Ev. *ǰūs* < *ǰū* + *-s* < *si* "thou", *ǰūn* "his house" < *ǰū* "house" + *-n* < **in* oblique stem of **i* "he" (cf. Ma. *in-i* gen., *in-de* dat.-loc., *in-či* abl., *imbe* < **in-be* acc.).

7.6. The parts of speech.

In the Altaic languages the parts of speech are less differentiated than in the Indo-European languages.

7.61. Two clearly distinct groups are the nouns and the verbs. Nouns do not act as verbs and, *vice versa*, verbal stems do not act as nouns. Thus as Grønbech says, Turkish does not have verbs like English *to face* or nouns like English *a find*. There are very few homonymous nouns and verbs like Turkic *āč-* "to be hungry" and *āč* "hunger". In many cases the homonymity is the result of loss of ancient endings as in Turkish *āri-* "to ache, to hurt, be painful" and *āri* "pain", the latter going back to **ayrïy*. It is known that in many cases Turkic has lost the final vowel, e.g., Turkish *gök* "blue", Yak. *küöx* < **kȫke* id. = Mo. *köke* id.; AT *qïs-* "to force, compel", Soyot *qïs-* < **kïsa-* "to squeeze, to be too tight" = Mo. *kisa-* < **kisa-* "to press, to oppress"; AT *as-* < **asa-* "to hang" = Mo. *asa-* "to stick to, to attach oneself to something" = Evenki *asa-kta-ǰa-* "to pursue", *asa-sin-* "to take the pursuit"; AT *qon-* < **qona-* "to spend a night, to dwell" = Mo. *qono-* < Middle Mongolian *qona-* "to spend a night", etc. Therefore it is to be assumed that *āč* "hungry" has lost its final vowel, whereas *āč-* "to be hungry" did not have a vowel at the end. Consequently, *āč* "hungry" may go back to **āčV*, *-V* being a suffix, namely, a suffix consisting of a vowel.

It is also a general rule that suffixes added to noun stems cannot be added to verbal stems and *vice versa*.

The same is true of Mongolian. There are very few homonymous verbs and nouns in Mongolian like *kele* "tongue, language" and *kele-* "to speak"; *alqu* "step" and *alqu-* "to pace, to step"; *balgu* "mouthful, gulp" and *balgu-* "to gulp", etc. However, *kele* "tongue" goes back to *kelen* (cf. Kalmuck *keln̥*,

Buriat *xeliŋ*), and *kele-* "to speak" goes back to *kelele-*, the form *kele-* being a contraction of two identical syllables. As for *alqu* and *balǧu*, there are two different derivational suffixes: *-ǧu* of nouns from verbs and *-ǧu-* of verbs from verbs. Likewise, there are two different suffixes *-qu* and *-qu-*.

In Mongolian, too, the same suffix never joins a nominal and verbal stem. The few exceptions can be explained easily. There is the suff. *-sun* which is added to nouns, e.g., *ayurasun* "utensil, household item", formed from *ayura* "appliances, property"; *aduyusun* "animal" from *aduyun* "herd of horses". The same suffix occurs also in Mo. *kögēsün* "foam" from *kögē-* "to swell, to foam"; *nilbusun* "tear, spittel" from *nilbu-* "to spit", etc. However, *kögēsün* goes back to **kögē-r-sün* (cf. Monguor *kōrdzę*) and *nilbusun* goes back to **nilbu-r-sun*, *-r* being a suffix of nouns from verbs to which *-sun* is added. It is known that the cluster *rs* > Mongolian *s*. Another example is the suffix *-ra-* of verbs from nouns and verbs of verbs, e.g., Mo. *kökere-* "to become blue" from *köke* "blue" and *ebdere-* "to go to pieces, to break" (intr.) from *ebde-* "to break" (transitive). This is, however, not one suffix but two different suffixes: the one forms verbs with the meaning "to become something" and the other forms *verba media*. Consequently, there are in Mongolian no suffixes which can be added to noun stems and verbal stems indiscriminately.

In Manchu-Tungus the nouns and verbs are clearly differentiated. Suffixes taken by nominal stems cannot join verbal stems and *vice versa*.

In Korean there are only three distinct categories of words: nouns, verbs, and particles. A nominal stem does not function as a verb, and a verbal stem does not function as a noun.

Consequently, the verb and the noun are two different categories and the boundaries separating them are clearly defined.

However, the other parts of speech which can be labelled as secondary parts of speech are much less distinct. They will be discussed in the following section.

Bibliography:

Avrorin, V. A., *Grammatika nanaĭskogo yazïka*, t. I, Moskva-Leningrad 1959, pp. 84–104.
Grønbech, K., *Der türkische Sprachbau*, Kopenhagen 1936, pp. 18–23.
Ramstedt, G. J., *A Korean Grammar*, Helsinki 1939, pp. 32–36, 60–69.
— *Einführung in die altaische Sprachwissenschaft*, II Formenlehre, Bearbeitet und herausgegeben von Pentti Aalto, Helsinki 1952, pp. 15–21.

7.62. The pronouns.

The personal pronouns are a distinct group among all the nominal parts of speech, i.e., among all that are neither verbs nor particles. The personal pronouns differ from the nouns, i.e., substantives, in that they have, in all Altaic languages, nominative forms which are different from the respective stems, whereas the nouns do not have a nominative form, the stem functioning not only as the subject form but also as a direct object form: Ancient Turkic *on oq budun ämgäk körti* "the people (*budun* stem and subject-direct object form) suffered (lit. saw sufferings)" and *az är itim* "I sent a few men (*är* stem and subject-direct object form)".

The noun does not have a nominative different from the stem in Mongolian either, e.g., Khalkha *šine ger baina* "[there] is a new house" and *šine ger bariǰ baina* "[they] are building a new house".

In Tungus languages the direct-object form occurs only with a suffix which the subject form does not have, e.g., Ev. *ǰū* "house" (subject form) but *ǰūwa* "the house" (dir. obj. form). However, the noun stem is identical with the subject form.

In Korean the subject form of many nouns differs from the original stem, but this is due to different developments of consonants in final and intervocalic positions, e.g., *kęt* "thing", *kęsi* "the thing", and *kęse* "at the thing"; *pat* "field", *pačhi* "the field", *pathe* "on the field", etc. In Korean, too, the direct object can be expressed by what is called the nominative, although there is a special direct object form (accusative).

The pronouns are different from the nouns in that they have nominative forms which function only as subject forms. They are different from the stems and they do not function as direct object forms.

In Chuvash the nominative forms of the personal pronouns and (in parentheses) their oblique stems are:

1 p. *epĕ* (*man*) "I", *epir* (*pir*) "we"
2 p. *esĕ* (*san*) "thou", *esir* (*sir*) "you"

The prefixed vowel *e* in the nominative is a particle. The original forms are **bi*, **si*, **bir*, **sir* respectively. The final *-r* in *epir* and *esir* is a plural suffix. The forms *man* and *san* go back to **män* and **sän* respectively. Consequently, the original forms are:

1 p. **bi* (**män*), **bir*
2 p. **si* (**sän*), **sir*

In Turkic the stems *män*, *sän* were generalized, and they replaced the original nominative forms. However, traces of a nominative form (without a final *n*) distinct from the stem (with a final *n*) are found even in Turkic, cf. the possessive suffix of the 3rd p. *-i* < **i* "he" (Turkish *ev-i* "his house", nominative) which is *-in* < **in* (oblique stem) in all oblique forms (cf. Turkish *ev-in-de* "in his house"). The suffix *-i/-in* corresponds to Mongolian **i* "he", *in* in *inu* "his" (*-u* is the genitive suffix) and Manchu *i* "he", *in* in *ini* gen., *inde* dat.-loc.

Other forms of nominative of pronouns are Turkish *o* "he" (but *onun* "of his", *ona* "to him", etc.), *šu* "this here" (but *šuna* "to this here"), etc.

In Mongolian the personal pronouns are:
1st p. *bi* (gen. *min-u*), Pl. *ba* (*man-u*)
2nd p. *či* (gen. *čin-u*),   *ta* (*tan-u*)
3rd p. **i* (gen. *in-u*),   **a* (*an-u*)

The pronoun of the 1st p. has one more stem, namely, *nama* (root *na*) which appears in the dative-locative, ablative, accusative, and instrumental. The root *na* was compared by Ramstedt with the Korean pronoun of the 1st p. sing. *na* "I".

The identity of the personal pronouns in Chuvash, Turkic, Mongolian, and Manchu-Tungus cannot be a result of borrowing.

7.63. It is difficult to draw a distinct line between the substantive and the adjective.

In Chuvash any noun may function as a substantive or adjective, e.g., *uyăx śutti pit śută* "the light of the moon is very bright" (*śută* "light, brightness" and "bright"). The same is found in Turkic languages, e.g., Yakut *ayïs sïl älbäx jïl kün* "eight years is many years and days" (*älbäx* "many"); *örü üräx älbäyä äxsïta suox* "the multitude of rivers and streams is countless "(*älbäx* "multitude").

The same suffixes can be added to what we call substantives and adjectives, e.g., Tatar *bašla-* "to begin" from *baš* "head" and *qarala-* "to blacken" from *qara* "black".

True, in modern Turkic languages there are adjectives which even have comparative forms, e.g., Tatar *yaxšï* "good" and *yaxšïraq* "better". However, a comparative was formed even from substantives, e.g., Manichean *täŋrim alpïm bägräkim* "my God, my Hero, my Prince" (*bägräkim* "my more prince"); Karai *ayarax* "the senior" (comparative of *aya* "chief"); Turkmenian *qïšrāq-daha yïɣnanïp-dïq* "we had a meeting still later in the winter" (*qïšrāq* comparative of *qïš* "winter").

Even pronouns can appear in the comparative form, e.g., Tatar *mindäräk* "closer by me" (comp. of *mindä* "at me, by me") etc.

In Mongolian no line between substantives and adjectives can be drawn, e.g., *temür* "iron" which functions also as an adjective, e.g., *temür saba* "an iron container". On the other hand, *sayin* "good", *maɣu* "bad", *ulaɣan* "red", etc. function as substantives, e.g., *sayin inu* "his goodness, kindness", *maɣu inu* "his evil", *ulaɣan inu* "its redness", etc. Therefore, it is more correct to avoid the terms substantive and adjective and, instead, speak of nouns as subject or compliment and nouns as attributes.

To proceed to Tungus, one may remark that Evenki *aya* is "good" and "goodness, kindness, property", cf. also *ərū* "evil, bad luck, disaster" and "evil, bad", *ŋonim* "long" and "length", *sagdi* "old" and "old man, oldster", etc. Of course, Tungus has words which are either only substantives, e.g., *mō* "wood" or only adjectives, e.g., *mōma* "wooden".

Korean has no adjectives different from substantives.

Bibliography:

Grønbech, K., *Der türkische Sprachbau* I, Kopenhagen 1936, pp. 23–27.
Ramstedt, G. J., *A Korean Grammar*, Helsinki 1939, pp. 34–35.

7.64. A characteristic feature of the verb in the Altaic languages is that the stem of the verb and the suffixless imperative form are the only purely verbal forms. All the other forms, i.e., tenses, participles, and gerunds (converbs) are of nominal origin.

The verbal forms are classified in imperative forms, verbal nouns or participles, and gerunds.

The imperative forms include that of the second person which is identical with the stem of the verb and is the only purely verbal form: AT *sabïmïn ädgüti äšid qatïɣdï tïŋla* "hear well my word, listen hard!" (*äšid-* "to hear", tiŋla- "to listen"); Mongolian *ire* "come!"; Korean *iri o* "come here!"; *čibe ga* "go home!".

The gerunds or converbs are petrified forms of verbal nouns, e.g., AT *ali* "taking", from *al-*; *iti* "making" from *it-*: suffix *-i*, cf. *körši* "neighbor" from *körüš-* "to see each other"; Mo. *surtala* "until [he] learns", a dative form in *-a* of the verbal noun in *-tal* (cf. *surtal* "teaching, doctrine") from *sur-* "to learn"; Evenki *hętękēmnęk* "jumping" from *hętękēn-* "to jump", with the suffix *-mnęk* < *-mnę* of verbal nouns (cf. *kikimna* "bite" from *kik-* "to bite") + *-k*.

It is to be noted that the converbs (gerunds) take possessive suffixes in Mongolian and Tungus, e.g., Khalkha *irsērē* "since he came (= since his own arrival)"; Ev. *soŋoknonmi* "until I started crying". The gerunds take in Tungus the plural suffix, e.g., *ičęwultękil* "being seen by each other".

The Altaic languages do not have indicative forms of the Indo-European type. The indicative forms, the tenses, are verbal nouns in origin, namely verbal nouns in predicative position, i.e., verbal nouns with personal endings, namely, possessive suffixes or predicative suffixes. Thus the Tatar future tense *kilərmən* "I shall come" is the participle *kilər* "one who will come" + the predicative suffix of the 1st p. sing. *-mən* (cf. *yazučïmïn* "I am a writer" from *yazučï* "writer"). Cf. Turkish *ačar* "key" from *ač-* "to open" and *ačar* "he will open"; Kazakh, Nogai *otar* "pasture" from *ota-* "to graze" and *otar* "he will graze", etc. The past tense is *-d* + possessive suffixes, cf. Tatar *birdəm* "I gave", *birdəŋ* "thou gavest", etc., cf. AT *bärtimiz* "we gave" (cf. Kirg. *olut* "chair" from *ol-* "to sit"). Likewise, one of the Mongolian present tense suffixes is *-m*, e.g., *olum* "he finds, he will find", *bolum* "he becomes", etc., (cf. *naγadum* "game" from *naγad-* "to play"). In Evenki the aorist has the suffix *-n*, e.g., *ŋenęm* < *ŋenę-n* + *-w* "I went", *ŋenę-n-ni* < *ŋenę-n-si* "thou wentst" from *ŋenę-* "to go", cf. *ŋenę-n* "motion, movement". The suffix *-n* = *-n* in Mongolian *siŋgen* "fluid" from *siŋge-* "to be absorbed" and *-n* in Turkic, cf. *aqïn* "current" from *aq-* "to flow".

7.65. A characteristic feature of the Altaic languages is the lack of prepositions. Instead, there are postpositions, i.e., auxiliary words which follow the word governed, e.g., AT *inim kültegin birlä* "with my younger brother, Kültegin"; *qutïm bar üčün* "because I had good luck"; Mo. *egünü tula* "because of this"; Ev. *tar ǰarin* "for the sake of that"; Korean *san aphe* "before the mountain", etc.

The postpositions are of diverse origin. Some of them are of nominal origin. Many nouns function as postpositions, e.g., Turk. *üstündä* "on". However, one should not confuse such nouns with true postpositions, because the latter do not take possessive suffixes.

8. BRIEF COMPARATIVE SURVEY OF ALTAIC LANGUAGES

8.0. The Altaic languages have more in common than general structural features. Numerous sound correspondences and suffixes common to all Altaic languages have been established. There is also a large body of words of common origin. In this chapter only the Chuvash-Turkic, Mongolian, and Manchu-Tungus languages will be discussed.

8.1. Sound correspondences.

The name of the language in question will be given in ( ). In instances in which there is no indication of language, the following languages are meant: Manchu-Tungus is represented by Evenki; Written Mongolian respresents Mongolian; and Ancient Turkic represents Turkic.

8.11. Consonants.

1. Consonants in initial position

Number	Manchu-Tungus	Mongolian	Chuvash	Turkic	Reconstructed common phoneme
1.	p (Go.)	f (Mng.)	Ø	Ø	$*p$
2.	t	t	t	t	$*t$ before any vowel but $*i$, $*ï$
3.	$č$ (Ma.)	$č$	$č$	t	$*t$ before $*i$, $*ï$
4.	k	k	k	k	$*k$ in words of front vowels
5.	k	q	x	q	$*k$ in words of back vowels
6.	b	b	p	b	$*b$
7.	d	d	$ś$	y	$*d$ before any vowel but $*i$
8.	$ǰ$ (Ma.)	$ǰ$	$ś$	y	$*d$ before $*i$
9.	g	g	k	k	$*g$ in words of front vowels
10.	g	$g̣$	x	q	$*g$ in words of back vowels
11.	$č$	$č$	$ś$	$č$	$*č$
12.	$ǰ$	$ǰ$	$ś$	y	$*ǰ$
13.	s	s	s	s	$*s$ before any vowel but $*i$
14.	$š$ (Ma.)	$š$	$š$	s	$*s$ before $*i$
15.	y	y	$ś$	y	$*y$
16.	m	m	m	b	$*m$
17.	n	n	$ś$	y	$*n$
18.	$ń$	n	$ś$	y	$*ń$

The correspondences are illustrated with examples. The numbers of examples correspond to those of corresponding consonants given in the table.

Examples:

1. Go. *pāra* "sledge", Ma. *fara* id. = Mo. *aral* "shafts of a carriage" = Tat. *ariš* id.; Mng. *fudur* < **purtu* "long", Mo. *urtu*, MMo. *hurtu* id. = Chuv. *vărăm* < **urun* "long" = AT *uzun* "long".

2. Ev. *tatigā-* "to teach" = Mo. *tačiya-* < **tatigà-* "to acquire bad habits" = Chuv. *tută-* "taste" = AT *tat-* "to taste".

3. Ev. *tikunŋi-* < **tikungī-* "to anger someone" = Mo. *čiqul* < **tikul* "anger" = AT *tiqil-* "to become angry"; Mo. *čilaүun* < **ti̯alagùn* "stone" = Chuv. *čul* < **ti̯āl* id. = AT *tāš* id.

4. Ev. *kẹpẹ-* "to swell" = Mo. *kȫge-* < **kȫpē-* id., *kȫgesün* < **kȫpērsün* "foam" = Chuv. *kăpăk* "foam" = AT *köpük* "foam", Alt. *köp-* "to swell".

5. Ma. *qarqa-* "to scratch, to play violin" = Mo. *qar-* "to dig, scratch" = Chuv. *xïr-* "to dig" = AT *qaz-* id.

6. Ev. *bōk-* "to detain, delay, prevent" = Mo. *boүo-* < **bogā-* "to bind" = Chuv. *păv-* "to strangle" = AT *boү-* "to strangle".

7. Ma. *delün*, Ev. *dẹ̄lin* "mane" = Mo. *del* < **dēl* id. = Chuv. *śilxɛ* < **yēlkei̯* id. = AT *yel* (*yil*) id.; Lam. *dal-* "to lick with the tongue", Ev. *dala-* id. = Mo. *doluүa-* < **dalugà-* id. = Chuv. *śula-* "to lick" = AT *yalүa-* < **dalugà-* id.

8. Ma. *jili* "the base of the antlers", Go. *jeli* "head", Ev. *dil* "head" = Mo. *jiluүa* "temples; reins".

9. Ev. *gẹdimuk* "the back of the head", *gẹtkẹn* id. = Mo. *gejige* < **gedikē* "cue" = AT *kedin* "after", Yak. *kätäx* "back of the head", Sag. *kizin* "behind".

10. Ma. *gala* < **gāla* "hand", Ev. *ŋālẹ* id. = Mo. *gar* id. = Chag. *qarï* "arm"; Lam. *gobja-* < **gubi-ja-* "to chase" = Mo. *guyu-* < **guyi-* < **gubī-* "to beg, to ask" = Chuv. *xăvala-* < **qubgala-* "to pursue" = AT *quw-* "to pursue".

11. Ev. *čāgū* "distant", Ma. *čālā* "on that side" = MMo. *ča'ada* "on that side"; Ma. *čikin* "edge" = Mo. *čikin* "ear" = Chag. *čikin* "the area between the neck and the scapula, nape"; Mo. *čigiqan* < **čibīkan* "a furuncle, swelling" = Chuv. *šăpan* id. = Turkish *čiban* id.

12. Ev. *ǰẹyẹ* "the edge of a knife" = Mo. *jegün* "needle" = Chag. *ignä* < **yignä* < **yegnä* "needle"; Ev. *jugu-* "to transport", Ma. *juve-* id. = Mo. *jüge-* id. = AT *yük* "load, baggage" from *yü-* "to transport"; Ev. *jiktẹ* "berry", Ulcha *justẹ*, Gol. *jusiktẹ* "blueberry" = Mo. *jigde* "jujub", *jedegene* < **jigdegene* "strawberry" = Chuv. *śïrla* < **jigdläk* "berry" = Alt. *yiläk* id.

13. Ev. *sẹlẹ-* "to awaken" = Mo. *seri-* "to awaken, to be sober" = Chag. *säz-* "to feel"; Mo. *saүa-* "to milk" = Chuv. *su-* "to milk" = AT *saү-* id.

14. Ev. *sirugī* "sand, a sand bank in a river" = Mo. *širuүai* "dust, earth" = Chuv. *šur* < **šār* < **si̯ār* "swamp" = Chag. *saz* "swamp"; Ev. *silgin-* "to rock, to tremble", Lam. *hilgin-* id. = Mo. *šilged-* "to shake" = Kum. *silik-* "to shake", Turkish *silk-* id.

15. Mo. *yada-* "to be unable", *yadaүu* "poor" = Chuv. *śuran* < **yadaүïn*

8.1. Sound Correspondences

"on foot" = AT *yaday* "pedestrian"; Ev. *yegin* < **yegün* "nine" = Mo. *yesün* < **yersün* id.

16. Mo. *meŋge* "mole" = Turkish *bänäk* id., *bäniz* < **mäŋiz* "face"; Ev. *moŋon* < **moingon* "neck" = Mo. *moyinog* < **moyïnak* "dewlap" = AT *boyun* "neck", Yak. *mōy* id.

17. Ev. *napta-* "to lie flatly", *naptama* "flat" = Mo. *nabtayi-* "to become flat", *nabtagar* "low"; Ev. *nęmęsin-* "to mend, to patch up" = Mo. *neme-* "to add".

18. Ma. *ńārxun* "young, fresh, green" = Mo. *nirai* < **ni̯ārai* "new born" = Chuv. *śur* < **yār* "summer" = AT *yaz* "spring"; Ev. *ńemumę* "soft, tender, gentle" = Mo. *nimgen* "thin" = AT *yïmšaq* "soft".

2. Consonants in intervocalic position

In Mongolian certain consonants 1. before an original unaccented (see p. 200)

Number	Manchu-Tungus	Mongolian	Chuvash	Turkic	Reconstructed common phoneme
1.	p	b/γ	p	p	*p
2.	b	b/γ	v	b	*b
3.	t	t	t	t	*t before all vowels but *i, *ï
4.	t, Ma. č	č	č	t	*t before *i, *ï
5.	d	d	r	ð	*d before any vowel but *i, *ï
6.	d, Ma. ǯ	ǯ	r	ð	*d before *i, *ï
7.	k	k/g	k	k	*k in stems of front vowels
8.	k	q/g	x	q	*k in stems of back vowels
9.	g	Kh. g/Ø	v	g	*g in stems of front vowels
10.	g	Kh. g/Ø	v	γ	*g in stems of back vowels
11.	č	č	ś	č	*č
12.	ǯ	ǯ	y	y	*ǯ
13.	s	s	s	s	*s before any vowel but *i, *ï
14.	s	š	š	s	*s before *i, *ï
15.	y	y/γ	y	y	*y
16.	m	m/γ	m	m	*m
17.	n	n	n	n	*n
18.	ń	n	y	ñ	*ń
19.	ŋ	ŋ/γ	n	ŋ	*ŋ
20.	l	l	l	l	*l¹
21.	l	l	l	š	*l²
22.	r	r	r	r	*r¹
23.	r	r	r	z	*r²

vowel (strong position) and 2. before an original accented vowel (weak position) show different developments. Note: b/γ means b in strong position and γ in weak position (see table on p. 199).

Examples:

1. Mo. *taba* < **tápa* "satisfaction" = MT *tap* "inclination"; Mo. *ebei* < **épe* + *-i* "dear mother" = Chuv. *appa* < **äpä* "elder sister"; Ev. *kępę-* "to swell", *kępęn* "swelling" = Mo. *köge-* < **köγē-* < **köpè-* "to swell" = Soy. *köp-* "to swell", AT *köpük* "foam".

2. Mo. *kebi-* < **kébi-* "to ruminate, chew the cud" = Chuv. *kavle-* id. = Turkish *gäv-* "to gnaw, chew", *gäviš* "cud"; Mo. *aba* < **āba* "hunt" = AT *ab* id.; Mo. *gaγurasun* < **gabùrasun* "straw, quill" = Turkish *qavuz* "chaff of millet"; Mo. *quwa* < **kubà* "light, yellow, pale" = Tel. *quba* "pale".

3. Ev. *ętirkēn* "old man", Lam. *ętę* "grandfather" = Chuv. *vată* < **öte* "old" = AT *öt-* "to pass"; Ma. *futa* < **puta* "rope" = Mo. *utasun*, MMo *hutasun* "yarn" = Yak. *utax* < **putak* "strands of which thick ropes consist".

4. Ev. *tatigā-* "to teach", Ma. *tači-* "to learn, study" = Mo. *tačiya-* < **tatīgà-* "to acquire bad habits" = AT *tat-* "to try, to taste".

5. Ev. *bodo* "the way of living" = Mo. *boda* "body" = AT *boð* "body, substance"; Mo. *čida-* "to be able, to vanquish" = Chuv. *čar-* "to detain" = AT *tið-* "to detain, to prevent"; Ma. *fatxa* < **padakai* "paw" = Mo. *adag* "end, the lower course of a river" = Chuv. *ura* < **adak* "foot, leg" = AT *aðaq* "foot, leg".

6. Ma. *fajilan* < **padïran* "partition, wall", Go. *pāji* "separated" = Mo. *ajira-* "to notice", *aji-* < **padi-* id. = AT *aðïn* "another", *aðïr-* "to distinguish between"; Ev. *gędimuk* "the back of the head", Lam. *gędękē* id. = Mo. *gejige* "cue" = AT *kädin* < **gedin* "behind", Yak. *kätäx* < **gedek* "back of the head".

7. Ev. *ękē* "elder sister", Lam. *ękęn* id. = Mo. *eke* "mother" = Chuv. *akka* < **äkä* "elder sister"; Ev. *bękę* "hump" = Mo. *böken* id. = Chag. *bükri* "bent"; Mo. *üker*, MMo. *hüker*, Mng. *fuguor* "ox" = Chuv. *văkăr* id. = AT *öküz* id.

8. Ev. *akā* "the younger brother of the father or mother" = Mo. *aqa* "elder brother" = AT *aqa* "elder brother", Yak. *aγa* < **aqa* "father".

9. Ev. *juguktę* "bee, wasp", *jugunuk* "wasp", Lam. *jęwęt* id. = Mo. *jögei* id.; Mo. *bögüji* "clasp, buckle", *bögüldürge* "loop at the end of a whip" = Chag. *bögüt* "button"; Ma. *fuxu* < **pögü* "wart" = Kh. *ū̃*, Mo. *egün* < **pögün* id. = Yak. *üön* < **pögün* id.; Kh. *bō̃* "shaman", Mo. *büge* id. = AT *bügü* "wise", Turkish *büyü* id.

10. Ev. *agī* "open place, plain, steppe, wilderness", Ev. *aglān* "steppe" = Kh. *agui*, Mo. *agui* "vast", Mo. *aglag* "uninhabited country, deserted place"; Ev. *sigī* "bush, thicket", *sigīma* "dense", *sigīkāg* "thicket" = Mo. *šigui*, Kh. *šugī* "forest"; Mo. *boγorla-*, Kh. *bōrlo-* "to cut the throat" = Chuv. *pïr* "throat" = AT *boγaz* "throat"; Kh. *sā-* "to milk", Mo. *saγa-* id. = Chag. *saγ-*, Yak. *ïa-* < **saγ-* id.

11. Ma. *ačan* "joint, juncture", *ača-* "to join, unite", *ačabun* "union, juncture" = Mo. *ača* "fork, bifurcation" = AT *ač-* "to open"; Ev. *mučū-* <

8.1. Sound Correspondences

*bučawu- "to return, to give back", mučūn "return, coming back" = Mo. buča- "to go back, to return" = Chag. bučmaq "angle".

12. Ma. fujuri "origin" = Mo. ijaγur, MMo. hija'ur / huja'ur < *pujagùr id.; Mo. oju- "to kiss, to have intercourse" = Kirg. oyun "game", AT oyna- "to play".

13. Ev. kęsę̄ "misfortune, suffering", kęsę̄ję- "to suffer" = Mo. kese- "to repent", kesege- "to punish", MMo. kese- "to warn" = Alt. käzän- "to make threatening movements, to threaten"; Ma. fusu- "to sprinkle", Go. pisinęsiu- id. Ul. pisūri id. = Mo. üsür- "to jump up, to fly", üsürge- "to sprinkle" = Sag., Koib. üskür- "to sprinkle with the mouth"; Ev. asaktaja- "to pursue", asasin- "to start pursuing" = Mo. asa- "to stick to, to impose oneself", Bur. aha- < *asa- "to start a quarrel" = AT as- "to hang".

14. Ma. fesin "handle", Ev. hęsin id. = Mo. eši, MMo. heši < *pesi "handle, stalk, trunk".

15. Ev. aya "well-being, welfare, good, good-natured" = Mo. aya "decency, everything suitable" = AT aya- "to pity, commiserate", ayaγ "esteem, reverence"; Kh. tūrai, Mo. tuγurai "hoof" = AT tuyuγ id.

16. Ev. kumtęw- "to topple, to fall down" = Mo. kömöri- id. = Alt. kömölö- "to upset, to overthrow"; Ev. amŋa < *amagai "mouth" = Mo. aman "mouth, opening"; Ev. omŋo- < *umga- "to forget" = Mo. umta- "to sleep", umarta- "to forget" = Kazakh umut- "to forget".

17. Ev. ęnūnil- "to become ill", Lam. ęńči "pain" = Mo. enel- "to be unhappy, to be sad", eneri- "to pity" = Sag. enig "suffering"; Ev. sūnŋi- < *sūngī- "to stretch" = Mo. sun- id. = AT sun- id.; Mo. sönü- < sön-ü- "to be extinguished", söni "night" = Ev. sī- < *söi- "to extinguish" = Turk., Chag. sön- id.

18. Ma. funexe < *puńekē "hair" = Mo. ünegen, MMo. hünegen < *pünekē "fox" = Yak. ünügäs < *ünekäč "welp"; Go. puńakta < *püńekte "ashes" = Mo. ünesün, MMo. hünesun, Monguor funiezę id.

19. Ma. qonsun "anus" = Mo. qoŋ "posterior", qoŋdolai "thigh", qonjiyasun < *koŋdigāsun "posterior" = Kaz., Alt. qoŋ "thigh"; Mo. šiŋge- < *siŋe- "to be absorbed" = AT siŋ- id.; Ma. nuŋgari "wool" = Mo. noγosun < *nuŋāsun "wool" = Küär. yuŋ id.

20. Ev. dala- "to lick" = Mo. doluγa- < *dalugà- id. = AT yalγa- id.; Ev. alas "thigh" = Mo. ala "the perineum" = AT al "front side", Alt. alïnda "under, underneath"; Ev. dul- "to warm" = Mo. dulaγan "warm" = MT yïlïγ "warm"; Ev. dę̄lin "mane", Ma. delun id. = Mo. del id. = Turk. yälä id.

21. Ma. dali- "to cover, hide", Ev. dal- "to cover" = Mo. dalda "hidden" = AT yašur- "to cover, hide"; Mo. čilaγun < *tįālagùn "stone" = Chuv. čul < *tįāl id. = Yak. tās, AT tāš id.; Mo. gölige "welp" = Turk. köšäk "young animal".

22. Go. pāra "sleigh", Ma. fara id. = Mo. aral "the bottom of a carriage" = Kirg. ariš "shafts"; Ma. ferxe "thumb", Ev. herbęk "finger", Lam. herégęn "thumb" = Mo. erekei, MMo. heregei < *perekei "thumb" = AT ärŋäk "finger", Yak. ärbäx "thumb"; Lam. burkun "blizzard" = Mo. boroγan < *burugàn "rain" = Turk. buran "snow-storm".

23. Ma. iri "edge" = Mo. ir "blade", irmeg "sharp edge" = Chuv. yěr "trace, trail" = AT iz "trace"; Ev. ur < *ör "stomach of an animal" = Mo.

örö < *öre "the inside, aorta" = Chuv. var < *ör "center, middle" = AT öz "oneself"; Mo. urtu "long", Monguor fudur < *furtu id. = Chuv. vărăm < *urun "long" = AT uzun "long".

8.12. Vowels.

Vowels of the first syllable

Number	Manchu-Tungus	Mongolian (Monguor)	Turkic (Turkmenian)	Reconstructed common phoneme
1.	a	a	a	*a
2.	ā	ā	ā	*ā
3.	o	o	o	*o
4.	ō	ō	ō	*ō
5.	u	u	u	*u
6.	ū	ū	ū	*ū
7.	i	i	ï	*ï
8.	ī	ī	ï̄	*ï̄
9.	e	e	ä	*e
10.	e	e	i	*ė
11.	ē	ē	ǟ	*ē
12.	ē	ē	ī	*ē̇
13.	u	o	ö	*ö
14.	u	ō	üö	*ȫ
15.	u, i	u	ü	*ü
16.	ī	ū	ǖ	*ǖ
17.	i	i	i	*i
18.	ī	ī	ī	*ī

Examples:
1. Ma. *ali-* "to take, accept, receive" = Mo. *ali* "give!" = AT, Trkm. *al-* "to take"; Ev. *arakūkān* "slow, a little bit", *arakūn* "gradually" = Mo. *arai* "hardly, scarcely" = Trkm. *az* "little"; Ev. *dal-* "to cover", *dalit-* "to obscure", Ma. *dali-* "to hide" = Mo. *dalda* "secret, hidden" = Trkm. *yašmaq* "veil", AT *yašur-* "to cover".

2. Mngr. *dāli* "shoulder", Mo. *dalu* "scapula" = Trkm. *yāl* "mane", Yak. *sāl* "fat layer under the mane"; Ev. *sā-* "to learn", *sāje-* "to know" = Trkm. *sān* "number", Yak. *āx-* < *sāq-* "to count".

3. Ev. *bodo* "life, the way of living" = Mo. *boda* "object", Khalkha *bodo* "the true nature, essence" = AT *boð* "body"; Ma. *tobgiya* "knee" = Mo. *toyig* "knee-cap" = AT *tobïq* "knee".

4. Mo. *bol-* "to become", Mngr. *ōli-* id. = Yak. *buol-* < *bōl-*, Turk. *ol-* "to be"; Mngr. *mōdi* "wood", Dag. *mōd* "tree" = Ev. *mō* "tree".

5. Ev. *omŋo-* < *umga-* "to forget" = Mo. *umta-* "to sleep", *umarta-* "to forget" = AT *unït-* "to forget", Yak. *umun-* id.; Ma. *ula-* "to transmit" = Mo. *ulari-* "to alternate" = AT *ula-* "to connect", *ulayu* "by the turn"; Mo.

8.1. Sound Correspondences

urtu "long", Mngr. *fudur* < **furtu* < **purtu* id. = Chuv. *vărăm* < **urun* "long" = AT *uzun*, Yak. *uhun* id.

6. Ev. *sūnŋī-* < **sūngī-* "to stretch" = Mo. *sun-* id. = Yak. *ūn-* < **sūn-* id.; Lam *ūru-* "to flow out" = Mo. *urus-* id. = Koibal *ur-* "to flow".

7. Ev. *ṅemumę* "soft", *ṅemkun* "thin" = Mo. *nimgen* < **ṅimkan* "thin" = Yak. *simnā-* "to become soft", AT *yimšaq* "soft"; Ev. *tikunŋi-* "to anger", *tikul-* "to become angry" = Mo. *čiqul* < **tüqul* "strait; anger" = AT *tüqïl-* "to become angry".

8. Ma. *irun* "furrow", *iri* id. = Mo. *iraɣa* id. = Chuv. *yăran* < **ïran* id. = Trkm. *ïz* "trace"; Mo. *isu* "soot" = Trkm., Yak. *ïs* "smoke".

9. Ev. *ękin* "elder sister", *ękī / ękē* "aunt", Lam. *ękęn* "elder sister" = Chuv. *akka* < **eke* "elder sister"; Ev. *ęri-* "to dig", Lam. *ęrdę-* "to row", *ęrūn* "wooden shovel, spade" = Mo. *erü-* "to dig" = Chag. *äz-* "to rub, to crush".

10. Ma. *delen* "udder", Lam. *dęlŋa* id. = Mo. *deleŋ* id. = Az. *yelin* < **yelin* id.; Ev. *gędimuk* "the back of the head", Lam. *gędęmęk* id. = Mo. *gede* id., *gejige* < **gedikē* "cue" = AT *kidin* "backwards".

11. Ev. *ŋēri* "light", Ma. *gere-* "to become bright" = Mo. *gerel* "light", *gere* "light; witness" = AT *kertin-* "to believe"; Mo. *ere* < **ēre* "man" = Chuv. *ar* < **ār* id. = Trkm. *ār* < **ēr* id.

12. Ev. *dęlin* "mane" = Mo. *del* id. = Chuv. *śilxe* < **yelkei* id. = AT *yil* id., Yak. *siäl* id.

13. Ev. *ugītmęr* "higher", *ugīlę̄* "above", *ugī* "top" = Mo. *ögede* < **ögède* "up", Mo. *ögse-* "to move upstream"; Lam. *kutęr-* "to climb upwards" = Mo. *kötel* "mountain pass", Kalm. *köti-* < **köteyi-* "to rise" = AT *kötür-* "to raise".

14. Ev. *sī-* < **sōyi-* "to extinguish", *sīw-* "to go out" (fire) = Mo. *sönü-* "to be extinguished" = Trkm. *sōn-* id.; Ev. *ur* "stomach" = Mo. *örö* < **ōre* "aorta" = Chuv. *var* < **ōr* "inside, stomach" = Trkm. *ōz* "oneself", Yak. *üös* < **ōz* "middle, marrow".

15. Ma. *fuče-* < **pürke-* "to be angry", Ulcha *puču-* < **pürkü-* "to jump up" = Mo. *ürgü-*, MMo. *hürgü-* "to be frightened" = Az. *hürküt-* < **pürküt-* "to frighten"; Ev. *jugū-* "to transport on sleighs", *jugūwūn* "caravan" = Mo. *jüge-* "to transport" = AT *yü-* id., *yük* "load".

16. Mo. *küli-* "to bind" = Trkm. *güyl-* < **kūl-* "to bind the hands and feet"; Ev. *tirękse* "leg of the boot", Oroki *tiyekse* id., Go. *tūrękse* id. = Mo. *türei* id.

17. Ev. *sippiy-* "to sweep" = Mo. *sigür* < **sipür* "broom" = Chag. *sipür* id., AT *sipir-* "to sweep"; Ev. *silgin-* "to shake" = Mo. *silged-* id. = Kumandin *silik-* id.

18. Ev. *bilę̄n* "wrist" = Mo. *bile* id. = Az. *biläk* id.

9. INDICES

(The numbers refer to the pages)

9.1. Languages, dialects, and scripts.

Abakan dialects 34, 40, 102
Ainu 138
Alar 12
Altai 34, 36, 42, 47, 102, 109, 110, 111, 118, 129, 130, 161, 183
Altaic 126, 127, 157
Anatolian (incl. dialects) 34, 51, 120, 162
Anatri 36
Anaulï 50
Ancient Chuvash 58
Ancient Kirghiz 60
Ancient Mongolian 21, 161, 162
Ancient Oghuz 60
Ancient Turkic 59, 60, 65, 106, 107, 111, 112, 116, 119, 121, 123, 158, 177, 178, 180, 185, 186, 191, 192, 193, 195, 196, 197
Ancient Uighur 60
Arabic (language, script) 37, 115, 122, 170, 171
Aramaic script 16
Armeno-Kuman 121
Azerbaijan Turkic 34, 49, 52, 162, 168, 183
Babylonian-Assyrian 170
Baraba 34, 102, 125
Bargu Buriat 12
Barguzin Buriat 12
Barguzin Tungus 97
Bashkir 2, 34, 35, 36, 45, 108, 161, 168, 181, 182, 187
Basque 125
Bayit 10
Beltir 40
Brāhmī script 59, 63, 116
Buinak 43
Bulgarian 58, 119, 136, 177
Buriat 2, 7, 8, 12, 82, 83, 84, 91, 139, 140, 158, 159, 193
Buzawa 11
Caucasian languages 125

Chaghatai 47, 109, 110, 121, 123, 161, 180
Chakhar 14
Chalkan 40, 41
Cheremis (= Mari) 130
Chinese 113, 137, 138, 165
"Chudic" 128
"Chudic-Tatar" 127, 128
Chulym 40, 41, 102
Chuvash 33, 34, 36, 37, 38, 58, 105, 108, 119, 121, 131, 133, 136, 139, 145, 146, 147, 148, 155, 157, 162, 169, 175, 178, 183, 186, 191, 194, 195
Chuvash-Turkic 2, 7, 33, 34, 197
Classical Mongolian 17
Common Turkic 33
Crimean Jews 44
Crimean Tatar 41, 44, 107
Cuman *vide* Kuman
Dagur 7, 8, 9, 21, 91, 139, 140, 160, 179, 188
Dambi-Ölöt 10
Danube Bulgarian 58, 119
Danube Turkish dialects 51
Dariganga 14
Dörböt 10, 11
Dravidian 126, 137, 138
Durbut-Beise 86
East Turki (= Modern Uighur) 34, 47, 48, 104, 105, 106, 107, 109, 118, 119, 120, 168, 182
Ekhirit-Bulgat 12
Elkembei (= Negidal) 31
English 171, 173
Ersarïn 49
Estrangelo 64, 69
Even *vide* Lamut
Evenki 21, 26, 31, 32, 83, 98, 99, 160, 161, 179, 180, 195, 197
Finno-Ugric 3, 82, 125, 126
Finno-Ugric-Samoyed 83, 127

French 171, 173
Gagauz 49, 50
Georgian 175
German 171, 173
Goklen 49
Golden Horde: literary language of 44, 45
Goldi (= Nanai) 26, 27, 30, 96, 97, 99, 131, 179
Gorlos 86
Greek 170
Hebrew 171
Hungarian 36, 37, 38, 58, 130, 132, 176, 177
Hunnic 57, 58, 119
ḥP'ags-pa script 21, 22, 23
Ili dialect 48
Indo-European 118, 126, 137, 138, 177, 196
Iranian 114
Italian 171
Japanese 127, 128, 137
Juchen 26, 27, 28
Jurchen *vide* Juchen
Kacha 40
Kalmuck 7, 10, 11, 12, 18, 81, 84, 85, 88, 125, 130, 184, 192
Kamass 175
Karachai-Balkar 34, 35, 41, 43, 109, 110, 119, 168
Karagas (= Tofa) 34, 39, 82, 118, 161
Karai (= Karaim) 34, 35, 41, 42, 119, 122, 171, 195
Karakalpak 36, 46, 110, 111, 117
Karakhanide 67, 68, 114
Kara-Kirghiz *vide* Kirghiz
Kashkai 52
Kasimov Tatar 45
Kazakh 21, 34, 36, 41, 46, 102, 106, 118, 161, 162, 163, 183, 187, 196
Kazan Tatar 45
Kazan Turkic 45
Ketsik 41
Khaidak 43
Khakas 40, 109, 110, 111
Khalkha 7, 8, 12, 14, 84, 88, 91, 130, 158, 159, 179, 180, 184, 186, 190, 191, 194, 196
Khanty (= Ostiak) 176
Kharchin 94
Kharchin-Tumut 14, 94
Khasarli̇ 50
Khasaw-Yurt 43

Khazar 36, 37
Khiva dialect 192
Khorchin 14
Khori 12, 82, 86, 140
Khwarezmian 67, 70
Kirghiz 2, 34, 36, 41, 47, 102, 118, 161, 196
Koibal 82
Komi 176
Korean 2, 7, 84, 127, 131, 136, 138, 145, 146, 147, 148, 157, 163, 165, 166, 180, 181, 185, 189, 193, 194, 196
Krymchak 44
Kuchan 168
Kuman (= Cuman) 34, 41, 42, 68, 72, 73, 114, 123, 161, 173
Kumanda 40, 41, 112
Kumyk 34, 35, 41, 43, 108, 168, 183
Kuznetsk Tatar 41
Küärik 41
Kypchak 34, 35, 41, 44, 118, 121, 123
Kypchak-Uzbek 118
Lamut (= Even) 32, 97, 98, 161
Lebed 40, 41, 102
Linhsia dialect 9
Lobnor dialect 48
Malayan 126
Manchu 26, 27, 28, 33, 96, 97, 125, 131, 139, 160, 161, 179, 180
Manchu-Tungus 2, 4, 7, 24, 95, 96, 126, 127, 145, 146, 147, 148, 155, 166, 179, 180, 181, 184, 189, 190, 191, 192, 193, 194, 197
Manichean script 59, 63, 116, 195
Mansi (= Vogul) 176
Mari (= Cheremis) 3, 120, 176
Middle Aramaic script 64
Middle Mongolian 21, 22, 23, 24, 89, 90, 91, 92, 131, 139, 188
Middle Persian 168
Middle Turkic 47, 67, 109, 115, 161, 162, 186
Mishar 45
Mingat 10
Modern Uighur (= East Turki) 34, 48
Mogol 7, 8, 10, 84, 92, 93, 120, 130
Mongol (Mongolian) 2, 3, 4, 7, 125, 126, 127, 145, 146, 147, 148, 155, 157, 158, 159, 161, 162, 166, 178, 180, 194, 195, 196, 197
Mongolian script 15
Monguor 7, 8, 9, 21, 90, 139, 140, 179
Mordvan 176

9.1. Languages, dialects, and scripts

Nanai vide Goldi
Negidal (= Elkembei) 26, 97, 179
Nerchinsk Tungus 97
Nižneudinsk Buriat 12, 82
Nogai 34, 36, 41, 44, 46, 110, 111, 118, 183, 196
Nohurlï 50
Nukha dialect 105
Oirat 7, 8, 10, 11, 81, 88, 139
Oirat script 18
Oirot 42, 47, 109, 110, 118
Old Anatolian 68, 73
Old Osman 68, 73, 123
Old Russian 106, 118, 174, 175
Old Tatar 173
Ölöt 10
Ordos (= Urdus) 15, 86, 90, 91, 139, 140
Orkhon inscriptions 59, 102, 106, 107, 112
Orochi 26, 27, 30, 98, 179, 180
Oroki 26, 27, 30, 31, 100, 179, 180
Osmanli (= Osman Turkish) 34, 51, 122, 123, 162
Ossetian 167
Ostiak (= Khanty) 176
Pahlavi 168
Palaeo-Asiatic 125
Palmyran script 64
Parthian 168
Permian 176
Persian 168, 169
Polovetsian vide Kuman
Post-Karakhanide 68
Pecheneg 123
Pre-Turkic 33
Proto-Bulgarian 173
Proto-Turkic 33, 57
Runic script 59, 60, 61, 107, 111
Russian 171, 173
Sagai 102, 118, 161, 180
Saka 167, 168
Salar 47, 49
Salïr 49
Samoyed 39, 125, 126, 175
Sanskrit 113, 167, 168, 169, 170
Santa 7, 8, 9, 21
Sarïk 49
Sart-Kalmuck 11
Sartul 12
Sayan Samoyed 3, 175
"Scythian languages" 125
Selenga Buriat 82

Semitic 126, 170, 171, 177
Semitic alphabets 16
Shor 40, 41, 102, 109, 180
Siamese 126
Sino-Tibetan 177
Slavic (= Slavonic) 117, 171, 173
Sogdian (Sogdic) script 3, 16, 59, 65, 113, 167, 168, 170
Solon 21, 26, 32, 160, 179
Soyot (= Tuva, Uriankhai) 39, 102, 104, 118, 161
Steppe Tatar 44
Sumerian 170
Syriac 64, 69
Tara 102
Tatar 2, 34, 35, 41, 45, 102, 120, 161, 162, 168, 181, 183, 190, 195, 196
"Tatar languages" 125, 128
Telengit 47
Teleut 47, 102, 118
Teptyar 45
Tibetan 126, 167
Tobol Tatar 102
Tofa vide Karagas 39
Tokharian 167, 168
T'o-pa 57
Torgut 10, 11
Trukhmen 50
Tsongol 12
Tuba 40, 41, 47
Tunghsian 9
Tungus 21, 82, 97, 98, 99, 125, 134, 139, 160, 161, 184, 185, 194, 195, 196
Tunka 12
"Turanian languages" 126
Turkic 2, 3, 4, 33, 34, 38, 126, 127, 129, 134, 139, 145, 146, 147, 148, 155, 157, 158, 165, 177, 178, 180, 181, 182, 183, 185, 186, 187, 189, 190, 191, 192, 194, 195
Turkish 34, 44, 49, 51, 52, 100, 101, 107, 110, 120, 121, 180, 183, 191, 194, 196
Turkmenian 34, 49, 121, 168, 177, 178, 183, 195
Tuva (vide Tuvinian, Soyot, Uriankhai) 34, 39, 104, 161, 162, 183
Tuvinian vide Tuva
Ude vide Udehe
Udehe 26, 27, 31, 179, 180, 181
Udmurt 176
Uighur, Uighur script 16, 59, 65, 66, 106, 113, 114, 116, 125, 141, 165

Ujumchin 15, 86
Ukrainian 173
Ulcha 26, 27, 30, 99
Ural-Altaic 5, 114, 128
Uralic 82, 127, 129, 175
Ural Tatar 45
Urat 14
Urdus (= Ordos) 15, 90
Uriankhai (*vide* Tofa, Tuva, Tuvinian)
Uzbek 2, 34, 47, 48, 109, 110, 116, 120, 161, 168, 169, 180, 192
Viryal 36
Vogul (= Mansi) 176
Volga Bulgar 36, 37, 38, 58, 176
Volga Finnic 176
Volga Tatar *vide* Tatar
Written Mongolian 12, 16, 21, 81, 91, 92, 93, 184, 197
Written Oirat 11, 81
Yaghnobi 167
Yakut 2, 34, 38, 101, 105, 132, 139, 161, 162, 177, 178, 180, 182, 185, 187, 192, 195
Yanalif 52
Yellow Uighur 40, 106, 107
Yenissei inscriptions 60
Yomud 49
Zakhachin 10

9.2. Authors.

Aalto 60, 79, 85, 136, 137, 138
Adam 95
Aganin 51
Akbaev 43
Aliev 43
Alijiv 50
Alkor (= Koshkin) 32
Amyot 95
Andreev 37
Arat 68, 114, 115
Aspelin 111
Aston 137, 138
Ašmarin 37, 52, 105
Atalay 68, 72
Austin 28
Avrorin 30, 98, 99, 185, 193
Axmerov 45
Babinger 80
Baičura 45
Bailey 63
Baïramkulov 43
Balakaev 46
Balhassan Oglu 68
Bammatov 43
Bang 65, 67, 68, 114, 117, 161
Bang-Kaup *vide* Bang
Banguoğlu 73
Barbier de Meynard 121
Barthold 87, 88, 103
Bartold *vide* Barthold
Baskakov 4, 5, 36, 38, 40, 41, 46, 47, 49, 50, 110, 111, 135, 136, 148
Batmanov 47
Bazin 50, 51, 121
Beknazarov 111
Belyaev 50

Benzing 4, 26, 36, 50, 142, 150, 151, 154
Bergsträsser 51
Bese 13, 92
Beveridge 70
Bidwell 48
Bobrovnikov, Aleksandr 79
Bobrovnikov, Alekseï 81
Bogoraz 32, 97
Böhtlingk 1, 3, 38, 101
Boĭcova 98, 99
Boller 127
Boodberg 57
Borovkov 43, 48, 49, 70, 109, 110
Bosson 12, 13, 14
Boyer 63
Beerijiv 50
Brockelmann 68, 72, 73, 115
Brondal 112
Budagov 72
Buge 129
Caferoğlu 51, 52, 72
Castrén 3, 39, 82, 83, 126, 127, 128
Ceahir 50
Cheremisov 2, 12
Chuvalkov 102
Chwolson 70
Cincius (= Tsintsius) 4, 26, 30, 32, 98, 142, 180, 181, 185, 189
Cïdendambaev 12
Clauson, Sir Gerard 72, 152, 154, 155
Cleaves 92, 93
Collinder 129
Cunvazo 49
Čeremisov *vide* Cheremisov
Čoban-Zade 44

Çağatai 114
Deny 51, 68, 72, 90, 121, 122
de Smedt 9, 91
Dien 14
Dïrenkova 40, 41, 47, 109
Dmitriev 38, 43, 46, 50, 108, 109, 142, 174, 178, 188
Doerfer 23, 28, 44, 52, 152, 153, 154, 155, 174
Donner 3
Duda 5
Dulling 50
Dulzon 41
Eckmann 72, 123, 124
Egorov 37, 105
Ellinghausen 52
Eren 123
Filonenko 43
Foy 43, 52
Fraenkel 53
Franke 89
Fuck 116
Gabain, von 48, 57, 60, 63, 65, 67, 72, 114
Gabelentz 95
Gauthiot 67
Gazizov 45
Gerhard 38
Golstunskiĭ 81
Gombocz 38, 58, 132, 133, 176
Gorcevskaya 98
Gorskiĭ 108
Grønbech (= Grönbech) 18, 70, 72, 112, 113, 149, 150, 154, 192, 193, 195
Grube 28, 30, 89, 96
Grunin 73
Grunzel 130
Guseĭnov 52
Haenisch 23, 28, 89, 90, 97
Haguenauer 76
Halasi-Kun 52, 73, 123
Haltod 18
Hambis 90
Hangil 76
Hangin 15
Harlez 114
Hartmann 117
Hattori 14, 93, 138, 142, 179
Hauer 28, 96, 97
Hazai 123, 124
Hebert 43, 47
Heikel 111
Henrikson 85

Honda 100
Hony 51
Houtsma 73
Hulbert 138
Hung 24
Hyungki 76
Ikegami 31, 100
Illich-Svitych 135, 136
Ilminskiĭ 102, 103, 104
Inkiželkova-Grekul 40
Isengalieva 46
Isxakov 39, 108, 178, 183, 188
Ivanov 104
Ivanovskiĭ 81
Iwamura 10, 93
Jaegher 95
Jagchid 14
Jarring 48, 49, 114, 120, 121
Jaubert 121
Jensen 137, 138
Joki 175
Junker 76, 137, 138
Jyrkänkallio 36
Kaidarov 49
Kakuk 49
Kałużyński 38, 162
Kanazawa 137, 139
Kanda 100
Kannisto 176
Kara 11, 15, 92
Karlgren 166, 167
Karrïeva 50
Kassatkin 18
Katanov 39, 102, 104 105
Kaya 44
Ki Sien-lin 67
Kibirova 49
Klaproth 3
Kohnova 73
Kōno 75, 76
Kononov 48, 51, 72, 110
Konstantinova 32, 98
Koppelmann 137, 139
Korsch 174
Kotwicz 11, 40, 80, 85, 88, 132, 133, 134, 135
Kotwiczówna 86, 135
Kovalevskiĭ *vide* Kowalewski
Kowalewski 1, 80
Kowalski 43, 51, 122
Kožurov 111
Kraelitz-Greifenhorst 73, 175
Krueger 18, 36, 37, 39, 91, 113, 149, 154

Kuleev 45
Kúnos 103, 123
Kurbangaliev 45
Langlès 95
Lebedeva 32, 98, 99
Le Coq, von 65, 67, 114
Lee, Ki-Moon 75, 76, 138, 163
Lee, Sung-Nyong 76
Leech 10
Lees 51
Lenormant 127
Lessing 18, 113
Levin 32
Lewicki 24, 63, 73, 86, 91, 92
Lidzbarski 65
Ligeti 10, 24, 28, 58, 135, 136, 137, 149, 154, 176
Loewenthal 4
Lotz 51
Luvsandėndėv 13
Maĭzeĺ 51
Malov 40, 49, 60, 67, 70, 106, 107, 175, 188
Mannerheim 40
Mansuroğlu 68, 73
Mardkowicz 43
Marquart 58
Martin 9, 76
Matrosova 4
Matsumura 100
Maxmudov 46
Megiser 101
Meillet 88
Melioranskiĭ 106, 175
Menges 36, 39, 40, 46, 47, 49, 50, 72, 105, 114, 117, 129, 167, 171, 173, 175, 183, 185
Meninski 100, 101
Menzel 107
Mikkola 58
Miklosich 175
Mil̓nikova 31
Möllendorff, von 28
Morawczik 57
Moshkov 103
Mostaert 9, 15, 90, 91
Müller, F.W.K 3, 67, 113, 116
Müller, Max 126
Murayama 93
Musabaev 46
Musaev 43
Nadžip 49
Nam 76

Nasilov 49, 63
Németh 52, 123, 132, 133, 159
Nerifi 50
Nikiforov 2
Nomura 14, 94
Novgorodov 38
Novikova 26, 32, 98, 99
Odabaš 44
Ogura 76
Okada 100
Okamoto 100
Orkun 63
Orlov 2, 3
Osada 10, 93
Paasonen 37, 176
Pallas 79
Paĺmbax 39, 178
Pang 76
Pavet de Courteille 72
Pavlov 37
Peeters 28
Peisker 175
Pekarskiĭ *vide* Piekarski
Pelliot 24, 67, 68, 88, 95
Petrova 30, 99
Piekarski 39, 105
Poceluevskiĭ 50
Podgorbunskiĭ 2
Pokrovskaya 50
Polivanov 138, 139
Poniatowski 30
Popov 18
Poppe 8, 9, 10, 12, 13, 18, 24, 33, 39, 45, 46, 49, 59, 72, 85, 86, 89, 91, 94, 98, 105, 135, 142, 148, 159, 162, 171, 176, 179, 181, 183, 184, 189
Poppe, Nicholas Jr. 48
Potanin 94
Poucha 85
Pozdněev 18, 81, 82
Preobraženskiĭ 174
Prince 175
Pritsak 10, 35, 37, 38, 40, 41, 43, 44, 46, 47, 49, 58, 59, 73, 91, 92, 103, 109, 113, 116, 119, 120, 137
Pröhle 44, 127
Quatremère 121
Rachmati (= Arat) 65, 67, 68
Rachmatullin (= Rachmati, Arat) 47
Rachmeti (= Arat) 67
Radloff 1, 3, 40, 67, 70, 102, 103, 104, 111, 112, 141, 142
Rahder 139

9.2. Authors

Ramstedt 3, 12, 34, 38, 63, 77, 83, 84, 85, 86, 87, 88, 91, 130, 131, 132, 133, 134, 136, 137, 138, 139, 142, 143, 144, 145, 148, 149, 151, 155, 178, 180, 181, 189, 193, 195
Raquette 49
Räsänen 36, 52, 114, 120, 129, 136, 141, 142, 176, 178, 181, 183
Rask 125, 126
Raun 176
Redhouse 52
Rešetov 48
Rišes 32, 98, 99
Ritter 53
Romaskevič 53
Róna-Tas 9, 14, 92
Rossi 73
Rudnev 28, 86, 87, 91, 132
Rupen 87, 91
Salemann 3
Samoilovich = Samoĭlovič 34, 36, 44, 106, 107, 108, 112
Sanžeev = Sanžeyev 94, 135, 141, 161
Sarïbaev 46
Sauvageot 128, 129
Schaeder 112
Scheel 117
Schiefner 83
Schindler 113
Schinkewitsch 70, 114, 115
Schmidt, Isaac Jacob 79, 80
Schmidt, P. 30, 31, 166
Schott 128
Schou 113
Schröder 9
Schurmann 10, 93
Schütz 73
Serebrennikov 136
Setälä 83
Sevortyan 52, 53, 188
Shimada 100
Shiratori 58
Shirokogoroff 128, 129
Simpson 53
Sinor 5, 30, 92, 97, 152
Sirotkin 37
Sjoberg 48
Skaličkova 77
Sprengling 63
Sternberg 97
Stönner 63
Strahlenberg, von (Tabbert) 125, 126
Street 12, 13, 24, 146, 147, 148

Sunik 4, 27, 32, 98, 99
Sunki 77
Sunoo 77
Swift 52
Szabó 92
Ščerbak 68
Ščerbatskoĭ 87
Šneĭder 31
Tabbert vide Strahlenberg 125
Telegdi 73, 123
Temir 63, 103
Teniševv 49
Thévenot 79, 95
Thomsen, Kaare 45, 49
Thomsen, Vilhelm 63, 68, 102, 111, 112
Thury 123
Todaeva 9, 12
Toščakova 47, 111
Trautz 113
Troxel 13
Tryjarski 73
Tsintsius vide Cincius
Tyulyaeva 4
Ubryatova 39, 107, 143
Unenseček 15
Uray 124
Vámbéry 123
Vasilevich = Vasilevič 27, 32, 98, 99
Vasmer 38, 117, 175
Velyaminov-Zernov 72
Verbickiĭ 104
Vladimircov = Vladimirtsov 12, 87, 88, 94, 132, 133, 134, 135, 139, 140, 143, 144, 148, 159, 171
Voegelin 52
Wang, Chung-Min 67
Ware 90
Weil 45
Weller 113
Wichmann 176
Windisch 101
Winkler 127, 130
Winter 65, 115
Wurm 36, 47, 48
Xamzaev 50
Xaritonov 39
Yadrintsev 111
Yakovlev 37
Yakovleva 4
Yamamoto 100
Yamasaki 10, 93
Yastremskiĭ 39

Yu 77
Yudakhin = Yudaxin 2, 47, 49
Yuldašev 46
Yusupov 38
Zaatov 44
Zach 96
Zajączkowski 43, 72, 73, 92, 114, 122, 123
Zakharov 95, 96
Zulfugarova 53
Zwick 18, 81
Žamcarano = Žamtsarano 87